FATAL
WEEKEND

FATAL
WEEKEND

Thursday 28th April - Sunday 1st May 1994

TOM RUBYTHON

For Ambrose
21st September 2012

First published in Great Britain in 2015
by The Myrtle Press

1 3 5 7 9 10 8 6 4 2

First Edition published on 12th November 2015

A CIP catalogue record for this book is available
from the British Library.

Hardback ISBN: 978-0-9934731-0-4
Softback ISBN: 978-0-9570605-93

Typeset in Garamond by: CBA Harlestone
Reproduction by: Fresh Vision, London

Printed and bound by
CPI Group (UK) Ltd, Croydon, CR0 4YY

Published by:
The Myrtle Press
Billing Wharf
Station Road, Cogenhoe
Northamptonshire
NN7 1NH, United Kingdom
Tel: +44 (0)1604 890 208
Web: www.themyrtlepress.com

Contents

Contents

Contents

Acknowledgements

I wrote *The Life of Senna*, between 2001 and 2003, with a big team and plenty of resources. For *Fatal Weekend*, I set about examining everything written and spoken about Ayrton Senna since 2004, and there proved to be a surprisingly large amount. The maturing of the Internet has seen even more information published, much of it privately on blogs, Facebook pages and the like. There were also another dozen or so books about Senna on the bookshelves that weren't there in 2004.

But I would still like to thank my original collaborators on *The Life of Senna*: Gerald Donaldson and David Tremayne for the work they did then on the nuts and bolts of Ayrton Senna's remarkable life. Gerry has written a lot on Senna's accident separately, which has proved incisive and informative.

Peter Collins, as ever, was a great source of information on everything Formula One. He was a close friend of Ayrton Senna and they often chatted about the sorts of things you don't expect such people to chat about – they both will know what I mean.

In the last weeks of his life, most of their chatter was about traction control, which they surmised separately, and correctly, that Benetton was using on Michael Schumacher's car. Collins was a former team principal of Benetton before Flavio Briatore took over and had special inside knowledge.

He was also a former team manager at Williams and was of great help to me in dissecting the culture of Senna's new team. Collins defended Patrick Head's role after Senna's death and told me that a man of greater integrity, or a more safety conscious engineer, could not be found in Formula One. I agreed with him. Invariably, when he told me something new, Peter immediately wished he hadn't. But that is Peter.

John Watson, as always, was a great help. He assisted me with insight into Senna's driving and into his character. John was at Imola right in the thick of it on Sunday 1st May, commentating for Eurosport. He told me of some of the hard realities of being a commentator that day. I questioned John closely, and also Bertrand Gachot, on the realities of driving a Formula One car round Tamburello curve at 190mph. Bertrand, in particular, concurred with almost every driver and said it was easy and that a monkey could get a Formula One car round Tamburello with little problem. The inference being that to not get round it meant something else had to have happened. Talking to them and other drivers, it struck me how serious mechanical failures in Formula One cars are routinely blamed on 'driver error' – something that the drivers seem to suck up whenever instructed to.

John Barnard is an excellent source of impartial technical insight. John is great because his opinion is never fixed like so many other observers. He reacts to the evidence and information put in front of him and questions his own judgement minute-by-minute, which makes him especially valuable to know to someone like me.

Jo Ramirez is a remarkable man, and arguably the person Ayrton Senna respected most in Formula One. It is clear leaving Jo behind at McLaren was one of the great regrets of Senna's life. It was obvious their love affair was mutual. Jo has a marvellous sense of perspective that is vital to any author writing about Ayrton Senna.

Andrew Frankl, the great Hungarian, who founded *Car* Magazine, was an out and out Senna fan and, outside of the Brazilian journalists, probably interviewed him more than any other writer. When anything is in doubt, Andrew can normally fix those doubts. He was also very handy with his camera in those days.

Julian Jakobi was at the heart of events that weekend. He was part of Team Senna and still is. So many people who were close to Senna in life now perform sterling work for the Ayrton Senna Foundation, the creation of Viviane Lalli, Senna's sister and a truly great woman.

Murray Walker was a huge help to me back in 2003 and his 10-year relationship with Senna went far beyond any normal media/driver collaboration. His extraordinary homily to Senna on the BBC Six O'clock News on the evening of 1st May is unmatched before or since.

Finally thanks to Dr Richard Abbatt for casting a glance over the chapters which focused on the medical aspects of the weekend.

I was surprised at the great number of people who still demand anonymity when speaking about the events of that weekend. 21 years has passed, but it seems that the wounds have not yet healed. Probably they never will.

Finally, to my own in-house team for the vital production skills that are needed to bring a book like this to its final form. I always say that publishing nonsense (polite word) is very easy, but creating properly researched and considered books is very difficult to pull off. Of course, only the reader can ultimately judge whether that is true, but what you have here is a tribute to Kiran Toor, our long standing sub editor; David Peett, even more long standing president of logistics and Will Adams who proof read the galleys expertly.

I thank everyone, named or not, for their help, but the words that follow – and any errors or omissions – are naturally my responsibility alone.

ACKNOWLEDGEMENTS

"He said to me: 'Isn't it, Josef, that we have a fantastic life - haven't we a good life?' I said to him: 'Are you afraid that this is going to stop one day?' He replied: 'No, because I have such a good life now so whatever comes, comes.'"

Josef Leberer
Thursday 5th May 1994

FATAL WEEKEND

Kennedy, Lennon, Diana
and Senna are icons all

This has been a very demanding book to write. Twice in the past few years I abandoned it because of the difficulties of writing about a subject so emotionally charged. Eventually, I put that to one side and just got on with what is essentially a book about four days in 1994. They are events that happened 21 years ago, which we should have forgotten but that somehow today still really matter. In the end there was too much still left unsaid.

Thursday 28th April to Sunday 1st May 1994 was the most infamous weekend in Formula One history and the third most infamous event in world sport after the Munich Olympics terrorist attack in 1972 and the Le Mans 24 hours crash in 1955.

Like the death of President John F. Kennedy in 1963 and Princess Diana in 1997, everyone can remember exactly where they were and what they were doing when they heard about the death of Ayrton Senna. The death of Senna brought Brazil to its knees just as Kennedy's death devastated the United States of America and Diana's death shook Britain to its very core.

Thankfully, the unexpected death of such icons suddenly and at their peak is rare. In the modern age, there have been Kennedy, Senna, Diana, John Lennon, Michael Jackson and Elvis Presley who have been with us one minute and literally gone the next. Jackson and Presley died in suspicious circumstances and when they were well past their best.

But Kennedy, Lennon, Diana and Senna were different because they were killed at the very height of their powers and cruelly struck down by events that were no fault of their own. And yet, by some strange coincidence, each had an innocent role in their own deaths. Kennedy should have insisted that the bulletproof glass bubble be placed on his car, especially in the hostile state of Texas, but for reasons best known to himself he did not. Lennon, one of the most famous personalities in the world, because he moved around New York with no security and let everyone know where he lived, set himself up for the lone-wolf nutcase. Even the simplest of security measures would have saved John Lennon's life. Diana should never have been in a car being driven at high speed late on a Saturday night in Paris. Never.

Senna, for very much the same reasons, should have insisted on tyre barrier protection for the concrete wall at Tamburello when he inspected the circuit on 9th March.

A glass bubble, some basic security, safer driving and a few hundred old tyres were such obvious precautions to take against the risk of death that they almost defy belief. It is fair to say that with such basic everyday precautions, all four would be alive and well today, old age permitting.

The death of Ayrton Senna was as inconceivable as was the death of John Kennedy and Princess Diana. The inconceivable events left large legacies and caused people to spend years and years trying to understand why and how.

Some people may think it bizarre to compare the death of a world statesman like Kennedy and a global icon like Diana to that of Ayrton Senna who was just a racing driver, a man who drove cars round in circles for a living. But Senna's worth was as an icon who gave hope to Brazil, then a very poor country with millions living in poverty. As Julian Jakobi says elsewhere in this book, you had to go to Senna's funeral to appreciate that fact.

Senna was an inspiration to a whole continent of South Americans. And no one should doubt that Senna's death and his subsequent funeral meant just as much to South America as Kennedy's death did to North America and Princess Diana's to Great Britain. And just as America was robbed of the future potential of John Kennedy, so Brazil was robbed of the future potential of Senna.

The saddest thing is that, by any measure you care to use, Senna should not have died. He raced in the safest-ever era of Formula One. He raced in an age when it was actually very difficult to die in a Formula One car. The era when no one died in a Formula One car, outside of 30th April/1st May 1994, spanned 30 years. It has become something that is incredibly safe to do.

This book records the list of circumstances that formed the chain of events that led to Senna's death. It is a long one.

Firstly, active suspension systems should never have been removed from cars that were designed to have them. Its removal made the cars (especially the Williams-Renault) unstable. The new regulations were well intentioned and were the right to do but should have been introduced in 1995, giving the teams due notice to design new cars. For this, Max Mosley must take the blame for railroading through this change without giving due notice. The way it was done at the 1993 Canadian Grand Prix was shabby and ill-thought through. Mosley and Charlie Whiting did an incredible amount of work to make Formula One safe, but they dropped the ball over active suspension.

Secondly, there should have been a treble row of tyres protecting the concrete wall at Tamburello. Why there wasn't is an inexplicable mystery and, for this, Ayrton Senna must take the blame as he carried out a safety inspection himself a few weeks before his accident. There are a lot of people who must also take some of the blame for this. Tamburello had been the scene of five major accidents – it should have had a tyre wall. 21 years later, no one wants to discuss this pretty basic imperative safety precaution.

Thirdly, the Williams car's steering system was suspect and probably failed at the point of the accident. If it had been in tip top order, Senna probably would have been able to steer himself out of trouble. The steering column had metal fatigue due to a scarcely believable, almost amateurish, modification made to it that went against everything Formula One stood for in maintaining safety in cars. Although they were not directly responsible, Patrick Head and Adrian Newey must take the blame for that.

The race should never have taken place at all. Roland Ratzenberger crashed and died on the previous day. Whatever anyone said afterwards, Ratzenberger was dead on impact, and Sid Watkins should have declared him dead in line with the law. However, Watkins was under pressure from Bernie Ecclestone never to declare a driver dead at the scene and always get them to hospital first. But if Watkins had acted properly, the race would have been cancelled and Senna would not have died that weekend. Watkins and Ecclestone must jointly share the blame for this.

Senna's helmet was almost certainly on the limit of legality. It was of lighter weight than a normal helmet and also had a thinner visor. With a heavier weight of helmet he would have had a much better chance of survival and this was entirely his own fault as he wore a lighter helmet looking for an edge.

Senna was overdriving his car throughout the 1994 season to keep up with Michael Schumacher's Benetton. After the season ended, Schumacher's car was to prove to be illegal for employing traction control, which give him the advantage. On lap seven of the San Marino Grand Prix, Senna was under the huge pressure of being chased by a much faster car. Without that, he may have gone into Tamburello more cautiously and been able to save his own life. As it was, he left himself no leeway. For this, the people who ran the Benetton team must take the blame as they were undoubtedly aware of what was going on, and it sadly contributed to Senna's death.

Senna was deeply troubled that weekend by the death of Roland Ratzenberger and the serious accident of his countryman Rubens Barrichello. Every violent accident upset Senna, and two in two days had undoubtedly unbalanced him. Anyone who studies the still photographs and video of that morning of the race can clearly see that Senna was in no state to get in a Formula One car.

The principal cause of that was Ratzenberger's death. Ratzenberger shouldn't have died. The Simtek team did not have enough money to go Formula One racing and therefore raced in a sub-standard car, which, for a myriad of reasons, caused Ratzenberger's death and, for that, many people, including team principal Nick Wirth, must take the blame. Ratzenberger's death, like many accidents in Formula One, was wrongly blamed on driver error. It was nothing of the sort. The front wing fixings failed and caused the wing to go under the car, denying Ratzenberger the ability to steer it.

Lastly, Senna was distraught over the conduct of his younger brother, Leonardo, who had stepped over the line by interfering in his brother's personal life, and he must take the blame for destabilising his brother in the days leading up to the San Marino Grand Prix.

So what can we learn 21 years later? There are still a few wrongs that need righting. The 1994 world championship was horribly tainted by the shenanigans of the Benetton team. The winning of Michael Schumacher's first world championship was a farce, and there is absolutely no doubt that Schumacher should have been thrown out of the championship for running an illegal car.

The Benetton team's cheating was the most blatant ever seen in Formula One. When Johnny Herbert joined the team later in the season, he was given a run in Schumacher's car when the traction control had been accidentally left on and could not believe the difference in Schumacher's car compared with his own Benetton-Ford.

The man mainly responsible for the blatant cheating, Tom Walkinshaw, is dead now but it is not too late for the FIA to do something retrospectively about the 1994 world championship. The outcome of the 1994 championship is an ongoing insult to the memory of Ayrton Senna.

The FIA could make a start by stripping the Benetton team and Michael Schumacher of that 1994 championship and handing it to Williams and Damon Hill. That championship does not belong to Schumacher or Benetton. Michael Schumacher later proved, six times, that he was the best driver in Formula One but in 1994 he didn't.

In many ways, the wrong has already been righted. Although Schumacher won the world championship seven times and for that reason alone should be regarded as 'the greatest', he is not. In 2004, I remember there was still a lot of debate about Senna's status in the history of Formula One. Now, 11 years later, that has changed and there is unanimity of the opinion that he was the greatest and fastest Formula One driver. So Ayrton Senna's true legacy has finally been established, and he has been recognised for what he was and is 'the greatest.'

And finally, as this book is signed off for printing, I mention in advance something you may read in the book and not particularly like. There is some mild criticism of Professor Sid Watkins later in these pages. Let me explain. Before he died, I spoke at length, more than once, to Professor Watkins about the weekend of 1st May. I was always mystified with the gaps in the Professor's answers. He was the man who lifted Senna's helmet from his head just before half past two on the afternoon of Sunday 1st May 1994. He was the first man to realise that the greatest driver of all time was dead. But Professor Watkins was never completely forthcoming about the details of Senna's or Ratzenberger's death. Now we know why – according to medical rules, both drivers should have been declared dead at the scene. True, he did get Senna's heart going again immediately so there was a valid reason to remove Senna to hospital, but certainly the existence of Ratzenberger's pulse was only in the Professor's imagination. Of course, if Ratzenberger's death had been correctly handled, then the San Marino Grand Prix would have been cancelled, and Ayrton Senna would in all probability be alive today, happily retired: a billionaire businessman and maybe a six or seven times world champion.

I am afraid Professor Watkins erred in not declaring Ratzenberger dead at the scene and thereby unwittingly creating a very unstable situation for the rest of the race weekend. Doctors must never again be put under such pressure just to ensure that the race goes on.

Some things are more important.

Tom Rubython
Olney Park
Buckinghamshire
25th October 2015

How to read this book

Fatal Weekend is four different books within one divided into six segments that can be read as one or separately. They all stand alone on their own merits. They are: 1) The love story between Senna and Adriane, 2) The technical story 3) Roland Ratzenberger's story 4) The story of Ayrton Senna's last week alive 5) The medical story and 6) the aftermath of his death. If you are really interested in the subject, then you will read all six, and I do advise this to get the full flavour, and it a story worth reading.

However, here is some guidance on how to read it if you are not interested in the love story or the more technical chapters or, indeed, about Roland Ratzenberger's story:

The love story:

The love story between Senna and Adriane, from their first to their last meeting, form the content of three chapters: Chapter 1, Chapter 3 and Chapter 6. Adriane comes into the story in other chapters but only as far as replaying her part in the weekend. If you are not interested in the love story and some of the Da Silva/Senna family machinations, then you may choose to skip these chapters. If you are interested, however, then Chapter 1 tells the story of when they first met to Senna's leaving for Europe two weeks later. Chapter 3 picks up the story of the love affair from the beginning of April 1993 until the last time Adriane saw him, on Friday 3rd April 1994. Chapter 6 details the efforts by the Da Silva family to derail his relationship with Adriane in the last few weeks of Senna's life.

The technical story:

The technical issues that affected the story are covered in four chapters and are a quite different read from the rest of the book. I apologise because this disturbs the natural rhythm of the book (particularly Chapter 22). These are Chapter 8, Chapter 12, Chapter 22 and Chapter 25. Chapter 8 deals with the Benetton team and cheating. Chapter 12 is the story of an investigation into the FIA crash test of Ratzenberger's Simtek car and the question of whether or not it should have passed. Chapter 22 explains how Patrick Head fought to get his hands on the data recorder boxes immediately after Senna's accident, and Chapter 23 goes into the causes of Senna's accident.

Roland Ratzenberger's story:

If you just wish to read about Roland Ratzenberger, then you only need Chapters 10, 11 and 12. It is the most comprehensive story ever written about Ratzenberger. But it is important as, aside from a few newspaper profiles, hardly anything has ever been written about him. Particularly, Chapter 10 is about Ratzenberger's background and his early life, and it also details the history of the Simtek team. Chapter 11 covers Ratzenberger's last few hours alive and his death. Chapter 12 is as above.

The medical story:

Chapter 17 deals with the medical details of Senna and Roland Ratzenberger's deaths and discusses the ethics of what happened. This chapter can be skipped and read later if you wish to avoid disturbing the flow of the story of that very sad afternoon.

Ayrton Senna's last week alive – 27th April to 1st May:

This is the pure story of Ayrton Senna's weekend, consisting of 21 chapters from the moment when he makes his secret visit to see Luca di Montezemolo on Wednesday 27th April to Friday 6th May, the day after Senna's funeral. The story picks up 10 days later when Senna's mother met Adriane at their shared São Paulo apartment and Adriane removed her belongings. This content is the subject of Chapters 2, 4, 5, 7, 9, 10, 11, 13, 14, 15, 16, 17, 18, 19, 20, 21, 23, and 24.

The aftermath:

These are the events after Senna died to the Friday after his funeral the 2nd May to 6th May and they are covered in chapters 26, 27 and 28.

The appendices:

I have included six appendices, which include material that originally appeared in the *Life of Senna* and is additional background reading to this story. Appendix 1 is the story of the close season 1993-94, when Senna moved from McLaren to Williams. Appendix 2 to 5 are about Senna's racing career and his beliefs from 1984 to 1993. Appendix 6 is the story of the trial and the official enquiry in Bologna three years after Senna's death. There is some repetition from the text of the main book, but it is more or less the full story of the trial.

The People
In order of appearance...

Adriane Galisteu b 1973
Adriane Galisteu was Ayrton Senna's girlfriend from 1st April 1993 to 1st May 1994. She was a model on the books of the São Paulo office of Elite Model Management. She became a celebrity in Brazil after Senna's death and now works as a television host as well as regularly appearing in magazines. She has been married twice, first to TV personality Robert Justus, and then to businessman Alexandre Iódice. They have a son called Vittorio, born in 2010.

Ayrton Senna b 1960 d 1994
Ayrton Senna was a Brazilian Formula One driver who competed in 162 races, winning 41 of them and becoming world champion three times in 1988, 1990 and 1991. He drove for Toleman, Lotus, McLaren and Williams in his 11-year Formula One year career.

Antonio Braga b 1926
Antonio Braga is a retired financier with a long and successful history in Brazilian banking and finance. He became very wealthy and acquired homes at Sintra in Portugal and Lyford Cay in the Bahamas. He met Ayrton Senna through his friendship with Emerson Fittipaldi and became his close adviser. He has been married twice, first to Vivi in 1953 and then to Luiza in 1968. He has six children, four from his first marriage and two from his second.

Leonardo Da Silva b 1968
Leonardo Da Silva is the younger brother of Ayrton Senna and a member of the wealthy Brazilian Da Silva family. He worked for the family businesses and was 26 when his brother died. After Senna's death, he worked for the company importing Audi cars into Brazil until 2005. He is the heir to the Da Silva family fortune.

Norio Koike b 1960
Norio Koike, a native of Japan was a Formula One press photographer before going to work exclusively for Ayrton Senna in 1985. He took over from Keith Sutton as Senna's official photographer after Sutton was fired. Koike went everywhere with Senna, on and off track. Known as an introvert, he was delighted to do his master's bidding and took over 40,000 photographs of Senna in nine years, which are now the property of the Ayrton Senna Foundation. In 1994, he bought a new Nikon F5. After Senna's death, he lost motivation and gave the camera away.

Luca di Montezemolo b 1947
Luca di Montezemolo comes from an aristocratic family from the region of Piedmont in Italy. He graduated in law from La Sapienza University in 1971 and studied at Columbia University in New York. He joined Fiat and then Ferrari in 1973 when he became head of the race team under Enzo Ferrari. He left in 1977 to re-join Fiat. In 1991, he was appointed president of Ferrari and started rebuilding the Formula One team, eventually taking it to multiple championships. He retired from Ferrari in September 2014. He has been married twice, latterly to Ludovica in 2000. He has five children.

Sir Frank Williams b 1942
Starting as a mechanic, he founded an unsuccessful Formula One team in 1966, which he

sold to Walter Wolf in 1976. With engineer Patrick Head, he founded a new team called Williams Grand Prix Engineering. The team's first win came in 1979 and first championship in 1980. The team has won multiple world championships since. He signed Ayrton Senna to drive for his team in 1994. He married Virginia in 1967, and she died in 2010. He has two children, Claire and Jonathan.

Patrick Head b 1946
Patrick Head's father, Michael, raced Jaguar sports cars in the 1950s and his son followed him into motor sport, graduating in 1970 with a mechanical engineering degree from UCL. He joined Lola Cars straight out of university, meeting up with John Barnard, with whom he later competed. In 1977, he co-founded Williams Grand Prix Engineering in partnership with Fran Williams and, in an incredible 17-year run, designed cars that won multiple world championship from 1980 to 1997.

Gerhard Berger b 1959
Gerhard Berger competed in Formula One for 14 seasons, starting 210 races, principally for McLaren and Ferrari. He won ten Grands Prix and 12 pole positions. He was Ayrton Senna's team mate at McLaren for three seasons, from 1990-92, and his closest friend on the track. The most interesting statistic of his career is that his first and last victories were also the first and last victories for the Benetton team, 11 years apart. After retiring from Formula One, he carved out a successful career as an executive with various Formula One teams.

Alain Prost b 1955
Alain Prost started go-karting at the age of 14 and progressed, winning in Formula Three before joining McLaren briefly in 1980 at the age of 24. He took his first race victory at his home Grand Prix in France a year later, driving for Renault. Re-joining McLaren, he was world champion in 1985: the first of three for the team. In 1990, he joined Ferrari for two unsuccessful years before driving for Williams in 1993, retiring after winning another world championship. He won 51 races from 199 starts. In 1997, Prost took over the French Ligier team, running it as Prost Grand Prix until it went bankrupt in 2002.

Betise Assumpcao b 1958
A Brazilian and former talented volleyball player, she came to Europe in 1988 and has worked in sports for over 30 years, first as a journalist before becoming Ayrton Senna's press officer in 1990. She kept Senna out of trouble and also kept his secrets. She is now an independent sports consultant. She married Patrick Head after Senna's death.

Owen O'Mahoney b 1951
Captain Owen O'Mahoney learned to fly in the RAF and, at the end of his service, moved on to fly private jets. He was employed by Ayrton Senna in September 1990 when he bought a HS-125 jet and worked for him until his death in 1994. Senna used to call him 'Mahny' after difficulty pronouncing Owen. He carried on flying Senna's plane for the family and also piloted for other drivers, including Michael Schumacher. After virtually retiring from flying, he now works for the Ayrton Senna Foundation.

Galvao Bueno b 1950
Galvao Bueno joined TV Globo in 1981 and is its Formula One commentator and a very well-known figure in Brazilian broadcasting. He became a personal friend of Senna and a member of his inner circle from 1980. Senna nicknamed him 'Parrot'. He is known as the Murray Walker of Brazil and apes Walker's broadcasting style. He has been married twice, first to Lucia and then Desiree. He has six children.

FATAL WEEKEND

Julian Jakobi b 1951
Trained as a chartered accountant, he worked with Mark McCormack at IMG handling the affairs of Alain Prost and Ayrton Senna amongst many other sporting stars. He left IMG in 1992 to become Ayrton Senna's business manager. His involvement with the Senna family continued after 1994 on both the commercial and charitable side of the family business. In 1997, he founded CSS Stellar PLC looking after the affairs of Prost, Jacques Villeneuve, Dario Franchitti amongst others and is now an independent sports manager. He married Fiona in 1983 and they have three grown-up children.

Viviane Lalli b 1958
Viviane Lalli is the sister of the Ayrton Senna and mother of Bruno Senna, currently racing in Europe. She is president of the Ayrton Senna Foundation, which was established after Senna's death with a cheque for $5,000 from Nigel Mansell. She graduated in Psychology at the Pontificial Catholic University of São Paulo in 1979. She worked in clinical psychology as a psychotherapist. She was married to Flavio Lalli, who died in 1994 in a motorcycling accident. They have three children: Bruno, Bianca and Paula who all work the Ayrton Senna Foundation.

Celso Lemos b 1957
Celso Lemos is a Brazilian businessman and was head of Ayrton Senna's brand licencing company from 1993 as Senna began to ramp up his business interests. After Senna died, he became head of the commercial side of the Ayrton Senna Foundation. He left in 2002 to pursue a business career and is now director of Allegro Participacoes SA.

Milton Da Silva b 1931
Milton Teodoro Guirado Da Silva was Ayrton Senna's father. He was a wealthy industrialist with a major share of the Brazilian car parts business. He also farmed thousands of acres outside São Paulo. A trained pilot, he financed his son's motor racing career in its early stages in the seventies. Now 84, he lives quietly on the family estate in Tatui with his wife, Neyde.

Neyde Da Silva b 1927
Neyde Senna married Milton Da Silva and produced three children: Viviane, Ayrton and Leonardo. When Ayrton Da Silva stared motor racing in Britain, he changed his name from Da Silva to his mother's maiden name Senna. Da Silva is the equivalent in Brazilian of the name 'Smith' and Senna wanted a more distinctive name.

Jo Ramirez b 1941
Jo Ramírez was born in Mexico City and studied mechanical engineering at UNAM. In 1960, he followed his friend Ricardo Rodríguez to Europe. After Rodríguez was killed at the Mexican Grand Prix in 1962, he worked at Maserati, Lamborghini, Ford, Eagle, Tyrrell, Copersucar F1 and, finally, McLaren, where he worked as a team manager from 1984 to 2001, when he retired. He is married to Bea and they have two children.

Josef Leberer b 1959
Josef Leberer was retained by Ayrton Senna full time and travelled to every race, looking after the physical well-being of his driver and attending to his dietary needs. After Senna died, he worked for many teams, ending up at Sauber looking after its drivers.

Nuno Cobra b 1938
A graduate of the School of Physical Education of São Carlos, he was professor of Bauru School of Physical Education until he became Ayrton Senna's personal trainer for most of

his racing career. Every winter, he ran a rigorous programme in Brazil that got Senna fit for the following season. He wrote a book called *The Seed of Victory*, in which he wrote about the theory of 'getting to the brain by the muscle and spirit through the body.' Cobra also trained Christian Fittipaldi, Rubens Barrichello, Mika Hakkinen and Gil de Ferran at varying times.

Xuxa Meneghel b 1963
Xuxa Meneghel is a Brazilian entertainer and television host. She is one of the best known celebrities in Brazil and has been for 30 years. At one point, she was Brazil's highest-paid woman. She dated Ayrton Senna for two years in 1989 and 1990. She was one of the three significant women in his life along with his wife Liliane and Adriane Galisteu.

David Brown b 1960
David Brown became Nigel Mansell's race engineer at Williams in 1987; then with Thierry Boutsen in 1989; Mansell again in 1991; Alain Prost in 1993; and then Ayrton Senna in 1994. He engineered Damon Hill's car after Senna's death, but then moved to McLaren to be David Coulthard's race engineer. He ended his Formula One career at Jordan in 2002.

Damon Hill b 1960
Damon Hill was Ayrton Senna's last team mate at Williams in 1994. He took the first of his 22 victories at the 1993 Hungarian Grand Prix. Hill became world champion in 1996 with eight wins and raced for Arrows and Jordan teams before ending his career in 1999. He is the son of twice world champion Graham Hill, and he is married to Georgie.

Rubens Barrichello b 1972
Brazilian, Rubens Barrichello competed in Formula One between 1993 and 2011 and holds the record for competing in the most Grand Prix races (331) and has the 11th highest points total in history. Starting at Jordan, then Stewart-Ford, he drove for Ferrari from 2000 to 2005, moving to Honda in 2006 and then Brawn in 2009, and ending his career at Williams in 2011.

Sid Watkins b 1928 d 2012
Professor Sid Watkins was a British neurosurgeon. He graduated from the University of in 1952 and served for four years in the Royal Army Medical Corps before specialising in neurosurgery. He was appointed the Formula One Safety and Medical Delegate in 1978 by Bernie Ecclestone and held the post for 26 years. He helped save the lives of Formula One drivers Gerhard Berger, Martin Donnelly, Érik Comas, Mika Häkkinen, Rubens Barrichello and Karl Wendlinger. He was married twice, latterly to author Susan Watkins, and has four sons and two daughters.

John Corsmit b 1915 d 2000
Veteran administrator, John Corsmit was the FIA security chief at the 1994 San Mario Grand Prix. This role gave him wide powers over the running of the Grand Prix alongside Roland Bruynseraede and Charlie Whiting, and he was effectively in charge of many aspects of the race management. He began his career marshalling at Zandvoort and headed the Royal Dutch Automobile Club. He was Ayrton Senna's nemesis and the two frequently clashed.

Richard Williams b 1947
Richard Williams, a former music journalist, was chief sports writer of *The Guardian* in the nineties, covering a full range of sports but becoming best known for his writing on Formula One. He exposed cheating at Benetton in the 1994 season in his book *The Death of Ayrton Senna*. He also wrote *Racers*, *Enzo Ferrari: A Life* and *The Last Road Race*.

FATAL WEEKEND

Peter Collins b 1950
Peter Collins was one of the Australians who came to Britain in the 1970s to pursue a career in motorsport. He was team manager for Lotus, Benetton, Williams and finally head of the Lotus Formula One team from 1991 to 1994. He was responsible for bringing Nigel Mansell and Mika Häkkinen into Formula One and became a very close friend and confidant of Ayrton Senna. Later a driver talent manager, he discovered the careers of Jenson Button and Kimi Raikkonen working with the legendary driver manager, the late David Robertson. Recently, he managed F1 drivers Giorgio Pantano and Tonio Liuzzi. He is married to Jane and has a daughter called Sam.

Tom Walkinshaw b 1946 d 2010
Tom Walkinshaw was a driver who came up through the ranks of motorsport until 1974 when he became a team entrant, in touring cars, GT and finally Formula One. He started TWR in 1975 and built it into a large engineering group. He entered F1 in 1991 as Engineering Director of Benetton. He bought the Arrows team in 1997 but TWR went bankrupt in 2002, forcing him out of Britain. He returned to Australia and raced saloon cars. He was married twice, to Elizabeth and then Martine, and has three sons: Fergus, Ryan and Sean.

Max Mosley b 1950
A qualified barrister, Max Mosley was president of the Fédération Internationale de l'Automobile from 1993 to 2009. Before that, he was a driver and team entrant, being a co-founder of March Engineering and, later, Simtek Research. Mosley is the youngest son of Sir Oswald Mosley and is married to Jean. They have two sons.

Bernie Ecclestone b 1930
Bernie Ecclestone is Formula One's undisputed supremo. He began as a driver and then driver manager, pursuing an entrepreneurial career in motorcycles, car sales and property development. He was the supreme opportunist and bought the Brabham team and gradually subsumed Formula One's finances and formed a team with Max Mosley, who became president of the FIA. His career as a driver manager and entrant saw Jochen Rindt become world champion and his own Brabham team win two drivers' championships. He has been married three times and has three children. His exploitation of Formula One's TV rights made him one of Europe's richest men. The Ecclestone family were very close to Ayrton Senna and often hosted him at their London home when he was visiting England.

Roland Ratzenberger b 1960 d 1994
An Austrian racing driver who raced in GT, Formula Nippon, Formula 3000 and Formula One. He died during qualifying for the 1994 San Marino Grand Prix, the same event at which three-time World Champion Ayrton Senna died the following day.

Nick Wirth b 1966
A trained automotive engineer and aerodynamicist, Nick Wirth founded Simtek Research in partnership with Max Mosley in 1989. Mosley resigned from Simtek in 1993 to become president of the FIA. Wirth launched his Formula One team shortly afterwards in 1994, but it quickly closed down a year after the death of its second driver, Roland Ratzenberger. After the demise of Simtek, he was technical director at the Benetton team and, later, the Virgin Racing Formula One team with no great success.

Roland Bruynseraede b 1939
Roland Bruynseraede is a Belgian motorsport official who for many years, from 1988 to 1995, was FIA race director. He previously worked as the FIA circuit inspector and Formula One safety delegate. Bruynseraede grew up in Germany and is fluent in French, Dutch,

German and English. Bruynseraede was controversial because he declared as safe the Imola circuit in 1994 ignoring the dangers of an unprotected concrete wall at the notorious Tamburello Curve. He was race director of the 1994 San Marino Grand Prix.

Gerhard Kuntschik b 1953
Dr Gerhard Kuntschik is head of sport at the Salzburger Nachrichten and, in 1994, was deputy sports editor and Austria's premier motor sport journalist. He was a close friend of Roland Ratzenberger and mentored his career.

Charlie Whiting b 1952
Charlie Whiting has many titles including Race Director, Safety Delegate, Permanent Starter and head of the Technical Department. It all means he is the most powerful man in Formula One after Bernie Ecclestone and Jean Todt. He started his career as a mechanic in saloon cars, then Formula 5000 and finally Formula One at Hesketh and as chief mechanic at Brabham, where he met Bernie Ecclestone. In 1988, Ecclestone appointed him FIA Technical Delegate to Formula One and, in 1997, FIA Race Director and Safety Delegate.

John Barnard b 1946
John Barnard is regarded as one of the top five race car designers of all time alongside Colin Chapman, Ron Tauranac, Patrick Head and Adrian Newey. He invented the carbon fibre chassis and the semi-automatic gearbox. Barnard met Patrick Head at Lola Cars in 1970, and they became best friends, dominating F1 car design in the eighties and nineties.

Adrian Newey b 1958
Adrian Newey is the doyen of British race car designers. He came to fame at Williams in partnership with Patrick Head in the 1990s. Together they formed a devastating partnership. He was lured away to McLaren in 1997 after being refused a directorship and shareholding at Williams. He almost joined Jaguar Racing in 2001 but opted to stay at McLaren. Then he almost re-joined Williams in 2006 but was again refused a shareholding and declined. He is currently the chief technical officer of the Red Bull Racing Formula One team. His cars have won 10 drivers' world championships.

John Watson b 1946
John Watson competed in Formula One, winning five Grand Prix races for Penske and McLaren. After his retirement, he became a commentator for Eurosport's coverage of Formula One from 1990 to 1996. He is currently one of motor racing's best known broadcasters.

Murray Walker b 1923
Formula One's British motorsport commentator for both the BBC and ITV from the early seventies to 2001. From 1980, he was the other half of a superb television double act with James Hunt, which ended with Hunt's death in 1993. Walker excelled as a commentator with an extraordinary breadth of knowledge and the ability to comment soundly on any issue to do with motor racing. His talents were never more obvious than the night Ayrton Senna died, when he delivered an extraordinary homily to the Brazilian driver on the BBC Six O'clock News. Their mutual respect was genuinely and enthusiastically held and endured right up to 1st May 1994.

Maria Theresa Fiandri b 1938
Dr Maria Theresa Fiandri was chief medical officer of Bologna Hospital on the day Ayrton Senna died. She was called to the hospital on the afternoon of 1st May 1994 and took charge of his treatment. She announced his death just before seven o'clock that evening after two bulletins confirmed he was gravely ill earlier in the evening.

"She has to be sensual, fascinating, intelligent, beautiful and assured of herself."
Ayrton Senna
March 1993

CHAPTER 1

Flashback: Adriane March 1993

Nothing would be the same again

It was just another beautiful Monday afternoon in downtown São Paulo when 19-year-old Adriane Galisteu popped into the offices of Elite Models, Brazil's biggest model agency, for an audition. Monday 15th March 1993 had nothing to distinguish it from any other Monday for Adriane. She loved every day of the week and was living her dream. Adriane had modelled since the age of 12, and she had been on Elite's books ever since it opened its São Paulo office in 1989. She was the daughter of a Brazilian mother and a Spanish father who died from a heart attack at the age of 50 when she was 15.

From when she could walk, Ema, her mother had entered her in beauty contests and she won some of them. As she remembered: "When I was nine, I found out I was beautiful and said, 'Mum, I want to be on TV.'" Ema Galisteu told her it would not be easy, but she got a photographer called Teresa Pinheiro to do her daughter's portfolio and, as soon as they saw the photos, she was quickly signed up by a children's agency called Pretty Models, in San Caetano.

She didn't disappoint her mother and, at 12, she won an audition to appear in a TV commercial for McDonald's hamburgers. Her career just took off after that, and she was signed by Elite when it opened its São Paulo office, four years later.

Adriane wasn't a top tier model, but she wasn't second tier either. At 19, she had already had two assignments abroad and could easily earn $500-$1,000 a day when there was work. She had a certain look that clients liked. She was not a classic beauty but was very ethereal with a magical smile. Her long blonde hair cascaded everywhere. She wasn't for everyone, but for some clients she fitted in perfectly. It meant she was always in demand and easily found work for at least two days every week. She had never known anything else, and she found modelling just one giddy round of auditions. There were other distractions, as she said: "Some invitations which can be accepted, a few proposals that must be refused."

By 1993, her earnings easily topped $50,000 and, at just 19, the world was at her feet. But suddenly that particular Monday, as she crowded into the Elite reception, she had a reality check. She was in company with a dozen other girls she realised were just as beautiful and desirable as she. She wondered what made her stand out in this company and came to the conclusion: "nothing."

Today, she was auditioning for an unusual assignment and had almost not bothered to come. Shell Oil wanted hospitality hostesses for the Brazilian Grand Prix and instead of going to a promotions agency had come to Elite Brasil because they wanted the best girls for a special assignment. Shell was ready to pay modelling rates for four days' promotional work. It had attracted 12 girls auditioning for 10 openings. Adriane had never lost a competitive audition and knew this job would be hers if she wanted it. But did she want it? She had done promotional work when she first started out but had moved beyond it. As she said: "Honestly, promotional girl didn't sound good to me. Not that I hadn't already done that type of work; it was not that, no prejudice, it's just that I was at a very special moment in my career and I felt I could choose my jobs. Besides Formula One, I thought it was a closed world, too masculine. It was as distant to me as rugby or baseball." She joked: "I would never want to exchange my perfume Roma by Laura Biaggotti for the smell of gasoline."

But $1,000 for four days' work was good pay for promotions work, and she was persuaded to accept the assignment, especially when she saw how many of Elite's top girls, including Nara Pinto, Patricia Teixeira and Laura Guiterrez, had also gone for it.

But the audition almost ended in tears when two Shell executives asked Adriane to model a swimsuit. She misunderstood and mouthed in the equivalent Portuguese, "I'm out of here." Just as she was walking out, the man in charge grabbed her hand and said: "No, you don't understand." She only calmed down when they told her the uniform for the job had the same cut as the swimsuit, which was why it was necessary.

She hadn't quite grasped how important the job was and that the three top directors of Shell in Brazil personally turned out at the audition to approve the girls. They were wooing some important clients that weekend, and even Ayrton Senna had agreed to help out with the process by coming to visit the hospitality suite.

Adriane kept hearing Senna's name being bandied about. She obviously knew who he was but hadn't quite grasped how important he was. The other girls were tittering about Senna and the fact that he currently did not have a regular girlfriend, and it was quite clear that they were all up for that role. In fact, she seemed to be the only one not interested. Adriane already had a boyfriend. It was continually on and off, but in a funny sort of way it was solid. Was she in love? – maybe, she thought. Was he in love with her? – unlikely, she also thought.

Adriane and nine other girls got through the audition. Afterwards, she left the offices to go shopping and have coffee with the girls. For her, it was just another assignment and a nice change from being in front of a camera all day. As she recalled: "It never crossed my mind that during that weekend I would find the love of my life."

Then, just as she was leaving, she suddenly remembered she was booked for a modelling job on the Thursday. She rushed back in and told them she couldn't make it on Thursday, expecting them to cancel the whole booking. But they didn't and just said she could start Friday. "Same money?" she asked cheekily. "Same money," the head honcho at Shell replied. "Done," she replied and shook his hand, delivering her unique, almost cheeky, smile at the same time. The Shell directors thought she was the pick of the bunch, with her street smarts combined with an unquestioned innocence, which was why they agreed to pay her four days' money for three days' work.

It was actually her second Formula One job – she had done a photo shoot in Portugal in 1990 when she was 16. It was her first trip overseas, and she had watched Nigel Mansell dominate the Portuguese Grand Prix in his Ferrari. She had become a fan of the Englishman. Up to then, she had always been indifferent to Senna, whom she barely noticed had come second. As she said: "I would be lying if I said I was an Ayrton Senna fan."

For no reason she could think of, Adriane found herself really looking forward to Friday. The modelling job on Thursday was straightforward enough and she was home early and went to bed straight after her mother had served supper.

The next morning, she was out of bed by 5am on Friday 19th March and straight into a taxi the agency had sent to bring her to Elite's offices for a 6am start. The other nine girls were already there waiting, and as soon as she walked through the door, they all piled into a minibus to get to the Interlagos race track circuit before the traffic built up.

She remembered: "At the circuit, we were quickly told how Formula One operates so that we wouldn't just stand there with our pretty faces and bodies. They introduced us to the jargon of the circuit: pitwall, cockpit, pitlane, etc." She was given her uniform, which consisted of Shell branded white shirt and hot pants. It was an easy assignment looking after Shell's important guests, showing them around the paddock and making sure they were happy. She found the whole scene very laid back, and it surprised her – everything seemed so calm. Where was all the excitement everyone talked about?

And there seemed to be no sign of Ayrton Senna.

After a 12-hour day, the minibus collected up all the girls at around six o'clock, and this time they had no choice but to thread through all the race traffic leaving the circuit. She didn't get home until well after eight, 14 hours after she had left the house that morning. She was exhausted, but her mother had kept supper hot so they could eat together. She then flopped down in front of the television eager to see some news about the Grand Prix, in which she had never been interested before. She was surprised to see that three quarters of the programmes were focused on Ayrton Senna as if he was the only driver in the race. Adriane realised that she knew very little about Brazil's national hero. She was surprised how good-looking he was and wondered whether she would see him tomorrow.

On Saturday, she went through the same routines again but noticed the step up in atmosphere and tension. In fact, by midday, she noticed a complete change from the casual indifference of Friday to the intense interest about what was happening on the track and in particular what was happening with Senna. Eventually, he qualified for the race in third place, which surprised her – "Didn't he always win?" she thought to herself.

After the guests had lunch and watched qualifying, the girls were allowed to eat, just after 2:30pm. But lunch was interrupted as whispers swept around the Shell hospitality suite that Ayrton Senna would be arriving shortly. It was exciting news for the guests, and Adriane was very surprised to see the change that came over some of Brazil's top business people, excited at the prospect of meeting Senna.

Some of these people she recognised from the newspapers and they seemed awestruck. "Who was this man?" she thought again.

None of the models had actually expected to meet Senna although all the talk in the rest room had been about him and how he was single again after having finally split up with his long-standing girlfriend, Xuxa Meneghel, the year before. They had actually split up three years before but Senna had kept his personal life under the radar since then.

There were whispers that he was interested in one of the Shell girls who had caught his attention. When it was confirmed that he was on his way, there was a rush to the bathroom and all the girls crowded around the mirror. Adriane was non-plussed. She wasn't a Formula One fan, and Senna held the least interest for her.

That was until she saw him.

Senna had always had his pick of Brazilian girls. He had had many girlfriends: many more than were apparent to the outside world. He went for Brazilian girls almost exclusively. When he liked a girl, his technique was to get his assistant to ask for her telephone number. If he got a good reaction, Senna would call. His gypsy lifestyle and constant moving around meant he was insulated from relationships that went wrong. Although there had been plenty of casual girlfriends, there had only ever been two serious women in his life before Adriane. The two were his teenage sweetheart and then wife, Liliane, between 1975 and 1981; and Xuxa Meneghel, a very famous (and rich) Brazilian TV presenter, between 1986 and 1991.

He arrived in a frenzy, surrounded by admirers with photographers clicking off flashbulbs. It was such a commotion and all Adriane could see was his blue cap. But she was immediately impressed with the way he seemed to manage to greet everyone personally and take in the whole scene. He shook hands with one guest whilst addressing another, then turned round and addressed that one as his hand shot out to another and so on. In the end, everybody had shaken his hand and said at least two words to him. No one felt short-changed and she noticed they all had smiles on their faces.

Adriane was extremely impressed with the way he pulled it off and realised his popularity with Brazilians was no accident – he was special. As she said: "His timing and control of the situation while he greeted everyone, looking around. I didn't move, I only observed. He was there, defenceless among fans and requests for autographs and no privacy. The life of Ayrton Senna must be very hard, I thought to myself."

Then, when the meet and greet was over, he got on a makeshift platform and was handed a microphone. Seemingly effortlessly, he made a short speech and then Adriane was certain he turned and looked over at her. She was standing in the middle of the group of Elite girls and they all felt the same thing afterwards – that he had looked at them. Afterwards, none of the girls could be sure who had caught his eye, but each girl was sure it was herself. Adriane remembered: "I felt he looked at me. But was it me or Nara who was just behind me? Or was it just an empty gaze?" Nara Pinto said to her: "He looked at you." Adriane replied: "It was at you." Nara said: "No, he prefers blondes."

She admits that all the excitement got to her, and by then she was very interested as to whether she was the chosen one, especially when the rumour mill started to buzz again that Senna was definitely smitten with one of the Shell girls. But which Shell girl?

Adriane had visited the pit garage with her guests on Friday and Saturday, both times without seeing Senna, and on the second day she was keeping a sharp lookout for him.

On Saturday evening, the routine of the journey home was repeated, but this time the circuit traffic was terrible and it was after nine o'clock before Adriane was back home. On Sunday, there was an even earlier start and the girls all assembled at the Elite office at 5:30am to catch the bus – it was the only way to get to the circuit on time.

At the circuit, she found the atmosphere and the tension ramped up again. The girls were so busy looking after many more guests than the Friday and Saturday. Adriane was shepherding groups of guests to the pit lane all morning.

On one of the trips, she was suddenly surprised by a tap on the shoulder from a man who introduced himself only as Jacir. He said: "I am Ayrton Senna's personal assistant for private matters. He has asked me to get your phone number." Adriane stared at Jacir for a few seconds and, then, without even thinking, she took the pad from his hands and wrote down her home number and Elite's office number. Then an older man, who introduced himself as Antonio Braga, came up and asked her for a fax number where she could be contacted. Braga hinted at Senna's interest in her.

Braga was a retired financier who lived in Portugal and the Bahamas; he was Senna's closest friend. Adriane didn't know it then, but it was the start of a lifelong friendship between Adriane and the Braga family.

Adriane was ecstatic and when she got back to the hospitality suite and couldn't help sharing her news with the other girls. However, her face dropped suddenly as half-a-dozen of the Elite girls told her they had had a similar experience that morning and that Jacir had also asked for their phone numbers. Adriane couldn't believe it and thought to herself: "Okay, so that's how Ayrton Senna plays the game."

But it was not the way she played.

Shell was a very important McLaren sponsor, and later that day, before the race, Senna came to the hospitality suite again. He made another speech and told Shell's guests: "I can win. I cannot guarantee victory though, but it is what I want." This time, the girls were all lined up right in front of him in a protective cordon as he spoke. When he had finished and was saying his goodbyes, Adriane got her first close-up look at him. Their eyes locked and he smiled directly at her – this time there was no doubt.

Although she was furious with him, she admits that she was hooked on him from that moment, although she was determined not to show it.

Adriane watched the change in atmosphere as the build up to the race began. Lunch was early and the guests all trooped off to the balcony or their grandstand seats, leaving the girls in the suite to watch the race on television. Adriane had never really watched a race and the experience was new to her. All the girls cheered as Senna's McLaren overtook Damon Hill's Williams-Renault to slot into second at the first bend. Prost drove off into the lead and by lap 11 Hill overtook Senna. On lap 25 Senna had a disaster and got a pit time penalty for overtaking cars during a caution period and found himself fourth behind Michael Schumacher.

Then Ayrton Senna got very lucky as the rain came down. Senna, Schumacher and Hill rushed into the pits for wet rain tyres while Alain Prost stayed out on his dry weather tyres. There were many accidents, and for the first time in Formula One, a Safety Car appeared on the track to slow the field of cars down whilst the accidents were cleared up. Then Alain Prost crashed, and the Safety Car came out again.

The rain had caused chaos, and Adriane and the girls were almost spell-bound in front of the television enjoying the excitement of a wet race. Adriane remembers: "My apathy about the race had turned into anxiety, and I only had eyes for that red and white McLaren car. I found myself frenetically cheering for him." Michael Schumacher went out of contention after a lengthy pit stop and the race was on between Senna and Damon Hill, who were back on normal tyres as the track dried. Hill was no match for Senna on a damp track and the hero of Brazil was back in the lead of his home race. The crowd, and it seemed the whole of Brazil, went wild as it appeared that Senna was going to win. In the end, he beat Hill by 16 seconds. As he crossed the line, the girls hugged each other, recovering just enough to welcome their elated guests back into the hospitality suite.

Senna's win triggered a whole host of celebrations and a party was quickly organised by Shell's marketing people for that night at the Limelight Club in the middle of São Paulo. The 10 girls were ordered to attend by their Shell bosses. Adriane was exhausted after her hectic three days and feigned tiredness, only going along reluctantly. She was resisting any more involvement with Ayrton Senna, and she was frightened by what was happening to her. She wanted to step off the ridiculous emotional roller coaster she had created in her mind.

She also didn't care for nightclubs: "I looked forward to lying down on my bed to regain energy after a hard day of work. But I had to go."

The girls arrived at the Limelight Club at around 11 o'clock to find the celebrations were already in full swing. The arrival of the girls from Elite caused a near sensation. For reasons not clear even to herself, Adriane deliberately dressed down in jeans, a black top with a red silk scarf and wore minimal make-up. Subconsciously, she had made herself look as unattractive as possible, especially against the other girls who were dolled up to their eyebrows.

No one was sure whether Ayrton Senna would come to the party, but soon after midnight, he was suddenly there. As Adriane remembers: "He arrived when the clock struck 12 as if it was an invented Cinderella story." For her, it may as well have been. The waiters formed a corridor for Senna, his brother Leonardo, and his assistant Jacir to get them to their reserved booth.

Adriane found him sitting in a padded banquette with his brother, Leonardo, talking to retired Brazilian footballer Pelé. Straightaway she resolved to say 'hello' to Senna and leave.

It was an extraordinary scene with the two most famous Brazilians together in one place. The excitement was palpable. The table was surrounded by at least a dozen girls, dressed to the nines, crowding around the three men. But Adriane found she stood out, precisely because she had dressed down.

She waited in the informal queue and shook his hand, congratulated him on his win and told him she had enjoyed the weekend and apologised for having to leave so early.

But Senna clearly had other ideas. He rarely drank, but for once he was drinking alcohol and appeared slightly out of control. He pulled her towards him as Leonardo moved up to make room. He persuaded her to stay for a drink. She remembers she was scared and retreated to her formal role as Shell's representative and babbled some PR-speak: "I said, 'You were great. I am here on behalf of Shell.' But he wouldn't let go of my hand: only briefly, to get a glass of champagne, which he handed to me." But Adriane didn't drink and had never touched alcohol in her life. As she protested, Senna said: "But it is a special day. I won. Won't you drink anything?" She explained she didn't like the taste of alcohol and asked for a Coca-Cola. Drinking it up quickly, she insisted that she had to leave as she had another assignment early in the morning. This time, Senna didn't persist but said to her: "Wait a minute, we are going to have a barbecue at Angra at the weekend, would you like to come?" She pretended not to hear and got up to go. She recalled saying to Senna: "I have to go. You have my phone number."

Adriane was playing it very cool and was acting counterintuitively – she wasn't prepared to stay and compete with all the other girls. By this time, she was very, very interested in him, and she knew that walking away was a risk. Senna grabbed hold of Jacir, who was sitting opposite him and said: "Go after her and make sure she comes at the weekend."

Jacir followed her out of the door and invited her to the beach house in Angra a few days later. He told her it was a going-away party before he returned to Europe for the European season. Adriane looked at Jacir and didn't say yes or no. She just nodded a 'goodbye' and rushed off to get into one of the waiting taxis that had been booked to get everyone home.

When Adriane left, Senna spent the rest of that evening with another model called Daniela, and she went home with him. Daniela was a blue-eyed blonde from southern Brazil and the following day was telling people that Ayrton Senna was her new boyfriend. But she was premature as Senna was actually smitten with Adriane.

As soon as she got back home that night, Adriane rushed to her bedroom and lay on the bed staring at the ceiling and imagining what was going on back at the Limelight. She couldn't believe how she had behaved. Eventually, she fell asleep in her clothes and woke up with a start at around four o'clock before sorting herself out.

At nine o'clock, she was in a deep sleep when her mother's maid shook her and woke her up.

Breathlessly, wearing a ridiculous smile, the maid told her: "Telephone for you. It's a certain Ayrton."

Adriane looked round the room, trying to remember the previous night. The maid couldn't understand why she was not excited, but Adriane knew it would be Jacir calling on behalf of Senna to ask her again to the barbecue. She was very annoyed at being woken up but grabbed her dressing gown and went to find the phone.

Picking it up, she paused and in the best sarcastic manner she could muster she said, 'So?' into the receiver. To her surprise, it was Senna, and she felt such a fool. As she remembers: "The sweet and calm voice in which he answered me back was like a cold shower cooling me down."

He said he had rung to invite her to his barbecue on Saturday personally and that he really hoped she would come. Her feigned indifference and sharp exit from the nightclub had surprised him and had exactly the effect she intended, and she resolved to continue her 'hard to get' stance. She was non-committal and told him she would "look at her diary."

Senna laughed as he was on to her and he said: "What are you doing now?" Realising she had overplayed it, she cut him off quickly before she could make a bigger fool of herself and told him she had to rush for an audition. That bit was true; she was due in a television studio at midday to audition for a part in a TV commercial that was being made, as coincidence would have it, with Nelson Piquet. He asked her to call him when she had finished and gave her his direct office phone number saying, "So call me right after the audition."

Any resistance she had, contrived or otherwise, ended then. He had literally melted her heart with one phone call, and she bought 15 phone tokens and couldn't resist calling him back from a public call box as soon as she got the chance. She was very nervous as she dialled the number and doubted she would be put through. A secretary answered the phone. When asked her name, she said "Adriane" and instantly regretted it, thinking he would be less likely to take the call if he knew it was her. But the secretary had clearly been expecting her call and put Adriane straight through to her boss.

Straightaway, Senna was very interested in the audition, and she decided to confess that it had been for a part opposite Piquet, his great track rival, advertising Tarantella tomato ketchup. Although she didn't know any details, Adriane knew there was bad blood between him and Piquet, which she had read about in the gossip columns. Senna told her that Piquet had spread rumours in the Formula One paddock that he was gay years earlier, which is why they didn't get on.

Suddenly, Senna got serious and started to question her closely about Piquet and what he was doing. His strong-arm methods upset her, and when Senna mentioned the barbecue again, she changed the subject. But he insisted on an answer, and she told him she was unsure of going to the barbecue because it involved an overnight stay and she didn't know him. He replied: "How can you say you don't know me, everybody knows me." She laughed and said: "As a man. As a person, I don't know you. I don't have the slightest idea of what you are like."

The she relented and told him she would have to be able to get back to

São Paulo on Sunday afternoon, and on that basis she accepted the invitation, making it quite clear she would insist on her own bedroom.

Then, on a whim, she asked him his star sign. "Aries," he replied. "Me too," she said.

Sensing her resistance, Senna invited her to dine that night with his friends at a restaurant called The Place in São Paulo. But later that evening, she heard other Elite girls had been invited too, and so she stood him up.

Senna had also invited Daniela to the dinner, and she thought he was trying to decide which girl would be his next girlfriend after weighing up both of them at dinner. When Adriane didn't turn up, he spent a second night with Daniela at his apartment.

The following morning, Senna dropped Daniela off at the Elite model agency, where Adriane was waiting to go on a job. Inside, Daniela talked about nothing else but her new boyfriend, and she left no one in any doubt as to what had happened the night before. She told Adriane: "He's great and I'm in love." Daniela went on to give all the girls a complete description of the night they had spent together. She said Senna had given her a foot, neck and hand massage. She told them he had even put toothpaste on a toothbrush for her in the morning.

Adriane was eaten up with jealousy. She had to admit Senna had good taste; Daniela was a lovely girl and a very successful model.

Tuesday passed, then Wednesday and Thursday, and still she had not heard from him. On Friday Adriane completely lost her nerve. She realised it was a deciding moment in her life, and if she didn't grab it now, it may not come again. She found that she was insanely jealous of Daniela and felt that she had overplayed her hand. It should have been her in his apartment on Monday night and now she had nothing to lose by calling him. When she did, he asked her to Angra again and, throwing caution to the wind, she told him she couldn't stop thinking about him.

Senna invited her to come over to his 17th-floor apartment at the Rua Paraguai in São Paulo. He told her to put her car in the basement car park below his apartment and described how to get in. She packed a small weekend bag and put it in the boot of her car, ready to go to Angra for the barbecue.

When she arrived, he was waiting for her and wiling away the time by doing grass slides with Leonardo across the two-inch shag pile carpet in his sitting room. She was shown in by his housekeeper, and she was surprised as he had no shirt on. He also seemed surprised to see her and bounded across the giant room and said: "I am pleased to meet you. My name is Ayrton Senna Da Silva. I am 33 years old, and I do not have a girlfriend." She asked: "How come I know your girlfriend?" He replied looking puzzled: "Me? Who is she?" Adriane said: "Daniela. Blonde. Blue eyes. Tall." After a pause, Senna replied: "So that's her name."

Adriane was not impressed and turned to go as Senna realised he had a lot of explaining to do. He grabbed her arm and apologised. He told her he rarely drank alcohol but had got very drunk the night before and was still celebrating his victory on Sunday. She called him a "sleazeball", and they both laughed.

He apologised for his lack of a shirt and said he was dressing to get ready to go to Angra when Leonardo had pulled him into the sitting room to do grass slides.

They sat down on a sofa and Leonardo disappeared. He asked her about Daniela as he continued to pretend he couldn't remember who she was. They talked for an hour and a half as he persuaded her to come to Angra. He said it would be a party with many people going and added: "I don't bite." Then she confessed that her overnight bag was already packed and in the boot of her car.

With that they went down to the basement, and she got her bag from her car and jumped into Senna's black Honda NSX to drive to his offices in the suburb of Santana, where his helicopter was waiting on the roof. She was surprised to see Daniela, along with another model who had also worked for Shell at the Grand Prix, plus Senna's personal photographer Norio Koike. Senna had hedged his bets, and Daniela was as shocked to see Adriane as Adriane was to see her, especially as it was apparent that she had arrived with him. But it was too late to turn back as her car was miles away.

It was Adriane's first trip in a helicopter, and once the girls' shock of finding each other on the trip subsided, the atmosphere was good as they all looked forward to a weekend by the sea. They were all nervous taking off from the rooftop but Senna told them: "Don't worry. I had lessons just before you came."

When the helicopter landed, they were met by Senna's Angra housekeepers Matesus and Maria, who grabbed the bags and escorted them to the house. Senna's dog, Quinda, rushed up to his master, and dog and master spent five minutes saying 'hello'. She quickly discovered that Senna was called 'Beco' by almost everyone, a habit she also quickly fell into.

The Angra beach house was a paradise on earth and Senna's private playground. It had a huge swimming pool and was situated directly on the beach. The waves came right up to the bedroom windows. By day, the resort was swamped in sunlight; by night, it was bathed in moonlight.

Senna's brother Leonardo and his assistant Jacir were also in residence for the weekend. They arrived at lunchtime and immediately sat down to a feast cooked by Maria. Senna virtually ignored Adriane, and he seemed embarrassed about Daniela. But she kept observing him and noticed he was looking at her too. After lunch, she put on a bikini and went down to the beach. Senna came and found her being intimidated by Quinda. Somehow, Quinda had perceived Adriane as competition and was biting her heels as she lay sunbathing. Senna eventually came to find her and they went swimming together: the ice broken.

In the evening, Adriane put on a white baggy sundress and flip flops. She came down with no makeup and hair still wet. She seemed determined not to impress him. Once again, she found the other girls dressed to the nines and wondered herself what she was playing at. But she remembers: "I was happy, and I felt I was looking good. It had been quite some time since I had allowed myself to forget all my worries and really relax. I felt light and free."

As night fell, they ate supper and watched Genesis videos on Senna's big screen. He came to sit beside her and said: "I like Genesis very much." As the others moved outside and left them alone, he leaned over to kiss her and she leaned away. Adriane fled to the bathroom. Behind the door, she heard one of Senna's friends ask him how he was getting on with Adriane, and he replied: "Nothing, nothing" and she thought he sounded desolate. The friend replied: "But you can't complain. Your little black book is full, isn't it?" Behind the door Adriane fumed quietly.

Adriane discovered that Senna had his own private discotheque in a wing of the house, and on the first evening, he and Adriane danced the night away. Afterwards, he escorted her to her bedroom and showed her where everything was. Daniela seemed forgotten, and Adriane had no idea where she was.

When Senna had exhausted the list of the room's features and told her three times where the fresh towels were kept, he went silent but didn't leave. She sat down on the end of the bed, and he came over and sat beside her. Neither moved a muscle. Quinda, his dog, pushed the door open, jumped on the bed and lay on the pillows, quietly growling at Adriane. Senna said: "Excuse her. She is very possessive."

Adriane had her mind on anything but the dog, as she remembered: "I felt that, each minute, the temperature between us kept rising. He sat by my side, and there was something special in his smiling tanned face. It was clear he found it very difficult to take the first step. And I felt, for the first time, the warmth of the proximity – real and spontaneous. Between us, there was something special: a long talk, a look, a touch. He tried to kiss me. I backed up – not yet."

They both lay down on the top of the bed looking at each other and seemed to be sinking into sleep when he grabbed her, stood her up and kissed her passionately, full on. This time, there was no going back and their lips hardly parted for an hour. She remembers it all vividly, as if she was counting: "He kissed me. The first kiss a real kiss and then one more, another one and another one. And another one: kisses, kisses and more kisses."

Adriane was in a dream and, for her, the world had stopped turning. The noise of the sea outside seemed to subside and the wind that had been blowing died away. She was in a trance. She had fallen head over heels in love, and that had never happened to her before.

When Senna started to undo a button on her blouse, she whispered in his ear: "Don't rush me." And he immediately stopped. They fell asleep in each other's arms. After a few hours, they both woke up and he got up to leave and return to his own room. She was bitterly disappointed he had left and was confused. She wondered if he had gone to Daniela's room to get what she had denied him. She would never know.

The next day, they were both embarrassed and Adriane kept her distance. Saturday was another perfect day with blue sky and perfect weather. They all went out on Senna's speedboat with Norio Koike, who clicked his camera seemingly non-stop. When they came back, more guests had arrived – more than they had expected – which meant Adriane had to vacate her own room and share.

Senna took his chance and moved her things up to his bedroom, saying: "This is my room. Now it is also yours. Make yourself at home."

She didn't demur.

When he left to greet his other guests, she was alone in his bedroom. The waves of the sea came right up to the window and as she looked around – everything was immaculate and precisely arranged. He obviously liked thick carpets and she couldn't find a speck of dirt anywhere. She wondered how many cleaners he employed.

His wardrobes were vast and covered one whole side of the bedroom. She counted over 100 pairs of shoes and 40 pairs of tennis shoes, scores of belts of every style, along with countless laundered shirts without a crease to be seen anywhere. She remembers thinking he had enough clothes in that room to change twice a day without washing anything for a year. He had far more clothes than she had.

Then she looked in the bathroom and saw the shelves were packed with jars of lotions, creams and perfumes. There they had something in common, and she was in heaven trying everything out.

When he returned, he said: "I am a bit fanatical about clothes." She told him she had noticed and said she had enjoyed trying out everything in his bathroom. He laughed.

She remembers her feelings that day: "To me, sharing his bedroom didn't necessarily mean that we'd have sex. I adored his paradise, and I wanted to make sure that I would be coming back there as a friend or a girlfriend."

And then they went off to enjoy a night of fun with his party of friends, which by now had swelled to 20 strong. They both kept their distance during the evening, and Adriane wondered what was coming later. She was sure of only one thing: that they would be sharing a bed that night for the first time. She tingled with excitement just thinking about it. As she remembered: "The night was perfect, the sky filled with stars: just like a fairytale."

But her thoughts and her actions were very different. That night, she donned what she called "armoured pyjamas", and they fell asleep. That is, until he woke her up and asked if he had to marry her to have sex.

He then began caressing her feet, her weak point. He told her: "You are the first woman in three years to provoke desire in me. I don't feel like kissing your feet; I want to kiss your entire body." She remembered: "The moonlight invaded our love nest, lighting up his handsome face, its delicate features, moist eyes that looked at me tenderly and lips that threatened a smile, a beautifully shy smile, perfect, as if sculpted by an artist."

Eventually, she succumbed, as she knew she would and, afterwards, they quickly fell asleep.

When she woke up, she put her hand out but no one was there. Surprised, she look round but he was gone. She was so insecure that she panicked and rushed to the window. And there he was, pacing up and down the pier, seemingly lost in thought.

As he looked up, she ducked down and went back to bed. After an hour, she got up and went to find breakfast. Everyone else was at the breakfast table, and she could hardly hear herself or think over the breakfast babble. No one seemed to have any idea she had spent the night with their host, and she was relieved to say the least. After breakfast, there was plenty of watersports, but she just watched from the beach. She noticed Quinda's attitude towards her had changed. She came up and licked her hand. Adriane smiled and thought: "She knows."

Most of the guests were staying on, but she had a photo shoot scheduled for the following morning. He asked her if she could break it, and she said she couldn't. She told him models were valued for their professionalism, and she had never let down anyone on a booking. So later that day, he took her in his helicopter to Angra airport to drop her off for the short flight back to São Paulo.

At the airport, he asked her if he could see her again. She just smiled. As soon as he returned to São Paulo, they were inseparable for the next few days until he had to leave for London for the European Grand Prix at the Donington racetrack in England.

Adriane remembers those few days spent at his apartment as the happiest of her life. She thinks they were for him also. It may have been a coincidence, but at the Grand Prix at Donington he drove what was undoubtedly the best race of his life and, for many observers, the greatest individual lap ever driven by any driver in the history of Formula One.

The stage was set for a new chapter in both their lives. But there was only 392 days left.

The fairytale had started.

FLASHBACK: ADRIANE - MARCH 1993

*"Ferrari is the myth of Formula One.
The tradition, the soul, the passion."*
Ayrton Senna
Wednesday 27th April 1994

CHAPTER 2

Dangerous Liaison in Bologna

Meeting with Luca di Montezemolo
Wednesday 27th April 1994

At a few minutes before 11 o'clock on Wednesday 27th April, Ayrton Senna's HS-125 800 jet with its personalised registration number N125AS touched down at Bologna airport. To all intents and purposes, Senna was arriving for the San Marino Grand Prix, if anyone was interested. In reality, he was headed to the Bologna country house of Luca di Montezemolo, the president of Ferrari.

The meeting with Montezemolo had long been planned and the San Marino Grand Prix was the perfect cover. If Senna had flown into Bologna on any other day, questions would have been asked and two and two would soon have been put together at Williams HQ in England. As it was, no one gave it a second thought as a helicopter collected him from the tarmac and whisked him off to Montezemolo's house.

The truth was that Senna had been less than impressed by his first few months at the Williams team. He had only agreed to move to Williams because it had the best car and he badly wanted to win the world championship again. But it was no longer the best car (the Benetton-Ford was) and, even worse, he found the team was not run to the same high levels to which he had been accustomed at McLaren. Whilst McLaren was a money-no-object highly professional operation, Williams by comparison was the equivalent of a Mom and Pop operation. Everything at Williams seemed to be done as economically as possible with an eye on the bottom line, the exact opposite of how McLaren was run. Worse, Frank Williams and Patrick Head treated Senna like he was just another employee. Ron Dennis, for all his faults, treated his drivers as very special people, and their every need was attended to. At Williams, Senna found none of his needs were attended to. When he wanted something done, like ordering a helicopter to take him to the airport, there was no one to do it. He found he was still asking Jo Ramirez, his old minder at McLaren, to get things done for him. Senna now realised why Nigel Mansell had walked out of Williams at the end of 1992. He confided to friends: "It has been difficult for me at Williams. It is very different from being at McLaren." Patrick Head and Frank Williams were blissfully unaware that Senna was unhappy and already thinking of leaving.

Senna had discussed his feelings about his new team with Gerhard Berger, his former team mate, and was very interested in how Ferrari was run. Berger told him it was run in the same way and with the same largesse as McLaren. Drivers were made to feel very special and there was even more money available, especially since Philip Morris started supporting the team and Marlboro branding had appeared on the cars.

Senna also knew that his old McLaren race engineer, Giorgio Ascanelli, was headed for Ferrari in 1995. Senna had tried to take Ascanelli with him to Williams, but McLaren boss, Ron Dennis, had held him to his contract and stopped it. Senna had felt totally at home working with Ascanelli, and although he got on with his new engineer, David Brown, he did not believe he was in the same class as Ascanelli. Ascanelli had more experience and more confidence – driver and engineer were of equal status, and Ascanelli was not afraid to tell Senna when he was wrong and to contradict him. He even nicknamed Senna 'boy genius' and wasn't afraid to call him that to his face – and not in a complimentary way. Brown was very different and he deferred to Senna on everything.

Senna had come to realise that he had arrived at Williams two years too late. In reality the car was poor, far slower than Michael Schumacher's Benetton, and only his skill and sheer bravery was making it work. Stripping the electronic gizmos from the Williams, made necessary by 1994 rule changes, had seriously compromised the performance of the car and made it very difficult to drive. Specifically, taking active suspension off the car meant it had to run a lot lower. He had put the car on pole for the first two races by driving out of his skin, taking too many risks and literally making the car perform. His own most private view was that the car without active suspension was dangerously unstable. He said: "I went through a lot to be able to finally sit in that car. Either I haven't adapted myself to the car or the car doesn't suit me." "Best car, best driver," he mused to himself publicly one day, "I don't know." In truth he did know, he was it wasn't.

There was also the question of money. Williams was paying him $8 million a year against the $16 million he had earned with McLaren in 1993. This compared unfavourably with the $8 million Ferrari was paying its current number one, Gerhard Berger; the $14 million Prost had earned in 1993 at Williams; and the $12 million Mansell had earned in 1992.

But Senna had only himself to blame as he had put himself in a very tricky position, having declared midway through 1992 that he would drive for the Williams team for nothing in 1993. After that, he had little room for negotiation when it came to his salary for 1994. Hence Frank Williams refused to pay him the then going rate of $12 million a year or the $14 million he was paying Prost. The best offer was $8 million, take it or leave it. This rankled Senna, especially as he was being paid $1 million a race by McLaren: $16 million in all for 1993. It was a similar offer to Nigel Mansell in 1992 that had caused him to leave Williams and that had also been caused by the whopping $14 million Williams had agreed to pay Prost.

As soon as they sat down on Montezemolo's overstuffed sofas, Senna wanted to talk about money. Montezemolo waved his arms and indicated Ferrari would match his salary at McLaren. Senna was very surprised. The most he had expected Montezemolo to offer was $12 million, but he wasn't going to argue.

Senna decided there and then that he wanted to drive for Ferrari in 1995 and effectively told Montezemolo that he would find a way to break his Williams contract, which expired in 1996, and to move to the Italian team at the end of 1994. Senna was no stranger to breaking contracts. In 1984, at the start of his career, he had signed a three-year contract with the then Toleman team and promptly broken it after one year to move to Lotus and risk the consequences.

But it wasn't only money that influenced him. He found increasing conflict between his own deal as Brazil's Audi importer and his own contract to drive a Renault-engined Formula One car. Audi was owned by Volkswagen, who were fierce competitors of Renault in Europe. There was all sort of pressure on Senna to drive Renault cars and give up his Audi road cars in Brazil. Senna knew that signing for Ferrari would eliminate this pressure.

But the most compelling reason to change was the performance of the new Ferrari car. Senna, being Senna, had examined more or less every single lap that he had driven in the Williams and that Berger had driven in the Ferrari in 1994. He knew from being his team mate at McLaren that he was, on average, half a second a lap faster than Berger. He could see from this analysis that in the Ferrari he would be just as quick as he was in the Williams.

It also suited him logistically to race for an Italian team, as it was much easier for him to commute from Portugal to Maranello than to the south of England.

Montezemolo and Senna also had a lot in common. They had been friends almost from the day Senna entered Formula One in 1984. In 1985, Montezemolo had introduced him to Gianni Agnelli, the head of Fiat as a "future Ferrari driver". They had allied the previous year, ironically, to successfully get rid of the electronic driver aids on cars and Senna had appreciated Montezemolo's support. Montezemolo said simply about their relationship: "I always appreciated Ayrton's style of racing."

With both Senna and Montezemolo united on what they wanted, it seemed that an outline agreement was reached. As Montezemolo revealed: "We were both in agreement that Ferrari would be the ideal place for him to further his career, which to date had been brilliant, even unique."

Senna believed that he could get out of his Williams contract and one way he could do it would be to tempt Alain Prost back to Formula One to retake his Williams seat for 1995. Senna resolved to try and make that happen. Montezemolo explains: "He wanted to come to Ferrari and I wanted him in the team. We spoke for a long time and he made it clear to me that he wanted to end his career at Ferrari, having come close to joining us a few years earlier. We agreed to meet again soon, so as to look at how we could overcome his contractual obligations at the time."

To all intents and purposes, Senna had agreed to become Gerhard Berger's team mate again in 1995, and Jean Alesi would be moved on. The only doubt was how much money it would take to buy Senna out of his Williams contract, which would have two years to run. That was a discussion for another day.

At 3 o'clock, lunch was over and the scheming was over. Montezemolo walked down with Senna to his helicopter, which was waiting to take him back to Bologna. It had been an extraordinary meeting and it was kept secret for 20 years until revealed by Montezemolo in April 2014 after he had left Ferrari himself.

Within half an hour, Senna was back in his jet waiting to take off for the three-hour flight back to Faro. On the journey back, he reflected on the meeting in his mind and the disruption that his move to Ferrari would cause in Formula One. He decided to start sowing the seeds for such a move right away. Senna told his girlfriend Adriane that night on the telephone: "Even if the Ferrari is as slow as a Volkswagen Beetle, I still want to be driving it on my last start, my last lap, my last race. Ferrari is the myth of Formula One. The tradition, the soul, the passion."

But Senna knew it had to be done and that the art of being a successful racing driver was always be at the right team at the right time. Although he knew he was a quarter of a second faster than Nigel Mansell, Alain Prost and Michael Schumacher, and half a second faster than drivers like Gerhard Berger, Damon Hill and Jean Alesi, having the right car under him was essential to win world championships. For only three of the 10 years he had been a racing driver had he been in that position, and in two out of these three he had been world champion.

As McLaren went into decline and Williams became ascendant, Senna had tried to join Williams in 1991 to take the seat that Nigel Mansell eventually got. Then Frank Williams was all ears and it was Senna who turned him down. Frank Williams said at the time: "I find Ayrton a fascinating character. For me, what sets him apart is his mental application, his ability to focus his mind on one thing. I've had experience of preparation for meetings and negotiations, and believe me, you've got to be ready. It's verbal terrorism – you can feel the bullets. Maybe if we ever did get together, we'd last three months, then kill each other."

Those words, heard now, are haunting. And so they should be. Had Senna stayed at McLaren, he may not have won any races in 1994 but he would still have been alive.

It was only a phone call from Soichiro Honda in the summer of 1990 that had persuaded Senna not to go to Williams and remain loyal to Honda. It proved a good call as the combination of him and the McLaren was good enough to win the championship again in 1991. And then the unexpected happened: on 5th August 1991 Soichiro Honda suddenly died of liver failure and Honda's directors almost instantly decided to remove the company from Formula One at the end of the 1992 season. The decision left Senna high and dry as Alain Prost had already been signed by Williams for 1993 and he was forced to stay at McLaren for a sixth season in an uncompetitive car. Prost had inserted into his contract that Senna could not be his team mate. And that clause was also valid for 1994, but it did not stop Williams and Senna talking all through the 1993 season about a contract for 1994.

But it was a one-sided negotiation. The only card Senna had to play was his own talent as he put in some stunning driving displays during the 1993 season. If Frank Williams had needed any proof of how good Senna was, he had given it to him that season. Driving an inferior McLaren with an inferior Ford Cosworth engine and a 100 horsepower deficit, he had on occasions run Prost ragged and had managed to win five races.

Frank Williams recalls how anxious Senna was to join his team in mid-1992: "A possibility for Ayrton to join us re-emerged towards the end of 1992, primarily led by him. Ayrton very much wanted to get in the car for 1993 and he just never left me alone. He was very persistent, very tough minded and occasionally I was frightened to go home because the phone would never stop ringing. He knew I was there so I would have to answer. I would get half-an-hour's conversation, mainly on his side, of why we should put him in the car."

Finally, at the beginning of September 1993, Senna and Williams signed a letter of intent for 1994. As part of the deal whereby he accepted a cut-price salary, Senna would have rights to sell a lot of space on his overalls and retain his cap and tee-shirt rights.

When Frank Williams informed Alain Prost that Senna would be his team mate for 1994, Prost was incensed. Prost was effectively pushed into retirement by Senna's arrival at the team. The Frenchman decided to depart midway through his own two-year contract even though he had a car good enough to enable him to equal Juan Manuel Fangio's record five world titles in 1994. Senna had pushed him out and as a result Williams had broken his contract and was forced to pay his full salary of $14 million even though he had left the team and would not drive the car.

It was an uneasy separation, and there was no mention of Senna's imminent arrival when Prost announced his retirement two weeks later at the Portuguese Grand Prix at Estoril. A few days after that, Senna revealed to journalists that he would be leaving McLaren without saying where he was going – as if the whole world did not already know.

Prost equally made clear that his retirement was final and inferred how hurt he was by Williams when he said: "The sport has given me a lot, but I decided that the game wasn't worth it any more. I have taken too many blows. I will not drive for Williams or anyone else. That goes for Formula One and all the other formulas. There will be no comeback."

It was all made official when a three-year contract was announced on Monday 11th October 1993 at the team's factory in Didcot, before the final two races of the season in Japan and Australia. Senna was by this time back in Brazil with his new girlfriend Adriane Galisteu, preparing for the last two races of the year. He appeared at the press conference on a special satellite link from São Paulo. Senna was clearly delighted to have at last got his hands on the equipment thought to be the class of the field, saying: "I am really looking forward to driving a Williams Renault in what I consider the beginning of a new era in motor racing for me. It is like a dream come true. I have been close to completing a deal with Frank many times now and am delighted it has finally happened. I've been waiting impatiently for this. I need it for motivation."

An equally satisfied Frank Williams said somewhat disingenuously: "In 1994 we need a team to defend the championships we have won this year. Alain Prost's retirement left us in a dilemma. He is a driver of immense talent who contributed so much to the team, both in and out of the car this year. Therefore his most appropriate replacement could only be Ayrton Senna. I have always admired him and his record speaks for itself."

After the announcement, Prost was depressed and Senna enthused. It showed in the results – Senna won the last two races of the season in Japan and Australia, with two of the greatest drives of his life.

*"Whenever I am with you.
I forget all my troubles"*
Ayrton Senna
Wednesday 26th May 1993

CHAPTER 3

Flashback: Ayrton and Adriane

The summer of 1993

As soon as the 1993 European Grand Prix was concluded, Ayrton Senna was back to São Paulo for a week before flying back to Europe for more testing before the San Marino Grand Prix. For a week, he and Adriane were inseparable, spending a few days at his apartment in São Paulo and the rest of the time at Angra.

On Sunday 18th April, it was Adriane's 20th birthday and he asked her if she would come to Europe in May for the Monaco Grand Prix.

When he flew back to Europe, Adriane was sure her future was with Senna, and she knew it was time to tell her on-off boyfriend, Cesar, it was definitely all over. She had continued to see Cesar casually. Cesar had only been her fourth boyfriend and the most serious. When she had first met him, 18 months earlier, she had fallen for him in a big way, causing him almost immediately to take her for granted. He controlled the relationship and there were long periods when she was lonely and didn't see him for days. She suspected there were other women but didn't push it. She said: "Beauty and glamour can hide a terrible solitude. When I met Ayrton, I was going through the end of a relationship in crisis. You can never choose when passion should vanish – it simply happens. With Cesar, I shared a year of day-to-day experiences. It was good while it lasted."

Cesar was close to a lot of the other Elite girls, and he started picking up rumours about Adriane and Senna. He suddenly became more attentive and realised how much Adriane meant to him. He dropped all his other liaisons and focused on her, becoming needy and bothersome to Adriane. When she finally told him it was over, she realised she still cared for him, but not in the same way, and let him down as gently as she could. He was heartbroken when she told him, and gradually, after hours of soothing phone calls, he started to get the message.

Adriane couldn't have been more excited about going to Monte Carlo. The Monaco Grand Prix was very social, and Senna liked to have a girl-friend with him at the race. He was certain he would win again for the sixth time. There was something about Monaco that was suited to his driving. He had won the last four races in the principality since 1989, and would have won in 1988 but for a silly mistake when he was dominating the race.

As soon as the Spanish Grand Prix was over, he flew back to São Pau-lo to spend some more days with Adriane. This time, they were com-pletely alone, and they spent the time getting to know each other better. They were both looking forward to Monte Carlo for her first race as his girlfriend. Before they went, she suddenly told Senna he had to ask her mother's permission to take her out of the country. Once he had got over the shock of that, he watched her mother help her pack and they left São Paulo together on Monday 17th May on a Varig flight to Paris.

She observed on the trip how Senna hated flying long distances. As she said: "He used to hate the routine, and he followed an automatic ritual. He would get changed in the toilet into a blue sweat top and protect his ears with plugs. He reclined in his seat and refused food, drink or the movie."

The flight to Paris took 12 hours, and Captain O'Mahoney was waiting with Senna's own jet to take them on to Nice. It was the first time Adriane met O'Mahoney, and they liked each other immediately. O'Mahoney had already noticed the change in his boss since March and was pleased to meet the reason why. When they landed at Nice, they took the helicopter shuttle direct to Monte Carlo and got a taxi for the 10-minute ride to his apartment, where they were greeted by his Monte Carlo housekeeper Isabel, who was Portuguese. He only stayed there for a week a year, for the race. He had sold the big apartment he used when Monaco was his permanent home, but for tax purposes, he still listed Monte Carlo as his base in Europe.

Isabel was all over Adriane and had already been given an advance brief-ing from Maria in Angra about what to expect. She was very impressed and said: "I can see why Maria told me you were beautiful." Adriane was used to being paid compliments, but this one mattered although she had no idea why it did.

Isabel, another excellent cook, already had supper on the table. They gulped it down, barely managing to stay awake. As Isabel chatted to Senna, updating him, Adriane was amazed how much she already knew about her. She worked out that Senna's three housekeepers, Maria in Angra, Juraci in the Algarve, and Isabel in Monaco, ran a network to keep each other informed about their boss. Apparently, they all spoke on the telephone whenever they could. She also realised that Senna was not their boss but a surrogate son.

Everywhere in the apartment, Adriane could smell fresh paint and the carpet looked new. She began to suspect a great deal of preparation had gone into getting the apartment ready for this week and she wondered what the cost of one week in Monte Carlo was for Senna.

But not everything was perfect. The bathroom had been retiled, and there was also work going on in the adjacent apartment. Adriane took a shower and could hear the drills, which were vibrating the walls. The drilling must have loosened the tiles in the shower which had not been properly fixed. One by one, they started falling off and smashing as they hit the floor. Adriane was petrified and cowered as the tiles came crashing down. They scratched her back and she cut her feet as they shattered on the floor. She grabbed a towel and ran out of the bathroom into the bedroom, trailing blood across the perfect white carpet. She screamed for help, thinking the apartment was about to collapse into the street. Senna was on the telephone and, hearing her screams, he dropped the receiver and rushed in. He was just in time to grab Adriane as she fainted at the sight of her own blood.

Senna called for Isabel, and they laid a comatose Adriane on the bed and cleaned her up. Isabel applied some antiseptic to her feet, and Senna bandaged them up as she started to come round. She apologised for staining his carpet and fainting, but he told her: "I loved it; no woman has ever fainted into my arms before."

Meanwhile, Isabel was scrubbing away at the carpet with not much success. She needn't have bothered as, the next day, Senna was putting an extra hole into a new belt and he stabbed himself with a screwdriver, thereby dousing the carpet with blood once again. Isabel couldn't believe it.

After nearly 16 hours of travelling and the shower drama, both were extremely tired and went to bed, waking up on Tuesday morning to blazing sunshine and a cool, refreshing breeze of the kind only found in the south of France. The circuit was all set up and the first Formula One trucks and motorhomes were beginning to arrive in the paddock. Monaco was the most important race of the year for entertaining sponsors, and McLaren's sponsors – Marlboro – had three big yachts in the harbour which were already filling up with guests for the race.

At midday, Senna walked Adriane around the Monte Carlo track, introducing her to the intricacies of driving a Formula One car on public roads. The circuit was closed to traffic for a few hours whilst white lines were being painted and there were no cars. The guards let Senna though the gates and they were able to walk in the middle of the road. They walked very slowly as he talked in detail about what it was like to drive his McLaren around Monaco. Adriane wished she could have taped his masterclass in driving a Formula One car, which took two hours from the start to finish line. At one point, he was describing the braking for a corner and lay down on the track looking for faint signs of tyre rubber marks from the 1992 race, which had long faded away.

That night, he proposed taking her to the famous Monte Carlo casino opposite the Hotel de Paris in Casino Square. The casino had been made famous by Greek billionaire Aristotle Onassis, who had owned it in the fifties and sixties. Then, Monte Carlo was like a down-at-heel French seaside town, and Onassis had single-handedly revived it, investing the modern day equivalent of hundreds of millions of dollars. Senna told her about Onassis, who he had read about when he had looked into the history of Monaco. It was clear Onassis was one of his heroes.

She asked him why they were going, as she knew he disliked gambling. He said: "Just today," and he went to his briefcase and took out $300.

When they got there, everyone knew who he was but no one bothered him. Adriane stuck to playing the machines and he went to the blackjack table, where he proceeded to lose $300 in an hour's play. Some friends joined him at the table, and Adriane watched as they all lost money. Adriane remembers that night: "Happiness was clear on his face. Waiters, croupiers, receptionists, and guests: they all bowed as we passed as if he was the highest member of the Grimaldi house." One of Senna's neighbours presented Adriane with a box of expensive Swiss-made truffles.

Senna hardly let go of her all weekend in Monaco. Wherever they went, they attracted the attention of photographers and fans. She was introduced to Betise Assumpcao, Senna's press secretary, who was Brazilian herself, and they immediately bonded. Like O'Mahoney, she had also noticed the positive effect Adriane had had on her boss.

For three days, they had a marvellous time, hopping from yacht to yacht for seemingly endless parties and ending the seemingly endless evenings in a nightclub, usually Jimmyz. Adriane dazzled in a short red dress at the Marlboro gala dinner in honour of Senna and his co-driver, the American Michael Andretti.

On Wednesday, Senna took Adriane out on the back of the Ducati 900 he kept at the basement of his apartment block. They travelled all round Monaco and then went into the hills in the glorious sunshine. She wore one of his spare race helmets.

But on Thursday, when the racing proper began, she noticed a sudden change in him. That night, he changed into his pyjamas and took the bible to read as he went to sleep. It was a different man from the one with whom she normally shared her life.

Practice and qualifying were held on Thursday and Saturday, with Friday being a rest day at Monto Carlo. On Thursday, it rained. That morning, he took her around the paddock and introduced her to everyone, especially his colleagues at McLaren. She also met his former team mate Gerhard Berger, who was now driving for Ferrari.

Wherever they went, they held hands and caused a sensation as photographers followed them, snapping away. The photographers were frustrated because they did not know who she was, and all enquiries were brushed away. Adriane found that even though she found it annoying, she also enjoyed the attention. As she said: "Ayrton held my hand more tightly and continued to show his love for me. It's always gratifying for a woman to be admired." At one point they were stopped by Giorgio Armani, who offered Adriane a modelling contract. Adriane wondered what the girls back at Elite in Brazil would say when she told them she had been offered a job personally by Armani himself. She says: "I got to know a different world in Monaco." She also noticed how different her boyfriend was as soon as he put on his racing overalls: "Ayrton would put on the helmet and overalls and turn into Senna." He told her: "It's the only way. I need to win. I have to win."

When Senna went to get into his car, Adriane spent time with Antonio Braga and got to know him better. He told her he predicted a wedding. She just giggled.

On Thursday afternoon, Senna lost control of his McLaren out on the circuit and crashed. His car suddenly turned to the left and went into the barrier head on at high speed, ricocheted off and carried on down the hill at St Devote. The car then hit the opposite barrier and lost two wheels in a very big crash. A dazed Senna bruised his thumb but walked away otherwise unhurt.

The official explanation was that he lost control of the car driving over a bump. But the reality was that the active suspension was playing up and pitched him off. Adriane was in the apartment and quickly ran down to the track, but it was nothing to worry about. Although, when she saw a replay of the crash later, it scared her to death.

On Saturday, Senna had endless problems with the active suspension on his car and could only qualify third at his favourite track, two and a half seconds slower than pole sitter Alain Prost. It was one of the biggest gaps of the year and not a good portent for the race.

It did not put Senna in the best of moods, and he was up early on Sunday morning. Adriane followed him down after she was woken up by the warm-up. Senna had another accident and damaged his car. Adriane was walking down when she heard it, and she eventually found him getting into his spare car unperturbed. She was disturbed by his second accident of the weekend. He had bitten his tongue during the accident and his mouth had swelled up. His thumb had also swelled up from the previous accident. It was then that she discovered what a genius Josef Leberer was as he got the swellings down and prepared his driver for the race.

She found race morning an extremely nervous time, especially the last hour before the start. She stood in the pit box in the narrow pit lane alongside the spare wheels. The pit boxes at Monaco were tiny in those days, and she was continually having to move out of the way of the mechanics. Finally, she was invited to watch the race from the commentary box of

Brazilian broadcaster TV Globo alongside Senna's friends Galvao Bueno and Reginaldo Leme. Before she went off, Senna kissed her and whispered: "Today's the day."

Senna's luck was in from the start, when Alain Prost was penalised for jumping the start and was effectively out of contention. Then Michael Schumacher retired with a hydraulic problem, and finally Gerhard Berger went out after touching Damon Hill's car, leaving Senna to inherit a very lucky win for a change.

Adriane was beside her self and ran down the road from the TV Globo commentary box. She cried as the Brazilian national anthem was played. When he finally made his way through the crowd on the track and found her, he whispered: "You know it was for you, don't you?"

Having won the race, they were due at the gala dinner at the Sporting Club to collect his prize. She had brought three evening gowns, and he chose for her. At the ball, she really noticed her lack of English for the first time. She could only converse in Portuguese as her English was very limited. She found it very difficult because her table companion one side was Prince Albert and on her other side was the American actor Michael Douglas. She spent the whole evening in virtual silence, smiling as they spoke and making frequent use of the words "yes" and "no" depending on the look on their faces when they spoke. She was also within conversational distance of Richard Gere, Cindy Crawford and Princess Caroline. She said: "I have never seen such a concentration per capita of beauty and fame."

Senna made conversation for her as much as he could and she just nodded when he smiled. She found it a "lovely ordeal" and was relieved when it ended and they were able to go off to Jimmyz, a nightclub with which she had already fallen in love from two visits earlier in the week. At the nightclub, they were surrounded by Senna's European entourage, all of whom could speak Portuguese.

They sat at a table next to the dance floor, and Adriane was astonished by the enormous number of girls who threw themselves at her new boyfriend, some quite brazenly. It was entirely different from Brazil, where a girl would respect another girl. In Europe, she found they just didn't care. It was something she would have to get used to. Aside from that, the entire day of Sunday 23rd May had been a complete dream from start to finish. When they got home and drifted into sleep, Adriane thought to herself: "Is it a dream? Is it true?"

The following morning, all of the world's newspapers were full of Senna's sixth win at Monaco. There were many pictures of him hand-in-hand with Adriane. But not one of the newspapers knew who she was, and they called her "the mysterious Brazilian blonde".

The week in Monte Carlo was over all too quickly, and she thought when they left: "Monaco is a principality and it is simply perfect for a fairy tale."

After Monaco, Captain O'Mahoney flew them from Nice to London in Senna's jet, where he had some meetings and some press interviews to do. They were accompanied by Betise Assumpcao and booked into the Berkeley Hotel in Knightsbridge. She remembers the trip to London because it was cold and raining every day, certainly too cold to swim in the Berkeley's rooftop pool.

On Wednesday 26th May, she flew home from London on her own. Senna begged her to stay on, but she told him she had commitments and earned her living as a model. As he waved her off, Senna whispered: "Help me to separate my professional life from my personal life. Whenever I am with you, I forget all my problems."

She promised to arrange her schedule to spend time in the Algarve that summer and as much time with him as she could.

On 10th June, she accompanied him and his brother, Leonardo, to the Canadian Grand Prix in Montreal. It was a period when she was getting on well with Leonardo, before all the bitterness started. On the flight, Leonardo, whilst Senna was asleep, wanted to talk about his own difficult personal life. He had been with his long-term girlfriend, Luciana Sargologos, a tall bunette, for many years, but he was unsure of whether he wanted to take the relationship any further. She said: "He was completely different from his brother, but I liked him." In fact, she initially got on well with all the family.

The family all came to London for the British Grand Prix, and Adriane spent quality time with them for the first time. After the race, Neyde Da Silva, Viviane Lalli and her two children, Paula and Bianca, went on a shopping trip to London. Then, on the 14th July, the five women flew to Paris

Above: Ayrton Senna and Adriane Galisteu in Paris for the Bercy charity go-kart race in December 1993. According to Bertrand Gachot they were very much in love and not afraid of people knowing. Gachot, a close friend of Senna, had never seen him like this with any other girlfriend.

Above: Adriane Galisteu attended half a dozen Grand Prix races in 1993 and she and Senna had a great summer around the race tracks of the world.

© Rex Features

Above: Ayrton Senna and Adriane Galisteu in Adelaide at the last Grand Prix of 1993. Nine months into their relationship they were looking forward to a winter together in Brazil before the 1994 season started.

Above: Ayrton Senna and Adriane Galisteu fishing on the lake at Tatui in Brazil. Tatui was Senna's parents' farm.

Above: Beside the swimming pool in Tatui at a photoshoot for *Caras* magazine. The photos appeared in magazines all round the world after his death.

Left: On horseback with Adriane at the Tatui farm. The winter of 1993 and 1994 was a time of great happiness and joy together.

Below: Senna and Adriane inspecting the pigs on his parents' farm. Farming gave him immense pleasure.

Helicoptering around Brazil in 1993 and 1994

Above and below: Ayrton Senna had gained his helicopter licence in 1992 and had flown over 103 hours by the time of his death. He used to fly off from the roof of his offices in Sao Paulo to his parents' farm at Tatui and his beach house at Angra.

Left: The Da Silva family farm at Tatui. It was a working farm but also a pleasure park for Ayrton Senna with a huge swimming pool and lake plus a full-size go-kart track.

Right: Senna kept a beach buggy for his personal use and loved taking it out on the remote sandy beaches with only Adriane and his dog Quinda for company.

Below: Ayrton Senna adored jet skis and spent many hours on them with Adriane. In his last winter at Angra he came off and knocked himself unconscious causing a momentary scare for her and his family.

Above: Ayrton Senna with his dog Quinda at the Angra beach house. Quinda's sister called Mouse lived at the house in the Algarve. Both dogs seemed disturbed at the time of his death although they had no physical means of knowing. The dogs waited for the next 10 years for their master to come home again, but he never did.

Below: Adriane Galisteu ticked all of Ayrton Senna's boxes from the moment he met her in March 1993 at the Brazilian Grand Prix. He thought she was sensual, fascinating, intelligent, beautiful and self-assured, all the virtues he demanded in a woman.

Above: Ayrton Senna and Adriane Galisteu met in March 1993 and enjoyed 14 months together. They vacationed together on the island of Bora Bora between the 1993 Japanese and Australian Grands Prix, both of which races he won.

Above and right: On 25th March 1994 the first clouds appeared in their relationship when Adriane appeared on the cover of *Caras* magazine in a major feature introducing her to Brazilians as Ayrton Senna's girlfriend. The family did not like the article or the photographs which were sultry and suggestive.

Above: Ayrton Senna photographed in early 1994 before the start of the racing season.

on Senna's jet for more shopping. Senna met them in Paris and counted 38 suitcases between them filled with shopping. Captain O'Mahoney had great difficulty getting it all on board the plane. They all went home to São Paulo together very happy.

Adriane flew back to Europe to attend the Hungarian Grand Prix in the middle of August. Her maternal grandparents were Hungarian and had emigrated to Brazil at the outset of the Second World War. Adriane wanted to absorb some of the culture of her heritage.

They booked into the Kempinski hotel in Budapest. The highlight of the trip was the after-race party at the Gundel restaurant thrown by John Hogan, vice-president of Philip Morris International, which sponsored McLaren. Senna and Adriane dressed casually, with him in jeans and polo shirt and her in a white vest. It was another magical evening.

They made a very glamorous couple, and as they went in, they were photographed by Andrew Frankl, the founder of *Car* magazine. Frankl had arranged for them to be serenaded by a Hungarian violinist in a maroon dinner jacket. Frankl's photo of the smiling couple was published all over the world. Adriane says now: "It was a photo of two people in love. We were in love."

Hungarian-born Frankl was a long-time friend of Senna's and remembered: "Ayrton was in tremendous form, clearly much in love, holding hands with Adriane. It was so obvious. I was convinced they would marry."

After the race, they flew home together to São Paulo. When they got back, she told him she was buying a new car, a secondhand Fiat Uno. She asked if he knew a mechanic who could look it over for her. He agreed to get it done but secretly went and bought her a brand new silver Fiat Uno. He arranged for the car to have a personalised number, *DRI 7770*. Adriane was overwhelmed and she got in the car and drove first to show it to her own mother and then to show it to Neyde Da Silva, who she took out for a drive. Senna, for reasons best known to himself, nicknamed the new car "tin of sardines."

The mid-August trip home proved to be a real family occasion as Adriane stayed at the Da Silva family farm at Tatui and shared a bedroom with Senna there for the first time.

She took Senna to the airport on 24th August so he could go to the

Belgian Grand Prix. Afterwards, she took his car back to Tatui, where she spent her first night with his family on her own. At that point, the relationship between her and the Da Silva family could not have been better.

Senna flew straight back to São Paulo after the race. When she met him at the airport, he was angry at only coming fourth. She picked him up in her new Fiat. Immediately, he asked for the keys, saying: "Where is the key to the tin of sardines?" They were pursued from the airport by waiting photographers keen to have photos of him with his new girlfriend. Senna's new relationship was the talk of Brazil. It was also getting her plenty of work – her picture was on billboards advertising jeans all over São Paulo.

All summer it was the same pattern, and Senna returned to Brazil after every race to spend time with Adriane at Angra. She made a few trips the other way to be with him at Quinto do Lago.

On 3rd September, they boarded a flight to Lisbon to spend a month together at Quinto do Lago whilst Senna competed at the Italian and Portuguese Grand Prix races.

In between, they spent a few days at the Braga family house in Sintra, where Senna had his own bedroom. Adriane could see this was his second family, and she immediately formed a close relationship with Antonio Braga's wife Luiza. They were joined by Galvao Bueno, and the principal discussion amongst the men was Senna's move to the Williams team.

A few days later, Captain O'Mahoney collected them from Lisbon in the HS125 to fly on to Faro before going to Lake Como for the Italian Grand Prix, the penultimate race of the European season. They stayed at the Villa d'Este, one of the finest hotels in the world. One of Senna's guests that weekend was tennis ace Monica Seles, who was recovering from being stabbed on court during a game in Hamburg. She was there to cheer her favourite driver.

It was another idyllic weekend by the magnificent lake, and Adriane did not want it to end. That is until the race when Senna retired halfway through. He drove straight back to the hotel from Monza, saying not a word to Adriane. Then he ordered room service, choosing for her without asking what she wanted. Only when crowds of fans began cheering his name in the car park did he snap out of his bad mood. He said to her: "But I lost – these Italians are crazy." She told him: "They're crazy for you." Sensing his mood, she asked: "Are you finding it too hard having me around?" He said: "I promise you that when we leave Italy, I will leave the frown behind." That night, she went to the hotel bathroom and wrote on the mirror in lipstick: 'Good Morning! Smile'.

The next two weeks were spent in the Algarve. Senna trained hard – the Portuguese Grand Prix was like his home race, and he wanted to do well. But this year, it was even more important. Inside his briefcase was a fax copy of a signed option with Williams to drive for the team in 1994, re-placing Alain Prost, who had decided to retire but would still receive his full $14 million salary from the team for 1994.

He was very moody during that period. The fax machine in the Algarve house whirred continually with draft contracts and notes from his man-ager, Julian Jakobi, in England. Senna was determined that every single detail of his relationship with Williams would be covered in the contract, easing problems that might occur later. Adriane remembers one phone call with Frank Williams in England lasting for five hours and 40 minutes. Senna couldn't sleep until the negotiations were over: when the document with Frank Williams' signature on it was faxed through, he signed it and faxed it straight back.

After the Portuguese Grand Prix in Estoril, Adriane flew straight home and would not meet him again until after the Japanese Grand Prix on 25th October.

The last two Grand Prix events of the year, in Japan and Australia, were a fortnight apart and they decided to take a holiday in between, joking it would be a honeymoon rehearsal.

Senna went into those two races feeling very unhappy. He hadn't won a race since Monaco in May, and he had been through the most gruelling negotiations to join Williams. He was also upset about leaving McLaren and all the friends he had made at the team. But suddenly, when he arrived in Tokyo, the problems fell away. All the deals were done, and he could concentrate on the racing.

Alain Prost took pole position by a whisper, and Senna was second be-side him on the grid. As so often in Japan, it was a wet race, and Senna led for most of it: coming in 11 seconds ahead of Prost. The Japanese fans went wild. They loved Senna like one of their own. The race was notable because of Eddie Irvine overtaking Senna whilst a lap behind, a no-no in Formula One.

On Saturday 22nd October, Adriane left São Paulo to fly to Tokyo via Los Angeles, a 28-hour flight. She slept all the way and was fresh as a daisy when she arrived at Tokyo's Narita airport on the Monday morning after the race. Japanese customs decided to give her a hard time, made worse by the fact that there was no common language. But a Brazilian at the airport recognised her and came over and told the customs officer that she was Ayrton Senna's girlfriend. All of the problems suddenly disappeared, and she was waved through.

Norio Koike arrived in a taxi and took Adriane to the hotel, which was located right by Tokyo's Disneyland. The manager of the hotel was waiting for Adriane and was determined to give Ayrton Senna's girlfriend the full red carpet welcome. When she asked where to register, he waved his arms and signalled to two bellboys to escort her straight to Senna's suite whilst others brought up her luggage.

When Senna opened the hotel room door, they fell into each other's arms. She remembers: "I exploded with happiness. I felt like a teenager." She took him straight to bed.

Afterwards, they ordered lunch in bed and he told her how, the day before, he had thumped Irish rookie driver Eddie Irvine. He told her he didn't like Irvine's attitude but admitted he had been stupid to have hit him. He said: "He doesn't have a good head on his shoulders, and he doesn't know what he is doing."

Later, they set out to explore Tokyo's Ginza shopping district in the one day they had together in the city. Then they flew to Bora Bora in Tahiti for a seven-day vacation before the race in Adelaide. It took three flights to get there: Tokyo to Wellington, Wellington to Tahiti, then by sea plane to Bora Bora. They were booked in for a week and didn't put on any shoes for the whole time. But then Senna fell ill and spent the last two days in bed. As they flew to Australia, his strength returned. At the airport, he bought a dozen belts, and Adriane knew he must be getting well again. In truth, the holiday was not a great success as even Bora Bora could not compete with the attractions of Angra. Christian Fittipaldi and his girlfriend, Mariana, who were originally going to accompany them to Bora Bora, had gone to Bali in Indonesia instead, and Senna realised they had made a mistake. As soon as they got to the hotel in Adelaide, help was at hand as Josef Leberer restored him to full fitness with some long massages. He was soon back on form. During qualifying, Senna suddenly remembered he had not won a pole position all season. Every single pole had gone to a Williams driver. In fact, the Williams team had won pole for the previous 24 races. He was determined to put that right and somehow wrestle his much slower McLaren-Ford around the Adelaide track fastest. He knew it was only down to his driving and later had that confirmed when it was revealed that the Williams cars were 9mph faster in a straight line.

It took three starts to get the race underway after incidents. After that, Senna led for most of the way, beating Prost home by nine seconds in his very last race for McLaren and the last race win of his career. After he won, there was an emotional farewell to the McLaren team and especially the team's Spanish manager, Jo Ramirez. Senna said in a small speech at the farewell party whilst looking directly at Ramirez: "My life is full of adventures and strife. I am moving but my heart remains here at McLaren." In truth, he loved and admired Ramirez, whom he affectionately called 'The Spaniard'. He wished he was coming with him to Williams. Ramirez was just one of life's 'nice men', and Senna knew it and appreciated it. He knew he would not find his like at Williams and not for the first time wondered whether he had made the right decision to leave the team.

They spent two days in Sydney and hired a speedboat to tour the harbour. Then they went Christmas shopping in the magnificent Sydney shopping malls. But both of them were looking forward to flying back home to São Paulo, where they had almost five months together before the new season started.

Adriane described it as five months of hedonism. It was a glorious routine, splitting their time between the family farm in Tatui, his São Paulo apartment and the beach house in Angra. They started with six unbroken weeks together. Adriane remembers: "Beco and I came back from Europe and were living together at the apartment in Rua Paraguai, sharing the same friends, going out to dinner, we were a typical boyfriend and girlfriend – although there was no wedding ring, there were intimacies like sleeping together in his parent's house. I felt he liked to show me off a bit."

At the beginning of December, they both flew to Europe for a celebrity go-kart race at Bercy in France in aid of various charities. Also competing was Belgian Formula One driver Bertrand Gachot, a close friend of Senna's. They spent some time together, as Gachot recalls: "I saw them at Bercy a lot, and he was very much in love with her. They didn't separate for one minute, and it was really nice to see."

Gachot, a controversial figure in Formula One, had a serious soft spot for Senna. He had been jailed for assault on a London taxi driver in mid-1991 after a stupid altercation at the very start of his F1 career. Eddie Jordan promptly dumped him from his team, and Senna was the only person in Formula One who supported him publicly. Whilst everyone else turned their backs, Senna came forward as a character witness, writing a letter of support to the English judge who jailed him. As Gachot recalled: "Ayrton wrote an amazing letter to the judge. It was so nice and well written. It really touched me." From Bercy, they flew to Heathrow and on to the Williams factory in Berkshire for a seat fitting. It was his first visit there, and the staff were sworn to secrecy as Williams wanted to make another splashy announcement for maximum publicity.

Frank Williams greeted them personally at the factory and Adriane noted that the close relationship with Frank Williams was totally different from Senna's relationship with McLaren Team Principal Ron Dennis. Senna told her he had found it increasingly difficult to cope with Dennis. Relations between them were strained, which Senna told her was a shame after so much success. But he added that, although the relationship between him and Dennis had cooled, he loved the McLaren team to the extent that he felt it was his real family and that he would return one day if circumstances were different.

But that was all in the past as Senna took her hand and toured the Williams factory, introducing himself and her to the Williams people – his new home for at least the next three years. His actions were a clear sign she was a fixture in his life and would be a part of his new life at Williams. But Senna was not happy when he left the Williams factory. He sensed a different atmosphere than at the McLaren factory, which had an air of quiet efficiency. He couldn't quite put his finger on the difference: only that he did not like it.

From Heathrow it was straight back to Brazil, and they were planning to spend a traditional family Christmas with the Da Silva family at Tatui. But Adriane decided at the last minute that she must return to her mother and 80-year-old grandmother, who was very ill, and she left on Christmas Eve. She borrowed Senna's mother's Volkswagen car to drive back to São Paulo.

For New Year, the whole family retreated to Angra with friends and the house was full. Brazilian women traditionally wore white on New Year's Eve, and Senna told her he felt like they were getting married rather than celebrating a new year.

For once, it was overcast at Angra and on the stroke of midnight they both told each other they wished they would be together for ever. They spent the next fortnight at Angra and during that time they spoke to each other about their past relationships. He spoke of his relationship with Xuxa Meneghel. He told her he had not seen or spoken to her since they had finally split, two years earlier. She told him about her ex, Cesar, and how she had had to let him down lightly once he realised that she had left him for Senna.

Nuno Cobra, his personal trainer, stayed with them for more or less the whole time. He was putting Senna through his usual winter fitness programme and both men took it very seriously. Cobra was a big fan of Adriane's and saw what a difference she had made to his boss. Adriane says of that time they had together at Angra over the holidays: "I felt I had been given a present by the gods." One day, whilst Senna was out waterskiing, Adriane and Cobra chatted on the beach. She asked him if he could make her fit enough to be able to run with Senna on his daily workout. Cobra agreed to take Adriane on as a client for a month once Senna had left for Europe for the start of the season.

On the 17th January, Senna went to Europe for a week, returning to Brazil on 24th January. He and Adriane spent a lot of their time at Angra, and, there, he told her: "One day, I will marry you and one day I will work for Ferrari. I will end my career there and end my life with you."

The idyll was only disturbed when Senna had an accident on his jet-ski, and hit the water very badly. Quinda, who had been keeping an eye on his master, immediately sensed danger and started nudging Adriane, who was sunbathing. Adriane shouted to the house for help, and they pulled in

Senna and laid him down on the pier. He momentarily stopped breathing and had to be quickly resuscitated. But it was only a momentary panic. He was badly bruised and in pain and had to rest for a week and take minimal exercise. A physiotherapist flew in to tend to him.

He was well enough to go to Europe again for a pre-arranged testing and a visit to Germany at the beginning of March. He returned to Brazil on the 11th. They then went back to Angra before returning to São Paulo for the last weekend of March 1994 and the Brazilian Grand Prix, the anniversary of their first meeting. It was his first race for Williams, and he was expected to win the race.

The Brazilian Grand Prix came and went. Senna got pole position but retired after a spin, and his new great rival, Michael Schumacher, won. The following Tuesday, he hired an aircraft hangar to announce he was introducing the German Audi range of cars into Brazil. His Senna import company had been appointed exclusive concessionaires.

Later, at an evening reception for the motor trade, Adriane accompanied him, this time dressed to the nines. Senna announced he would also have deals with Ducati motorcycles and Mont Blanc pens for Brazil. Audi cars would be the first of many products he would import to Brazil for his new business life when he planned to effect a seamless change from top racing driver to top businessman. He had seen the demoralising effect of retirement on drivers, and he did not intend that to happen to him. He had already predicted he would retire from Formula One in 2001, at the age of 41 and, by then, wanted his business to be earning enough money to replace his earnings from racing.

They then enjoyed their last week together before he flew to Japan on 3rd April 1994. He was competing in the Pacific Grand Prix on the 17th April and her 21st birthday was on the 18th. But inexplicably he failed to call her on the day, which upset her. She waited in his apartment in vain for the phone call that never came. As she remembered: "10, 11, midnight, nothing. I couldn't sleep, and I was sure he had not forgotten. It was the saddest birthday of my life." It was six o'clock in the morning before he called and asked her how her birthday had gone. She said: "How do you think it was? The most important person in my life didn't phone me."

She guessed he had been very depressed about the result in the Grand

Prix when he was knocked off the track at the first corner. She suspected he had locked himself in his hotel room in the dark whilst he got over it and didn't want to admit how disappointed he was. Now he assured her it didn't matter, and he would win the next race. He said to her: "20 points behind doesn't mean much. The next one is mine."

She stayed on for a month in São Paulo to take an intensive English language course. If she was to settle in Europe for half the year, she would have to be able to speak English. She was cramming English lessons into the evenings as well. Nuno Cobra was also calling on her everyday for intensive physical training. She carried on with the lessons and the training right up to when she left for Europe on Friday 29th April.

They spent the last month of his life apart, but she says it took their relationship to a new turning point: "There was no way back. I had lost my fear. I was no longer afraid of being the girlfriend of a myth, an institution, and having to share him with the world. In truth, my boyfriend was my man and, as a man, he was only mine."

Adriane still remembers the last day they were together, 3rd April: "It was a very special day, and I didn't know why at the time. Before he went, we had a long afternoon of love. We got to the airport early and we stayed in the car and talked, hugged and kissed. He said to me 'I'll keep an eye on you, little girl.' He said 'goodbye' and gave me a long kiss in the car."

Before leaving, he told her he planned to leave Williams two years hence, when he believed the team would peak, and move to Ferrari, which he believed would then have its act together after the return of Luca di Montezemolo as boss. He said he would be meeting with Montezemolo soon.

It was the last time she saw him.

"Life would be very boring without feelings, without emotions. And there are some feelings that only drivers can experience. It is a fortunate and unique position to be in, but it is stressful at the same time."

Ayrton Senna
October 1988

CHAPTER 4

Waking Up in Paradise

The Algarve - Morning - Thursday 28th April 1994

Thursday 28th April 1994 was just like any other early spring day at Quinta do Lago in the Portuguese Algarve as its most famous resident, Ayrton Senna, woke in his house to the sound of his Portuguese housekeeper, Juraci, squeezing orange juice and brewing coffee in the kitchen.

The sun shone as it always did in the Algarve at this time of year. Senna got out of bed, grabbed his shorts and a t-shirt and went straight out for an early morning run around the resort's sand dunes and golf greens. He preferred to run at midday in the heat of the sun but as he was leaving in an hour he had no choice but to take his exercise when he could that day. In 1994, he was arguably the fittest driver on the grid after a winter of highly regimented intensive exercise at his beach house in Brazil under his trainer, Nuno Cobra. As he ran out of the house he left his younger brother Leonardo in bed, still asleep.

Senna loved his Portuguese home almost as much as he did his beach house at Angra. Quinta do Lago was his European paradise and was still a well-kept secret as far as Senna was concerned. The four-bedroomed white-walled villa sat in its own grounds, protected by high walls and electric gates, in a dream resort of around 2,000 acres. With golf courses on one side and a beach on the other, interspersed with lakes, Senna had bought the house a few years earlier and had it completely renovated during the previous winter.

The house was managed by a woman known only as Juraci, and even Senna didn't know if she had any more names. She was a one-woman powerhouse in permanent residence and her duties were to cook, clean and chauffeur. She did them all admirably.

The Quinta do Lago resort had been opened in December 1971 by André Jordan, a developer of mixed Polish and Brazilian parentage. The original 550-acre site was a farm, and the old farmhouse was rebuilt as a restaurant. The beach-lined estate had been owned by the Pinto de Magalhães family for the previous 300 years and Jordan commissioned a talented Brazilian architect called Júlio Neves to design much of the infrastructure and to turn it into a pleasure paradise. Only people who had been to Quinta do Lago understood the unique atmosphere and climate. The resort had a five-star hotel, four championship golf courses, a multitude of good restaurants and even its own night club.

Jordan's genius had been to build a footbridge to connect the beach to the estate. He then asked famous architect William F. Mitchell to design a golf course. The resulting course was such a success that in 1976 the Portugese Open was held in Quinta do Lago for the first time.

In 1987, sensing a recession just around the corner, Jordan sold Quinta do Lago to British entrepreneur David Thompson for a huge profit. Thompson had sold his food wholesaling business a year earlier and had the money and resources to complete the development to a very high standard. Thompson was delighted when Senna bought a house on the resort, and he bent over backwards to accommodate his needs.

Whenever Thompson showed a potential client around, the first thing he always mentioned was that Ayrton Senna owned a house on the resort. It seemed to add at least 10 per cent to the price of the villas.

Quinta do Lago gave Senna the anonymity he craved. He was never bothered there, and that was exactly how he liked it. It was the only place in the world outside Brazil that he felt at home. It was a complete bonus that many of the people also spoke his native language, Portuguese.

Senna felt good every time he drove past the rainbow-coloured 'Q' logo statue that rotated slowly inside a fountain at the main entrance to the complex. He felt he was entering a unique environment where nature was in complete harmony with his design for living a Brazilian lifestyle in Europe. His garden was a breathtaking vista of exotic tropical plants: palms and banana trees; giant hibiscus; vivid yellow mimosa; whole walls of bougainvillea; and orange, lemon and avocado trees. The area, legally protected since 1987, was a unique natural habitat for more than 200 resident or migratory birds, including a number of rare and endangered species. The lakes were a rich repository for shellfish and other marine life.

When he wanted, he could jet-ski or windsurf on the lakes and run for hours along the nature trails or the beach. The wonderful climate and beautiful surroundings made his fitness regime more bearable. And when he needed a social life he went to the golf club, where the locals and residents knew him but, more importantly, knew not to bother him. At the restaurants and nightclubs on the complex, the same rules applied. Senna regarded the security firm that looked after the site as his own personal one, and it was so effective in ensuring his privacy and security that petty crime in Quinta do Lago became virtually non-existent.

When Senna returned from his run after half an hour, he showered, dressed and packed a small overnight bag for the three nights he was going to spend in Castel San Pietro near Bologna. He put a jacket and tie on for the day's work he had ahead, but there were no formal dinners or commitments that weekend, so his clothing needs were minimal. But there was a small irritation in his life that glorious morning. His brother, Leonardo, was staying until Sunday and would be coming with him to Imola. Leonardo was on a mission from his family to try and persuade Senna to give up his girlfriend, Adriane. For all sorts of reasons, the family, with the exception of his mother, Neyde, who loved what he loved, detested Adriane.

It was no surprise that in 1994, for the first time in his life, Senna planned to spend the entire season at Quinto do Lago and not return to Brazil until the season was over.

"Nobody else can, considering that in our profession we deal with ego a lot, with danger, with our health, continuously, second after second, not just day after day or month after month or year after year. Our life goes by in seconds, even milliseconds."

Ayrton Senna
October 1988

CHAPTER 5

Taking Care of Business

Afternoon - Thursday
28th April 1994

No one could disguise the sense of anticipation and excitement in the Senna household that morning as Juraci brought the car round to the front of the house to collect Ayrton Senna and his younger brother, Leonardo da Silva, for the 25-minute drive to Faro airport to drop the brothers off for their flight to Munich.

He remarked to Juraci that life couldn't get any better than it was that bright sunny morning in the Algarve. But he was always saying that to the people around him, reminding them, and not least of all himself, how lucky they all were to be sharing the life Formula One had given him.

The journey to Faro was a 12.5-mile trip Juraci had made many times before. If Senna was driving, it took 15 minutes; for her it was nearer half an hour.

Juraci had lost count of the number of times she had made the trip as she picked up or dropped off his friends and family from the airport that served the Algarve. Juraci preferred it when it was just her and the boss in the car – then he was polite about her driving. When he wasn't alone, Senna liked to supply a running commentary on her driving for the amusement of the passengers. Although she always enjoyed having a driving lesson from the best driver in the world, she also found it mildly embarrassing. She was also scared, especially when they left the house with only 10 minutes to get to the airport and he was driving. Senna could easily make Quinta do Lago to Faro in 10 minutes. He possessed extraordinary eyesight that enabled him to see things others simply couldn't imagine. Only Jackie Stewart, of modern day Formula One drivers, could match it. He put that superior vision to good use on the road and his judgement of distance was so honed that overtaking manoeuvres horrifying to ordinary road users could be accomplished with absolute ease. Professor Sid Watkins once described a trip in his hire car with Senna, after they had arrived in Italy together on Senna's plane for the San Marino Grand Prix. He offered Senna the keys to his hire car with his mother, Neyde, and sister, Viviane, in the back seat. As Watkins described: "He went off on the Autostrada Tangenziale like greased lightning. There was a long line of two lanes of traffic at an intersection. Without hesitating, or slowing, he shot up the middle with a centimetre or so of clearance on each side. The traffic lights changed and we'd gone before any outraged motorist could blow his horn. I sat with clenched jaws in the front passenger seat and my jaw muscles were sore by the time we reached the hotel." After that experience, Watkins never offered the keys of his car to Senna again.

This Thursday morning was much like any other morning drop-off. Usually Senna sat in the front, his windows open and shirtsleeves blowing. But today he was dressed smartly in a dark green sports jacket and cream trousers with a grey patterned tie. He had a full day of business meetings and was dressed appropriately.

His brother, Leonardo, skulked in the back. Juraci noted there was some bad blood between the brothers that day, not that it was any of her business, although she sensed that the disagreements between them were centered on Adriane. Juraci was firmly in Adriane's camp. She loved Senna's new girlfriend and was looking forward to her imminent arrival in Portugal almost as much as her boss was.

At Faro, Captain Owen O'Mahoney was already waiting on the tarmac with Senna's distinctive BAe HS125-800 jet, painted white with three graded black and grey stripes with its personalised registration N125AS. Senna used his jet almost every day, like a taxi flying to various destinations in Europe, either for a race or testing or on business and sometimes even for pleasure.

O'Mahoney had started flying for Senna straight after he bought the HS-125 in 1990. He spent more time with Senna than anyone else, continually flying him around Europe. The 46-year-old was a pilot straight out of central casting, with a honey baritone voice reminiscent of Richard Burton and each word he spoke being perfectly enunciated. His years in the RAF had taught him everything he knew, including coping with crises, which was more common than most people thought in a private light jet. Of the 14 pilots with whom he had learnt to fly, only three were still alive. He had learned to suppress emotion, a trait he would find very valuable before the weekend was out.

Before Senna, O'Mahoney had kept his distance from his employers, never getting close to them. But he found Senna very different from the people he usually flew around, and the two had quickly become firm friends. Sensing a reticence to communicate, Senna said to him after their first ever flight together: "Owen, in future, just talk to me."

O'Mahoney saw it as part of his job to ease the pressure on his boss's existence as much as he could. He made sure he never complained about anything. As he recalled: "I was just the means to an end. He was the star, and with everyone wanting a piece of him, he didn't want one extra guy bleating at him all the time. I was old enough to be his father, which was perhaps why we got on so well. Many was the time we would sit on journeys and he would ask me questions about this and that."

They enjoyed a little game whereby Senna would never tell O'Mahoney the result of a race as they flew home together: "I could never tell from his manner on a Sunday whether he had won or lost. The only clue was that if he'd won, he might ask what the weather was like in Faro and that was a coded message. Sometimes, if he'd not had a good race, it took time to get something out of him."

O'Mahoney gradually became his closest friend and confidante, and he knew more about Senna than anyone else. As he recalled: "I can remember parking behind hangars so he could sneak into Frank Williams' plane without anyone seeing him." O'Mahoney was also one of only three people who knew about his trip to see Luca di Montezemolo the day before.

Surprisingly, Senna never got his pilot's licence although he was a newly qualified helicopter pilot with 103 hours under his belt. But he took informal lessons from O'Mahoney whenever he could, planning to get his licence when he retired. As O'Mahoney said: "He didn't have a licence, but I would often sit in the co-pilot's seat while he took the controls."

That morning, as Senna was still packing his bag, O'Mahoney had already filed a flight plan for Munich and was anxiously looking at his watch to make sure they didn't miss the planned takeoff and landing slots he had pre-booked. Booking in the slots to suit Senna's hectic schedule was not always easy and the cost of missing a slot was up to half an hour waiting on an apron with the engines running. No one enjoyed that, least of all O'Mahoney.

Senna had devoted the whole of Thursday 28th April to pursuing his new career as a business entrepreneur. He wanted to put his fame and his money to good use and carve a career out for himself when he retired from racing. Senna had worked out that when he retired at around the age of 40 he would still have half his active life in front of him. He had used 1993 to build the foundations of a life after motor racing, and now he was tying up details of all the commercial deals he had found and signing off on the contracts. He had already allocated $47 million of his own money in commitments to his new ventures plus hundreds of millions more of borrowed money for capital. He planned to import Audi cars, Ducati motorcycles, Mont Blanc luxury goods and Carraro bicycles into Brazil starting in 1994 and he already employed a large number of people at his Senna Import company in São Paulo.

To start the day, Senna had an early morning meeting with executives from Audi at its Ingolstadt headquarters, half an hour's drive from Munich airport. The meeting was to finalise car orders and shipments for the rest of 1994. His deal with Audi to become its sole Brazilian importer had been signed on 18th November 1993 in Ingolstadt and had been consummated on Monday 28th March 1994, the day after the Brazilian Grand Prix. That day 2,000 people were entertained in a giant aircraft hangar owned by Varig at the Congonhas airport in São Paulo as Senna introduced all the Audi models to Brazil.

Importing cars was easy but making money from it was the hard bit. Selling Audis in 1994 was nowhere near as easy as it became 20 years later, and the brand was unknown in Brazil. But Senna could see into the future and knew, with Volkswagen's backing and its long-term plans for the brand, that there was lots of money to be made when he retired. Senna knew that this deal would make him more money in a year than he had ever earned as a race driver. But becoming Audi's sole importer meant the outlay of tens of millions of dollars in capital and startup costs even though projected sales for year one were less than 2,000 cars. Starting it up from scratch was more money than Senna had and would mean a commitment to borrowing a lot of money from banks. There were plenty of details to sweat, and Senna's speciality was sweating the details. Audi's executives were astonished at his grasp of detail.

The meeting with Audi was quickly concluded, and everyone was excited as Senna said his goodbyes and headed back to the airport.

Just over four hours after they had landed in Munich, O'Mahoney steered the HS125 down the runway and headed for Italy. He was less worried about this leg of the journey. The Italians were far less bothered about punctuality and landing and takeoff slots. There was flexibility in the Italian system that did not exist amongst German air traffic controllers, especially when he mentioned to Italian controllers that he had Ayrton Senna on board. Then, anything seemed to be possible.

They were headed for Forli Airport near Bologna, where a chartered Augusta helicopter was waiting for them. The flight was over quickly and the Augusta was on the tarmac to take Senna straight to Padua and the Carraro bicycle factory. It was a very quick transfer and he didn't even have to show his passport.

Senna had a new deal with Carraro to manufacture a carbon-fibre bicycle called the Senna, which would carry his now famous double 'double S' logo. It had been planned for some time and was one of many new products he planned to sell under the famous 'double S' Senna brand. Separately, he was going to import the whole range of Carraro bicycles into Brazil.

The Augusta landed at around four o'clock in the fields surrounding the Carraro Industrial factory. As Senna alighted, he was immediately surrounded by factory workers and photographers. He worked his way through the crowd towards the offices to shake hands with Giovanni Carraro, the managing director. They went into a small conference room to formally sign the contract. Afterwards Senna was interviewed for a short promotional film and effortlessly read a four-minute script in Italian to launch his new bike. Then he and Giovanni Carraro took a car to the Sheraton Padova Hotel where they were due to hold a press conference.

When Senna sat down, he looked around and saw that there were no journalists he recognised. That was good, as he wanted to focus on his new business career and not answer endless questions about Formula One. But he was surprised as the journalists were not interested at all in bicycles and all they wanted to talk about was motor racing.

In the end, Senna gave up trying to bring the subject round to his agenda and went with the flow of questions. He told them: "The world championship is just beginning for me in Imola, with a handicap of two races."

Senna was very surprised at the level of knowledge the writers had about Formula One when he started to get questions about Benetton's supposed illegal traction control. He answered carefully, saying: "I really can't say much about it," but then couldn't resist adding: "It's difficult to talk about things one cannot prove." He had not expected questions about Benetton's suspected cheating, and he realised that knowledge of it must be more widespread than he thought. He quickly wrapped up the questioning and realised he had already said too much.

At around 5:30pm they drove back to the Carraro factory and Senna got back on board the Augusta and flew straight to the Imola circuit. On the way, they picked up Mike Vogt, the marketing director of TAG Heuer. Senna and Vogt knew each other well from his McLaren days. During the ride, they discussed a new Senna watch that the company wanted to develop. Even though Senna had left the McLaren family, of which TAG Heuer was a part, Vogt still wanted to do business with him. He knew he could sell plenty of Senna watches at $2,000 apiece. This was an easy deal for Senna to make. He got a big cut of every watch sold, and if it went well he knew he could earn a million dollars out of the deal for doing virtually nothing. The watches also enhanced his brand.

At six o'clock the Augusta landed on the infield at Imola. Although he had no commitments at the track on Thursday, Senna wanted to show his face to the team. He also wanted to see the results of a programme of aerodynamic modifications that had been planned from the last test session a week earlier in France.

After he had checked in with his engineer, David Brown, he chatted to Williams' marketing chief, Richard West, about how the Carraro launch had gone. After barely an hour, he was back in the Augusta for the short flight to his hotel. He was booked in for three nights at the Hotel Castello, a typically modest Italian hotel in Castel San Pietro, a spa town about 10 kilometres west of Imola.

The hotel was run by Valentino Tosoni and his wife, Luiza, both of whom Senna had got to know ever since he first started staying there with McLaren in 1988. When he got there, he discovered Luiza was nine months pregnant and due to give birth any day. She told him the most likely time was 1st May, the date of the San Marino Grand Prix. He wished her well in case their paths didn't cross again.

It was the hotel of choice for McLaren's top executives. Although he was no longer a McLaren team member, he had booked his usual room, officially called Suite 200, although in reality it was a standard room and bathroom barely deserving the description as a suite.

Interestingly, Frank Williams was staying in the room directly below him and Ron Dennis in the one directly above. The hotel was far below the standard that the Formula One fraternity usually stayed in, but they loved it for the convenience and the attitude of the proprietors who went out of their way to service their every need. But most importantly for Senna, he could land a helicopter in the grounds at any hour of the day and night with no problems, even if it meant waking up every guest in the hotel.

That weekend, there were seven friends and colleagues staying with him at Imola, the first European race of the year. Apart from his brother, Leonardo, the company included Julian Jakobi, his manager, Antonio Braga, his close friend and neighbour in Portugal, Galvao Bueno from TV Globo, Celso Lemos, managing director of the Senna brand licensing company in Brazil, Josef Leberer, his personal physio, and Ubirajara Guimaraes, head of the Senna import company. They were all making their own way to the hotel, and all would meet later for dinner.

Soon after he checked in, Josef Leberer arrived to give Senna his regular massage and tell him the arrangements for the evening. At Senna's request, they would all dine at the hotel, as he had no desire to go outside. He asked Leberer if they could do the same for Saturday evening, but Leberer informed Senna there was a wedding party that had taken over the whole restaurant. There was always a wedding on a Saturday night in the Castello. Senna told him to book a table at the Romagnola restaurant instead.

After dinner, Senna was back in his room just after 10 o'clock. As soon as he got in, he picked up the phone and dialled his apartment in São

Paulo, where it was just after seven o'clock in the evening. He wanted to speak to his girlfriend, Adriane.

When he got through, he found she was packing to fly out to Portugal the following day. She couldn't disguise her excitement, and her enthusiasm was infectious. After chatting for another 15 minutes, he put the phone down and got undressed and into bed. Almost immediately, he was asleep. It had been a very long and very fruitful day.

TAKING CARE OF BUSINESS

"I didn't move. Any argument would have been in vain. Dozens of times I had seen him like that, but never as a victim. I never thought it would be directed at me."

Adriane Galisteu
23rd March 1994

CHAPTER 6

Leonardo vs Adriane

The family persuader overplays his hand

Normally, the weekend of the San Marino Grand Prix was a very successful and joyful time for Ayrton Senna. It was the first European race of the season, and the teams brought their own motorhomes to races for the first time. Senna enjoyed having his own dressing room and rest area; at the Imola track everything was to his convenience, and he didn't have to think for a moment about his routine. He adored the Italian way of life, and it was a weekend where he could anticipate and react to anything that was thrown at him. And it was a track where he really enjoyed racing.

His previous results reflected that. In his nine previous races at the circuit, he had been on pole position seven times and won the race three times. He knew it like the back of his hand and, barring events outside of his control, he was certain he would win on Sunday.

But there was a shadow over the weekend. There was a fight going on with his family over his girlfriend, Adriane Galisteu. The family wanted him to give her up because they did not think she was good enough for him. So much so that they had sent his younger brother, Leonardo, over to Italy to insist that he make the change and end the relationship.

Senna was annoyed and distraught at the same time, as he had planned to take Adriane to every European race in 1994. At the last minute, he had been forced to cancel her visit to San Marino because of the presence of Leonardo. If she did come, then there was the danger of a public row; and Ayrton Senna did not air his family's dirty linen in public.

Senna had known for some time that a major conflict was coming between him and his family. He had come to realise that even in the closest knit families there are jealousies, and for the first time they were coming to the surface in the Da Silva clan.

The Da Silvas were quite a family. They owned thousands of acres that they farmed in Brazil and they also ran a car parts manufacturing business. The businesses had made family patriarch Milton Da Silva extremely wealthy.

The family was tight, very tight, and usually everything was everyone's business within a circle of six people – Senna; Milton, his father; Neyde, his mother; Viviane, his sister; Leonardo, his brother; and his sister's husband, Flavio Lalli.

The family had supported him and made possible his rise in motor racing, but now he felt he had paid his dues and should be set free. But they weren't letting him go so easily, and Adriane was where they chose to make a stand. They were jealous that Adriane was displacing them in his life, and there was no one more jealous than his 26-year-old brother, Leonardo. But Adriane was not the only source of conflict. Leonardo was envious of the influences of Senna's European-based friends, a tight group dominated by Antonio Braga. They supported him in Europe and had embraced Adriane.

Basically, Leonardo thought Adriane too young for his brother and the age gap, 13 years, too much. She was a lot younger than his own girlfriend. He just thought she was a dumb blonde, and he hated her more and more as each day passed. Whereas Leonardo was always at Senna's side in the past, now it was Adriane. He was consumed with envy.

It hadn't always been that way, and it had been very different when the relationship started in March 1993. Then the Da Silvas had welcomed her into the family. They believed it would be like all Senna's other relationships and end after a few months: a year at the most. It was, at the beginning of 1994, when they realised it was not going to end quickly, and that she had effectively moved in with him as his full-time partner, that their attitude changed dramatically. They were dismayed that Adriane and Senna were now firmly established as a couple living together in Brazil at his São Paulo apartment and his beach house in Angra. As if this was not enough, the family had really become upset when they learned that he planned to spend the entire summer together with Adriane at his European base on the Algarve. Worse still, he would not be returning to Brazil to see them during the whole of the summer, something he had never before neglected to do.

Their like had suddenly become dislike, especially on the male side of the Da Silva family. The main reason for the dislike seemed to be that she was born into the lower classes, and they called her "the peasant girl". It didn't seem to matter that her family had made good and become prosperous.

The family had been totally dismayed when Senna told them about his travel plans for the coming season, and they redoubled their efforts to try and split them up. The decision not to come home for six months was received especially badly, and they blamed Adriane's influence. But in truth, it had been Senna's decision, and Adriane had simply gone along with his wishes. He wanted an uninterrupted summer with her in the Algarve.

At 34, Senna finally wanted to live his own life, and some people close to him believed a total split with his family was inevitable if they ultimately refused to accept Adriane in his life.

They felt they were losing him. And to some extent, they were; although at one point it had looked as though their campaign might work. In the middle of March, alone in Europe and feeling battered by the family, he had written a letter to Adriane ending the relationship, but he had second thoughts and never sent it.

In those few days, Senna worked out in his head that Adriane was the most important thing in his life, and the family now came second. If necessary, he believed he would choose her over them although he hoped that it would not come to that.

The 1994 European season marked the start of a long period living together. The six-month trip to Europe was a trial run: if it didn't work, she would return to Brazil, and if it did, they would probably be married.

Later it was revealed that the family were worried that he would do something rash and marry Adriane suddenly, and then it would be too late for them to do anything about it.

The issue had been festering since the start of the year but didn't come out into the open until just before the Brazilian Grand Prix, when the family saw their chance to strike. On Tuesday 22nd March 1994, a new issue of the weekly *Caras* magazine hit the newsstands in São Paulo. *Caras* was the Brazilian equivalent of *Hola* magazine in Spain and *Hello* in Britain.

Published in the week of the Brazilian Grand Prix, it contained Adriane's first media interview since she had started going out with Senna, and she was on the cover.

In Brazil, Adriane was becoming famous as Senna's girlfriend, and he had already warned her about being exploited by the media. But his words of warning had apparently fallen on deaf ears.

When she was offered the chance of a photo-shoot with *Caras*, Adriane seized upon it. It was to be a swimwear shoot on Camburi beach. Realising it could be sensitive, she asked Senna's permission and, when he learned that the photographer would be Fabio Cabral, he agreed she should do it.

He even approved of the photos he was shown on 21st March, as he and Adriane celebrated his 34th birthday. At a family gathering that day, Adriane showed them to his mother, Neyde, who thought they were beautiful.

But that all changed when the magazine was published, two days later. The photos had been arranged in a provocative fashion over a 12-page feature, and Adriane was splashed all over the cover. *Caras's* editor was delighted and believed he was introducing the beautiful girlfriend of the national hero to the Brazilian public. He was unprepared for the Senna family's outburst of disapproval.

Adriane was very pleased with the article when she first saw it, but she was equally unsure whether it had all been a good idea. As she said: "I felt a shiver down my spine. The article was beautiful. The text was perfect. But I kept asking myself whether I should have done it?"

Adriane got her answer when Senna returned to the São Paulo apartment that evening waving a copy in the air. In her own words, he "exploded" and shouted, as he threw the magazine against the wall, "How could you let them do this?"

Adriane remembers: "I didn't move. Any argument would have been in vain. Dozens of times I had seen him like that, but never as a victim. I never thought it would be directed at me."

She told him she was a model, and that was what she did. She told him she needed the work and the money. He shot back: "You must understand that you are not the same person any more, Adriane. Now you are my girlfriend. You don't have to show the world you have a beautiful body, this other side of Adriane Galisteu."

At that moment, she knew she was in real trouble, as he had never called her Adriane before. He had always called her by her shortened name, 'Dri'. And he was far from finished. He told her: "You were too sexy. You don't have to show the world you have a beautiful body. You should show your beautiful body only to me."

It was their first row. She was used to his moodiness and periods of silence, but his open anger towards her shocked her to the core. She genuinely thought their relationship might be over and started packing her things for what she was certain would be a speedy exit from his life.

But after half an hour, Senna calmed down and admitted to her he was just another jealous boyfriend. He told her his anger would pass. It did pass, but he was not the problem; the family had sensed blood in the water and sought to take full advantage.

Adriane went on a charm offensive with the family and had the uncomfortable job of apologising to Milton and Neyde Da Silva for the *Caras* photos. But after a heart-to-heart discussion, she thought they had put it behind them. She couldn't have been more wrong.

As for Senna, he had forgotten about it in 24 hours as he focused on the Brazilian Grand Prix. The night of his birthday, he asked her to give up her career as a model and become his full-time girlfriend. He agreed to give her a $5,000 a month allowance to make up for her lost earnings. Senna was fully aware that Adriane was now a hot property for the Brazilian media, and he wanted to avoid any more situations like the *Caras* photoshoot.

He also persuaded her to take a crash course in English before she came to Europe. Adriane couldn't have been happier, and she said "yes" to it all straight away. The next day she telephoned the Elite Models office and told them she would not be available for the rest of March and all of April. She had already told them she would be away for the whole of the summer.

Senna believed his family's reaction was a storm in a teacup, reflecting the fact that they knew he really cared for Adriane and that something even more serious than Formula One was afoot in his life.

But Senna had made a serious mistake by discussing his dissatisfaction with his family. He had inadvertently given the family the excuse they needed to go after Adriane.

Soon after the *Caras* article, Leonardo decided to bug the telephone at Senna's apartment and to listen in on Adriane's calls to try and get some dirt on her to present to his brother. It produced endless conversations between Adriane and her friends, mainly with her telling them how much she loved Senna and how happy she was. However, one series of conversations produced exactly what Leonardo wanted. They were tapes of conversations between Adriane and Cesar, her old boyfriend she had been dating for a year and a half before Senna, and with whom she had enjoyed a close relationship. She had given him up for Senna, but it had been a very difficult parting. The former boyfriend had been devastated, and the parting had also upset Adriane. She had stayed in touch with him and attempted to do all she could to assuage his feelings. In the process, she entered into conversations she probably shouldn't have, discussing her love life with Senna. In an attempt to spare his feelings and make him feel better about himself, she inferred that he was better in bed than her new boyfriend.

Leonardo spent all his time before he left for Europe listening to the cassette tapes. He was delighted when he heard these conversations, and as soon as he got to Portugal, he handed a copy of the tape to his brother. Senna was barely interested as Leonardo began playing the first tape to him. But as soon as he grasped what was happening, he took them off him and said he would listen to them later.

Senna was totally exasperated that Leonardo had taped Adriane's phone calls but declined to argue with his brother. Instead, he resolved to have the locks changed on his apartment so that only he, Adriane and his housekeeper had keys.

Leonardo had started arguing with Senna as soon as he arrived from Brazil, and it continued right up to race morning at Imola. Annoyingly for Senna, the argument about Adriane continued on the aeroplane on Thursday morning. As the weekend went on, Leonardo became more fractious and emotional. For his part, Senna simply could not understand why Leonardo and his family were so upset and what had suddenly changed.

Especially as he couldn't have been happier, despite the *Caras* blip. For Senna, Adriane was the real thing, and he believed she could be the love of his life. She was everything he liked in a woman, good-looking but ethereal rather than beautiful. She was blonde, small-breasted and long-legged but not too tall. But most importantly, she had no attitude. In fact, her naiveté was refreshing, and their sex life was stimulating and compatible.

She was also intelligent in an unobvious way, with a perception of things that weren't always clear. She understood the things that mattered, and she understood what mattered to him. Senna knew instinctively that she was special and that he could even end up marrying her, which was why Leonardo's mission was a waste of time. It also meant that his last words with his brother on Sunday morning were fractious ones – a continuing cause of great regret for the rest of Leonardo's life.

On the morning of Sunday 1st May, Leonardo had tried again to persuade his brother to change his mind and some very rare harsh words were exchanged between them. But Senna would not be moved. He told him he was staying put for the summer, even if it meant seeing far less of his family, especially him. For the first time, instead of ignoring him, he had let loose and told his brother his personal life was none of his business and he was fed up with his interference.

In truth, the seemingly never-ending and ongoing aggravation was beginning to wear him down. He was eight years older and felt his brother had overstepped the mark. But he also felt unable to make the break. He wished it would go away and couldn't wait until Leonardo stepped on to the flight to go home to Brazil. He fervently hoped that would be the last he would see of him for the summer.

"You leave a lot of things behind you when you follow a passion"

Ayrton Senna
August 1989

CHAPTER 7

Barrichello Avoids Death

Qualifying - Friday 29th April

O n Friday morning, Senna caught a helicopter for the short trip to the circuit at 8:30am, ready for the start of practice and qualifying. Senna had much on his mind that Friday morning. Since his meeting with Luca di Montezemolo two days earlier and his tacit agreement to join Ferrari for the 1995 season, he had thought of little else. He kept trying to think of ways he could get out of his Williams contract. He had come to the conclusion that the return of Alain Prost could be the key to Williams letting him go.

He was also thinking about his relationship with the FIA and the motor racing establishment. Ever since the start of 1994, he had felt persecuted. With Prost's retirement, he was the only world champion left racing and therefore the senior driver on the grid. He was also the driver's unofficial spokesman. But the FIA hierarchy hated him for it. He thought the new FIA president Max Mosley was orchestrating the opposition to him, and he wasn't sure where Bernie Ecclestone stood either. Ostensibly, Ecclestone was his friend and they were almost like family. He often stayed at his London house overnight and Ecclestone's children, Tamara and Petra, knew him as 'Uncle Ayrton.'

But Ecclestone was not keen on anyone who he thought might challenge his authority or be more powerful than him. Where power was concerned, his ego was huge and Senna could see that sometimes he resented him. He wondered if Ecclestone was behind the aggravation he was getting and the hate he felt from race officials. He thought Ecclestone may well have told Mosley to "tweak Senna's tail a little bit". He had seen him do it with other drivers and now it was his turn.

As he walked to the motorhome on another wonderful Italian spring morning, he tried to clear his mind and forget his problems. He was here to race and he knew he must never forget that was his priority and, for him, everything else was just kabuki, and he didn't want to waste any more of his time on it.

In between Japan and Imola, Williams had been testing intensively at the Nogaro circuit in south-west France to find the source of the Williams car's multiple problems. A number of changes were promised for Imola, but Senna was sceptical that the modifications would make any real difference. The new car had been consistently slower than the Benetton despite having a much more powerful Renault engine.

Both Senna and his team mate Damon Hill had said openly that the car was horrible to drive. Hill remembers: "We were always changing the set-up of the car in an attempt to find that perfect combination which would turn the promise of a great car into a reality. But it is difficult to become familiar with a car if it is constantly being changed – it becomes a vicious circle."

It was clear from the difference in Senna's and Hill's times that Senna was driving through the problems. As Hill admits: "Ayrton had enormous reserves of ability and could overcome deficiencies in a chassis."

At just after 9:30am, Senna climbed into his car and completed 22 laps, posting a fastest time of 1m 21.598secs, more than a second quicker than his team mate. Hill was pleasantly surprised by the behaviour of the modified chassis. Senna was not. He thought the team was going in the wrong direction with the car and spent a lot of time afterwards with his engineer, David Brown, writing down a whole list of notes about the car's performance on his A4 pad.

At 1pm, the first qualifying session began and Senna was soon fastest. But 15 minutes into the start of the session, the Jordan of Rubens Barrichello hit the steep kerb in the middle of the 140mph Variante Bassa chicane. The kerb acted as a ramp, lifting the Jordan up, and it flew through the air. The car was out of the driver's control, and Barrichello lowered his head the best he could and covered the front of his visor with his hands as he waited for the inevitable impact.

The car hit the tyre barrier and glanced off it before smashing against a debris fence, slowing down with tremendous force against the flexible barrier before hitting the ground.

The crash was horribly violent, but the tyres had taken some of the pace out of it as Barrichello bounced around upside down and ended up suspended unconscious in the car. The accident couldn't have looked worse over the pit lane monitors, and Team Principal Eddie Jordan feared he might have lost his number one driver.

Damon Hill remembers the shock of Barrichello's accident: "What shook us most was the rate at which the car took off; at one stage it looked as if it was going to smash through the fence and fly into the grandstand." The Jordan, more by luck than anything else, finished on its side, upside down and against the barrier. That was bad enough, but the marshals promptly tipped the car over without any care at all and it thumped down hard on its wheels, visibly sending the driver's head from side to side. Hill says: "You could see Barrichello's head thrashing around in the cockpit."

A red flag was immediately shown and the session was stopped. The medical car was sitting at the chicane, and immediately Mario Casoni sped round to the accident in the car containing Professor Watkins and Dr Baccarini, an Italian anaesthetist. The accident had happened behind them, and they had heard the car thump the tyre barrier. They weaved through the Formula One cars that were still on the track slowing down and got there first before the other medical and safety cars. Watkins knelt down by the side of the car and could hear Barrichello breathing hard. That was a good sign although he was clearly unconscious. Watkins cut the helmet strap whilst Baccarini held the driver's head firmly. His nose was bleeding, but Watkins was concerned with his breathing and thrust a tube down his neck to clear the airways. He rotated the tube to ensure airflow. He put a cervical collar on and the special extrication team arrived to get Barrichello out of the car. The team fitted a spinal splint as a precaution and got him out and laid him on the grass for Watkins to diagnose any problems and plan his immediate treatment. Three minutes later, Barrichello woke up on the grass wondering where he was. Watkins did his assessment, and he was whisked by ambulance to the circuit's medical centre.

The Imola facilities were as good as many small hospitals, and Franco Servadei, a neurosurgeon, was on hand to put Barrichello through an immediate scan and then into a recovery room.

Senna had not seen the accident but Betise Assumpcao, his PR chief, went off to investigate Barrichello's condition as she knew her boss would want to know all about it as soon as he stepped out of his car.

Senna got out of his car and went straight to the medical centre. Burly security men barred his way. But Senna very much believed in the principle that if the front door is closed, you immediately try the back door.

So, undeterred he climbed the chain link fence at the back and bypassed the guards, who didn't see him until it was too late and he was inside. Professor Watkin shooed them away, and after a quick chat with Watkins, Senna went straight in to where Barrichello was laying. Barrichello had momentarily nodded off, and when he woke up, he found Senna looking over him. He told Barrichello: "Stay calm. It will be all right." Barrichello remembered: "The first face I saw was Ayrton's. He had tears in his eyes. I had never seen that with Ayrton before. I just had the impression he felt as if my accident was like one of his own."

As soon as Senna knew Barrichello was okay, he quickly left – this time through the front door – and ran back to his garage ready for qualifying to restart.

Barrichello was quickly shipped off to San Maggiore hospital by helicopter – the first of three that weekend. Nobody dared to believe that he had got away with just a broken nose and bruised ribs.

Damon Hill, for one, was mightily relieved when he heard the news, although he was still furious with the marshals a few hours later: "I was astonished that the marshals did that, particularly in view of the neck and spinal injuries received by J. J. Lehto and Jean Alesi during test sessions earlier in the year. Barrichello could have sustained similar injuries. He should have been left as he was or, if there was a risk of fire, then at least the car should have been put down gently."

Senna got back in his car to resume the session and was back on track at 1:40pm, when the qualifying session resumed. Senna bettered his time immediately and, just before the close, set a very fast lap time of 1m 21.548secs at an average of 138.2mph. In the emotional aftermath of Barrichello's accident, it was a repeat performance of what happened in 1990 when Martin Donnelly crashed.

Senna had been the only driver to stop at the scene of the enormous accident in qualifying at the 1990 Spanish Grand Prix when Donnelly's Lotus car disintegrated against the barriers. After that accident, he had gone faster than ever and eventually won yet another, his fiftieth, pole position, but he found such bravery came at an emotional price. As he said: "As a racing driver, there are some things you have to go through, to cope with. Sometimes, they are not human, yet you go through it. Some of the things are not pleasant, but in order to have some of the nice things you have to face them. You leave a lot of things behind when you follow a passion." As one observer put it: "It was an emphatic reminder of Senna's supreme skill and courage."

At the end of the session, Senna climbed out of the car and left the pit garage for the motorhome to do some prearranged press interviews. Senna sat down with the BBC commentator Murray Walker in the Williams motorhome to record a preview to be broadcast during the run-up to the Grand Prix on Sunday.

Senna had a great affection for Walker, and it was mutual. He always made time for him on a Friday afternoon. Walker remembered: "Over the winter, I'd got out some tapes of the 1983 Formula Three duel between Senna and Martin Brundle just to amuse myself. I realised as I was watching them that I had been correctly calling him I-Air-Ton Senna. And I had realised that I had become sloppy and had been calling him Ayrton at the Grand Prix races. So, at the Brazilian Grand Prix in 1994, I started to call him I-Air-Ton again. Well, I got a torrent of abuse from the British public along the lines of who is this bloke, I-Air-Ton? Why can't you call him Ayrton like the rest of us? So during the Pacific Grand Prix I reverted to calling him Ayrton and thought no more about it.

"At Imola I sat down with him to do my usual pre-race interview in the Williams motorhome. 'Well, Ayrton,' I said. 'You lost out to Schumacher in Brazil, you went off the track. You lost out to Schumacher in Aida when Larini drove you off the track. You are 20 points behind, what are your feelings?' Senna replied: 'What happened to I-Air-Ton?' 'How could you possibly know about that? You are in the car,' I said. Senna replied simply: 'I keep in touch Murray.'" Walker was astonished that he picked him up on such a small detail and even that he was aware it: "I thought that incredible.

With everything in his life, he could be troubled to raise such an insignificant detail. But, then, no detail was ever insignificant to him." When he had finished, Senna walked back to his transporter to get changed.

As he walked, a few fans shouted to him from the Paddock Club balcony above the Williams transporter. They said: "Now's your chance to show Schumacher who's the champion." He acknowledged them but didn't stop. Inside the motorhome, he greeted the waiting journalists but told them there was a problem with his car and that he needed an hour with David Brown.

They agreed to wait. In with Brown, Senna produced the usual two-page hand-written A4 list of jobs he believed needed doing on the car. For all the speed, he was clearly not happy with it.

An hour later, he joined the journalists and briefed them on the business interests he was building for when he retired. Shadowing him for the weekend was Mark Fogarty of the new *Carweek* magazine, who also had a photographer inside the Williams pit. Fogarty said afterwards that he thought Senna was not focused at all: "Usually, if Senna agreed to do an interview, he would give it his full attention. This time he just wasn't focused. His answers were halting and he looked glazed, as if he was mentally worn out." When *RTL* TV reporter Kai Ebel asked him about Rubens Barrichello, he began a sentence three times but kept losing the thread of his thoughts. He then ominously changed the subject and told the journalists that Imola was a dangerous circuit, that there were a few places that were "not right as far as safety is concerned." They asked him why the drivers hadn't done anything about it and he told them: "I am the only world champion left – and I have opened my big mouth too often. Over the years I have learned that it's better to keep my head down."

His pilot Owen O'Mahoney was also surprised at some of Senna's actions that day. He had often mentioned that he would like some signed photos of the two of them together, but he had never got around to it. So he was very surprised when Senna called him over as he passed by the Williams garage, fished some photos out of his briefcase and signed them for him. O'Mahoney says: "The odd thing was that he gave them to me in the middle of practice. It was so out of character for him to think about anything other than racing. It was almost as if he wanted to tie up loose ends."

When the journalists left, Senna was back to work with Brown again and they were together for two hours. It was eight o'clock by the time he left the circuit and returned to San Pietro. Again, Josef Leberer arrived in his room for the regular massage. The two men chatted about Barrichello's accident. Senna told him he thought Barrichello was very fortunate not to have sustained more serious injuries. Leberer found Senna more distressed about it than he might have expected.

That night, he dined with his brother and friends at the Trattoria Romagnola restaurant but was interrupted throughout by autograph seekers once word got out he was there, albeit in a private alcove at the back.

Afterwards, he walked quickly back to the hotel to telephone Adriane before she got on the Varig flight to Lisbon that night. He told her: "I can't wait for you to get here." Adriane said later they had a long discussion about their relationship and she told him she was no longer scared of being his girlfriend as she had been at the start.

During the conversation he mentioned he had written her a letter but hadn't posted it. She asked why not and told him to fax it so she could read it before she left for the airport. He replied that it was unimportant and the moment had passed. The truth was that he had written the letter ending their relationship after a period of particularly heavy pressure from his father and brother. His father had said to him he had to choose between them and Adriane. After putting the letter in an envelope he couldn't bring himself to post it and tucked it in the inside pocket of his bag. Now, when he had time, he intended to replace it with a different sort of letter, expressing what he really felt. He knew now that given a similar ultimatum in the future, he would defintely choose Adriane and that it was a big turning point in his life.

But she was never to know any of that.

Then, according to her, he burst into tears and started recounting the details of Barrichello's accident and the speed that he had left the track. She recalled: "Can you imagine what it is like to receive a phone call from Ayrton Senna when he bursts into tears?" She said the call showed his despair at what had happened. She said of the moment: "I felt absolute panic and kept asking him what happened, what happened." In the end, she had to break off the call in order to catch her flight.

"Do you feel that you're likely to stray into any of these new grey areas of illegality?" He answered: "I don't think so, no. I'm fairly confident we're kosher."

Ross Brawn
March 1994

CHAPTER 8

The Dodgy Benetton

Senna suspects cheating

Ayrton Senna had a myriad of problems niggling him when he arrived at the Imola track on the Thursday evening. He seemed even more intense than usual and his issue was not his family problems or even his team problems; it was the unusual speed being demonstrated by Michael Schumacher's Benetton-Ford car.

By then, Senna was almost certain that he knew the reason why. He believed the Benetton was gaining an unfair advantage by using traction control, an electronic system that had been banned by the FIA for the 1994 season.

Traction control was a wonderful piece of software that measured wheel rotation and effectively used sophisticated counter methods to eliminate wheelspin. It had been invented in America by Buick and Cadillac in the early seventies for use on their road cars.

Advanced versions of traction control were tailor-made for Formula One cars where wheelspin was a consistent problem in corners. Traction control systems optimised grip during acceleration by reducing engine power, allowing the car to accelerate smoothly even on wet surfaces.

When traction control was banned, precise throttle control by a driver became critical again. But inevitably a driver was not as efficient as a computer, and the cars were slower.

But it proved to be almost impossible to ban traction control because it was not at all obvious when it was being used and, since it was software, there was no way of detecting it without access to a car's software source codes.

The ban relied on honesty. Tom Walkinshaw was the first engineer in the paddock to really understand this and, together with the Benetton software engineers, he devised a system that would keep traction control on the Benetton cars but make its use undetectable. It was the ultimate cheat.

But it required the co-operation of a small group of people in the team to keep the secret. Nobody knows who knew and didn't know this was going on in the team. However, one person who must have known and gone along with it was the driver Michael Schumacher. Schumacher had to know because he turned the system on and off from his car. He dismissed the claims by saying: "The only thing I can think of is that they are jealous."

Cheating had always been practiced in Formula One and across all motorsport. The challenge was not to get caught, and this is how certain people at Benetton played the game.

Right from the start of testing in 1994, Schumacher knew he had a superior car. And he knew why. At the last test session, at Silverstone, before the Grand Prix season started in March 1994, he was keen not to show the potential of the car and give anything away. Richard Williams, who first exposed the Benetton team's cheating in his book *The Death of Ayrton Senna*, was present at that test and said: "He was not silly enough to overplay it when told that people were speculating about how he was now faster than Senna."

That day, Richard Williams also noted that there were three different coloured buttons on the steering wheel of the Benetton car, and when the mechanics were asked what they were for, they all clammed up in unison. Williams remembered: "It was curious, but it didn't seem very important at the time."

Richard Williams appeared to be on to something as he later interviewed Benetton technical director Ross Brawn before the start of the season. In Brawn's office at the team's headquarters in Oxfordshire, he specifically asked him about the possibility of cheating using traction control: "Do you feel that you're likely to stray into any of these new grey areas of illegality?" It was a curious question to ask the senior technical person of a leading Formula One team. Effectively, he was asking him: "Are you going to cheat?" One might have expected immediately to be shown the door, but Brawn didn't miss a beat as he answered: "I don't think so, no. I'm fairly confident we're kosher." Looking back on his answer now, one might make a different interpretation: that Brawn didn't want to know what was going on in his software department or what Tom Walkinshaw was up to.

Schumacher's apparent speed had baffled Senna at first. Senna knew he was personally the faster driver – he knew the Williams car was faster, he knew the Renault engine was more powerful and he knew that Williams was a better-funded and a better-run team. So he couldn't make out how the Benetton car was still proving quicker than his Williams-Renault when it counted. He was also amazed how much slower Schumacher's team mates, J. J. Lehto and Jos Verstappen, were in the same car. Schumacher consistently went two seconds a lap quicker than either of them.

In fact, Senna knew the Williams-Renault package was superior to the Benetton. Ross Brawn and Rory Byrne of Benetton were good designers, but not in the same league as Patrick Head and Adrian Newey, who were arguably the best design combination ever seen in Formula One. Renault had a huge budget for its engine and top-line speed indicated to him it was far more powerful than the Cosworth-built Ford HB engine, which was being produced on a relative shoestring compared to Renault.

Senna was puzzled until he ran into Peter Collins of Lotus at another Formula One test session. Collins casually mentioned to him that he thought he had detected the use of traction control when he had been watching the cars out on the track. "Who do you think is using it?" asked Senna casually. "Schumacher," replied Collins equally casually. At that stage, Collins thought it would be stripped off by the time the season started and that Benetton were trying to unsettle the opposition with some fast times. After all, the team could do what it liked in private testing.

But suddenly, a light went on in Senna's head. Immediately, everything was clear. Later, he asked his own software engineers how it could be done. They told him if the software was on the system, it could be turned on and off with a switch. Like Collins, he didn't think Benetton would dare use it in a race even though he knew Flavio Briatore, the team principal, had few scruples in that direction. By all accounts, Senna didn't have a lot of time for the Benetton team principal, believing Briatore to be an Italian huckster who had arrived in Formula One after a career selling fluffy cardigans in America. But he hadn't considered him to be a cheat. Senna knew Briatore was an astute operator, well capable of embracing a skewed interpretation of the rule book, and he knew there were many grey areas in the rules that could be exploited within the spirit, if not the letter, of the rules.

That all changed at the first race of the season in Brazil at the end of March. Senna led until the first pit stop. On lap 21, Schumacher and Senna had entered the pit lane a second apart. Despite both drivers putting the same amount of fuel in, Schumacher's stop was so much faster than Senna's stop, so Schumacher left the pit lane in the lead and drove away with the race, leaving Senna in his wake. Senna was suspicious of how much faster the Benetton team was at its pit stops and how he had just been able effortlessly to extend his lead once he was in front.

When he got back to his motorhome after the race, he again asked one of his software engineers how Benetton could be using traction control. The answer to Senna's question this time was one word: "Walkinshaw."

Senna didn't really know who Tom Walkinshaw was. But he soon found out. Tom Walkinshaw, who was in ultimate charge of Benetton's engineering, was anything but an honest man. He was a man who almost prided himself on the opposite. When Senna asked around, he soon found out that Walkinshaw was a serial cheat. He had been caught cheating more than a few times in the lower formulae. In 1983, he had competed with a team in the British Saloon Car Championship. His team won all 11 races and the championship. But he was stripped of the title for blatant cheating. The rules had required the engine to be sealed at the beginning of the season. Walkinshaw blatantly unsealed it and enhanced the performance.

He had also swindled the British Racing Drivers Club (BRDC) out of £5 million over some car dealerships. The BRDC had sought to diversify its commercial interests, which at that time consisted of running Silverstone Circuit. Walkinshaw, a member of the BRDC, had been trusted with the project and had trousered £5 million of the members' money. He had also cheated Ford, Jaguar and Aston Martin out of millions and left a trail of financial destruction in his native Australia. Few people had a good word to say about Walkinshaw.

Senna questioned Peter Collins closely about Benetton. Collins had run the Benetton team before Briatore. Collins told Senna he had signed confidentiality agreements when he left and felt he had to honour them and so could not really comment. Senna respected that and didn't press it.

When he asked him about Walkinshaw, Collins just rolled his eyes.

But from that point on, for the last five weeks of his life, Senna was obsessed with proving that Schumacher's Benetton was using traction control. He took his fears to Patrick Head, but Head just poo-pooed the idea. Head was naive and thought everyone was as honest as him. He even thought Walkinshaw was straight. It took until the French Grand Prix, after Senna had died, and halfway through the season, for him to realise that Senna had been right and something was up.

Senna knew that only his extraordinary and risky driving skills had kept him at the head of the grid in qualifying, and he became consumed with exposing Benetton's secret advantage. He became more and more determined to find out what was going on. Betise Assumpcao confirmed it was a big problem for him: "It was all that was on his mind; Ayrton was not alone in thinking there was something dodgy about Schumacher's Benetton."

After Senna was punted off at the first corner of the Pacific Grand Prix in Japan during the second race of the season, he stayed out on the side of the track as he wanted to observe the behaviour of Michael Schumacher's Benetton. He watched for lap after lap and compared Schumacher's car to that of his team mate's. Schumacher's car, in comparison to its rivals, looked like it was on rails, and the difference going round corners was clear. Afterwards, he became even more convinced that Schumacher was using traction control.

Senna wondered to himself why the FIA was not doing anything about it as, by now, rumours were rife in the paddock and it appeared that some of the Benetton engineers had not managed to keep their mouths shut and had let some things slip. Especially as at the start of the season, Max Mosley, the president of the FIA, had promised draconian punishments for anyone caught cheating: they would be thrown out of the championship, he said.

But Mosley believed there was no possibility of cheating because it would need a switch to turn traction control on and off. He was confident the FIA scrutineers would be able to find such a switch and prevent its use.

But eventually Mosley could not ignore the obvious after Schumacher's third easy victory in a row at the San Marino Grand Prix, where even the FIA scrutineers were suspicious.

The FIA called in a data analysis company called Liverpool Data Research Associates (LDRA) to investigate the allegations of cheating using traction control and launch control. The FIA had to be seen to be fair and not just target Schumacher. Instead, it took the top three placed cars of Michael Schumacher, Nicola Larini and Mika Häkkinen for investigation by LDRA. The three teams were asked by the FIA to surrender their computer source codes.

Ferrari immediately complied for Larini, but Benetton for Schumacher and McLaren for Häkkinen refused, citing copyright law. The two teams claimed they did not own the source code and said they would be infringing the intellectual copyright of their third party software suppliers if they handed it over. They also cited their own commercial confidentiality rules.

The two teams were immediately fined $100,000 by the FIA and threatened with more fines for every day they didn't comply with the order. Eight days later, both teams capitulated – especially when it was pointed out that LDRA worked for government departments and its directors had signed the Official Secrets Act. Then their resistance crumbled.

It turned out that both teams had good reasons for not to wanting to comply. Straight away, LDRA discovered that McLaren were running a programme that allowed automatic gear downshifts but the FIA declared this was legal.

LDRA then set out to find the traction control on the Benetton that they were certain existed after studying video film of the car on the track. That wasn't easy as, once it was turned off, it was invisible.

Benetton stated that traction control and launch control, even if they hadn't wiped it from the system, could only be switched on by "recompilation of the code".

LDRA personnel were annoyed and insulted by what it saw as patronising behaviour by Benetton engineers. They knew full well that it was untrue and that its launch control could be switched on by connecting a computer to the gearbox control unit. When that was suggested, Benetton's response was to agree it was possible but that it had come as a "surprise to them."

In the event, Benetton had found a better way to activate it than attaching a computer as LDRA eventually discovered. Its subsequent report stated: "In order to enable launch control, a particular menu with 10 options has to be selected on the PC screen. Launch control is not visibly listed as an option. The menu was so arranged that, after 10 items, nothing further appeared. If however, the operator scrolled down the menu beyond the 10th listed option, to option 13, launch control can be enabled, even though this is not visible on the screen. No satisfactory explanation was offered for this apparent attempt to conceal the feature but when Schumacher went through the correct sequence of button pushes, it allowed computer assistance to completely take over the driving of the car and match gear changes to engine speed without any driver intervention. It made sure his car got to the first corner in the shortest possible time before the driver took over again.

Benetton's response this time again was that it was surprised, but the team said it definitely hadn't been used.

Finding the traction control software was much more difficult for LDRA. It effectively became a search for the switch that turned it on and off. But it wasn't a conventional on and off switch they were looking for; it was a software switch, which meant pressing a combination of buttons in a certain order would trigger it on and off. It was like turning the combination of a safe to open it.

Eventually, LDRA investigators found it. They found it could be turned on by pushing the throttle pedal to the floor and holding it there whilst simultaneously pressing other buttons and paddles on the steering wheel in a certain order.

Once again, Benetton didn't deny it was there but firmly stated it had never been used.

They then came up the remarkable excuse that it hadn't been wiped from the computer because it would have been too difficult to do so. They said that when they had tried, other programmes had become corrupt so they had left it.

And then Benetton came out with the best joke of all. They said they had designed the complex on-and-off system so that the driver couldn't find how to turn it on accidentally and start using it. It was a farcical response.

Benetton's excuses were blown apart when another team said it had taken two days to expunge its system of illegal software and one software engineer had been able to achieve it easily on his own with no adverse effects on the rest of the software system.

LDRA's report made it apparent that cheating in Formula One was easy and virtually undetectable. The only defence against it was honesty, and there didn't seem to be much of that present in the Benetton team. There is no doubt that the FIA should have applied the draconian penalties and thrown Benetton out of the championship. No one knows why it didn't.

Benetton came up with a remarkable defence when it appeared in front of the FIA World Motorsport Council. The team successfully argued that the regulations only required that traction control must not be used, not that it must not be present in the software. When the FIA checked its own rules, it found they were wanting and it was forced to back down.

The FIA World Council subsequently announced that no evidence had been found to suggest Benetton was using illegal electronic systems, but it did confirm that an illegal system existed on the car, which could be activated at any time.

It was a ludicrous let-off.

By the time of the French Grand Prix, even Patrick Head was suspicious. He watched Schumacher make a perfect start from the grid, driving around the all Williams-Renault front row to take the lead. Schumacher's start, from fourth on the grid was the most brilliant driving Head had ever seen at the start of a race. He also realised that it could only have been done with computer assistance. Head repeatedly played back Schumacher's start on his television. He had originally dismissed Senna's observations as paranoia, but now he changed his mind. Head had also had noticed an unnatural season-long dominance by Schumacher over his team mates J. J. Lehto, Jos Verstappen and Johnny Herbert. Between them, they scored 11 points that season to Schumacher's 92, the implication being they didn't have traction control to help them.

However, there was much more to come and Schumacher and Benetton were continually exposed as serial cheats as the season went on. First, they were found to have removed the filter from their fuel rig, enabling the fuel to flow 12.5 per cent faster through the hose, thereby saving them a second on every pit stop. Benetton claimed a junior mechanic had accidentally removed the filter when assembling the rig. Benetton were found guilty of removing the filter but faced no punishment because of the extenuating circumstances. It was another ludicrous let off.

At the Belgian Grand Prix, Benetton was found to have a thinner than allowed underbody on Schumacher's car, giving it an aerodynamic advantage. It was 2.6 millimetres thinner than the regulations, and Benetton claimed that excessive wear on the underneath of the car during the race had caused it. In another ludicrous decision, the FIA accepted their excuse and let them off without any punishment.

That made it three times the team had been caught cheating and three times it had been let off.

Perhaps worst of all, there was some evidence that Max Mosley, the president, and Bernie Ecclestone had colluded in getting Benetton off on one of the charges of removing the filter from its fuel rig. That came when a biography of the top barrister George Carman, who had died in 2000, was published by his son, Dominic, a couple of years later. The book recalled how Carman was acting for Schumacher and the Benetton team at the FIA World Motorsport Council hearing. In the book, it was alleged that Mosley and Ecclestone had met Carman the night before and cooked up the result of the hearing with him. If true, it would have been highly irregular. But there was no evidence to say it happened and Carman was dead.

But Benetton and Michael Schumacher were not finished cheating. The world championship came down to the last race of the season between Schumacher and Damon Hill. The Australian Grand Prix in Adelaide saw Schumacher leading Hill by only one point. Hill only had to beat the German to be world champion. Throughout the event Schumacher's Benetton had traction control turned on according to Keith Wiggins, team principal of the Pacific team. Wiggins watched part of the race from the first chicane and could hear it cutting in. But Schumacher led for the first 36 laps and, doubtless, he was being told on the pit radio that he must not let Hill pass him at any cost.

But Hill was putting him under intense pressure, which caused the German to make a mistake and his car glanced a concrete retaining wall. Although still drivable, Schumacher knew immediately he had no chance of finishing the race. Whilst he was still moving, Hill went to pass and

Schumacher deliberately turned the car into his path, which caused Hill to quickly switch sides. Then Schumacher turned the other way and this time Hill could not avoid him, there was a collision and both cars retired, making Schumacher the world champion by a single point. In his defence, Schumacher said his steering was damaged and he was not in control of the car. It was an absurd excuse for what was effectively indefensible dangerous driving. Although Schumacher's action was witnessed by millions of people on television the FIA took no action and Schumacher was declared world champion.

THE DODGY BENETTON

"The perfect lap is achieved when the driving becomes automatic because your brain controls the throttle, it knows your braking ability, your gear-change points. It depends on your eyesight before a corner, on your judgment of your speed into a corner."

Ayrton Senna
October 1989

CHAPTER 9

The Last Pole

Fastest in qualifying
Friday 29th April 1994

In the old days of Formula One, when the sport was a lot more of an event that it is today, qualifying sessions were held over two days of practice. Drivers ran in four sessions over Friday and Saturday, meaning qualifying and practice were as exciting as a race. Drivers also had the use of their spare cars. It was a simple, uninhibited quest for speed: an understandable process that made full use of the whole three days of a Grand Prix weekend.

That Friday morning at 9:30am, Senna climbed into his car and would complete 22 full laps, posting a fastest time of 1m 21.598secs, more than a second quicker than his team mate Damon Hill, and a very fast time indeed.

Although he was comfortably fastest, Senna was shocked again how poor the car was. He wondered what had been going on in the past few weeks at Williams as it seemed to him that no progress had been made despite a test session in France and a programme of aero updates.

It was obvious to Senna that the problem was not aerodynamic but mechanical, and the team had been chasing shadows. Adrian Newey's talents were then not as appreciated as they are today and it was clear that, under Newey's direction, the aerodynamics of the Williams Renault FW16 were as good they were going to get. It was the suspension that was the problem.

Newey had designed the optimum shape to push through the air and in the process had compromised driver comfort. The cockpit was very cramped in the footwell and the steering wheel area where there was barely room to clear a knuckle. There were also vision problems. Senna could only just see over the top of the cockpit. Damon Hill was a lot more comfortable in the car. He was taller and the car had been designed around his shape over the winter, and he had worked closely with Patrick Head and Newey. For Hill, the car was much improved and he was pleasantly surprised by the behaviour of the modified bodywork.

Senna knew that the core problem remained, and that was the stripping out of the active suspension from the car. Without the computerised assistance, the suspension needed a complete redesign and until that happened no progress was going to be made. He was frustrated because he was sick of telling Patrick Head about the problem and not being listened to. Head had never worked with a driver like Senna and was not used to being second guessed or having his views challenged.

Senna was deeply frustrated and missed the set-up at McLaren. Senna knew that eventually the suspension would be reworked but, until then, he knew he was going to have to drive every lap out of his skin and that was not comfortable even for Ayrton Senna, a man who normally loved being on the edge of his abilities and often sought risk and possible danger even where none existed.

At one o'clock, the first qualifying session began, and Senna was immediately fastest. 15 minutes later, the session was stopped for the Barrichello accident. Formula One held its breath for 35 minutes and the track was cleared as they waited for news of the injured driver. In the end, Barrichello regained consciousness and was okay and Senna was a mightily relieved man.

After all the drama, Senna was pumped up and in the best shape physically and mentally to drive the perfect lap. The sheer relief of knowing Barrichello was safe rushed through his mind, and it relieved him temporarily of another concern: the strange competitiveness of the Benetton team.

By then, he knew for sure that the Benetton team was cheating and that it had a way of turning traction control on and off so that it couldn't be detected. It meant he was having to compete against a vastly superior car in the hands of the second best driver on the grid. To beat the Benetton, he needed the perfect lap. And there was no better driver able to do it than he.

But Senna didn't believe the perfect lap existed and knew he had never driven one. As he said: "A fast lap requires a high level of sensitivity between body and mind. It is the combination of the two that gives the performance. But I have never done a perfect lap because I know that there was always room for improvement."

The spine-tingling spectacle of Ayrton Senna on a qualifying lap had provided some of the most thrilling moments in the history of motorsport. Before or since, there has never been a faster driver over a single lap than Senna, nor had anyone felt or thought so deeply about how to achieve a fast lap. John Watson, who briefly raced against Senna in the mid-80s, is adamant that Senna was the greatest qualifier of all time: "There was no other driver that approached his skill. His qualifying laps were events in themselves. I was mesmerised every time I watched him qualify. He did things in a car other drivers could only dream about."

Senna's passion for pole position was palpable ever since he drove to his first pole nine years earlier at Estoril in a Lotus. He had said: "I always wanted to be in pole position for a Grand Prix. And when I got it was an amazing feeling. Then I just keep trying the same."

From then on, he got a deep sense of pleasure every single time he did it. Despite all his problems at Williams, his 65th and final pole was no different. For people watching, it brought back memories of perhaps the fastest series of qualifying laps anyone has ever driven, and that was his own lap-after-lap performance during the final qualifying session at Monte Carlo in 1988.

It was only his third race for the McLaren-Honda team and he was already comfortably on pole, out of reach of any other driver, including his team mate Alain Prost in an identical car. At one stage, he was an astonishing two seconds faster than Prost, the world champion. An embarrassed Prost tried to close the gap but was still 1.427 seconds slower at the end.

Afterwards, Senna said of that sequence of laps, the quickest comparative series of laps any driver had driven ever in Formula One: "One lap after the other, quicker and quicker and quicker. I was, at one stage, just on pole, then by half a second and then by one second – and yet I kept going. Suddenly, I was nearly two seconds faster than anybody else, including my team mate with the same car. And I suddenly realised that I was no longer driving the car consciously." In Monte Carlo, Senna recounted that he had taken a wild ride through a surrealistic tunnel into the great unknown. In his description of what followed, Senna said he had struggled to contain an other-worldly experience within physical parameters that could be understood: "I was kind of driving by instinct only. I was in a different dimension. It was like I was in a tunnel, not only the tunnel under the hotel, but the whole circuit for me was a tunnel. I was just going and going and going and going – more and more and more and more. I was way over the limit, but still I was able to find even more."

Something similar was going on at Imola where Senna, just as he had at the Monte Carlo street track, always excelled. The only difference was that, this time, he was fighting a difficult car and his main rival had vastly better equipment.

In his first lap out, he improved his previous best. He improved on every lap, and when the session finally ended at 1:35pm just before the close, he set what was to prove the quickest time of the whole weekend: a 1m 21.548secs lap at an average of 138.2mph.

It was one of Senna's dream laps, in which he felt detached from the act of physically handling the car and became a passenger along for the ride. Senna admitted he got into a trance on a really fast lap until the dangerous reality of the situation snapped him out of it. John Watson, commentating for Eurosport, was once again mesmerised by Senna's qualifying lap.

That qualifying session in the emotional aftermath of Barrichello's accident was just a repeat performance of what happened in 1990 when Martin Donnelly crashed. Then, Senna had claimed his 50th pole. He said afterwards: "Suddenly, something just kicked me. I kind of woke up and I realised that I was in a different atmosphere than you normally are. Immediately, my reaction was to back off, slow down. I drove back slowly to the pits and I didn't want to go out any more that day.

"It frightened me because I realised I was well beyond my conscious understanding. It happens rarely, but I keep these experiences very much alive in me because it is something that is important for self-preservation. It is important to know what fear is because it will keep you more switched on, more alert. On many occasions, it will determine your limits."

Senna had put everything he could into getting that last pole at Imola just as he had in all of the previous 64 poles. He understood perfectly what it took. As he said: "The perfect lap is achieved when the driving becomes automatic because your brain controls the throttle; it knows your braking ability, your gear-change points. It depends on your eyesight before a corner, on your judgment of your speed into a corner. Sometimes you're not even looking at the rev counter when you change a gear, but using only your feeling, your ear, which tells you how to be on the right revs. This is vital because, in a high-speed corner, if you look at your revs for a split second you will not be as committed to your driving as you should. So your ear then plays an important part of it. It's not easy to. I think it is a matter of putting in everything that I have and everything that I am still finding that I *can* have."

There was no more to be said.

"He was very shaken, crying. He was
vulnerable like I'd never seen him before.
I wanted to help him. He looked lost."
                                    Betise Assumpcao
                                    Saturday 30th April 1994

CHAPTER 10

Simtek and Ratzenberger

A fatal combination

I t's true to say that Roland Ratzenberger was desperate to get into
Formula One any way he could. He was 33 years old and time was
running out. At the start of 1994, it literally was now or never for the
Austrian. It had to be now.

At the same time there was another man also desperate to get into Formula One but this time as a team principal. Surprisingly, at only 28 years
old, Nick Wirth also thought his time was running out. Like Ratzenberger,
he was also in a desperate hurry.

Both men had another thing in common: they both had nowhere near
enough money with which to achieve their dreams. As both were so desperate, they took what they could with what they had.

Simtek Research Ltd was set up by Nick Wirth on 14th August 1989.
The company was an unlikely partnership between Nick Wirth and former
March Engineering founder, Max Mosley. Wirth was just 23 and Mosley
in his late 40s. They were equal partners in the venture. Mosley invested
because he believed that Wirth had star quality. Tim Clowes, the insurance
broker who was friends with both of them said: "Max was close to Nick
and certainly treated him like a son. He made him smile a lot."

For Mosley, it was an ideal opportunity to do something meaningful
again with his life, which had stalled. He was at a loose end in 1989 after
ten years of acting as secretary to Formula One Constructors Association
(FOCA), the teams' association, and helping out Bernie Ecclestone doing
the legal drafting for the Concorde Agreement. But in 1982, he had left
Formula One to go into politics. Between 1983 and 1985, he tried to find
a British parliamentary seat to become an MP for the Conservatives. It

was unsuccessful, and the door was slammed in his face at every turn. His problem was simple: he was the son of the late fascist leader, Sir Oswald Mosley and Diana Mitford, a woman who was widely believed to have Hitler sympathies. In the end, the British Conservative Party rejected his overtures.

After three years, he returned to motorsport helping out Ecclestone again. Ecclestone steered him towards the FIA and he became head of the manufacturers commission, an internal committee. But it was a non-job and did not satisfy any of his ambitions.

That is, until he and Wirth established Simtek in the summer of 1989. Mosley was delighted to be involved with something meaningful again. He recruited an accountant he knew, the then 57-year-old Donald Hughes, to keep Wirth on the straight and narrow.

The idea behind the company was to conduct research and development for external clients in motorsport. Simtek was an abbreviation of the words 'simulation technology'. The company began modestly enough, in Wirth's garage, with one employee, named Darren Davis.

Everything looked very promising at first, and there was no doubt that Wirth was a very talented man. He was born in Wimbledon, London, on 29th March 1966 to John and Mary Wirth. His parents remember him being obsessed with Lego from the age of three, a fascination with creative construction that quickly developed into making weedkiller and sugar-powered fireworks by the time he was six years old. He was fascinated with science and engineering from an early age.

Educated privately at public school, Wirth was a rebel and taught himself to drive on public roads at the age of 14 and was nearly expelled as a result. He won a place at University College, London, to study mechanical engineering and naval architecture. During the summer breaks, he had temporary jobs – first with March Engineering and then engine builder Brian Hart.

He graduated from university with first class honours and secured his first job in the aerodynamics department at the March Formula One team in 1987, where he met Mosley and worked with such design legends as Robin Herd, Gordon Coppuck and Adrian Newey. Wirth was regarded as a prodigy. Such was his progress that, 18 months later, he reputedly turned down an offer to be chief designer at the Ligier Formula One Team. Soon after that, he got together with Mosley.

Simtek quickly acquired a factory in Banbury, Oxfordshire, and got a real lucky break when the company secured a contract to design a prototype Formula One chassis for BMW, which was considering making a return to Grand Prix racing as a manufacturer in its own right. It had withdrawn from the sport as an engine supplier four years earlier. Mosley had strong links with BMW from his days at March, which helped swing the contract Simtek's way.

BMW also financed the building of an innovative, but rudimentary wind tunnel in Banbury, which Wirth designed with help from another supporter, Adrian Reynard.

The prototype BMW car was designed and built through 1990 and 1991, with BMW paying all the bills.

But the world went into recession, and as the BMW board of directors looked to make cuts, it suddenly and unexpectedly decided it was not the right time to enter Formula One and cancelled the project. It was a devastating blow for Wirth although, by then, Mosley was out of the picture as he had been elected as President of the FIA, the governing body of motor sport after ousting incumbent Jean-Marie Balestre in a series of strongly contested elections. As president, Mosley immediately had to resign all his commercial interests, which included Simtek. Mosley sold his shares back to Wirth and resigned his directorship. But he left behind a good solvent company with lucrative research and development contracts. Wirth struck out alone with Donald Hughes.

As part of his deal with BMW, Wirth retained ownership of the Formula One project and put it up for sale. He found a buyer named Andrea Sassetti, an Italian shoe manufacturer who ran a company called Andrea Moda. Sassetti had dabbled in Formula One unsuccessfully in 1991 but had a very bad car built in Italy.

The ex-BMW chassis was fitted with a Judd V10 engine for the start of the 1992 season. It took until the sixth race of the season, at Monaco, for the car even to qualify. But that was the peak, and it all ended in tears when Sassetti was arrested for fraud. In August of that year, the team was thrown out of the championship with only one race to its name. The chassis could not have had a more dreadful debut.

Simtek Research, however, was thriving and won another BMW contract to modify its 3-series model for the German touring car championship. It also got to run the team for three years. Mosley helped with contracts from the FIA, and Simtek also won a contract to design and build a wind tunnel for the Ligier Formula One team in France.

Wirth owned a thriving and profitable company with plenty of money in the bank and a great future ahead. But there was just one problem: Wirth had caught the Formula One bug and it would ultimately destroy him and ruin his life.

At the age of 28, Formula One was a colossal leap of ambition, but everything in his life up to that point had been a huge success. He was young enough and arrogant enough to believe he could succeed in Formula One as a team owner despite his youth.

In fairness to him, it was not a wholly unreasonable assessment to make. People were always whispering complimentary things in his ear. In particular, Mosley told Tim Clowes that Wirth was the "next Colin Chapman". It was heady stuff.

The only problem was money. Even in 1993, it took a lot of money to succeed in Formula One. Even experienced operators like Peter Collins, who had taken over the Lotus team, were having difficulties and only getting by on a wing and prayer.

Wirth already had a design for a new car ready and the monocoque had been built at SMPE, a specialist factory in France. The rest of the parts were gradually manufactured and ready to be assembled.

But Wirth was unsure whether he should go ahead, and in a moment of indecision he sold the chassis to a nascent team called Bravo, founded by Jean Mosnier. But Mosnier unfortunately died soon afterwards in mid-1993.

Believing Mosnier's death to be an act of fate and a sign, Wirth finally decided to create his own Formula One team and, on the 29th October 1993, he founded a new company called Simtek Grand Prix Ltd. On the exact day the company was legally formed, a ritzy launch party was held at the team's new factory extension, and it was revealed that its number one driver would be David Brabham.

The team had no start-up capital. Its income was from profits of Simtek

Research and money from Sir Jack Brabham, effectively paying for his son's drive in 1994.

Wirth recruited a good team of engineers for the new team, including Humphrey Corbett, Charlie Moody, Rod Nelson and Harry McCourt.

Wirth had the carbon fibre chassis of the first Simtek car, designated the S941, ready to be tested in December 1993.

David Brabham did the early testing as Wirth cast around for a second driver who could bring some more cash to the team. But the world was in recession and there were six other teams with up to 10 Formula One drives for sale. Competition for good drivers, with cash to spend, was intense. Wirth realised he would have to take what he could get.

The basic cost of running a two-car team in Formula One in 1994 was approximately $6 million, some $400,000 a race. Wirth realised he had little chance of getting that sort of money together but believed he could get as much as $3 million, half of it from sponsorship and half from his drivers. But that was a wing and a prayer budget. Lotus, one of the smaller teams, was spending $13 million and the big teams Williams, McLaren and Ferrari, well over $45 million plus the cost of engines.

The American music TV channel MTV was launching in Europe and was signed as title sponsor. This was not thought to be worth more than $500,000 a year plus advertising slots that could be used to barter for sponsorship, which brought in another $200,000.

With Jack Brabham's money, plus around $500,000 from Bernie Ecclestone's prize fund, the team had just under $1.5 million to go racing with – one quarter of what it needed. It was foolhardy to say the very least, but Nick Wirth was a man on a mission and believed he could make it happen.

Then, along came Roland Ratzenberger out of the blue with $500,000 burning a hole in his pocket. Ratzenberger was also a man on a mission to become a star of Formula One although, by the age of 33, he had left it very late to make his mark.

Ratzenberger was born in Salzburg in 1960. His father, Rudolf, was an insurance broker. There was no motor racing background in his family, but the young Roland became obsessed with it. He flunked university and enrolled at the Walter Lechner Racing School at the Österreichring and devoted himself to racing.

His breakthrough came in 1986, when he won the Formula Ford Festival at Brands Hatch. It brought him to the attention of the movers and shakers in motor sport and won him a works drive with BMW in the 1987 World Touring Car Championship. Then he joined West Surrey Racing and drove two seasons in the British Formula Three series. He rented a house in Northamptonshire, where many of the British race teams were based. West Surrey had been Ayrton Senna's team, and Ratzenberger thought some of its star quality would rub off on him.

But he was to be disappointed, and after a mixed time with West Surrey, he moved to Japan where he became a professional race driver in the Japanese equivalent of Formula 3000, earning half a million dollars a year for his services and eventually getting a reputation as one of the quickest drivers outside of Formula One. During that time, he competed against other Formula One hopefuls such as Eddie Irvine, Johnny Herbert, Mika Salo and Heinz Harald Frentzen who had also gone to Japan to enhance their careers.

In 1991, Ratzenberger thought he had his chance and made a deal with Eddie Jordan to drive the second car alongside Bertrand Gachot in his new Formula One team. But his sponsorship fell through at the last minute, and he carried on racing in Japan. He was bitterly disappointed and believed that his time had passed.

He was by then earning close to $700,000 a year and moved to Monaco in order to pay less tax. He bought a studio apartment in Monte Carlo and became a permanent resident. He also bought a larger apartment in Salzburg, which he rented out as an investment for the future.

In 1991, he got married and divorced inside two months. He then met a Somalian model called Khadija Qalanjo, and they were together for three years until his death.

The relationship was up and down, but they lived together at his Monte Carlo studio.

At the same time, he was also involved with a wealthy German widow called Barbara Behlau, who ran an international talent and promotions agency very successfully from the principality. Behlau was in her late 40s, and she took a liking to Ratzenberger. It was she who made the breakthrough for him into Formula One. She paid $500,000 for him to take part

Above: Ayrton Senna at Imola for the 1994 San Marino Grand Prix as he ponders the weekend ahead. It would turn out to be the most infamous weekend in Formula One history.

Ayrton Senna's European home at Quinta do Lago

Above and below left: Ayrton Senna spent the summer at his Portugese villa called Sunset on the Algarve. It was within the Quinta do Lago resort.

Below: Senna in his office at home on the Algarve. He called it his European headquarters.

Bottom: A large Q marked the entrance of Quinta do Lago and Senna always felt good when he passed it.

Below: The gates of the villa and high surrounding walls afforded Senna seclusion and security.

Ayrton Senna's jet flew him around Europe

Left and below: Senna splashed out $8 million on his own jet, a British built Hawker Siddeley HS125-800, carrying the personalised registration N125AS.

© J Library

Above: Captain Owen O'Mahoney was Ayrton Senna's pilot for four years. When in Europe, he used his private jet most days like other people would use a taxi.

Right: Ayrton Senna in his HS125-800 private jet he bought in 1990.

© Rex Features

Visit to Carraro bicycle factory – Thursday 28th April 1994

On Thursday 28th April Ayrton Senna flew to Bologna airport and then by helicopter to the factory of Carraro, the famous Italian bicycle manufacturer, where he posed for photographs with Giovanni Carraro, the managing director. Senna had a new deal with Carraro to manufacture a carbon fibre bicycle called the Senna, which would carry his now famous 'double S' logo.

Above: Senna had been heavily involved in the design of the new bicycle that carried his name.

Above: The same day he attended a press conference at the Sheraton Hotel to launch his new deal with Carraro and show off the new Senna carbon fibre bicycle.

Left: Ayrton Senna photographed with Ferrari president, Luca Di Montezemolo. The two had a secret meeting the day before his visit to the Carraro bicycle factory. Senna was already unhappy at Williams and was planning to leave the Williams team and join Ferrari in 1995. On his flight home back to Faro he pondered the impact his move would have on Formula One.

Ayrton Senna at Imola in 1994

 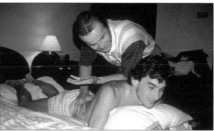

Left: Julian Jakobi, Ayrton Senna's business manager.

Right: Josef Leberer, Ayrton Senna's personal physiotherapist.

Antonio Braga, his close friend and neighbour in Portugal, was at Imola on 1st May 1994.

Leonardo Da Silva, Ayrton Senna's brother, travelled to Italy to try and persuade his brother to end a relationship.

Mike Vogt, the marketing director of Tag-Heuer, was discussing a new Senna watch that weekend.

Ubirajara Guimaraes, head of the Senna Import Company, was responsible for Senna's business activities.

Last supper at the Trattatoria Romagnola

The Trattoria Romagnola restaurant in Castel San Pietro was the eating place of choice for Senna and his friends at the San Marino Grand Prix. He ate his last supper at the restaurant on the evening of Saturday 30th April 1994. It was typical Italian and very basic, but Senna always picked up the bill for his party. Senna rarely ate anything else but pasta served to him personally by the owner.

Rubens Barrichello accident – Friday 29th April 1994

Above and below: 22-year-old Rubens Barrichello was 10th fastest in the Friday morning practice session but in afternoon qualifying on his first flying lap he lost control of his car in the second part of the fast Variante Bassa chicane just before the pits. He caught an outside kerb at 140mph and was launched into the air. Barrichello hit the final row of tyres at the top of the barrier, which, together with the wire fence, absorbed the momentum and tipped over his Jordan, which rolled over twice before coming to rest upside down. He was knocked unconscious and the session was immediately stopped with Ayrton Senna the fastest. Irresponsible marshals righted the car and it landed violently on its wheels, risking further injury to the driver. Professor Sid Watkins and his medical team quickly arrived at the crash site to stabilise him. Watkins's main task was to prevent Barrichello from swallowing his tongue, which was blocking his airway.

Above: Rubens Barichello's Jordan Hart overturns as it comes to rest. In contrast to Senna's accident, he was fortunate that there was a double wall of tyres to absorb the impact, thereby saving his life.

Left: Senna was one of the first to go and visit him in the medical centre before he was taken by helicopter to Bologna San Maggiore hospital and released the next day.

Left: Barrichello returned to Imola on Saturday and spoke with Senna and Betise Assumpcao, who was his press relations adviser and who wrote a syndicated column for journals all over the world on Senna's behalf.

Suite 200 - Hotel Castello, San Pietro

Above and left The Hotel Castello in Castello San Pietro, seven miles from the Imola circuit where Senna had stayed since 1988, when he joined McLaren. He always had the same room, the grandly named Suite 200. But it was very basic accommodation, far below what he was used to. But he liked the proprietors and enjoyed the atmosphere of the hotel.

Above: Ayrton Senna and Leonardo Da Silva leave the Imola track and arrive at Hotel Castello on the evening of Friday 29th April after Barrichello's accident.

in the first five races of 1994 at the Simtek team. If he was successful, she had a provisional deal for the balance of the season.

So Ratzenberger finally arrived in Formula One at the grand old age of 33, at the Brazilian Grand Prix in 1994. By doing so, he became part of a proud heritage of Austrian Formula One drivers. Jochen Rindt was the first successful Austrian, becoming the sport's first posthumous world champion in 1970 in a Lotus. Soon afterwards, Niki Lauda arrived in Formula One and was world champion three times. Gerhard Berger reached the top of the tree with Ferrari and McLaren but was destined never to be world champion. Ratzenberger joined Berger and Karl Wendlinger as Austrian Formula One drivers in 1994. With such a rich driving heritage for such a small country, expectations in Austria were extremely high for Ratzenberger.

Ratzenberger went to the first race at São Paulo in Brazil at the end of March but failed to qualify for the grid at the Interlagos circuit. The car was unprepared, and Ratzenberger was unaware of all the drama surrounding getting the car through the FIA crash tests. It was not a good start, and Ratzenberger naturally worried whether he would be able to qualify for any races that season. He was at least a second per lap slower than his team mate David Brabham who did qualify – albeit last on the grid.

Two weeks later, in Japan for the Pacific Grand Prix, Ratzenberger qualified comfortably at the Aida circuit. In the race, he finished 11th – last of the cars still running. It was starting to look more promising.

And then he headed back to Europe for his date with destiny at Imola.

*"Let's finish this in the evening.
I have no more time."*
Roland Ratzenberger
Saturday 30th April 1994
12.30pm

CHAPTER 11

Ratzenberger Dies

Saturday 30th April 1994
Afternoon

At just after midday on Saturday 30th April, Roland Ratzenberger sat down with Austrian journalist Gerhard Kuntschik in the Simtek motorhome to eat his last meal. Kuntschik was deputy sports editor of the *Salzburger Nachrichten* newspaper and its specialist Formula One correspondent. Kuntschik was very close to Ratzenberger and had followed his career from the start; he had been an unofficial cheerleader. In fact when they first met in December 1980 at the Saalbach winter rally, the 19 year-old had asked him, "How do I become a racing driver?" It was Kuntschik who recommended Walter Lechner's racing school as a good starting point.

Ratzenberger's easy-going manner and unpretentious attitude had made him very popular with everyone in Formula One. Even though he had only been around for three races, the journalists had taken to him, which was not always the case for new drivers.

As he ate, Ratzenberger was excitedly telling Kuntschik how he had met Ayrton Senna for the first time just the day before. They had bumped into each other when they both arrived at race control at the same time. He said Senna had engaged him in conversation and had mentioned that Josef Lieberer had talked about him many times. Senna had told Ratzenberger that he would be in Monaco for a whole week for the Grand Prix in May and that they should get together for a meal. Senna asked him where he lived in Monaco, and they exchanged phone numbers. Ratzenberger was very excited at meeting the three times world champion and didn't try to hide it from Kuntschik.

He also told Kuntschik that he believed that his Simtek team mate, David

Brabham, had a much better car than him; one that was fitted with the latest development parts. He was worried that he would seem much slower than Brabham, and he was frustrated. He didn't think he would be able to prove himself good enough inside the five races he was contracted to drive the Simtek, and his Formula One career would be over as soon as it began. Ratzenberger was elated and frustrated all at the same time.

Then, according to Kuntschik, he suddenly stood up without warning and said: "Let's finish this in the evening, I have no more time."

Kuntschik is still haunted by those last words: "I have no more time." With that, Ratzenberger sprinted off to the garage, leaving Kuntschik to finish eating alone.

At ten minutes to one o'clock, Ratzenberger grabbed his helmet and got ready to go out on track, at the same time getting a last-minute briefing from his mechanics. Ratzenberger's mission was simply to qualify, since the two slowest drivers would not be allowed to start the race. Barrichello's withdrawal had made it easier and now only one driver would fail to make the cut, but he didn't want it to be him.

Ratzenberger was effectively fighting Bertrand Gachot and Paul Belmondo in the Pacific cars for the last slot. The stakes were just as high for him at the back of the grid as they were for Ayrton Senna at the front fighting with Michael Schumacher for pole.

Returning to Imola was poignant for Ratzenberger as it had only been seven weeks earlier that he had first driven a Formula One car at a private test session at the circuit. He remembered it well as he had posed for a photograph on the pit wall with Austria's two other Formula One drivers, Gerhard Berger and Karl Wendlinger. Berger and Wendlinger didn't really care for each other. Ratzenberger had kept the peace by standing in between them, arms crossed, keeping at least four feet between the two protagonists who looked as though they were about to put on boxing gloves and fight it out. Ratzenberger didn't understand the animosity between the two countrymen, but he put it down to the pressures of competing at the highest level of Formula One. He wondered if it would end up the same for him if he would be lucky enough to establish himself as a regular driver.

As soon as the clock struck one o'clock, Ratzenberger was out on the track for some exploratory laps. After a few laps, he returned to the pits to have some adjustments made.

At just after ten minutes past one o'clock, Roland Ratzenberger pulled out of the Simtek team garage to try and make certain of qualifying to compete in the 1994 San Marino Grand Prix. In reality, he had already done enough to qualify when he set a time of 1:27.657 the previous day, but he didn't know that then.

Gerhard Kuntschik was watching qualifying in the media centre on one of the many monitors strung up above the journalists' heads. The Imola media centre was the smallest in Formula One, and it was packed with journalists looking forward to an exciting qualifying session.

He watched Ratzenberger drive out of the pit lane and join the circuit. On the first lap, his car rode the kerb at various points around the circuit as he tried hard to post a better time, but there was nothing unusual about that, and it worked, as he posted a new time of 1:27.584 – an improvement on anything he had done before.

Normal procedure when that happened was to come into the pits and get the nosecone and the front wing fixing checked out. If there was some damage, the team would simply replace the nosecone with a new one. The Simtek team had been having problems with the front wing assembly of Ratzenberger's car all weekend. It kept coming loose on the mounts and they kept tightening the fixings each time. They were short of spares, which exacerbated the situation. After that hard lap it was likely the front wing would need tightening up again at least.

Inexplicably, the team kept Ratzenberger out and he did not come in. It was to cost him his life as, by all accounts, the cause of the accident was the front wing detaching from its mounts and becoming wedged under the car, negating any steering control and leaving Ratzenberger a passenger as his car careered down the track completely out of control. Many reasons have been put forward for that decision. Perhaps the team did not have a spare nosecone that was serviceable and he would miss the rest of the session and that he might be bumped from the grid. Or perhaps the spare nosecone was an earlier design and slower. Or perhaps they did not know how loose the front wing fixings had become. Certainly the assembly needed constant attention as the mounting retainers in the carbon fibre nose were gradually disintegrating with use.

Whatever it was, he carried on for another lap and paid the ultimate price. Martin Brundle said later that he thought he saw some damage to the nose before the accident. Jean Alesi, recovering from neck injuries from a recent testing accident, was a spectator out on the track near where the crash happened. He said that he believed the front wing of Ratzenberger's Simtek had become detached just before the accident. Alesi's account chimes with other eyewitnesses, who said the front wing was partially detached. That account is corroborated by video evidence.

That explanation certainly fits the circumstances of the accident. As Ratzenberger approached Villeneuve Curve, the steering wheel failed to react to his command as the front tyres lost contact with the track. Then the car turned 90 degrees and the front of the car took off. It flew through the air at a speed of around 200mph, and then slammed into a concrete retaining wall on the inside of the Villeneuve Curve before being thrown back into the middle of the track with one of the detached wheels running down the track. The car came to rest slowly in the middle of the Tosa hairpin. It had been an extremely violent accident but of the sort many drivers had walked away from in the past.

Everything was shown on television back to the pits and a silence descended as people stared at the monitors. Ratzenberger's head leaned lifeless on the side of the cockpit. If the chassis had held up, Ratzenberger may well have got away with it, but it didn't. The chassis had failed in the seatbelt area and it had also broken behind the dashboard bulkhead. His legs were exposed though the side of the chassis. The failure of the chassis was catastrophic and caused injuries that no human being could withstand.

The qualifying session was immediately halted by race directors Roland Bruynsaede and Charlie Whiting, who immediately alerted the medical cars to go to the scene.

Bernie Ecclestone was sitting in his motorhome chatting to Lotus Team Principal, Peter Collins, when the accident happened. As they both looked at the monitors above their heads, Ecclestone turned to Collins and said: "This looks bad." Ecclestone grabbed his walkie-talkie and headed off to see Whiting as Collins went back to the Lotus garage.

Senna was out of his car when the accident happened and was watching replays of the accident on the monitor in the Williams pit garage. He visibly flinched when he saw the scale of the impact and cried "no"; he stepped back six paces in the garage grimacing with his eyes closed. He knew it was bad but no one could conceive that the driver might be dead, as that didn't happen in Grand Prix racing any more. But Senna's reaction was extreme.

He rushed into the pit lane and ran down to where the course cars were parked. He grabbed a driver and told the driver to take him to the scene of the accident. It was strictly against regulations but this was Senna asking, and everyone had seen the accident on the monitors and was in a state of shock. The driver just got in the car and they drove round past the Tamburello bend to the scene.

Unlike Senna, Damon Hill was on the track when the accident happened and drove past the wrecked car and the debris. He also realised it was bad, as he said: "You would be doing around 200mph when you brake for Tosa. So that's the kind of speed Roland would have been doing when he went off the circuit. I could see where the debris had started and, judging by the distance travelled, it was obvious it had been a very big accident. As I went by, I had a strong sense of foreboding about his condition because there was so much destruction. With Barrichello, we had been lucky. This time it was clear that poor Roland was not going to be let off so lightly."

Gerhard Berger was sitting in his car with the monitor resting on top of the chassis so he could view the progress of qualifying. He had become increasingly close to Ratzenberger as they were both Austrians living in Monaco. They had spent a few days in the previous week on his boat: "I knew how bad it was when I could see Professor Watkins doing heart massage on Roland. For the first time I found myself shaking after an accident." Berger got out of his car, and when he saw that an ambulance, not a helicopter, had been called to take Ratzenberger away, he knew exactly what it meant. As he said: "I went to the motorhome and I felt sick."

Mario Casoni got the medical car to the scene of the accident 25 seconds after it happened. Professor Sid Watkins leaped out with Dr Baccarini by his side. Immediately, they could hear that Ratzenberger wasn't breathing. Baccarini cradled Ratzenberger's limp head in his hands and Watkins frantically cut his chin strap to remove his helmet. Ratzenberger's eyes were closed. Watkins lifted his eyelids and could immediately discern that Ratzenberger was clinically dead, having suffered massive head injuries. There was no pulse and no heartbeat – Ratzenberger was beyond help. The situation was grave, and he ordered his men to extricate him and try resuscitation. Watkins laid him out and began to massage his heart. According to Watkins, they were successful in getting his heart going. An ambulance arrived seven minutes later, and he was quickly taken to the medical centre. The resuscitation team managed to keep his heart beating long enough to get him into the medical centre, although according to some eye witnesses, this was entirely artificial and Ratzenberger was dead at the scene, and blood and brain matter were pouring from his nose. If there was any sign of life, Watkins would have ordered up the helicopter to get him straight to San Maggiore. But he knew there was no point, so an ambulance took Ratzenberger's inert body straight to the medical centre. As soon as he was wheeled inside, Franco Servadei must have realised he was dead and there was nothing he could do, so he packed him straight off to San Maggiore hospital by ambulance. The fact that the medical helicopter was not used for the transfer from the circuit medical centre to San Maggiore hospital spoke volumes. There was simply no point as the driver was dead.

Watkins was under strict orders from Bernie Ecclestone that a driver was never ever to die at a track. In following those orders, Watkins violated his own Hippocratic Oath as he should have declared Ratzenberger dead at the scene as required by law. He should also have noted the time of death for official records. On that basis Dr Servadei went along with it. He had sent a dead body to hospital.

Gerhard Kuntschik went to the gates of the medical centre to wait for news. He wasn't under any illusions and said: "I feared right away Roland was dead."

When Ratzenberger arrived at San Maggiore at seven minutes past two o'clock he was taken straight into the resuscitation unit. But he was already dead, and eight minutes later, having realised that the procedures had not been properly followed, the hospital announced his death as quickly as it could. Within 10 minutes of him being wheeled in, a statement was being issued.

As in most things medical, there is of course plenty of latitude in life and in death. The significance of delaying the announcement was not lost on anyone. If Ratzenberger had been correctly declared dead at the scene, the San Marino Grand Prix would have been cancelled.

By the time Ayrton Senna arrived at the accident scene, Ratzenberger had gone in the ambulance. He inspected the wrecked Simtek car.

He then got the driver to take him back to the pit lane and immediately marched off to the medical centre for the second time in two days. He went through the same scenario – he was not allowed to enter the front way so jumped over the fence at the back. Once he was inside, this time he found his way barred by Sid Watkins, who grabbed him and took him outside. After a few seconds to compose himself, Watkins told Senna that Ratzenberger was clinically dead. Watkins remembered: "Ayrton broke down and cried on my shoulder."

Watkins realised then that Senna had not been in close proximity to death before. He said of Senna: "He was very shocked. He had never faced the reality of his profession before so starkly because no one had been killed during his time in Formula One. He was always fatalistic about death; he was a religious man and intelligent enough to think it through. But this was the first time it had come so close."

Watkins recalled saying to Senna as he was crying on his arm: "Ayrton, why don't you withdraw from racing tomorrow? I don't think you should do it. In fact, why don't you give it up altogether? What else do you need to do? You have been world champion three times, you are obviously the quickest driver. Give it up and let's go fishing." Watkins recalled Senna's response to him in his book *Life at the Limit*: "Sid, there are certain things over which we have no control. I cannot quit. I have to go on." Watkins said that those were the last words he ever spoke to him.

On Senna's way out, Martin Whitaker, then press officer of the FIA, brushed past him. Whitaker remembered: "I asked Senna if he knew what had happened. He didn't reply. He just looked at me and walked away, but I won't forget that look."

After leaving the medical centre, Senna went straight to the Williams pit garage and signalled to Damon Hill and Patrick Head to join him. He told them Ratzenberger was dead and said: "From what I witnessed, there is no doubt about it."

Frank Williams overheard the conversation and said they should carry on qualifying as normal until they heard anything officially, but Senna just refused to go out again. Williams said he had asked him "more as a matter of form than expectation" and didn't argue. Senna went into the transporter to change out of his racing overalls.

The situation was rather different for Hill, and he would have to do as he was told. However, after Senna's blank refusal to drive, Frank Williams thought about it again and withdrew the team from the rest of qualifying. Benetton and Sauber also withdrew their cars as their drivers were all deeply affected by the news. It was the first fatality at an actual Grand Prix since Riccardo Paletti was killed at the Canadian Grand Prix in Montreal in 1982. The last Formula One driver to die had been Elio de Angelis in 1986 during private testing.

Damon Hill took the news of Ratzenberger's death more calmly than Senna. As the son of Graham Hill, he was much more used to sudden violent death and had been from an early age. As he said: "I thought Ratzenberger's accident was serious, but it didn't strike me as just how serious. After all, Gerhard Berger had been off at Tamburello in the past; Nelson Piquet had gone off in the air and hit the wall at Tamburello. Drivers had been walking away from big accidents for a long time. Carbon fibre really was an amazing invention. It saved a lot of lives. But what it meant, I think, was that people felt safer. Among drivers, there had grown perhaps a sense of complacency; a lot had gone through the sport without encountering a fatality."

Like Sid Watkins it also dawned on Hill that Ayrton Senna had never experienced death before. This was his first. Michael Schumacher was also deeply affected and J. J. Lehto was crying. Lehto said: "I drove up here with Roland from Monaco." Heinz-Harald Frentzen, who raced with Ratzenberger in Japan, went straight back to his hotel and said: "I don't want to talk to anyone."

Fifty-seven minutes after the accident, at 2:15pm, Ratzenberger's death was announced at the circuit, although by then everyone in the paddock already knew. Senna ran from the transporter to the Williams motorhome, where he found Damon Hill and his wife Georgie with Betise Assumpcao.

Assumpcao remembers: "His spirits were so low. I just stroked his head and talked to him a little, but he was very quiet."

Andrew Longmore, a *Times* journalist, wrote in an article published later that Senna broke down again in the Williams motorhome and lay down on the floor crying his eyes out. Damon Hill lifted him up, but he was not in a good way in the immediate aftermath of the accident. His mood was bad enough for Frank Williams to be concerned about his emotional state, and he asked Betise Assumpcao to arrange for a meeting with him later that evening back at the hotel.

In Salzburg, Rudolf Ratzenberger and his wife Margit had just that morning returned to their home from a holiday in Acapulco. Realising that his son would be racing, Rudolf had switched on his television, tuned to Eurosport, and was listening to commentators discussing the Formula One qualifying. In those days, Eurosport covered every session of a Grand Prix weekend. Suddenly, he shouted to his wife: "Margit, there is a big crash in Imola." They quickly realised it was their son's car. Within an hour, they had been telephoned to say their son was dead. The two sat on their sofa for over an hour in stunned silence before family and friends started arriving at the house.

Ratzenberger's fatal accident was especially shocking because modern day Formula One had never experienced death before. Hardly any of the drivers had raced with De Angelis and Paletti. It would have been better for all if the race had been cancelled there and then. But that was never an option, and Max Mosley knew Bernie Ecclestone would never agree to it.

If Professor Watkins had done his job as the law required, it would have been out of Ecclestone's hands and the race would have automatically been cancelled.

But at a Grand Prix, Watkins answered to a higher authority than any government – he answered to the authority of Ecclestone. His failure to declare Ratzenberger dead at the scene of the accident was to haunt Watkins for the rest of his life and he never discussed the circumstances of Ratzenberger's death with anyone. The events of the following day made him realise that, but for his actions, his friend, and the man he admired most in the world, would still be alive.

Qualifying duly restarted but, unsurprisingly, no one bettered Senna's Friday time so he was on pole for the race the following day. But he seemed not to care and told race officials he would not attend the obligatory post-qualifying press conference. That should have attracted a fine, but in the circumstances the FIA officials declined to punish him. However, the officials were angry that Senna had commandeered a course car in flagrant breach of race regulations. When tackled about it, Senna told them he didn't care.

At three o'clock, the permanent FIA steward, John Corsmit, a Dutchman, called him to a meeting in race control. Betise Assumpcao handed him the official notification. Normally, Senna would just have ignored the request out of his general contempt for FIA race officials, which he had harboured since the days when Jean-Marie Balestre ran the FIA. But this time he grabbed the piece of paper from Assumpcao and rushed out of the motorhome. He ran up the metal stairs to race control, determined to have a row with Corsmit and the stewards.

Senna was in no mood to accept the censure of the FIA, and when Corsmit read out the complaint, Senna launched into him viciously with every personal insult he could muster. He told Corsmit a driver had died that day and all he was interested was petty breaches of rules. A visibly shocked Corsmit realised he had got it wrong and immediately backed down. Corsmit said: "He seemed bothered by lots of other things."

Senna was privately disgusted with Corsmit's attitude and stormed off in disgust, and the stewards took no further action.

Outside race control, Niki Lauda was waiting for Senna. Lauda told him the drivers had to present a united front on safety issues and that he planned to hold a meeting at the next race in Monaco in two weeks' time. Senna promised his full support and said he would do anything he could.

Senna retreated back to the motorhome, drew the blinds and lay down in one of the small offices. He spent a couple of hours on his own in the dark waiting for his helicopter to take him back to the hotel. Outside, Betise Assumpcao stood guard. He would speak to no one, not even her. Assumpcao said later that he seemed to be fighting a battle inside his head, asking himself whether he should retire there and then and start enjoying his life. But she said he quickly realised it was a waste of emotions, as he already knew what the answer would be. Senna had always been scathing of sportsmen who retired too early and then spent the rest of their lives wondering what to do with themselves.

After his third championship, he had often pondered retirement but the example of Niki Lauda was much in his mind. Lauda had sacrificed two, maybe three world championships through muddle-headed thinking. He had left Brabham just as things were about to come good with the Ford engine and handed two world championships to Nelson Piquet in the process. With all those thoughts rushing around in his head, Senna finally fell asleep until Assumpcao woke him up to catch his helicopter back to the hotel.

He walked to meet his helicopter shortly before 5:30pm, and nobody dared go near him. People who saw him said he had an aura of absolute isolation and inapproachability about him after the row with Corsmit.

Hill decided to stay at the circuit and eat in the Williams motorhome but found it difficult to think of anything other than the accident. He said at the time: "Look, I'm not going to stop racing; I'm looking forward to the Grand Prix. I enjoy my motor racing just as Roland did. Every second you are alive, you've got to be thankful and derive as much pleasure from it as you can."

"There is no way that we would have raced if we hadn't passed the FIA crash test."
Rod Nelson
September 2004

CHAPTER 12

Doubts About Ratzenberger's Car

Was the Simtek safe?

T hroughout 1994 there was increasing talk in the Formula One
paddock about the integrity of Roland Ratzenberger's Simtek car
and particularly the apparent weakness of the carbon fibre chassis. The chatter had started because during the accident on Saturday 30th
April, the chassis had effectively broken and been breached – the driver's
legs could be clearly seen through a hole in the carbon fibre

The Ratzenberger accident could have just been a one-off failure. But
after a second serious chassis failure occurred a month later, it was clear
something was amiss.

The second accident happened when Ratzenberger's replacement,
30-year-old Italian Andrea Montermini, driving a new chassis, lost control
of his car during practice for the Spanish Grand Prix, less than a month
after Ratzenberger had been killed.

The accident on his first lap happened at the exit of the final corner, entering the start-finish straight. Montermini's Simtek hit the concrete wall at
the exit of the corner at the right side of the old grandstand. Although the
wall was protected by a tyre barrier, the front of the car completely disintegrated, exposing the driver's feet. If the tyres hadn't been there, a second
Simtek driver would have died. Miraculously, Montermini suffered just a
broken toe and cracked heel and escaped any serious injury.

Coming so quickly after Ratzenberger's crash, the accident caused people
in the paddock at the time to openly question whether the Simtek car had
passed the official FIA crash test before it was allowed to race. This time,
the chassis had failed and disintegrated well beyond the line of the nosecone
and broken open. The driver's seat was visible when the car came to rest

with the driver still in it, in the middle of the track. The damage was so great that the chassis couldn't be repaired and had to be written off it was never raced again.

People who saw the damaged car and were familiar with FIA crash test procedures were aghast at the state of the chassis after the accident, and the rumours gained credence. Some Simtek mechanics, admittedly without direct knowledge of the tests, told friends that they did not believe that the car had passed the tests. People began openly questioning the race-worthiness of the Simtek S941 chassis and whether it should have been on the track at all.

After Ratzenberger crashed, his car Chassis S941-02 was withheld by the Italian authorities, but unlike Aytron Senna's accident, an investigation was never ordered. When the chassis was returned to England, it was cut up by an engineer called Roger Evans and buried in a secret location, taking its secrets to its grave. The chassis (03) from the second accident was also written off and destroyed. The following year, Simtek went into liquidation.

And that might have been that except when, in the summer of 2004, reporters from *BusinessF1* magazine, tipped off by senior paddock figures, began investigating the Simtek S941 and in particular the crash testing programme it went through at the start of 1994. The object was to find out definitively whether or not the car had passed the FIA crash test.

The magazine's investigation was the biggest it had ever mounted. It began in April 2003 and took 17 months to complete. The magazine spent over $100,000 on it, involving two journalists virtually working full time on the story. It was money well spent, and the journalists managed to piece together the circumstances of the procedure the car went through to pass its crash test programme. They also managed to obtain copies of all the crash test documents from FIA insiders who were also concerned about the validity of the tests. These documents were closely examined by two retired Formula One technical directors who gave an expert opinion.

In the subsequent article, the magazine's journalists were scathing about the lack of co-operation they received from the two Simtek men in charge. They were Charlie Moody, the Simtek team manager, and Harry McCourt, the Simtek engineer in charge of the crash test procedure.

McCourt later worked for Ferrari after he left Simtek and then went to live in California. Charlie Moody, who left Formula One when the Simtek team closed down, moved to MotoGP. But he died of motor neurone disease in 2011 at the age of 53.

Both men were sought for comment by *BusinessF1* journalists. But the writers found doors slammed in their faces and phone receivers put down on a regular basis. It was unclear why.

Two former employees who were more open and up front were Humphrey Corbett and Rod Nelson. Both were senior Simtek employees and both were unafraid to talk to the magazine. They were not directly involved in the crash tests but were ambiguous about whether or not the car had indeed passed the tests. Nelson, in particular, became angry with reporters at the suggestion of the possibility that he might have been involved in a team that raced an unsafe car and said: "There is no way that we would have raced if we hadn't passed the FIA crash test."

In that period when journalists were asking difficult questions, Richard Woods, then FIA director of communications was forced to issue a statement in September 2005 that stated: "The Simtek S941 passed all the FIA crash tests before its first race. No Formula One car had ever been permitted to race without first passing the required FIA crash tests." Woods's statement was true. The Simtek S941 had passed the FIA's crash test, but the question that really needed answering was: should it have?

Despite Woods's statement, the *BusinessF1* journalists carried on digging and then got lucky when an anonymous FIA insider handed them all the documentation from the crash tests ten years earlier. Included in a brown envelope that was delivered by courier to the magazine's offices, sender unknown, were around 20 photographs taken of the chassis during the various tests. It was an incredibly lucky break, and without those documents, the investigation would probably have gone nowhere. To this day, the journalists have no real idea who sent them the documents although they have their suspicions.

The 8,000-word article, published in October 2004, told the whole story, starting in January 1994. It told of how, with the first Grand Prix in Brazil scheduled for 27th March, Nick Wirth and his team fought a desperate race against time getting the Simtek car through the tests.

In 1994, crash testing was a relatively new innovation in Formula One and certainly not the same procedure that teams go through now. As then Williams technical director, Patrick Head, recalled: "It is certainly true to say that crash testing in 1994 was not what it is today."

Back then, it was relatively simple: the teams had to present a reference chassis, which was required to pass seven tests, six static load tests with pressure against various parts of the chassis, and one moving impact test where the chassis of the car was secured to a trolley on wheels and the nose of the car slammed into a wall at speed. The most difficult by far was the moving impact test, but two of the static tests were no cakewalk either. The difficult tests were tests one to three, done only on a reference chassis and which covered all subsequent chassis. The other four lesser (routine) tests were required to be carried out on all the chassis that were built.

Of the seven tests, tests one to three were the main 'chassis integrity' tests. In order to complete and pass the programme, it was necessary to achieve a 100 per cent pass in all tests. The other four lower rated tests that every chassis subsequently manufactured had to pass before it could be raced were relatively easy to pass.

But initial failure, first or even second time around, in any of the tests was not the end of the world. If any of the tests were failed, a team was allowed to have the chassis retested after strengthening. In almost all cases, strengthening a chassis would require adding weight, and only a catastrophic failure in the tests would require the redesign of a chassis.

To ensure integrity of the tests, the reference chassis had to be rigorously weighed to make certain that each subsequent chassis manufactured was to the same specification as the reference chassis actually tested. Weighing and correct recording the chassis and nosecone weight was an essential requirement at every test, otherwise FIA scrutineers and officials would have no idea whether subsequent chassis were built to the 'tested' specification.

After each chassis was tested and had passed the four lesser tests, an FIA inspector bonded a small 'certification' plug to the chassis behind the driver's seat.

The Simtek team was fortunate in that it owned a crash test chassis jig that it had bought cheaply from the Brabham team, which had gone bankrupt at the end of 1992. It enabled Simtek to do its own 'static load' tests on site at its own factory in Banbury, Oxfordshire, with an FIA official present to observe. But the moving impact test could only be done at a specialist impact centre such as Cranfield in Bedfordshire, England.

The first tests scheduled for the Simtek were the lesser rated four tests that every race chassis had to undertake. This was for Chassis No S941-01 (ID no 17FCD9D7C0) which was a production race chassis that had first run on the track in December.

These tests could easily have been undertaken at the factory on the jig. But strangely the team chose not to do this and booked Cranfield Impact Centre at Cranfield University for the test on 2nd February 1994. There was no logical reason to book expensive time at Cranfield for a routine test that every chassis raced had to undertake. It would also have been logical for the team to do the main moving impact test on the same day on the reference chassis which had been designated as Chassis S941-02.

Now, 21 years later, a lot of people with knowledge of the situation believe that Chassis S941-02 was at that Cranfield test on 2nd February, took the test and failed it very badly and that this test was not officially recorded. They believe that the failure was so great that a redesign and new chassis would have been needed.

The records back up this assertion. On the Cranfield record sheets for 2nd February, Chassis S941-01 was recorded as weighing 50.6kg. This was compared on the sheet with the weight of Chassis S941-02, which was recorded as being 48.2kg and named as being the reference chassis.

The fact that its weight was noted indicated that either Chassis S941-02 was there on the day or that there had been a previous test which had not been recorded.

As it was, Chassis S941-01 easily passed the lesser rated tests that day; it would have been very surprising if it hadn't. But it seems clear that Chassis S941-02 was present on 2nd February and had undertaken the moving impact test. Otherwise, there would be no logical reason to be at Cranfield, as the test could have easily been run on the ex-Brabham jig in the Simtek factory. But for reasons unknown, the results of that test were not recorded. The only possible reason for not recording it was that it failed catastrophically. A less sinister explanation was that it was intended to do the test of Chassis S941-02 but it was abandoned for reasons unknown.

There were other anomalies. Chassis S941-01 was now individually cleared for racing, but it could not actually race until reference Chassis S941-02 had passed the main test.

Whichever way it was looked at, it was an illogical way of doing it. Logically the team would have focused on getting S941-02, the reference chassis, through the main test and then do the routine tests for the production race chassis at their convenience.

But the strangest occurrence that day was the presence of Charlie Whiting and Nick Wirth at the Cranfield routine test. A former team principal in 1994 recalls Whiting attending only one in four crash tests personally. And it was inexplicable that he would have attended a routine test such as supposedly occurred at Cranfield on 2nd February.

A former team principal around the time gave an opinion to the magazine's reporter. He said he believed that Chassis S941-02 was tested and had failed the moving impact test badly enough for it not to be recorded. Then one of Formula One's foremost crash test experts was asked for a possible explanation of what really happened on 2nd February at Cranfield and could not suggest one. He said: "Usually, if you send the chassis for testing, you do all the tests. It is impossible to know why they only did those tests. I don't know why they were not done. I have no idea."

After a gap of nearly four weeks, surprising in view of the urgency of passing the tests, the programme resumed on 28th February at the Simtek factory in Banbury – this time on the former Brabham test rig. The only tests that could be done on the rig were tests two to seven, the static load tests. All six were scheduled to be carried out. This was an important day in the programme and again Charlie Whiting was there, this time his presence being fully justified. Also present was Peter Duffy, a composites specialist. Surprisingly, Simtek's head of its crash test programme, Harry McCourt, was not listed as being present – nor was Nick Wirth.

The chassis to be tested was Chassis S941-02 (ID no 17CDC2370), the officially designated reference chassis. Ostensibly, this was its first test and its weight was recorded as 48.2kg, exactly the same as had been recorded on the 2nd February sheet. The nose weight was recorded as 4kg. The chassis was recorded as passing tests four to seven successfully, as one would have expected.

But the main static tests, tests two and three, were a different matter. On test two, the roll hoop integrity test, the carbon fibre roll hoop split after a load of 28.00kN was applied. This failed at only 38 per cent of 72.08kN pressure needed to pass. In fact, the failure was catastrophic and the roll hoop actually split in half.

On test three, called the nose push off test, with pressure applied to the side of the nose, it also failed at a pressure of 23.00kN – 23.4 per cent away from the required 30.00kN. This failure was described in the official report sheet as "core crushed under pad."

The failure of both tests at such low levels again indicated that Simtek was in deep trouble. In particular, the roll hoop had failed at a ridiculously low level. It was a catastrophic failure and probably should have been completely redesigned, but there simply wasn't time.

Simtek had just 25 days before the first practice session of the Brazilian Grand Prix, the opening race of the season. Chassis S941-02, the reference chassis, was scheduled to be Roland Ratzenberger's race car. It could not leave for Brazil until the tests were passed. And it had to leave for Brazil, at the latest, in 18 days' time. The team was really up against it.

Meanwhile, Chassis S941-01 was being tested by David Brabham. But the car was potentially unsafe. If it had turned over during an accident, the roll hoop would almost certainly have failed, leaving the driver unprotected. On safety grounds, Chassis S941-01 should have been withdrawn from testing. But it wasn't. Strictly speaking it did not have to be, as the rules about private testing and crash test approved chassis are very vague. Simtek was doing nothing wrong by continuing to run the car. But it was taking what many people would have considered an "unacceptable risk".

On 7th March in Banbury the static load tests, tests two and three, which the car had failed on 28th February, were run again. Charlie Whiting and Nick Wirth were again present at the Simtek factory to witness the tests.

In the week preceding, the team had cut off the split roll hoop about 30cm below its top. They constructed a steel plate horseshoe-shaped roll bar approximately 10cm wide and had bonded it to the stub of the old roll hoop and then covered the joint with carbon fibre. It was a botch job but nonetheless entirely legal as teams could do what they wanted to pass the test – so long as every subsequent chassis was also converted similarly.

The steel roll hoop imposed an obvious weight penalty in a place the team didn't want it. But in the circumstances it had little choice. The nose side and cone were also strengthened with additional carbon fibre.

The modifications appeared to work and the chassis passed the tests, easily exceeding the required pressures. It appeared to easily pass test two, the roll bar integrity test, with a maximum load 72.25kN being applied with displacement of only 14mm. Test three also appeared to be easily passed, with the maximum load of 30.05kN applied.

The magazine deemed the description to have "appeared" appropriate because it got experts to examine photographs of the chassis before and after the steel roll hoop was added. The experts were all adamant that the way the steel hoop was bonded to the carbon fibre, it would have been unlikely to pass the test. One former team principal said: "This should have been bolted through. There was no way it would have been strong enough." Close examination of the photographs show no sign of any bolts, indicating it was not. The thickness of the steel used also seems inadequate.

BusinessF1 journalists also discovered a serious anomaly in the day's testing. There were no chassis or nose weights recorded on the official test forms. Without these weight records, the tests were almost meaningless. It meant that in the future FIA officials could not check where a similar spec chassis which had passed the tests was being used if there was an incident. Adding the steel roll hoop would have significantly increased the weight of the chassis, and it is very hard not to add weight at the joint between the monocoque and the hoop whether it is bolted or glued. Without a recorded weight, it would have been all too easy at a later date for the team to strip off the additional weight that had been added to ensure a pass.

The whole purpose of the FIA crash test is that in the event of a problem (i.e. a serious accident), the investigators should be able to go back and weigh components to verify that they were made to the same level of the test components. That the weight of the chassis is not recorded is inexplicable and hardly satisfactory.

An expert involved in crash testing in 1994 explains: "The idea is that you weigh the chassis when you test it and again after that. If a chassis gets crashed that has not been tested, you know you can bring that chassis and nosecone back and you could weigh it and assess whether this was the chassis or nosecone specification that tested."

On 8th March, 17 days before the car was due to for practice in Brazil, the Simtek Chassis S941-02 arrived at Cranfield Impact Centre for its final, and most daunting, test – the moving impact test. Ostensibly, it was the first time it had taken the test.

The key measure in this test is the deformation of the nosecone, with no incursion or damage to the chassis allowed. In the Simtek case, it would not be allowed to deform more than 670mm, the full length of its nosecone. Even a millimetre over that would have classified as a fail. G-forces in the test are rigorously measured. But in reality it could not deform more than 620mm to ensure a pass. This is because collapsed debris would build up during the impact, eventually becoming solid, and then impact directly on the chassis face, damaging it before the 670mm was reached.

All of the measurements in this sort of test are made electronically and recorded and displayed on four graph lines printed out on a sheet that goes with the official test report sheet, which would have been completed on the day. As well as measuring the graphs, a pass or fail would also have been easily identified by eye. If the chassis was damaged in any way, it would be a fail, even if the graphs reported otherwise.

According to the figures entered on the official test report sheet, the chassis easily passed the test, with the nosecone only deforming 470mm, calculating the peak g-force of 24g and average g-force of 13g.

BusinessF1 reporters had the four graphs analysed by scientists and crash test experts who were involved in Formula One at the time.

The first graph on the printout was a measure of the g-force recording the impact of the nose on the solid object. The Y-axis of the graph had an upper limit of +31.25g. The graph is divided into 20 equal divisions that equal 3.125g per division. The peak printout line from the test corresponds to 24.2g on the graph. The mean average is calculated at 13g to equate from the deformation of 470mm. The curve is 38 divisions long (length of impact time) and multiplied by 2.5 milliseconds.

The second graph is a deceleration graph, velocity against time, which indicates where the deceleration stops. It measures the distance from when the nose starts to hit to when the trolley holding the chassis completely stops, measuring deceleration as opposed to g-force. The Y-axis of the graph has an upper limit of 15.7m/s (metres per second) and a lower limit of -15.7m/s. The graph is divided into 20 equal divisions that equal 1.57m/s per division.

The third graph measures the distance travelled and the exact point at which the chassis stops. The Y-axis of the graph has an upper limit of +0.8038m (metres) and a lower limit of -0.8038m. The graph is divided into 20 equal divisions that equal 0.08038m per division (80.38mm per division). Observing the peak of this line and transcribing across to the Y-axis, a reading is found between 670mm and 680mm (8.5 units multiplied by 80.83). If one counts 38 divisions, the time when it stopped is estimated at 670mm, not the 470mm that was recorded on the sheet.

The fourth graph is a measure of peak g-force and is not of any great significance.

Put very simply, it has taken 0.095 seconds, being the deceleration time from the beginning of impact, to stop. All three graphs point to the same time, equalling a crush distance of 660-680 millimetres. At an impact speed of 11.03 metres per second, the actual mean average g-force would be 9.4g not the 13g stated.

This is confirmed if the same time is taken from all the X-axes. All the graphs tie up to a point where they all stop, even the g-force recording on the nose, where there is a bounce at the end. If this line is tied back to the curve, it is where the curve goes flat – in other words, it has stopped. If a straight line is drawn off to the Y-axis, a reading can be taken that shows that the nosecone has deformed as much as 680mm. This was a definite fail.

As the report is filled in from the analysis graph, it appears the report form has been filled in incorrectly. If the deformation is 680mm, or even 660mm allowing for error, against the 670mm length of the nosecone, the main chassis would definitely have been damaged. In the schematic line drawing of the chassis, the length of the nose box is given as 670mm, therefore deformation of 680mm is a clear fail and the nosecone would effectively have disappeared with the bulkhead face showing damage.

The analysis conforms with visual inspection of Chassis S941-02. There has clearly been damage to the lower half of the front of the chassis, which has been repaired, yet Chassis S941-02 was never recorded as having any frontal accident damage during its racing life.

The rules clearly state that the monocoque should remain undamaged. At an actual 680mm deformation, the chassis failed on the electronic reading and presumably also the visual damage inspection.

It could have been that the FIA inspectors simply misread the graph. There is an anomaly on the graphs where there appears to be no data recorded for the first five divisions on the X-axis, which adds 12.5 milliseconds. It is possible that the measurement in the first graph was triggered early and this is why it doesn't start with a zero. If one takes the time as 12.5 milliseconds, it is possible that equals the five divisions where nothing happens. Therefore, the time axis is no longer 38 divisions, but 43 divisions. Where previously there was a time of 0.095 seconds until the end of the impact, now it is 0.1057 seconds, which equals an average of 11.6g with a deformation of 660mm, but even on that measurement, the deformation has been inaccurately recorded on the test report sheet.

Convention is that zero is the point of impact, and there is no reason for the graph to be represented differently. It seems inexplicable that on impact, a g-force did not begin to be measured. One explanation is the g-reading output was offset on the X-axis by a set-up error. It is possible that the electronic graphs were incorrect, indicated by the 12.5 milliseconds at the start of the first graph where nothing happens.

In reality, the nosecone had disappeared in the impact and the calculation of 470mm could not possibly have been correct. To make absolutely sure, the nosecone deformation should have been measured manually. However, it is also possible that the deformation was 470mm but the read-out was wrong. In this instance, a re-test should have been ordered as something had clearly gone wrong. Additionally, if indeed 470mm is the correct figure, it was simply too good to be believed that the nose safely protected the chassis from damage with 200mm spare. A technical director at the time told *BusinessF1* reporters: "With the expected performance of a nose box at that time, it would have been a magic nose box to have stopped with 200mm to spare." There are simply too many 'ifs and buts' for this result to have been defendable. As one leading expert of the day, who has examined the data and the findings of this report, says: "I would put my house on the results recorded here being incorrect."

In addition, once again there was no chassis weight on the official test sheet for the second day running. It seemed an inexcusable second lapse. However, the form did record a nosecone weight at 4.35kg; 0.35kg heavier than previously.

In the end, the magazine's reporters could not prove conclusively either way if the Simtek S941 had properly passed the FA crash test. What it did know was that the team could not afford for it to fail. The team was in a desperate financial condition. It had neither the resources, the time nor the money to do it properly. In an effort to be competitive, it took too many chances with the design of the chassis. Many people believe that the chassis was too light and too flimsy. They believe the design compromised the integrity of the chassis to save weight and to be able to ballast the car the way that the team wanted to on the track.

In normal circumstances, if the test had failed and the chassis was damaged it would not have been a particularly big deal. No car, before or since, had ever failed the crash test. The team would have simply gone away, repaired the damage and strengthened the nose components, returned a week later having done simulations on a computer, and passed the test.

But Simtek was short of money and planned to use Chassis S941-01 and Chassis S941-02 at the opening races, and the team had run out of time. In the event of a failure, the team would not have been able to enter the first race of the championship. It would have therefore faced tough FIA sanctions and repercussions from its drivers and sponsors. In its fragile financial condition, it would probably not have been able to continue.

The Brazilian Grand Prix was looming. It was less than 14 days before the car had to be shipped out. Before that, it had to be painted, built up and tested. If it had failed the test, there would not have been time to modify the production race cars to match the test.

John Barnard, who invented the carbon fibre chassis and was responsible for saving many drivers from death and serious injury, says: "The tests were an absolute total burden for a small team."

Of course, if the Simtek team had got through the 1994 season without any major accidents, it would not have mattered whether the car had passed or not. No one would have known and probably no one would have cared. The secrets of the 1994 Simtek S941 crash test programme would have remained secret forever. The significance of a successful crash test is important in Formula One only when there is an incident. If there had been no incidents, no one would have been concerned.

There is also the question of FIA president Max Mosley and Charlie Whiting's role. Mosley was undoubtedly close to Wirth, and there is a question as to whether both men should have recused themselves from having anything to do with the tests. Charlie Whiting attended every Simtek test personally. If anything was untoward, then there is the question as to whether Whiting knew about it. No one knows if he was under any pressure from anyone.

One good thing that did come out of the chassis failure that caused Ratzenberger's death is that crash testing was vastly extended, and all Formula One carbon fibre chassis were redesigned to make them much safer.

Since the 1995 season, when these changes were instigated, there has not been one serious injury to a driver in a Formula One car because of a chassis failure: an extraordinary record. There is absolutely no doubt that many drivers' lives have been saved because of Roland Ratzenberger's death and the Simtek chassis failures.

Patrick Head says: "It is the case that the weekend of the Imola race in 1994 had a major effect on attitudes to safety throughout Formula One and motor racing generally. And although safety developments are always advancing, the events of that weekend were a catalyst for many developments undertaken between the FIA and the teams." He added: "Charlie Whiting was instrumental in many of these developments."

"I want to spend the night awake. We will talk until morning comes. I want to convince you I am the best man in your life."
                              Ayrton Senna
                              Saturday 30th April 1994

CHAPTER 13

The Last Supper

Saturday 30th April 1994
Evening

That night every one of the drivers had the same thoughts and every one of them came to the same conclusion. They all thought about withdrawing from the San Marino Grand Prix and then all decided not to. Even the Simtek of David Brabham would take part in the race, and that was unprecedented after the death of a team mate.

When Senna arrived back in San Pietro at the Castello, he found the inevitable Italian Saturday night wedding in full swing and having taken over the whole hotel. He was so upset that when he was asked to pose for a picture with the bride and groom, he uncharacteristically refused. But the sight of the joy of a wedding and everyone having a good time brightened his mood considerably. It reminded him, just when he needed reminding, that there was always a brighter side of his life.

As soon as he got back to his suite, he telephoned Adriane, who by then had arrived at Antonio Braga's house in Sintra near Lisbon and was sitting with his wife Luiza. She asked him how he was, and he replied: "It's like shit. Shit, shit, shit," before he started to cry. Adriane thought he was still upset about Barrichello's accident the day before until he told her about Ratzenberger's death. Then he broke down completely and told her he was not going to race the next day. He said: "I have a really bad feeling about this race, I would rather not drive." Adriane had to rush catch an 8:30pm flight to Faro that night so didn't have much time to talk. He told her he would catch her later when she arrived at the house in the Algarve.

As soon as he put the phone down, Josef Leberer knocked on the door and asked him if wanted a massage. But he was in no mood for that and sent Leberer away. Leberer asked him if he wanted to talk about the accident but he said he didn't. Leberer had been good friends with Ratzenberger and had brought him to Senna's attention as a promising new and talented Austrian driver. Senna told Leberer he was too upset about Ratzenberger and even more upset by the callous attitude of the race officials. He was furious at the treatment he had received from the stewards. He told Leberer: "How dare they tell me what I could do? I am driving the car, and they tell me about safety."

Leberer asked him if he would still be coming out with them to celebrate his birthday. He said "Of course" and shouted down the corridor to Leberer "Happy Birthday".

Senna met the rest of the party at the Trattoria Romagnola. The meal had been planned for some time but few felt like celebrating. Instead, Senna spent the evening questioning Leberer about Ratzenberger. The general mood of the evening was very sad and at the end, Leberer wished he had cancelled it.

When Senna returned to the hotel, he found a message under his door from Frank Williams reminding him to go downstairs for a chat before he turned in. He talked to his team principal, who found him a lot calmer than he had been earlier. After 30 minutes or so, he went back to his room. Leberer popped by and offered to do his massage before he went to bed but Senna said he wasn't in the mood.

Meanwhile, Adriane had finally arrived at Quinta do Lago, after nearly 24 hours of travelling. She made straight for the shower. As she got out, the phone rang. It was Senna. He told her he had decided to race after all, and when he won he would uncoil an Austrian flag and fly it on his victory lap in honour of Roland Ratzenberger. During the call, his housekeeper Juraci shouted to Adriane to tell him she was preparing his favourite meal of grilled chicken and steamed vegetables for when he returned on Sunday evening. She handed the phone to Juraci, who told him the meal would be waiting for him when he got back. He then said to Adriane: "I want to spend the night awake. We will talk until morning comes. I want to convince you I am the best man in your life." As the conversation got lighter, she laughed and said to him: "But you don't know the others." He said: "I will prove to you I am the best." She said: "If necessary, I will join the queue like any other fan." Senna appeared to be referring to Leonardo's tapes, but of course Adriane had no idea about them and it went over her head.

Adriane told him she had looked inside his wardrobes and chided him for buying even more belts and training shoes. She reminded him again that he had enough clothes to change twice a day without washing anything for a year. He replied, "I can't help it – I'm addicted." Then she asked him about Leonardo, and Senna told her to "forget him."

Her last words to him were that she had news for him. Jokingly, he asked her if she was pregnant. "No," she shouted; the news was that she had been training and would be running with him on Monday. During their conversation, Senna said he had changed from being deeply depressed to being happy again. He asked her to come out to Faro Airport with Juraci when she picked him up on Sunday evening and told her to be there at 8:30pm.

They were the last words they ever spoke.

"You are relying entirely on the car and, in the light of Roland's accident, it brings it home that sometimes you are just a passenger, putting your faith in the components."
                              Damon Hill
                              September 1997

CHAPTER 14

Rendezvous With Death

Race day dawns

On Sunday morning Ayrton Senna was wakened in his hotel room by the sound of a telephone ringing. He knew precisely who it was. The clock showed 7:30am and it was Captain O'Mahoney. As soon as Senna picked up the receiver, O'Mahoney greeted him as he always did on race mornings: "Baggage collection here." It was Senna's wake-up call. Senna answered, "Okay Mahny" as he always did.

O'Mahoney asked him what time he could pick up his bags at the hotel. Senna replied: "Give me 45 minutes." With that, Senna got up, jumped in the shower, towelled off quickly and changed into a fresh shirt and his familiar cream trousers. He threw the rest of his things in a bag. By the time O'Mahoney had arrived and they walked down to reception, it was 15 minutes past eight.

In reception, Valentino Tosoni had been waiting for him and rushed over, apologising for the noise and confusion of the wedding the night before but at the same time imparting the news that his wife Luiza was in hospital and that their second son was about to appear. Senna thought about the inevitable context of life: a death and a birth within his orbit inside 24 hours. Senna asked him to pass on his best wishes to Luisa, and Tosoni said he was sorry about Ratzenberger. Senna thanked him and said, "See you next year" as he walked out the front door into the car park.

Senna waved O'Mahoney goodbye and went to his waiting helicopter to take the short flight to the track. By the time he arrived, the sun was shining and a beautiful day was developing.

As he walked to the Williams motorhome, he saw Alain Prost on the other side of the paddock. He waved and walked over, greeting him extremely cordially.

It shocked Prost to hear how kind Senna was being to him. Although they had spoken a few times since Prost had left Williams, more often than not Senna would walk right past him without even an acknowledgement. But now something had changed.

In Senna's head it certainly had. Prost had something he needed, and that was his presence in Formula One. In his mind, Senna had already decided to leave Williams at the end of 1994. By then, he knew it was not the team for him and the meeting with Luca di Montezemolo had turned his head. He liked Frank Williams but didn't care for the rest of the people in the team – they were not his kind of people. If he stayed five years, he knew he could probably change the culture and win some world championships along the way. But he didn't have five years. He had turned 34 and the most he could expect was another six seasons, including this one.

After his meeting with Montezemolo on the previous Wednesday, he knew that he wanted to spend that five years making Ferrari into a winning team and being world champion again with them.

But that meant breaking his three-year Williams contract. The best way to do that was to lure Prost back to the team to take his place – hence the charm offensive on the Frenchman. Senna knew that Prost hadn't really wanted to retire but the thought of earning $14 million for doing nothing appealed to his nature. He was certain he could persuade Prost to come back to Williams so he could leave discreetly. He wasn't sure how he would pull that off, however.

Senna told Prost they should talk later as he was short of time and running late for his briefing with David Brown. Prost told him he would be in the Williams pit garage for the warm-up as part of his commentating duties for French broadcaster TF1.

In morning warm-up, Senna was once again considerably faster than the rest of the drivers. Damon Hill described his performance in that warm-up as "blindingly fast". In fact, he was nine-tenths quicker than the next best. His speed disconcerted Hill who, as soon as warm-up was over, went to the motorhome and started studying the telemetry to see how he was so much slower than Senna. He said: "I felt I had to take a closer look at the difference between myself and him."

During warm-up, Senna continued his Prost charm offensive. He sent a message over the pit radio to be relayed to Prost: "Hello, my friend. I've been missing you." Prost was bemused, but he didn't complain. In his new role with TF1, a good relationship with Senna was essential.

For once, Senna was pleased with his car. When he returned to the pits, he told David Brown not to touch the settings; finally, the set-up was right.

During the half hour he was out on the track, Betise Assumpcao had sat talking to Karin Sturm in the media centre. The German journalist was one of the few female reporters on the Formula One circus and she and Assumpcao were very good friends – she trusted the German. As Sturm listened, Assumpcao laid out the whole story of how she believed John Corsmit and his race officials were trying to intimidate Senna. She told Sturm about the course car incident, which was not public knowledge and then the threat to disqualify him. She explained: "But it's like that the whole time." She said it was because they knew Senna was the driving force behind the re-forming of the Grand Prix Drivers Association (GPDA), which Corsmit called a "drivers' trade union".

Sturm was grateful to get the inside line although she knew she couldn't use it or else her relationship with Assumpcao would be at an end. But it was nice to know for background purposes. She had also confided to Sturm about her growing closeness to Patrick Head, the Williams technical director, who she had met when she moved with Senna to the Williams team. But neither woman had any idea it would eventually end in marriage after Head split from his wife.

Damon Hill had found the warm-up very difficult that morning, especially driving past the corner on the circuit where Ratzenberger had crashed. As he remembered: "I could imagine the force of the impact because I was actually travelling at the same speed he had been doing before he went off. Under normal circumstances, I wouldn't have given it a second thought because, even though speeds reach 200mph, it is not a part of the circuit where you come close to the limit; it is not a place you worry about. You are relying entirely on the car and, in the light of Roland's accident, it brings it home that sometimes you are just a passenger, putting your faith in the components." By then, it was known that the front wing had failed, taking away the steering on Ratzenberger's car. It had compounded Hill's biggest fear: that of being a passenger without any control of a Formula One car at 200mph.

For once, Senna's chat with David Brown was short, and he knew he was free until 11 o'clock. He went to the Ferrari pit where Gerhard Berger was chatting with his engineers and asked him to swing by the Williams motorhome to collect him for the drivers' briefing later. He told Berger he had something he needed to discuss with him before the meeting started. Berger was still very upset about Ratzenberger's accident and was in no real mood to talk.

Then he went to his changing room in the transporter and got back into his shirt and slacks. After that, with nothing to do, he casually wandered into the Williams motorhome, where he spotted Alain Prost at a table on his own waiting for his breakfast. He asked if he could join him. A very surprised Prost said, "Of course."

It was the start of 30 minutes of what people who were there describe as "animated conversation". Ostensibly, Senna lobbied him to help with "urgently needed" safety improvements in Formula One, and Prost agreed that they would meet before the Monaco Grand Prix in two weeks' time to discuss it. Prost asked him if he would do a voice-over for a lap of Imola later for TF1 to broadcast before the race. He readily agreed.

Prost was wholly surprised at Senna's attitude towards him that weekend. As he said afterwards: "I was very surprised as normally he did not even say 'hello' if I crossed his path.

"It was always Ayrton's rules; if it's your rules, it follows you believe they are correct. Now it was different, and Senna wanted to talk: he talked a little about the car, a little about safety matters. It seemed he just wanted to share time with me."

Senna thought it too early to introduce his real agenda. Prost later recalled: "For the first time in ages, we had a really normal conversation – we set aside the differences between us."

Senna suggested they do the voice-over straight away, and he and Prost went to the TF1 broadcast tent where he recorded it. During the recording, Senna repeated his earlier greeting: "I would like to say welcome to my old friend, Alain Prost. Tell him we miss him very much."

With that, he strolled off back to the office in the motorhome to write a letter to Rudolf and Margit Ratzenberger. When he had finished, he took it to Betise Assumpcao and asked her to fax it straight off. Then he went to the same room he had been in yesterday, drew the blinds and tried to sleep for an hour before the driver's briefing at 11 o'clock.

Gerhard Berger arrived at 10:45am, and Betise Assumpcao went to wake up Senna and bring him down. They chatted at a table briefly and then walked off to race control for the briefing. Senna asked Berger to bring up a safety point about the pace car on the formation lap. Senna wanted the idea scrapped and Berger agreed. Senna didn't want to do it himself because he believed there was now considerable personal animosity between him and the FIA officials and that he would not get a fair hearing.

At the briefing, Senna sat at the back, away from Berger. Most of the talk was of the events of the day before. Then Bernie Ecclestone stood up and suggested a minute's silence in memory of Ratzenberger. Sid Watkins, standing at the side, was mortified and whispered to the person standing next to him: "That is the last thing the drivers need now." Watkins thought to himself that Bernie didn't often get things wrong but this time he had. Predictably, Senna was deeply affected and was openly crying during the minute. Watkins scowled at Ecclestone, who immediately realised he had made a mistake.

Then Berger raised the point about the introduction of a pace car during the final parade lap leading to the start. He said that he felt it was nothing more than a gimmick and contributed little else apart from making the cars run far too slowly and therefore less able to put heat into their tyres. Berger said: "Going that slowly increases risk as everybody's tyres and brakes are too cold at the start." He demanded forcefully that it shouldn't happen in future, starting with today. The other drivers supported Berger, and Roland Bruyneraede reluctantly agreed to abandon the idea. John Corsmit stared at Senna throughout, well aware who had initiated the idea and put Berger up to it.

After the briefing, Senna stayed behind and chaired a brief discussion about safety with some of his colleagues, notably Michael Schumacher, Gerhard Berger and Michele Alboreto. He told them about his discussions with Niki Lauda and Alain Prost, and they agreed to hold a meeting on safety issues with all drivers in Monte Carlo on the Friday before the next race.

There was no dissent, but Hill believes that the talk of a drivers' meeting about safety to take place before Monaco rang alarm bells with the FIA. He said: "Whenever drivers group together, there is the potential for trouble. We were all together in the pre-race drivers' briefing as usual, and we weren't happy."

With that, Senna went back to the Williams transporter to get dressed for the race. As soon as he was ready, he joined Richard West in the motorhome and, together with Damon Hill, they walked to the Paddock Club to talk to Williams' sponsors and their guests for half an hour.

Normally, Senna didn't see his sponsor work as a chore at all and enjoyed it as long as he was not taken for granted. But he preferred his team mate to be there to share the heavy lifting. The performance was well rehearsed as they described a typical lap with the help of a map of the circuit on an easel. Senna and Hill gave a corner-by-corner commentary, which went down very well with the guests.

Just after midday, he was back at the motorhome and ate a light lunch of fish and pasta cooked for him, as usual, by Josef Leberer, and then he shut himself away in the motorhome with his just thoughts for company. 15 minutes later, he picked up his spare overalls from the debrief room and waved to Frank Williams on the way out. It was the last Williams saw of him. He went off to the Ferrari motorhome for another chat with Gerhard Berger with some more thoughts he had had after the meeting.

Half an hour before the start, Senna walked to the Williams garage. Jaime Brito, a Brazilian broadcaster with Globo TV, was in the garage and had three photos he wanted him to sign. Brito had known Senna for years, from when he first started karting and was usually around in the garage before the start of the race looking for background material to use during Globo's long broadcast. Senna was very supportive of all the journalists and photographers who had been close to him on the way up with the exception of one: Keith Sutton, a photographer, who had been Senna's unofficial PR man when he first came to England in 1981. They had fallen out when Sutton was reluctant to give Senna access to all the photographs he had taken of him as a young up-and-coming driver even though Senna had paid him at the time.

From that day, Senna hardly exchanged a word with Sutton and never liked him taking his photograph. He never forgot what he saw as a betrayal. After Senna died, Sutton cashed in on their relationship with books and exhibitions. He became the go-to guy for photographs of Senna's early career in motor racing – all sold at very handsome fees.

Senna later employed the Japanese photographer Norio Koike to do that job and reportedly paid him $350,0000 a year to follow him around snapping his life. But he made sure he owned the copyright to the photos. Koike subsequently took some extraordinary photos, delighting Senna for the rest of his life. Reputedly there are more than 40,000 photographs taken by Koike in the Ayrton Senna Foundation archives.

Jaime Brito did not think Senna was his usual self that day. He watched as he paced round the car, examining the tyres and resting on the rear wing, silent and alone: "He did something that day I had never seen him do before. It was as if he was very suspicious of the car." But Brito thought little of it and was delighted to get his photos signed.

Betise Assumpcao also thought he was different that day: "He usually had a particular way of pulling on his balaclava and helmet, determined and strong, as if he was looking forward to the race. That day, you could tell just from the way he was putting on his helmet that he didn't want to race. He was not thinking he was going to die; he really thought he would win, but he just wanted to get it over with and go home. He wasn't there, he was miles away."

But Assumpcao has dismissed any speculation of his mood that he was thinking of refusing to race or even retiring: "At a race, Ayrton was often intense and stressed. He would carry the weight of the world on his shoulders. At the beginning, this was because of how important Formula One was to him; as time went by, it was because of how important it was for everybody and he knew how much was at stake every time he went out in the car. In Brazil, Ayrton was bigger than Pele. When Pele was achieving greatness, there were not so many people who had television sets. Every Sunday, people expected Ayrton to win in what was by then a TV age. He was the only certainty of some goodness in the country."

Damon Hill was on the other side of the garage, but they didn't speak:

"There was so much pressure on Ayrton that weekend — he was not going to come second again to Schumacher. The death of Roland Ratzenberger had heightened his passion to be Ayrton Senna — and to win. It's how he approached his sport. And his life. It was his mission not to give in to any form of fallibility."

Hill believed that Senna put a force field around himself before a race, and he never attempted to communicate with him or even wave to him in that period. As he said: "I didn't get close to Ayrton in the moments leading up to a race. People gave him space. He was on his own. He kept a protected wall."

Whilst Senna was pacing the garage, Sid Watkins climbed into his medical car and ordered his driver Mario Casoni to drive round the circuit on his normal inspection lap to make sure the medical intervention cars were in place and the people manning them alert. When he returned to the pits, he inspected the medical centre. Everything was perfect. Roland Bruynseraede, the FIA race director, also went through his starting rituals.

A few minutes later, Senna asked Josef Leberer for his helmet. He was strapped into the car by his mechanics as all the cars gradually left the pit garages, did a lap and formed up on the grid. Leberer walked into the pit lane ready to meet Senna on the grid. Betise Assumpcao went up to the media centre to watch the start of the race with the journalists.

Senna's modus operandi on the grid was to sit quietly belted up with his helmet on in his car for the 15 minutes or so before the start, preparing mentally for the first corner and replaying in advance over and over in his head what he was going to do. This time, he broke his usual routine by taking his helmet off, removing his nomex fireproof balaclava, and loosening his seat belts whilst remaining in the car. Josef Leberer stood guard, protecting him from the sun with an umbrella and shooing away any well-wishers who might inadvertently interrupt Senna's concentration. On the grid, Williams technical director Patrick Head talked briefly with him, and there was a hint of a smile as they spoke.

As usual, the circuit commentator announced the names of all the drivers on the grid, and when he came to Gerhard Berger's name, because he was a Ferrari driver, the San Marino crowd cheered wildly. Senna turned around and smiled at Berger, who was alongside him on the grid. Berger remembers: "It was the smile of a friend who was pleased to see the people's support and love for me. That is the last thing I remember of him."

Leberer gave him a last drink and then handed Senna his helmet and he put it on for the last time. With his helmet on, Leberer checked Senna was happy, the mechanics started the engine and Leberer waited a few moments before running back to the Williams garage to watch the start on the monitors.

Meanwhile, at Senna's house in the Algarve, Adriane and Juraci settled in front of the television to watch the race whilst eating their lunch.

In the medical car, four men were belted in their seats, waiting to follow hard on the heels of the pack of cars on the opening lap in case of an incident. In the front were Watkins and Casoni. In the back seat, Dr Baccarini had his IV infusions ready, the cervical collar, and the paraphernalia of resuscitation. Next to him was Dr Domenico Salcito, deputy chief medical officer for Imola.

Up in the BBC commentary box, Murray Walker made his customary preamble to British TV viewers: "Ayrton Senna in pole position. Michael Schumacher next to him on the grid. So now, with just seconds to go, the grid is being cleared and you will see the cars going around in less than 30 seconds' time."

"There's going to be a fucking awful accident any minute."
Sid Watkins
Sunday 1st May 1994
2.15pm

CHAPTER 15

Lap Seven

The end of the road

A t exactly two o'clock, 26 drivers pulled away on the pace lap of the 1994 San Marino Grand Prix and raced around the circuit back to the grid, trying desperately to keep the heat in their tyres. The procession of Formula One cars went past Professor Watkins's medical car and took their places on the starting grid.

Ayrton Senna's Williams-Renault was on pole and beside him was Michael Schumacher in his Benetton-Ford. Gerhard Berger in his Ferrari and Damon Hill, Senna's team mate, completed the second row. One of these drivers would certainly win the 1994 San Marino Grand Prix, and Ayrton Senna was determined it would be him.

Senna could not have been more motivated than he was on Sunday 1st May. He described the first lap of a race as being like "an explorer finding a different world. You have this desire to go into places you have never been before. The situation is extremely absorbing. When I push, I go and find something else. I go again, and I find something more. I have experienced on many occasions the feeling of finding new things – even if I thought, 'okay, that is my maximum.'"

He was as mentally alert and as ready as he could be for the start. He didn't have long to wait as the lights went red, then four seconds later turned green and the cars streamed into the first turn.

Senna sped off into the lead, but behind the lead cars there was mayhem; almost immediately, yellow flags were waving everywhere. Pedro Lamy's Lotus-Honda had got a great start from the 11th row and run straight into the back of J. J. Lehto's Benetton, which had stalled on the start line. It was a violent accident and bodywork was spread around the start line. A wheel became detached and rolled down the track.

Mario Casoni took a few seconds to react, then pulled out in the medical car and drove it straight through the debris, passing the wrecked cars on each side. He paused, just so long that Professor Watkins could observe that the drivers were out of their cars uninjured. Then, on Watkins's say-so, he tailed the main pack of cars while marshals started to clear up the mess. Watkins was in no doubt that the race would be red-flagged and restarted when the track was cleared. But the red flag never came out and instead, at 2:03pm, the safety car emerged, driven by Massimo Angelini, and picked up the pack of cars. This struck Watkins as less than satisfactory. However, the safety car was a relatively new innovation and race officials were keen to use it at every opportunity, and this was one such opportunity.

Senna led the cars round with Michael Schumacher, Gerhard Berger and Damon Hill following. But the Opel pace car was painfully slow and tyre temperatures were dropping dramatically. Senna, Berger, Schumacher and Hill would have been fuming under their helmets at having to run so slowly for five laps.

The medical car finished its lap uneventfully, and as it reached its permanent position in the chicane, the leading Formula One cars were completing their second lap. The marshals had cleared the circuit in less than six minutes and swept up the best they could with Formula One cars still on the track. The risk of punctures was huge.

At 2:15pm, David Brown told Senna over the pit radio that the safety car was about to pull off. Senna acknowledged him and these were the last words he ever spoke to anyone.

With the safety car finally off the track, Senna put the hammer down. He seemed even more motivated now than he had been 15 minutes earlier. With a full load of fuel in his car, he clocked 1m 24.887secs on the sixth lap on cold tyres. It was an extraordinary time and only two drivers, Damon Hill and Michael Schumacher, had bettered it by the end of the race.

Senna knew he had to put space between him and Schumacher who was running a lighter fuel load and appeared to be able to refuel his car a lot quicker at pitstops.

As Senna passed the pit wall, his car fed a burst of digitised information to the tiny radio dishes on the wall in front of the Williams pit. It was instantly relayed to the computer screens of the data engineers in the rear of the garage. The sensors had recorded a very fast lap as he attempted to put space between himself and Michael Schumacher in second place. The data captured showed the behaviour of the most significant components of the car during the preceding minute and a half of lap six: the temperatures, speeds, pressures, wear rates, steering and hydraulics. Crucially, the steering angle was being measured by a potentiometer placed on top of the steering column, just behind the dashboard. Any steering-wheel movement was registered by the sensor. A pressure sensor mounted on the hydraulic steering system was measuring the performance of the power steering.

On board the car were two data-recording black boxes, one belonging to the team and one belonging the engine-maker, Renault. They were unrelated systems which would collect data for the whole race as a back-up to the telemetry transmitted to the pit wall.

Schumacher couldn't keep up with Senna and fell behind immediately. But the fast pace of the race suddenly worried Sid Watkins – so much so that he turned to Mario Casoni and said: "There's going to be a fucking awful accident any minute."

14.4 seconds later, there was.

At exactly 2:17pm, Senna approached the Tamburello curve on lap seven. Senna was driving out of his skin, experiencing extraordinary feelings and emotions. He had described it many times in the past: "There is the feeling of 'Oh! I have just almost gone over the limit'. It is fascinating and even attractive in a way. But it is a challenge for you to control it and not to exceed those things. So the feeling of living in that narrow band, of overdoing it and being too easy, is very small. The challenge to stay within that band is very much a motivation."

Senna was about to stray out of the narrow band with terrible consequences.

As he approached Tamburello, the onboard computer was recording hundreds of pieces of data every second. At 9.1 seconds into the lap, Senna's foot was flat to the floor round the Tamburello curve. Beyond the track was a small area of grass, then a smaller area of tarmac, then a solid concrete wall – there was no tyre protection. If something went wrong at that moment, a driver was in a lot of trouble with nowhere to go.

In 1994 a Formula One car ran millimetres from the surface of the road, and on sticky slick tyres, with the aid of sophisticated aerodynamics, it had the ability to corner at almost unbelievable speeds. At close to 200mph, 11 seconds into the lap, Senna's car was on the very edge, and the aerodynamics were so efficient that it was almost being crushed into the tarmac by nearly four times its own weight in downforce.

The car was generating huge grip, enabling the Tamburello bend to be taken flat out. In fact, the car was set up in such a way that the bend was safer taken flat out. Anything else could have been simply dangerous.

Some people say that the worst thing a driver could have done in 1994 was lift off. It would throw the aerodynamics out of kilter, and on the limit the car could not be guaranteed to steer properly.

Sensors on board Senna's car indicated a force of 3.62G at Tamburello. If something went wrong now, the car could literally fly off the road. And at that exact moment, something did go wrong. At 12.6 seconds into the lap, 1.6 seconds before impact, something unknown had reduced the ride height of the Williams. Television viewers saw an intermittent flash of sparks from Senna's car. This was normal behaviour for a car in 1994, and it caused Senna's car to scrape along the track. The telemetry showed that Ayrton Senna had lifted off the throttle momentarily and the back of the car appeared to step out. With lightning reactions, reacting exactly as would be expected, Senna appeared to steer into the slide. The car gripped and turned to the right – but whether or not this was under Senna's control is debatable.

And then definitely it all went wrong. The telemetry shows the brakes were hard on, with Senna appearing to try and keep the car on the track. But other forces had taken over; other than trying to slow the car by urgently downshifting the gears, he was by then just a passenger. In any case, his focus was keeping the car on the track and winning the race, not saving his life. But Tamburello was the one unforgiving part of the Imola circuit, with no run-off and no protective tyre wall.

He veered off the track in a straight line just after the apex of the bend. He was doing 190mph, and as he braked he slowed the car to 130mph before he slammed sideways into the unprotected concrete wall. Because the accident took less than two seconds from start to finish, few saw him leave the track and did not notice the accident until he had bounced off the wall and was coming to a halt. He had gone into the wall at a 45-degree angle, and the car immediately ricocheted back on to the run-off area. All in all, it had taken exactly 1.8 seconds from leaving the track to coming to rest. There was a pause as everyone, including the marshals, froze.

But Senna didn't move again. A wheel had become trapped between the chassis and the wall before catapulting up and hitting the Brazilian in the head, forcing it back hard against the carbon-fibre headrest. At the same time, part of the suspension block on one of the wheels snapped off and broke through his visor, hitting his forehead like a bullet. The FOCA TV onboard camera caught the whole incident, bar the last 0.9 seconds of impact. Senna had been killed instantly the car hit the wall.

The next moment the red flags were out again and Mario Casoni put his foot to the floor and steered towards Tamburello. Sid Watkins thought to himself: "Somehow, I knew it was Senna."

At exactly 2:18pm, Watkins' Alfa-Romeo pulled up at Tamburello behind the wreck of the blue and white car. Life had suddenly gone wrong for one of the best drivers the world had ever seen. He had driven his last lap.

The TV cameras were further away than they had been at Ratzenberger's accident, and the first time the 65 million TV viewers watching the race realised that Ayrton Senna had failed to complete lap seven of the San Marino Grand Prix was when Michael Schumacher's Benetton-Ford swept into their screens at the exit of Tamburello. All they could see was a cloud of dust in the background.

Murray Walker was commentating on British television: "Well, we are right with Michael Schumacher now, and Senna, my goodness, I just saw it punch off to the right, what on earth happened there I don't know." Walker's shock and surprise was down to Senna being out of his third race in succession with no points on the board. He had no reason to worry about Senna's safety; he had seen many, many accidents worse than this.

Betise Assumpcao shot up from her seat in the media centre when she saw Senna's car rebound off the wall: "I had hardly sat down in the media centre when Ayrton went into the wall on lap seven. My first thought was, oh, he is out of the race again. Now that's three races and no points; he's going to be in a really bad mood now. I grabbed my handbag and ran as my first thought was that I had to be there when he walked back to the pits."

But one man felt immediate concern: Brazilian commentator Galvao Bueno, in the TV Globo cabin. Bueno was more knowledgeable than most journalists and quickly worked out Senna's crash speed. He told Antonio Braga, who was sitting next to him: "You know, when you hit a wall at 130mph, already the deceleration is lethal."

He and Braga simply looked at each other, and they were the first to realise the accident was probably going to be fatal. They were Senna's best friends along with Reginaldo Leme, another Brazilian journalist, who was also in the commentary box with them.

Bueno made no attempt to play down the situation. He said to millions of Brazilians straight away: "Ayrton has hit [the wall] badly. It's serious. It's very serious."

But before the marshals could get to Senna and the first medical car had reached the scene, his head moved forward in the cockpit and unknowing viewers were encouraged that the champion was intact. But it wasn't movement; it was a spasm.

Another man, sitting thousands of miles away, watching television in Balcarce, Argentina, knew different. Five-times world champion, 82-year-old Juan Manuel Fangio, knew the spasm was a sign of a massive head injury. He said: "I knew he was dead." He switched off his television.

In describing the split-second before the car hit the wall, Bueno had been spot on. Senna had managed to slow the car by 60mph before it hit the wall, and the impact speed was estimated at 130mph. The right-hand front of the car took the full brunt of the impact, and as the suspension crumpled, it acted as a spring and the Williams had catapulted back onto the track. The monocoque was split by the force of the impact but was otherwise intact.

As a helicopter with an overhead camera was soon hovering, pictures of the car were being transmitted live to an avid audience. The BBC director, Mark Wilkin, sensitively switched to its pitlane camera, but other broadcasters did not and stayed glued to the scene. It was starting to become very unpleasant.

Senna's girlfriend Adriane Galisteu was at Senna's home in Portugal, watching the race on television. When his car hit the wall, she remembers a selfish thought went through her mind: "Oh that's good! He'll be home sooner." She waited for him to throw off his gloves, undo the steering wheel and leap from the cockpit. It didn't occur to her for a second that he wouldn't. Even in the 18 months she had known him, similar accidents had happened a few times, and always with the same outcome. She remembered when he had hit the barrier hard at Monaco in 1993 and got out of the car straight away – this seemed no different.

Captain O'Mahoney, who had moved Senna's plane to Bologna for a quick departure, was also watching the race on television in the executive jet centre. He stood up and started to get ready to leave early when he saw the crash. But when his boss didn't get out of his car, he quickly sat down again.

Josef Leberer was in the Williams garage. He remembered: "I said c'mon, c'mon, move, move, get out of the car, boy." Suddenly a heavy feeling enveloped Leberer, who knew something was very wrong.

The Portuguese TV commentators gave Adriane no cause for concern, and there was nothing that suggested to her that the accident was anything out of the ordinary: certainly no more serious than other crashes he had survived. She remembered: "I jumped up from the sofa, holding the plate on which I was having my lunch." But that soon changed. She grew more anxious as he stayed in the car. She shouted out to Senna's Portuguese housekeeper, Juraci: "What are they waiting for?" She said: "He must have broken his arms or a leg." She screamed at the TV: "Get out of the car, get out!" After a few minutes when he had not moved, she recalled: "I was motionless, and I started to sob."

"He arrived at the hospital with no hope"

Dr Maria Teresa Fiandri
Sunday 1st May 1994

CHAPTER 16

No Hope

Sid Watkins removes the yellow helmet

As Professor Sid Watkins approached Tamburello in the medical car, he somehow knew it was Ayrton Senna who had crashed. Mario Casoni parked the car directly behind the first intervention car that had arrived a few seconds earlier. Watkins hesitated for a few moments before he opened the door and looked at the wreck of the motionless car. Aside from his wife, Susan, this was his best friend in the world, and he was sure he was not going to find anything good.

The doctor from the first intervention car was already with Senna and cradling his head, aware from the condition of his helmet and seeping blood that he had suffered a bad head injury. Senna's head was resting on the cockpit side. There was no sign of life and no sound of any breathing. He was just slumped in the Williams. The two men just looked at each other, unsure of what they would see when they got the helmet off.

Watkins frantically cut the chin strap and lifted the helmet gently, whilst others supported his neck. Blood poured out. His forehead was a mess and, more worryingly, blood and brain matter had started to seep from his nose. It was not as serious an injury as Ratzenberger's the day before, but that was small comfort.

Watkins appraised him visually. Senna's eyes were closed and he was deeply unconscious. But, according to Watkins, there was a faint pulse. Unlike Ratzenberger, Senna was technically not dead. In that event, Watkins's duties were crystal clear; he had to do everything to keep him that way. From that point of view, Senna could not have been in better hands. Watkins didn't know it then, but Senna had suffered a burst temporal artery and had already lost a lot of blood.

Instinctively, Watkins forced a tube into his mouth to obtain effective airflow. He knew he would need a tracheotomy. He grabbed a scalpel from his bag and cut a small slit in his neck and inserted a tube directly into his trachea and then left it to Dr Pezzi, one of the trackside medics, to get on with intubating Senna.

Watkins shouted for blood – his team already knew Senna's blood type: B+. Senna had lost at least one litre during the accident, and he was still bleeding profusely from the wounds above his eye and where Watkins had cut his neck. He was surprised at the amount of blood that rushed out where he had made the incision for the tracheotomy. Watkins put a cannula into his arm and squeezed the blood in as quickly as possible. All in all, before he died, Senna had 4.5 litres of blood replaced.

Under Watkins's supervision, the team inserted several IV infusions into the inert form. Before they removed him from the car, the four doctors worked to keep the respiratory passages clear, stem the blood flow and replace lost blood as they completely immobilised the cervical area.

The crowd at Tamburello were absolutely silent as Watkins and his team worked on Senna.

After all that was done and Senna was stabilised, Watkins checked again for a pulse. It was faint, but it was there. Senna looked serene as Watkins did what he knew he had to do and raised his eyelids so he could assess the state of his head injury. He remembered: "It was clear from his pupils that he had had a massive brain injury. I knew from seeing the extent of his injury that he could not survive." In reality, Senna was dead on impact and brain activity had instantly ceased. But because this was Ayrton Senna, and because Watkins had his orders from Ecclestone, he kept him artificially alive.

Watkins gave the all clear for the extraction team to lift him out of the car. As they did, blood spilled onto the tarmac from his wounds. They laid him on the ground as marshals held up plastic sheets to shield him from view. Watkins said: "As we did, he sighed, and though I am totally agnostic, I felt his soul departed at that moment."

As chance would have it, there was only one photographer at Tamburello that afternoon – Angelo Orsi, a close friend of Senna's and the picture editor of *Autosprint*, the Italian racing magazine. He leapt over the wall when the car came to rest and started snapping. He took close-ups of Senna in the car before and after his helmet was removed, and then when he was being treated on the ground, before marshals blocked his view. Galvao Bueno also knew Orsi and was watching him on his television monitor. He knew the photos he was getting would be controversial. He said: "He aimed and shot without even seeing exactly what he was getting."

Meanwhile, Betise Assumpcao had made her way back to the pit garage. When she got there someone shouted to her across the garage: "Don't worry, he has moved his head." She explained: "I didn't see the end of the accident: I just saw him going off the track and hitting the wall. I didn't see the wheels flying. All I saw on TV was a fog of sand, then his blue and white car and yellow helmet."

As soon as she heard that he had moved his head, she stopped worrying and turned her attention to his mood when he got back to the garage, which she knew wouldn't be good: "I thought he must be conscious, and I didn't even think he might be badly hurt. My only thought was to get back and make sure he didn't cause chaos or something like that."

But when the race was red-flagged, it suddenly occurred to Assumpcao that it might be more serious: "I knew he was not coming out of the car but I did not think for a second that he was dead." But she added: "I could feel the tension in the garage. Alain Prost was just staring at the monitor."

Adriane Galisteu, watching anxiously on television in the Algarve, stared at her boyfriend's feet as he was laid on the ground, looking for signs of life. She understood what she called "the language of feet". She saw no movement, and his feet told her he was dead, but she put that thought completely from her mind. By then, Juraci, the Algarve housekeeper, was a screaming wreck. Senna's close neighbours had started to arrive at the house to see if there was anything they could do.

Although people at the circuit were calm, viewers on television had seen everything. The sharper-eyed had seen blood seeping from the car like oil; it carried on as Senna lay on the ground, staining the track red. It was not obvious unless you knew what to look for. In the TV Globo cabin, Bueno could not see what Watkins could, but he was reading the body language of Watkins and the doctors: "At the moment of the disaster, by the way it happened and by the way he was rescued, I knew that it was extremely serious, but I had to continue to commentate on the race until the end. Bueno had already had a difficult time on Friday when the young Brazilian driver Rubens Barrichello was taken to hospital.

Frank Williams was watching in the Williams pit; Alain Prost was alongside him. They anxiously scanned the monitors. Williams had experienced death at the track when his driver Piers Courage lost his life in 1970; 24 years on, the same emotions stirred within him.

Roaming around the garden at Quinta do Lago, Senna's other dog, called Mouse, strangely seemed to sense that his master was in trouble and started barking loudly. Mouse was the sister of Quinda who lived at Angra. The neighbours' dogs started to bark as well.

Neyde da Silva called Adriane from the farm at Tatui to see if she had more information. But Brazilian viewers were getting the best information possible from Galvao Bueno. Adriane had nothing to tell her. After that, the telephone never stopped, and neighbours congregated at the house. The peaceful retreat, half an hour before, had suddenly turned to bedlam.

Journalists and photographers had started to gather at the back door of the Williams pit garage. Assumpcao was still of the opinion that Senna would soon be back and out of his wrecked car. She was concerned to intercept him before he said too much to the reporters, who were already gathering at the garage door. As she said: "I thought he's going to be angry when he gets back, swearing at everybody, whingeing about the engine, the car, the tyres. I told myself, I need to be there."

Back on the track, Watkins followed procedure and decided Senna should go straight to San Maggiore Hospital for urgent treatment in intensive care conditions although he knew it would be fruitless. He radioed for the medical helicopter and asked Dr Giovanni Gordini, the intensive care anesthetist in charge of the circuit's medical centre, to accompany Senna to San Maggiore. Watkins decided not to go there immediately as there was nothing on earth he could do to help Senna now. He knew it was just a matter of time before his heart gave out and he could not be revived.

During the short helicopter journey, Dr Gordini spoke to Dr Maria Teresa Fiandri at San Maggiore on the radio. He told her Senna had died instantly on impact. Fiandri said: "Dr Gordini warned me that there was little to do. Even though the track doctors had done their best, the picture was irreversible. From the brain standpoint, there was no more activity immediately after being hit."

She added poignantly: "He arrived at the hospital with no hope."

"Whether or not Ayrton was removed from the car while his heart was beating, or whether his supply of blood had halted or was still flowing, is irrelevant to the determination of when he died."
                                    Professor Pinto da Costa
                                            January 1997

CHAPTER 17

Resuscitation

A terminal injury and medical ethics

There is no doubt that Ayrton Senna died instantly when he hit the wall. He was not breathing and there was no heartbeat and therefore no pulse, when Professor Sid Watkins reached his car. But according to Watkins, there was just a very faint pulse, barely detectable. There is some debate now 21 years later whether that was true. Many people now feel there was no pulse and that Watkins, with his considerable skills and experience, brought Senna back to life and literally played God. No one wishes to disrespect the memory of Professor Watkins, who died in September 2012, but it is now almost certain he was economical with the exact truth. It is highly unlikely that Senna had a pulse when Watkins got to him, and that the correct medical procedure would have been to check his pupils and declare Senna dead at the scene. But Dr Richard Abbatt says it may not have been as simple as that: "It might be difficult to be certain about presence or absence of a pulse in the pressure and activity of the moment."

But bringing people back to life is quite a regular thing. It is often the case that people die and then are resuscitated, sometimes as much as an hour later. But these are not people with fatal injuries. One extreme case was that of English businessman Kevin Threlfall, who collapsed on a golf course after a severe heart attack and was without a pulse for nearly an hour. He was given continuous CPR and then defibrillated, which somehow kept his brain functioning for nearly 60 minutes. By the following morning, he had made a full recovery.

Senna was different because he was brain dead. But Watkins chose not to establish that until after he had got his heart going again. Only then did he lift his eyelids to see the extent of the injury.

It appears that after clearing his airways and intubating him, getting IV lines in and some new blood into his arm, Watkins massaged his heart and got a pulse.

But should Watkins, once he saw the extent of his injuries and knew that brain death had occurred, have been doing any of that?

Again Dr Abbatt says: "If Professor Watkins thought there was the possibility of a pulse i.e. cardiac output, he would try to resuscitate even in the presence of a brain injury because a brain injury causing unconsciousness might subsequently be treatable for example by evacuation of an intracerebral blood collection, which would only be identifiable on brain scans."

There was no better man in the world at this sort of thing than Sid Watkins. His surgical skills were no different from those of any other experienced neurosurgeon, but his great gift was knowing what to do and when to do it in an emergency. He could assess an injured patient and make decisions, taking in all the factors, to get them the right treatment as quickly as possible, which made a huge difference to the long-term outcome. Watkins directed the rescue doctors like a top conductor would direct an orchestra. Once when someone called him the 'Burt Bacharach of medical science', they weren't joking.

Watkins had saved many, many lives by quickly planning treatment and sourcing the best doctors and hospitals to get a patient well again after brain injuries. Many people believe that the outcome of Michael Schumacher's 2013 skiing injury would have been a lot better if Watkins had still been alive and able to take charge of his treatment.

But Watkins's resuscitation of Ayrton Senna had huge and immediate implications for the organisers and promoters of the race. Italian law required the race to be cancelled in such circumstances. But the official and actual times of death were over four hours apart and became the source of huge disagreement in the medical profession.

The day before, Ratzenberger was dead on impact. There was really no argument about that. All the medical rules had been broken, and he was not declared dead until an hour later when he was safely at San Maggiore hospital. Short of a stake through the heart, it is more or less impossible for drivers to die at the circuit now that fire, once the leading cause of driver death, is almost extinct in Formula One. Ratzenberger had the equivalent of a stake through the heart, but Watkins followed his instructions from Ecclestone and got him away from the circuit, officially still alive.

Those instructions endure today. When Jules Bianchi, the French driver, crashed in the 2014 Japanese Grand Prix, he was effectively dead at the scene but he did have a pulse and was correctly taken to first the circuit medical centre and then to hospital, ostensibly to be treated. The fact that he was taken to the medical centre and then hospital by ambulance was a strong indication that there was no hope for him. Otherwise, he would have been immediately airlifted from the crash scene. Officially, the reason the helicopter could not fly was attributed to the weather, but Bianchi was apparently brain damaged with no chance of recovery. When he got to hospital, he was immediately connected to life support machines to await a miracle that would have been medically impossible.

But the machine was kept on, seemingly at the request of his family, hoping for that miracle. The media were misinformed that he might recover, which the doctors issuing the statements must have known was impossible. Eventually, 10 months later, the machine was turned off.

Senna's injuries were much worse than Bianchi's and he was kept artificially alive by the extraordinary medical expertise available to Formula One, and Dr Fiandari, Bologna's chief medical officer, was adamant that Senna was still breathing on arrival in Bologna. Professor Watkins is equally adamant he had a pulse when he was put into the helicopter at the circuit, and Dr Gordini has vividly recalled the need to restart his heart during the helicopter trip.

But it is clear that, by any normal standards, he was dead on impact with the wall, and 200 million TV viewers saw his last spasm of life in the cockpit. The spasm was a sign of death.

But Watkins and his team supported his life as he lay on the ground at the circuit; apart from his head, his body was untouched. But had he regained consciousness, the brain damage would have left him severely handicapped and totally incapacitated, and Senna would never have wanted that. Accidents such as Senna's are almost always fatal, with the few survivors suffering terrible, irreversible brain damage. This is due to the effects on the brain of sudden deceleration, which causes structural damage to the brain tissues.

Estimates of the forces involved in the accident suggest a rate of deceleration equivalent to a 30-metre vertical drop, landing head first.

Medical personnel attending anyone with severe head injuries, such as Senna's, and believing the heart is still beating, have a three-step procedure.

The first is to ensure that the respiratory passages remain free so that the patient can breathe, usually by means of an emergency tracheotomy. This was performed on Senna immediately. The second is to stem the loss of blood and replace it. Senna lost a lot of blood, which was replaced. The third is immobilising the cervical spine. This was done as he was lifted from the car and onto the ground. After that is done, the urgent need is to reach the intensive-care department of a major hospital with the best facilities. It is for that reason that Sid Watkins ordered that Senna be removed straight to San Maggiore hospital and not to the circuit's well-equipped medical centre.

When he got to San Maggiore, brain scans were immediately performed. Dr Fiandri told Sid Watkins when he arrived that Senna had multiple fractures at the base of the skull, where his head had smashed into the carbon-fibre headrest of the monocoque. What had likely happened was that the right front wheel had shot up after impact like a catapult and violated the cockpit area where Senna was sitting. It impacted the right frontal area of his helmet, and the violence of the wheel's impact pushed his head back against the headrest, causing the fatal skull fractures. A piece of upright suspension attached to the wheel had partially penetrated his helmet and made an indent in his forehead. In addition, it appeared that a jagged piece of the upright assembly had penetrated the helmet visor just above his right eye. Any one of the three injuries would probably have killed him. The combination of them all made it certain. Only Senna's extremely high level of fitness meant he had momentarily survived. He suffered brain death on impact, but the lack of any physical injury to the rest of his body meant that his heart and lungs continued to function.

The neurosurgeon who examined Senna at the hospital said that the circumstances did not call for surgery because the wound was generalised in the cranium. But an X-ray of the damage to his skull and brain indicated he would not last long, even with a machine maintaining his vital functions. When Watkins got to the hospital after the race, he looked at the monitors of blood pressure, respiration and heart rate and realised the end was near, probably within the hour, and it was decided not to restart Senna's heart again when it stopped.

The autopsy done the following day found that the impact of the 130mph crash caused multiple injuries at the base of the cranium, resulting in respiratory insufficiency. There was crushing of the brain as it was forced against the wall of the cranium, causing diffuse bruising and oedema, increasing the intra-cranial pressure and causing brain death. The rupture of the artery caused blood loss and obstruction in the respiratory passages and the consequent heart failure.

With that sort of terminal injury, the ethics of applying the best medical talent to bringing someone back to life and not allowing them simply to pass on are highly questionable. But at a racetrack, with the best talent and the best facilities available, it is the natural thing for doctors to do. As Dr Abbatt said: "The difficulty is that you might not be able to assess fully the extent and severity of brain injury until cardiovascular resuscitation had been achieved and the patient stabilised sufficiently to undergo brain scans etc."

Professor Pinto da Costa, a Portuguese expert, noted: "From the ethical viewpoint, the procedure used for Ayrton's body was wrong. It involved dysthanasia, which means that a person has been kept alive improperly after biological death has taken place due to brain injuries so serious that the patient would never have been able to remain alive without mechanical means of support. There would have been no prospect of normal life and relationships.

"Whether or not Ayrton was removed from the car while his heart was beating, or whether his supply of blood had halted or was still flowing, is irrelevant to the determination of when he died. The autopsy showed that the crash caused multiple fractures at the base of the cranium, crushing the forehead, rupturing the artery and obstructing the respiratory passages.

"It is possible to resuscitate a dead person immediately after the heart stops through cardio-respiratory processes. The procedure is known as putting the patient on the machine. From the medical-legal viewpoint, in Ayrton's case, there is a subtle point: resuscitation measures were implemented. From the ethical point of view, this might well be condemned because the measures were not intended to be of strictly medical benefit to the patient but rather because they suited the commercial interest of the organisation.

"Resuscitation did in fact take place, with the tracheotomy performed, while the activity of the heart was restored with the assistance of cardio-respiratory devices. The attitude in question was certainly controversial. Any physician would know there was no possibility whatsoever of successfully restoring life in the condition in which Senna had been found."

Another expert, Professor Jose Pratas Vital, a neurosurgeon and a doctor who had been a long-standing member of the team at Estoril for the Portuguese Grand Prix, has a different view: "The people who conducted the autopsy stated that, on the evidence of his injuries, Senna was dead. They could not say that. He had injuries which lead to his death, but at that point the heart may still have been functioning."

The pathologist, Dr Carrado Cipolla, had his own definite view. He recorded Senna's official time of death as 2:17pm on Sunday 1st May 1994. It was the time of his cerebral death under Italian law under, the exact moment Senna impacted the wall at Tamburello. But he added that there was no doubt that cardiac death had occurred at 6:40pm. Cipolla said Senna's injuries were caused by a massive blow above the right eyebrow. Senna had not died from the impact of the crash but from a blow from part of the front suspension. Cipolla was in no doubt that the blow crushed the front part of Senna's brain, killing him instantly.

The FIA and the Automobile Club D'Italia still maintain that Senna was not killed instantly but died in hospital. The two organisations have little choice but to maintain that position as they could have been in serious trouble had it been ruled that they violated medical ethics and national Italian law in handling the deaths of Ratzenberger and Senna.

In truth, they were probably on the right side of the law with Senna and the wrong side with Ratzenberger. On both occasions, as he had done many times in the past, Sid Watkins found himself playing God.

Because a great driver, possibly the greatest driver, died on Sunday 1st May 1994, endless resources, time and effort have been put into establishing the exact circumstances of his death. The definitive answer, like the cause of the accident in the first place, has never been found.

CHAPTER 18

Watkins Tells Ecclestone

"He's dead"

As Adriane Galisteu watched Senna's motionless body being loaded into a helicopter on television at Ayrton Senna's house in the Algarve, the lounge was beginning to fill up with people, mainly neighbours concerned for the well being of Juraci, his housekeeper.

Some of the neighbours handled the situation tactfully and others seemed to have no sense of what was going through the two women's heads. One idiot pointed out the red stain on the ground after Senna had been moved. It startled Adriane before another neighbour tried to reassure her, saying it was a new kind of fire extinguisher foam. She hadn't noticed the stain but was under no illusions as to what it was and later remembered thinking to herself at that moment: "Nobody ever thought Ayrton Senna would die in a racing car. Neither had I."

In truth, Adriane knew he was dead but did not choose to accept reality. She carried on as if he would be coming home soon with something relatively minor like his arm in plaster.

That afternoon, Dr Maria Teresa Fiandri was watching the race on television in her apartment in Bologna. The mother of five boys, she was Bologna's Chief Medical Officer and head of the Anaesthesia and Resuscitation Department. She had worked at the San Maggiore for 29 years. As soon as she saw Senna had hit the wall, and from the movement of the head, she concluded it was something very serious. She grabbed her white coat and 32 minutes later was pulling her car into the courtyard car park at San Maggiore reserved for doctors.

Meanwhile, Sid Watkins had to deal with Bernie Ecclestone. As he watched the white and orange helicopter take off from Tamburello with his friend in the back, he wanted to grab his bag and get out of Imola as fast as he could. But he had responsibilities to the drivers still left in the race, and Sid Watkins took his responsibilities very seriously.

It didn't take long for Ecclestone to call. His personal radio buzzed at 2:41pm. He didn't need to look down to see who it was; he knew it would be Ecclestone. Once again that afternoon, Watkins hesitated and held the radio to his ear for a full 20 seconds before speaking.

He had grim news and knew there was no point sugar coating it. As soon as he heard Ecclestone's voice, he cut him off and just said, "He's dead."

Ecclestone understood immediately, and there was a long silence as he took in what must have been absolutely devastating news. Neither man spoke for at least a half a minute until Ecclestone asked: "How?" Watkins started to tell him the details until Ecclestone stopped him and said he had heard enough. Ecclestone didn't really need to know any more as he trusted Watkins implicitly to handle things in the right way. He also knew that there was no doubt about what Watkins was telling him – that Senna was effectively dead even though he also told him he had a pulse and would not survive for very much longer. The two men spoke for another two minutes and neither has ever revealed what was said.

After speaking to Watkins, Ecclestone immediately went to race control where he found the room in absolute chaos. The local Italian officials had received news direct from the accident site and knew the situation was grave, although they did not quite understand how grave. They were unsure what to do next. Ecclestone grabbed Charlie Whiting and told him to get the race restarted. As he left, he bumped into Williams team manager, Ian Harrison, telling him he knew nothing.

Sid Watkins had done his job perfectly, and now he knew Charlie Whiting would get the race restarted and over with so that Formula One could get on with dealing with the death of its superstar.

As soon as he had finished with Ecclestone, Watkins spoke to Martin Whitaker, Formula One's press delegate and chief spokesman. Watkins was more circumspect with Whitaker and told him that Senna had received a bad head injury but was alive and had been taken unconscious to San Maggiore hospital and to await further news. Why Watkins did not tell Whitaker the truth is uncertain, but it is likely that he and Ecclestone had concocted a version of events they wished to be released to the media in those two minutes of conversation. This is speculation but it is the only logical reason why Watkins delivered two different versions of the same story to two different people.

As Ecclestone walked back to his motorhome, he was a complete mess inside but he knew he had to carry on and that the whole place would fall apart unless he was strong. He had experienced all these emotions 24 years earlier on the afternoon of Saturday 6th September 1970, when 28-year-old Jochen Rindt was killed in a remarkably similar accident to Senna's. Like Senna, Rindt was Formula One's superstar, and Ecclestone was Rindt's personal manager, his business partner and his best friend. They couldn't have been closer.

It had been a beautiful Italian Saturday, and Rindt had all but won the world championship after a dominant season. His wife Nina was sitting on the pit wall as Rindt went out in the final qualifying session. Like Senna's Williams-Renault, Rindt's Lotus-Ford was unstable, and he left the road inexplicably and hit a barrier sideways at high speed and rebounded back onto the run-off area. The reason for the accident was never known although it was apparent a brake shaft had failed and likely caused it. Rindt was technically alive when he was put in the ambulance but died on his way to hospital. Ecclestone was devastated and left motor racing altogether for a period while he got over it.

It is likely that those thoughts were going through his head as he walked back. On the way, he ran straight into Betise Assumpcao and Leonardo Da Silva, who were going to race control.

Whatever other people were being told, Ecclestone decided it was his duty to tell them the truth. But then once again that weekend, Ecclestone's thinking got muddled. Ecclestone is a much more emotional man than many believe. In a highly charged situation, his first thought is not always his best thought. He failed to see the necessity of going along himself with the fiction he had created externally. He got himself into a very atypical muddle when he told Leonardo da Silva that his brother was dead straight after Martin Whitaker had made a statement to the press that Senna was gravely injured but alive.

It was to cause Ecclestone immense trouble that has continued to this day because he then launched into a full-scale cover-up, where lie was told on top of lie, which made things worse. Only after Sid Watkins's death did the truth to come out. And it was all so unnecessary.

As all this drama was unfolding, Sid Watkins directed the clean-up of the accident scene. As the race was clearly going to be restarted, the scene of the accident had to be made perfect. In ideal circumstances, it would have been cordoned off and a canvas cover erected over the car and everything around it whilst investigators got to work. But Watkins knew that was not the way Formula One worked. He knew the race would go on.

As he surveyed the scene, he realised no one had touched the area where they had treated Senna. The marshals were waiting for Watkins's lead. He went and picked up Senna's helmet. But as he looked around, he couldn't find either his own gloves or Senna's, and neither pair was ever seen again. A souvenir hunter had picked them up: probably one of the many Italian officials who attended the scene.

As they finished off, another drama was happening in the air. The 20-minute helicopter ride was barely three minutes old when Senna's heart stopped. Dr Gordini worked on him frantically in the very cramped conditions of the helicopter bay and quickly got his heart going again.

Then, with a last glance at the place where his very good friend had been killed, Watkins got back to the medical car and Mario Casoni drove it straight to the medical centre, where more journalists were waiting after having been told that Senna would be taken there.

Watkins ignored the journalists, went straight in and started talking to Dr Servadei with details of Senna's condition. Servadei got on the phone and gave the waiting trauma team a full briefing of what to expect when the helicopter arrived.

Watkins was having to deal with his own personal grief at the same time as organising Senna's care, and as he turned round he saw that Josef Leberer had come into the medical centre. They didn't need to exchange words. Leberer remembered: "I saw Professor Watkins and he just looked in my eyes, and then I knew it was going to be a very serious thing.

"He didn't say anything." After the silence, Watkins briefed him. At that moment, Pasquale Lattuneddu, Bernie Ecclestone's assistant, walked in and asked Leberer to follow him to Bernie Ecclestone's motorhome.

WATKINS TELLS ECCLESTONE

"I really did not know what to do.
I had never seen such a raw pain."
Betise Assumpcao
Sunday 1st May 1994

CHAPTER 19

He's Dead. "No, It's His Head"

Bernie Ecclestone juggles death

A s the drama unfolded, Leonardo Da Silva walked from the TV Globo commentary box, where he had been watching the race, down to the Williams garage. Leonardo had been with his fellow Brazilians but came looking for Betise Assumpcao as soon as Senna went off. Despite accompanying his brother to many races in Europe, Leonardo had never learnt to speak English. As he stood in the garage watching the monitors he was getting increasingly agitated and fired questions at Betise Assumpcao, but she had no answers. Leonardo was a confident young man, used to getting his own way. He was not at all overawed by his brother and his lack of English was considered a blessing by people who knew him in Europe. He acted the part of a scion of a very rich family and did not have the perceptive nature, the natural humility and keen sense of the awareness of life possessed by his brother.

Up to then Assumpcao had focused on waiting for Senna to return and controlling his response to the accident. When she realised he was not coming back to the garage and had been airlifted to hospital, she turned her attention to keeping control of Leonardo.

As Leonardo looked around, he could tell by the look on everyone's faces that the situation was becoming increasingly serious. Assumpcao stood by Leonardo's side, but they couldn't tell what was happening any more than TV viewers could in Brazil. TV Globo were running non-stop coverage of the rescue scene although other broadcasters, including the BBC, had cut the transmission out of respect for Senna once they realised the accident was serious. The BBC had the benefit of its own roving pit lane camera and had an alternative feed, which gave Murray Walker a chance to talk about anything but the accident. But many other broadcasters did not, including Eurosport, which was receiving pretty graphic images from a low-flying helicopter. Eurosport's production team was based in Paris controlling the feed. John Watson, its lead commentator, spoke to them and asked them if they could cut to another feed as he was finding it very unpleasant and disrespectful to Senna when there was really little he could add. He was told in no uncertain terms that this was the only feed and, if he didn't feel up to it, they could take over the commentary in Paris. Watson, a veteran of the Grand Prix circuits and a five-time race winner, could sense the situation was critical and the outcome could be fatal. But he could not say that without first-hand knowledge, which he did not have.

As Betise Assumpcao was soothing Leonardo and keeping him quiet, suddenly the possibility that Senna might be seriously injured hit her when she saw him lying by the track: "They got him out of the car and laid him on the ground. I saw his feet just falling open and I just knew as your feet don't do that unless you are completely unconscious. I knew, even if I didn't want to know." But she said nothing to Leonardo, hoping against hope that her amateur diagnosis was wrong.

Phone calls were coming into the Williams garage from Viviane, Senna's sister, who was watching the race in São Paulo with the Da Silva family. Viviane had 101 questions but Leonardo could not answer any of them. Although Senna was driving for Williams, the team had no information at all. Frank Williams sent team manager, Ian Harrison, off to race control to see what he could find out. But all he found was chaos and the stewards running around like proverbial chickens with their heads cut off. Eventually, Bernie Ecclestone was called to race control by Charlie Whiting as he sought to calm them down so he could think about restarting the race.

As soon as Senna was loaded into the helicopter, Betise Assumpcao grabbed Leonardo and they headed off to the only place they could think of to get information: the race control tower.

As they walked, they passed by Bernie Ecclestone's blue and grey motorhome just as he was going back up the steps. Ecclestone was stopped in his tracks when he spotted Leonardo, and he froze, staring straight into his eyes. After a moment he said simply: "I need to talk to you" and, as Betise translated, Ecclestone grabbed him by his shirt and literally hauled him up the steps into his motorhome. Betise followed, but just as she was about to enter, Ecclestone barked, "No, not you," and barred her way. Ecclestone did not realise that Leonardo hardly spoke a world of English and that he would need Betise to interpret. Quickly, she explained: "Leo does not speak a word of English."

Ecclestone immediately understood and, nodding, beckoned her to follow him also. The two men had never talked before, although Leonardo had sat by the side of his brother many times in meetings in the motorhome.

The three of them stepped into the main saloon surrounded by multiple TV monitors, feeding every live camera that was operating. Sitting around the table was Slavica Ecclestone, rubbing her eyes. She had clearly been crying. Betise wondered why, but she was soon to find out.

Ecclestone sat down in his swivel chair, faced them and said calmly: "He's dead." It was the only way he knew to impart the news. For him, there was no point in disguising the news or trying to soften it. He also knew he had a duty to tell Senna's brother the truth.

Ecclestone himself was trying to come to terms with something he had heard only 10 minutes before. Senna was one of his best friends, one of less than two dozen people in the world he regarded as a friend. His wife doted on him and he was like an uncle to his two daughters, Tamara and Petra. He couldn't remember how many times Senna had stayed overnight at his house in Chelsea Square when he was in London. Of all the drivers Ecclestone had known, save for Jochen Rindt, he was closest to Ayrton Senna.

But his two words gave Betise Assumpcao an enormous problem. Firstly, she was absorbing the news and suppressing her own feelings. Her boss, a man she loved more than life itself, was gone and, in an instant, she knew her own future would be very different after that day. She also knew that she had the biggest challenger of her life handling the PR of her own client's death – the ultimate task for any human being. But she knew she had to remain calm and do her job and contain her own grief. She thought for a few seconds and said to herself: "How can I translate it and tell Leo in a more adequate manner, considering he only spoke two words?" As she remembered: "I turned to Leo and, in the most gentle and caring way I could master, said: "I am really sorry to have to translate this to you but Bernie is telling us Ayrton has died."

Leonardo was absolutely stunned, it was not what he was expecting to hear. He did not have the sort of personality that could handle the bald truth without masses of sugar coating.

But there was no sugar coating she could apply. Her job, at that moment, was simply to translate what Ecclestone had said. After a few moments, Leonardo started to cry uncontrollably, and she wanted to put her arms around him but was too stunned herself to do anything. According to Assumpcao, Ecclestone then told her: "But we are not announcing it yet, so the race won't be stopped."

It may have been the truth, but they were words that Ecclestone would vehemently deny later. He also denied telling Leonardo his brother was dead, insisting he had said: "It's his head."

Then Ecclestone and his wife watched silently as Leonardo became more and more distraught, screaming and crying out. He started shaking as if he was having a fit.

Assumpcao said: "I really did not know what to do. I had never seen such a raw pain." Leonardo's crying set Slavica off, and the two wept openly together. Even Assumpcao lost her self-control for the first and last time that day, crying openly. Only Ecclestone was calm, and he casually picked out an apple from the bowl on the table took a few bites and threw it back down. He put his arms round his wife's shoulders and stared at the ceiling. He remembered she was shaking like a leaf.

When she recovered her poise, Assumpcao worked on Leonardo, trying to calm him down. It took more than five minutes. Then he sat frozen to the spot in a stunned silence, seemingly incapable of doing or saying anything. She held his hand tightly and said: "Leo, I am truly, truly sorry. I don't know what else to say to you, but one thing is certain. You have to pull yourself together as well as you can, and you need to call your parents in Brazil and tell them. They'll be worried sick, and I cannot be the one to do that. They will need to hear it from you. I am sure it will be more comforting for them as well."

Ecclestone got the number from her and dialled it himself, handing her the receiver. She passed it to Leonardo, who tried to get his words out to

Viviane on the other end of the line over 7,000 miles away.

At that moment, Martin Whitaker burst in, and he and Ecclestone talked quietly beyond Assumpcao's earshot for a few minutes. She could tell it was not an easy conversation. She and Whitaker were very good friends and former colleagues at McLaren when Whittaker had been head of communications at the team and Senna had been number one driver.

Talking to Whittaker, straightaway Ecclestone realised he had made a mistake telling them the driver was dead. In fact, it was the exact opposite of what Whittaker had just announced to journalists a few minutes earlier in the media centre. He motioned for Assumpcao to join them and told her: "What I said in the press room is that Ayrton has head injuries and has been taken to the hospital." She replied: "Bernie just told us he is dead. Leo is on the phone telling his family Ayrton has died."

Whittaker was adamant: "No, what I informed the press is that he had severe head injuries." Assumpcao replied: "Yes, I know that, but we already know he's dead."

In reality, both were in their own way correct. Senna had suffered cerebral death but not cardiac death. Only later would the official time of death be declared as 2:17pm.

It became obvious what had happened. Sid Watkins had spoken to Ecclestone and told him the blunt truth that Senna, although technically breathing and with a pulse, was brain dead and gone. He had told Whittaker a different version that he had a severe head injury and was alive but in grave condition. Of course, Whittaker had the truth as it was at that moment. Ecclestone had the truth as it was and would be in a few hours time. It was a momentous miscommunication that would come back to haunt Ecclestone later.

Realising that they were in the middle of a very difficult situation, Assumpcao and Whittaker went off to a small back room to talk. She remembers: "I pulled him into the small room at the back of the motorhome. We had worked closely few years back when he was McLaren's press officer, so I thought I could rely on him." She told him: "Martin, I don't think you understand the importance of the situation. Leo has already told his family in Brazil Ayrton is dead. They are already going through extreme pain." Whittaker replied: "Betise, I understand that. But I have told the press he has head injuries and has gone to hospital. I did not tell them he is dead." She said: "Yes, Martin, but what I am trying to tell you is that, if you insist on this, I will have to leave this room, go and tell Leo that Ayrton is still alive and, consequently, give his mother and father, some hope that might not exist."

Whittaker, not fully aware of what had gone on 15 minutes earlier, was adamant: "Betise, he is not dead. That is the information I'm giving out."

With that, she went back to the saloon and sat down and told Leonardo that his brother was not dead and to call Brazil again and relay the latest situation.

In scenes that, if they had not been so serious, were more worthy of a Brian Rix comic stage farce than the stark tragic reality of what was really unfolding, Leonardo told Viviane that he had got it wrong and that their brother was alive. Viviane passed the phone first to Neyde and then to Milton who were naturally delighted to receive this news, pleased there had been a mistake and that there was now some hope.

At that point, even Betise Assumpcao became convinced and believed that Ayrton Senna might recover from his injuries. Only Watkins and Ecclestone and the doctors attending Senna knew different. Martin Whitaker was clearly of the opinion that Senna might recover.

Meanwhile, Leonardo put the telephone down and completely lost it. Having to tell his parents their son was dead and then he was not dead, and handling his own emotions at the same time, put him over the edge. For once, Ecclestone had no idea what to do and how to control the situation he had created. Sensing his discomfort and that he was not used to not being in control, Betise Assumpcao suggested they find Josef Leberer to come and calm Leonardo down and take charge. Ecclestone immediately sent Pasquale Lattuneddu, his then minder, off to find Josef Leberer and to bring him to the motorhome. Lattuneddu quickly found Leberer wasn't in the Williams garage and someone told him to try the medical centre, which is where he found him talking to Sid Watkins. Watkins had already told Leberer Senna was dead. But he was mightily relieved to be told, when he reached Ecclestone's motorhome, that Senna was not dead and that his task was to take charge of Leonardo. He said: "I had to calm his brother down." At that point, Leonardo didn't know what to believe. Leberer told him he was in a serious state but still alive and they should get to San Maggiore hospital as soon as possible. Leonardo calmed down enough to make another phone call to his parents in Brazil from the motorhome telephone. He told them he was leaving for the San Maggiore hospital. Meanwhile, Ecclestone arranged for his helicopter to take them all to the hospital. They left immediately with Julian Jakobi and Celso Lemos, who were waiting outside the motorhome, following in his hire car.

After his motorhome emptied, Ecclestone went off to talk to Max Mosley, the FIA president. Afterwards, he toured the pitlane, assuring everyone that everything was being done for Senna. What he was sure of was that the race would restart and run to a conclusion. It always did. That was the way of Formula One.

Then he went into the Williams garage to talk to Frank Williams. He told him that everything possible was being done for Senna but that it didn't look good. He was not about to repeat the mistake he had made with Leonardo Da Silva. Just as with Ecclestone, emotions from 1970 were flooding Frank Williams's memory, taking him back to the day Piers Courage was killed in a Williams team car. Ironically he had, like Senna, been killed by a flying wheel hitting his helmet.

But no one could sense Frank Williams's turmoil nor Bernie Ecclestone's, who was doing what he had always done for Formula One: creating stability in a very unstable environment.

*"They were all listening to me, hoping
I would say some good news."*
Galvao Bueno
Sunday 1st May 1994

CHAPTER 20

Tragedy and Chaos

Four hours of misinformation

Just after four o'clock, with the noise of the race still in their ears, Leonardo Da Silva, Betise Assumpcao and Josef Leberer were waiting at the track heliport for Bernie Ecclestone's helicopter to take them to San Maggiore hospital in Bologna, 35 kilometres away.

Antonio Braga had taken charge of the immediate family arrangements and was particularly concerned about getting Adriane to Bologna. He knew Senna would want her at his bedside.

Braga racked his brains as it was not going to be easy to get a flight from Faro or Lisbon directly to Bologna on a late Sunday afternoon. He thought about asking Captain O'Mahoney to fly to Faro to pick her up, but that would have been a round trip of seven hours. Finally, Braga used the phone in the McLaren motorhome to call his wife Luiza, who was in their house in Sintra near Lisbon with their teenage daughters, Joanna and Maria. Like everyone, Luiza had been watching the race on television and wanted an update. After Braga told her what he knew, he told her to phone Adriane and tell her she had to get to Bologna as soon as possible. Between them, they decided the best option was to charter a plane in Faro to bring her to Bologna. By this time, Braga was almost certain that Senna was dying but thought there would be time for her to say goodbye.

As soon as she put down the phone to her husband, Luiza called Quinta do Lago. She told Adriane: "Braga called me from Imola. It's extremely serious. You have to go there immediately." Adriane replied: "Luiza, come with me. Don't leave me alone."

Luiza agreed to accompany her there; she said she would charter a jet in Lisbon and pick Adriane up at Faro. She told her she would be there at around five o'clock. The flight to Faro would only take half an hour, but renting a jet at short notice on a Sunday proved difficult, and it would take three and a half hours for Luiza Braga to hire the plane and fly to Faro.

After putting the phone down to his wife, Braga returned to the TV Globo cabin and discussed with Galvao Bueno what they should do. They agreed to leave for the hospital as soon as the race was over. Then he went back to McLaren's motorhome and called Senna's father, Milton, who, along with his wife Neyde, and like every other Brazilian that morning, was following events on television. Braga told them it was serious and for them to stand by to come to Bologna. Milton told Braga he would also try and charter a jet to get them all to Bologna as quickly as possible. It was now a race for Senna's nearest and dearest to get to San Maggiore to say goodbye before he died. Braga was praying they would all make it.

In Brazil, it was just after 10 o'clock in the morning and the streets of the major cities were quiet on that Sunday morning. Brazilians had woken up to the news from Europe that their favourite son had been gravely injured in an accident. It seemed the whole country was glued to their television sets awaiting news. As the word of the accident spread, people huddled in front of their sets, hanging on Galvao Bueno's every pronouncement.

Bueno was well aware that he was broadcasting to half of the Brazilian population, who were listening to his words. He also knew that Milton, Neyde Da Silva and Senna's sister, Viviane, would be watching. He found it a terrible responsibility, as he said: "They were all listening to me, hoping I would say some good news. Reginaldo and Antonio, who was like a father to Ayrton, kept looking at me speechless, having the same worry. Through my earphones I was constantly being pushed forward by our manager, and also from our studios in Brazil, they kept asking me to go on. At least three times, I left the cabin to catch some breath. And because I had this great friendship with Ayrton, people started coming to our cabin: Barrichello's manager, Christian's Fittipaldi's girlfriend, Marianna, everybody apparently expecting something to hope for."

TV Globo had the best sources of information, and even though Bueno was reluctant to tell what he knew, a news reporter at the studio had already given two bulletins on Senna's condition. It was stark news and Brazilians were told at 10 o'clock that Senna had severe brain damage and would

likely never race again. As Senna struggled for life, and TV Globo commentators predicted the worst, millions of Brazilians held their breath, not
quite believing what they were witnessing on live television. The streets of
Rio de Janeiro and São Paulo stayed eerily deserted.

Ten minutes before the end of the race, Bueno realised that it would take
them too long to get to the hospital by car with all the race traffic. He told
Braga to go and find a helicopter. Braga went off and asked Jo Ramirez,
the McLaren team manager, if he could organise it. Ramirez told them
they could have the helicopter he had booked to take Senna to the airport.

Brazilian driver Christian Fittipaldi sent a message to Bueno over his pit
radio asking him if he could accompany them all to the hospital. When the
Arrows mechanic arrived with the note, Bueno sent a message back to the
Footwork Arrows pit telling him to be ready as soon as the race was over.

As soon as Michael Schumacher crossed the line, Bueno threw off his
headphones and ran out of the cabin. He left the studio back in Brazil
to carry on broadcasting. He didn't care any more about his job; he just
wanted to be with his friend at the end of his life. He also wanted to play
no part in the reporting of Senna's death on television. That was a burden
for others, not him. He left Reginaldo Leme in charge of the TV Globo
cabin and said he should come to the hospital in the hire car when the
broadcast was finally finished.

Braga went straight to the McLaren motorhome where he knew he could
use McLaren's phone and pick up any messages as Bueno rushed to the
Arrows motorhome where he found Fittipaldi half dressed. Bueno took
one look at him and said they were off. Fittipaldi pleaded with Bueno to
wait. Bueno told him to come to the McLaren motorhome, where he was
meeting up with Antonio Braga.

At McLaren, he found Braga surrounded by a group of people including
Ron Dennis, Gerhard Berger and Jo Ramirez. Berger was recommending
that Braga call a neurosurgeon he knew in Paris who had once saved Jean
Alesi from brain damage after an accident. Berger said that he could organise a jet to bring the doctor from Paris. Braga told him to get on with
it. Then Berger asked if he could hitch a ride with them to the hospital.

Bueno waited impatiently for Fittipaldi to arrive, and as soon as he did,
they ran for the helicopter. Suddenly, Bueno realised he still had the keys

to the hire car in his pocket. Luckily at that moment, he bumped into Jose Pinto of the Portuguese TV company, threw him the keys and told him to give them to Reginaldo Leme with instructions to meet him at San Maggiore.

As they rushed to the helicopter pad, Fittipaldi, who had a cell phone, phoned a TV Globo bureau reporter who was already at the hospital and who told him he had heard that Senna would not last long.

After a short wait for the helicopter to touch down, Braga, Berger, Fittipaldi and Bueno took off for San Maggiore. The trip was made in absolute silence. These were four men as close to Senna as it was possible to be. The tragedy that had unfolded that afternoon defied any meaningful words.

Meanwhile, at the family farm in Tatui, Viviane Senna's husband, Flavio Lalli, had arrived and had taken charge of a distraught family. Milton Da Silva was trying to charter a jet but was finding it difficult to get one big enough to make the 7,000 mile journey non-stop.

In Portugal, Luiza Braga tried frantically to charter a plane, as Juraci helped Adriane pack enough clothes for three days. She told herself she would be by his bedside, waiting for him to recover. It was the only possible thought, and it kept her going.

As she waited, a neighbour told her she had heard he had recovered consciousness. Adriane's mother, Ema, phoned from São Paulo and asked what was happening. Adriane told her she hoped Senna would recover and that it was not as serious as was thought. Her no-nonsense mother immediately disabused her of that and made her face reality. TV Globo was delivering far more accurate information to Brazilian viewers than the European television channels, which were waiting for an official bulletin and shying away from the reality. Adriane's mother told her that only a miracle could save him. After putting the phone down from her mother, Adriane felt her emotions going out of control. She had a terrible headache and took some tablets.

Adriane then phoned a distraught Neyde Da Silva at Tatui in Brazil and tried to calm her down by telling her she had heard her son had recovered consciousness. Neyde told her the family had chartered a plane to Bologna and would leave in mid-afternoon but would probably not arrive at the hospital until six o'clock the following morning.

Meanwhile, as soon as the race was over and the cars had stopped, Sid Watkins ran to the medical centre. He found Lotus Team Principal Peter Collins waiting for him. Collins and Watkins were close friends, and he was closer to Collins than to any other team principal. Collins had come to find out about Senna, but he feigned concern over his mechanics, which he already knew were alright. When Watkins told Collins his mechanics would be fine, Collins said sheepishly, not really wanting to ask: "Is Senna in a bad way?" Watkins simply said: "Yes". Collins replied: "Is there any hope?" Watkins shook his head and replied: "No". Collins was the first of the Formula One fraternity to find out the truth that all the others feared.

With that, Watkins threw his overalls on the floor. He knew his place was at the hospital, and he told Dr Franco Servadei they would take the medical helicopter, which had returned from San Maggiore.

Just as Watkins and Servadei were about to leave, two Italian policemen arrived and demanded entry to the medical centre. The police had been tipped off that the accident would probably be fatal and they requested that Watkins hand over Senna's helmet. He had no choice but to comply. With that, they took off straight for the hospital. Watkins desperately wanted to get away from the gloom that had fallen over Imola. It was a terrible place to be at that moment.

Separately, Julian Jakobi and Celso Lemos got into their hire car and started the drive to San Maggiore. Surprisingly, the traffic was thin and, instead of rushing off after the race, fans had stayed on to hear news of Senna and talk about the awful events they had witnessed that day. Like everyone else, they hoped for good news.

The 12 of them – Betise Assumpcao, Leonardo Da Silva, Josef Leberer, Sid Watkins, Dr Franco Servadei, Gerhard Berger, Dr Gordini, Galvao Bueno, Antonio Braga, Christian Fittipaldi, Celso Lemos and Julian Jakobi – would join together at San Maggiore in a vigil for their friend. They all silently prayed for the miracle they knew would not come. Strangely no one from the Williams team came to the hospital.

Back at Imola, word of Senna's desperate condition had circulated around the media centre. The journalists from over 50 countries, who all knew Senna personally, were enveloped by a shroud of dread. They knew he would never race again, and many were under no illusion that he would be dead before midnight.

The British writer David Tremayne had been tipped off by Peter Collins, and he was starting to write an obituary for the next day's edition of the London *Independent*. Other British journalists with national newspaper contracts followed suit. In truth, many of them hadn't much cared for Ayrton Senna when he was alive – they tended to favour Alain Prost – but the enormity of his imminent passing weighed heavily on them. Suddenly, any lingering enmity was forgotten.

TRAGEDY AND CHAOS

"I was just thinking 'shit'
what is happening now."
Gerhard Berger
Sunday 1st May 1994

CHAPTER 21

The Show Goes On

Schumacher takes victory

The Formula One drivers had little idea as to the severity of Ayrton Senna's accident when they lined up on the grid for the restart of the race. Those that were interested knew, like Christian Fittipaldi, but the other drivers just focused on the restart and not on Senna. Fittipaldi had sent his girlfriend Marianna to the TV Globo cabin as he knew Galvao Bueno would know what was going on.

The other drivers knew that Senna had had an accident and that there was no big problem and that he had been taken to hospital as a precautionary measure. Team principals, managers and engineers were not keen to burden their drivers with information when there was still a race to be run.

Even Gerhard Berger was not aware of the extent of his friend's injuries. As he remembered: "At the time, I didn't realise how bad it was. I didn't see his accident as I was in the car behind him, but you get a feeling from the atmosphere. And there was a strange atmosphere." Bertrand Gachot, another close friend, recalls he was told that Senna had only broken his leg: "They said he was going to be okay."

Professor Watkins calmly went about his business talking to as few people as he could. He replenished his medical bag from the stores in the medical centre and walked back to his car to await the restart. They went through the normal pre-race routine exchanging few words with Mario Casoni and his two doctors in the back.

Race regulations at the time in the event of a restart meant that the sixth lap would be cancelled, the seventh lap ignored and the San Marino Grand Prix would be restarted from the beginning of the sixth lap. The overall result would now be decided on aggregate of the first five laps and whatever laps were run in the second part. In the event, the second race ran to a total of 53 laps plus five from the first race: 58 laps in all.

At 2:55pm, 37 minutes after Ayrton Senna's accident, the race restarted. The formation lap saw Heinz-Harald Frentzen stall his Sauber-Mercedes on the grid, and he was forced to start from the pit lane behind the other cars. The rest of the cars started from the grid in the order they were when the race was stopped.

For once, Michael Schumacher's Benetton-Ford made a poor start and Gerhard Berger's Ferrari took the lead although he was technically second as Schumacher still led the race overall due to his being ahead of Berger before the race was stopped. It was very confusing for spectators, but the Italian crowd went wild as usual as a Ferrari led the race.

Damon Hill, from third on the grid, ran into Schumacher attempting to overtake him at the Tosa corner. Hill had damaged his nose, ruining the aerodynamics, and dropped back to last place before being forced to make a pit stop in order to fit a new nose cone. His chances of winning were gone.

A very fast Schumacher took the lead on track on lap 12 when Berger ran wide, before almost immediately relinquishing his overall race lead to Berger when he made his first pit stop. Schumacher was running a three-stop strategy, which was why he was able to run so fast and keep the pressure on Senna earlier in the race. When he came back out after a lightning stop, he really put the hammer down. Berger pitted at the end of lap 15 for his first of two scheduled stops. But then he just retired a lap later, citing a "handling problem".

So Mika Häkkinen led his first ever lap of a Formula One race before he pitted at the end of lap 18. After the pit stops had all finished, Schumacher was in the lead. Schumacher's extra pace as a result of a lighter fuel load meant he was able to pull out enough of a gap to Häkkinen, which enabled him to make his extra pit stop.

Häkkinen's pace was very slow, allowing Nicola Larini to leapfrog him when the second round of pit stops were made. By then, Schumacher was already off into the distance and his remaining pit stops didn't matter – he had all the time in the world.

On lap 48 overall, Michele Alboreto came in for his second pit stop, but as he left, the rear-right wheel came loose from the Minardi as it left the pit lane. The wheel bounced down the pit lane, hitting two Ferrari mechanics and then two Lotus mechanics, who were immediately carted off to the medical centre for urgent treatment.

Berger remembered: "I was just thinking 'shit, what is happening now?'"

Alboreto was glad it was over and he leapt out of his car, made sure the mechanics were being looked after, and then threw his helmet down in the pit garage and ran straight to the medical centre to talk to Dr Servidei. Servidei didn't see any point in holding back and told him Senna would soon be dead. Servidei told him the full truth of what had happened and Senna's condition.

Alboreto, one of Senna's closest friends, walked straight back to the Ferrari garage to speak to Gerhard Berger, his old team mate at Ferrari. Berger was hanging around in the Ferrari garage, watching the race and waiting for a lift to the hospital with the TV Globo people. Alboreto told him: "It's very bad with Ayrton, he's in hospital in Bologna and very critical." He said he was certain from speaking to Dr Servidei that Senna would not make it and would be dead by nightfall. Berger said to him: "Why are all these things happening?" Berger resolved to try and get to the hospital straight after the race.

The only interest left in the race was the battle for third place. Häkkinen's McLaren-Peugeot could not maintain the pace of the race, which was slow anyway, and Karl Wendlinger started to catch him in the Sauber-Mercedes. The Sauber team had never had a podium finish and it injected some excitement. Somehow, Häkkinen held off Wendlinger's charge and he came home fourth, still a good result for Sauber. Ukyo Katayama ended up fifth for Tyrrell, and Damon Hill was able to battle back to finish sixth for one point: a point that would prove vital as the season wore on but didn't seem much consolation then.

Michael Schumacher won the race ahead of Nicola Larini. It proved to be the absolute highlight of Larini's career, his only podium, and he would only score points once again. No driver who has come second in a world championship race ever had a worse career than him.

As for Schumacher, he maintained his 100 per cent season, which no one had predicted or foreseen at the start of 1994. Schumacher had 30 points after three races.

Karl Wendlinger rode back to the pits on Mika Häkkinen's McLaren after his car broke down on the slowing-down lap.

For Sid Watkins, the one and half hours of the race had been terrible as he watched the cars go by. It seemed interminable. But he breathed a sigh of relief as the race finally ended at 4:20pm with no further incidents, and he rushed out of the car leaving the door open and Mario Casoni alone to finish up.

The podium ceremony was a very sombre affair. It had already been decided to dispense with the Moet et Chandon champagne ceremony out of respect for Roland Ratzenberger. Michael Schumacher had been told that Senna wouldn't make it by Flavio Briatore, who had been told by Bernie Ecclestone. But both were warned not to say anything publicly until it was announced.

So no champagne was sprayed by Schumacher, Larini or Häkkinen. It should have been the greatest day of Larini's life, but he felt nothing for coming second. The drivers were very upset and wished they weren't there.

The post-race podium press conferences were very difficult affairs. Michael Schumacher was deep in thought. He looked dazed. It must have been running through his mind that he was now favourite for the championship but that the star of the sport was gone. He hardly made any sense as he took in the news and said: "I hope we learn from this. I think there is a lot to learn from this. And we have to use this and things like this. They shouldn't happen without taking the experience from it."

Meanwhile, Murray Walker, who would have been packing up and leaving the circuit as quickly as he could, prepared for a long night assisting with BBC news bulletins. The story would be leading the news, and Walker went to the media centre to prepare to deliver his own homage to his great friend, which ultimately would prove to be the most eloquent words he ever delivered on television. Walker had lost his favourite ever driver in Formula One, and he had known all of them.

THE SHOW GOES ON

"I have seen thousands of these devices and removed them for checks. The two boxes were intact even though they had some scratches."

Fabrizio Nosco
Sunday 1st May 1994

CHAPTER 22

The Battle of the Boxes

Patrick Head is desperate to retrieve the data recorders

A s soon as Ayrton Senna was taken away in the medical helicopter, a circuit truck arrived with a crane and hoisted Senna's car on to it and propped it up on the detached wheels. It was driven round the circuit hanging off the crane bouncing on the tyres until it arrived at the parc fermé, where it was officially impounded and put in the steward's garage. Fabrizio Nosco was in charge of the garage that day and took sole responsibility for the car. He knew what his duty was. In Italy, racing car accidents are covered by the same laws as road accidents. Already things had been done wrong. Senna should have been declared dead at the scene and the area cordoned and sheeted off to await accident investigators. But that was not the way of Formula One. At a Grand Prix track, the law was played by Bernie's rules. Sid Watkins had done his job and brought Senna back from the dead so his death could be recorded away from the track. Now, Nosco could hear the sound of the race restarting – that was the way it was done in Formula One. The fact that one of the most famous people in the world had just died was of little consequence in comparison to the necessity of the show going on. Nosco knew Senna was dead, the Italian grapevine had told him that – all the Italian officials knew.

Putting a car into isolation to await the attention of accident investigators was standard procedure when a driver had not walked away from an accident. If Senna had got out the car, it would have, more than likely, been returned straight to the Williams team. In fact, the gravity of the accident was confirmed when the car had not been taken straight back to the Williams garage.

Patrick Head was aware of how serious the accident was. He and Frank

Williams had almost certainly been briefed by Bernie Ecclestone as to Senna's condition. Head was very anxious to see the telemetry as he was almost certain it would tell the story of what had happened to the steering. He was desperate to see it before anyone else did and knew his best chance of getting possession of the two data recorders was there and then. He knew that if Senna died, he would never get to see them, and Italian police would swoop and seize everything. Head was equally worried about Damon Hill still out on the circuit.

Head was right to be concerned. Italy was the worst country in the world for a racing driver to die in a car because it was treated like a car accident, and anyone found to be responsible would be charged with culpable homicide. But at that stage, Head must have been very worried. The consequences were too horrible to contemplate.

In 1994, there were no black boxes on the cars that recorded all data in the event of an accident. The black box would not become mandatory until four years later. All that was available to investigators were the team's own data recorders.

The Williams-Renault FW16 had two data recording boxes. The first, belonging to Williams, was designed to record data from the chassis and gearbox; the second, belonging to Renault, primarily stored information from the V10 engine. The data recorder that belonged to Williams recorded hundreds of functions of the car, including the steering. It was only the 12.7 seconds of data on lap seven that Patrick Head was interested in. The rest of the data had already pinged back to the pits as Senna crossed the line on every lap. The Renault box recorded mainly engine functions, but on its spare channels it also recorded some car functions, including apparently the steering.

Head knew that whoever controlled the data recording boxes would control the agenda, and he wanted it to be him rather than an Italian prosecutor. The next 30 minutes would define his whole life and career and everything he had achieved. He had to get those boxes.

Head immediately sent Simon Scoins, a Williams electronics engineer, to the garage to fetch the two data recording boxes. Scoins knew exactly where the boxes were: attached to the car and the engine. Head told him to make it sound like a routine request and not display any urgency. Scoins ran off with a big pair of pliers to the parc fermé.

But Scoins found an unavoidable object in the shape of Fabrizio Nosco barring his way. Nosco was keen to cooperate, but he knew the law. He wasn't fooled by Scoins's laid back approach.

Fabrizio Nosco is, by all accounts, a lovely man, liked by all he comes into contact with, but he had a steely side and was very correct in the way he did things. He politely refused Scoins entry. He told him that, under FIA rules and Italian law, no one could touch the car. Although Nosco was absolutely right to refuse to give him entry to the garage, he guessed (correctly) that might not be the end of it.

Scoins scurried back to the Williams garage to report to Head. By now, Patrick Head must have been scared stiff of what had happened and would have been desperate to see the telemetry before anyone else did. He would have been very worried about Damon Hill and the possibility of his steering being faulty. He had reason to be fearful; the power steering system Williams was using was new that season and he might have remembered the welding that had been done to Senna's steering column and wondered whether the modified rod was still being used on the cars. He would have prayed it wasn't.

The memory of Jochen Rindt's accident at Monza at the Italian Grand Prix in 1970 also haunted him. Then, he had been a young 24-year-old engineer, newly graduated from UCL, working at Lola Cars in Huntingdon, England. Rindt's accident was probably caused by a faulty brake shaft that hadn't been properly crack tested due to manufacturing problems, and Lotus team principal Colin Chapman was charged with culpable homicide. It must have run through his mind whether the same fate might await him. He had to get hold of those boxes.

A now desperate Head rushed off to race control with Scoins in tow. He explained to race director Roland Bruynseraede, and to Charlie Whiting, that he must see the telemetry so that he could be assured that the same thing wouldn't happen to Damon Hill's car, which was taking part in the restarted race. He argued furiously it was a safety issue and that it must override all other considerations. Formula One insiders have been very critical of Head for allowing Damon Hill to take the restart when he didn't know what had caused the accident. Bruynseraede and Whiting undoubtedly knew the law and took a few moments to weigh up the situation. It is not known whether Whiting consulted Bernie Ecclestone or Max Mosley, only that he decided to ride roughshod over Italian law and his own regulations, a decision made in the name of safety.

Whiting bought Head's argument and accompanied him and Scoins back to the garage. He ordered Nosco to remove the boxes and hand them to Scoins, telling him he had full authority to act.

Nosco knew this was wrong and hesitated, but he realized when faced with such firepower that he had little choice but to comply. He said: "Whiting told me to open up the garage and that he had permission from Roland Bruynseraede, the Italian race director. He told me to remove the black boxes."

Whiting never denied that he had authorised the Williams engineers to remove the two data recorders immediately after the accident. When asked to explain why he had allowed the data recorders to be removed from the car by the team before it was handed over to officials, Whiting replied that he had done so because of the overriding need to make sure the other Williams car might not suffer the same strange loss of control that had apparently affected Senna's.

Nosco remembered that the Renault engine box was situated behind the cockpit, saying: "I removed it with a pair of large pliers." The Williams box was trickier as it was behind the radiator near the back wheel, on the right sidepod of the car, but he was able to remove it intact. As he said: "I have seen thousands of these devices and removed them for checks. The two boxes were intact even though they had some scratches. The Williams device looked to have survived the crash."

Simon Scoins was looking over Nosco's shoulder as he removed the boxes and disagreed with his assessment: "I was shocked when I lifted the material cover from Senna's car. The Williams data recorder was above the gearbox, 18cm from its natural position. Three of the four connectors were disconnected or damaged."

Back at the Williams garage, Scoins tried to retrieve the data. But according to his version of events, the power had been lost to the box and wiped the memory. He also said that although the box was basically intact, the connectors had been badly damaged in the accident. The problem appar-

Roland Ratzenberger: 4th July 1960 – 30th April 1994

Above: Roland Ratzenberger in his Simtek racing overalls before the start of the 1994 season. A late starter, at the age of 33, he finally got the money together to pay for a Formula One drive and found a team that could afford to run him for the money he had, which wasn't much. But three races into his five-race contract, his luck ran out and a combination of his and his team's inexperience caused him to crash the Simtek car.

Ayton Senna and Roland Ratzenberger qualify for the San Marino Grand Prix at Imola on Friday 29th April 1994. Together on the track, they were at the opposite ends of Formula One. Senna was striving for pole position and Ratzenberger was struggling to qualify for the race. Senna was driving for the best team in Formula One and Ratzenberger was driving for the worst.

Above: The three Austrian drivers involved in Formula One in 1994, Gerhard Berger, Roland Ratzenberger and Karl Wendlinger, pictured together at the mid-March 1994 test session at Imola. Berger and Wendlinger were not friends.

Below: The last photograph taken of Ratzenberger as he waits to qualify for the race. In truth, the car was not good enough to be competing in a Formula One Grand Prix. But both driver and team were desperate to succeed at the top level of motor racing.

Above: In the pit lane on Friday 29th April 1994 as Simtek's team principal Nick Wirth briefs Ratzenberger before he goes out to try and qualify for the race. Max Mosley, FIA president, is in the background. Mosley was a co-founder of Simtek and, although he sold out his shares on joining the FIA, he took a keen interest in the team.

Left: On Saturday 30th April, Roland Ratzenberger went out to qualify for the San Marino Grand Prix. It was a desperate situation for him and the team as non-qualification had grave consequences for both.

Above: The Simtek car was originally called a Bravo and built for a different team to race in 1993. When that team collapsed, Nick Wirth adapted the car for the 1994 season. It was a good design but hampered by an outdated gearbox and engine, which meant it had no chance of success.

Left: Roland Ratzenberger's Simtek comes to rest after leaving the track at a speed said to be 190mph.

Below: Roland Ratzenberger hit unprotected walls twice and suffered lethal injuries, including a transection of the aorta and a basilar skull fracture. As in Senna's accident, tyre protection of the concrete walls probably would have saved him.

Below: Ayrton Senna runs down the track after Roland Ratzenberger's accident. He commandeered a course car and went to the scene. He was anxious to know as much as he could about what had happened.

Above right: Ayrton Senna stands with Professor Sid Watkins at the scene of Ratzenberger's accident. By then, both Watkins and Senna knew that the driver was dead. It was a shock as no driver had died at a Formula One race for 12 years since Gilles Villeneuve and Ricardo Paletti were killed in 1982.

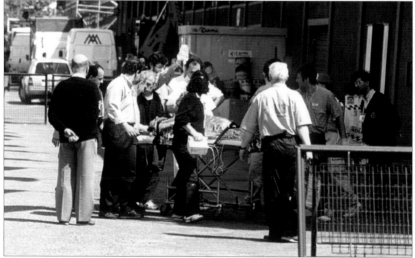

Above: Roland Ratzenberger is stretchered to the Imola medical centre. Sid Watkins made the decision to send him there as he had been killed outright on the impact and there was little point sending him to hospital. However, Bernie Ecclestone had long before decreed that a driver was never to be declared dead at a race track, and he was shipped to San Maggiore Hospital in an ambulance to be declared officially dead.

© Sport Magazine

© Getty Images

Above and left: The Simtek chassis broke up under the force of the impact, leading some insiders to question the integrity of the chassis. Ratzenberger's legs were clearly visible through the chassis after the accident.

Below: Ayrton Senna and Patrick Head wait on the pit wall after Ratzenberger's death to see if qualifying will be resumed. In the event, Senna elected to play no further part in proceedings that day.

© Sport Magazine

Above: Roland Ratzenberger's girlfriend, Somalian model Khadija Qalanjo, was interviewed and photographed by *Paris Match* magazine in the week after the accident. She is photographed in the sparse studio apartment in Monaco where they lived together until April 1994.

Above: Roland Ratzenberger's grave at Maxglan, near Salzburg, in Austria. His funeral, held on the day after Ayrton Senna's, was attended by drivers Karl Wendlinger, Heinz-Harald Frentzen, Johnny Herbert and Gerhard Berger.

ently was that the separate battery that powered the data box had become disconnected, wiping all the memory. Scoins said: "I carried it to the garage, where I attempted to connect it. It was useless. I tried inserting the RAM card but without success." The team had more luck with the Renault box, and the data was transferred to a diskette. Curiously, Scoins claimed he had nothing to do with this, saying later: "I have no knowledge of the Renault data recorder."

Bernard Duffort, a Renault engine-electronics expert, saw both boxes and backed up Scoins's story. He claimed that the Williams box showed signs of impact and had been damaged, and he confirmed that when it was examined it contained no data. Duffort said the data from the Renault box was transferred onto a computer disk on the day of the crash and a copy handed to the Italian authorities on 18th May 1994, along with the data recorder. By that time, however, the recorder's information had mysteriously been wiped from its hard disk. Duffort said that tests done on the recorder in Paris shortly after the accident, on an engine test bench, had erased its data. Taken at face value, it was all scarcely believable. But perhaps it was never explained well enough. Renault engineers maintained its black box was merely a recording device, and once the data had been downloaded to a floppy disk the recorder was totally irrelevant. A lot of people didn't believe it, but it was probably true.

Renault had no interest and saw no need to preserve the box, which was a standard instrument and undamaged. The interest was in the data, and this was removed from the Renault box in the usual way and put onto a computer disk. The box was then re-used.

But Williams' credibility had been stretched by Fabrizio Nosco's insistence that the box was virtually undamaged. And then an independent electronics expert, Marco Spiga, also said he felt the data should have been available. He also criticised the time lag and the whole month it took for Williams and Renault to hand over the boxes to the investigators. Spiga said: "The Williams box was totally unreadable when we got it back."

There was also surprise that a large quantity of the car's performance data was found by Williams on the engine data recorder box. One former team principal said: "Our engine data recorders of the time just recorded engine data. That surprised me a lot when they found all that car data on the engine box." But, of course, it was very convenient for Williams. The fact that the car box was blank severely damaged the Williams team's credibility in the later enquiry.

But Patrick Head breathed a sigh of relief that the data recorders were back in his team's possession. Now he could control the flow of information rather than others and ensure there were no problems on Damon Hill's car.

It was to prove crucial in the investigations that followed.

THE BATTLE OF THE BOXES

"It has happened before and it will happen again."

Murray Walker
Sunday 1st May 1994

CHAPTER 23

Clinically Dead

The BBC tells the world

At three o'clock, the helicopter carrying Ayrton Senna approached San Maggiore hospital. Dr Maria Teresa Fiandri, who had just arrived at the hospital, got out of her car and watched it pass overhead. When it landed, doctors rushed out and surrounded the gurney, helping Dr Gordini who was still working feverishly to keep Senna alive. He was not conscious, but there was a pulse.

They wheeled him straight to the CT scanner for a brain scan that would only confirm the diagnosis Sid Watkins had made at the track.

At 3:10pm, his heart stopped again but the doctors were able to quickly restart it before putting him in a clean room on a life-support machine.

Dr Fiandri took immediate charge. She was immediately accosted by a local Bologna reporter she knew, who was first on the scene, and she quickly told him all she knew: that surgery was out of the question.

Fiandri was calm and already knew she had to go through the motions as there was nothing she could do to save Senna's life. As she said: "Dr Gordini warned me that there was little to do. From the brain standpoint, there was no more activity immediately after being hit. He arrived at the hospital with a very weak pulse, almost without blood pressure. So it was just a matter of time for him to be considered legally dead."

She was surprised at how small the facial injury was and remembers he had a cut on his forehead of three or four centimetres. She said: "There was nothing else, and it was the only wound." Equally, she was surprised at the amount of blood from such a small injury. But she soon realised it had come from the back of his head and from the tracheotomy opening performed by Professor Watkins.

She remembers every detail of Senna from that day: "He came to me pale, but beautiful and serene. A handsome young man with dishevelled hair and his eyes closed. It is the image that I keep."

As soon as they were all together, Fiandri, Watkins, Gordini and Servadei gathered around to look at the results of the CT scan, and all of them knew immediately, if they didn't already, that there was nothing more they could do. There was no turning back although Senna's pulse and blood pressure had by then returned to something approaching normal levels.

Several dozen reporters and some TV crews had arrived and at just after 4:30pm, Dr Fiandri stepped outside to read out a clinical bulletin. She said Ayrton Senna had brain damage, with haemorrhaged shock and was in a deep coma. She told the reporters there would be another bulletin at six o'clock. "Deep coma" were the two words picked up by news crews, and they were repeated in countless news bulletins across the world.

Watkins also learned from X-rays that Senna had multiple fractures of the base of the skull where his head had smashed into the carbon-fibre headrest of the monocoque. It appeared that the right front wheel had shot up after impact like a catapult and violated the cockpit area where Senna was sitting. It impacted the right frontal area of his helmet, and the violence of the wheel's impact pushed his head back against the headrest, causing the fatal skull fractures. In addition, it appeared that a jagged piece of the upright assembly had penetrated the helmet visor just above his right eye. It was apparent that he suffered brain death on impact, but the lack of any physical injury to the rest of his body meant that his heart and lungs continued to function.

The circumstances did not call for surgery because the wound was generalised in the cranium. But the X-ray showing the damage to his skull and brain indicated he would not last long, even with a machine maintaining his vital functions. Watkins looked at the monitors of blood pressure, respiration and heart rate and realised the end was very near.

Meanwhile, people were starting to arrive from the Imola track. Although their helicopter had left well before Watkins and the doctors, Leonardo Da Silva, Betise Assumpcao and Josef Leberer arrived five minutes after them. Then Julian Jakobi and Celso Lemos turned up in a car.

Betise Assumpcao immediately took charge of communicating with the media, which had gathered outside, and she huddled with Dr Fiandri as Leonardo and Leberer sat in the corridor trying to hear what they were saying. Leonardo was surprisingly calm, and Leberer held his hand. Sid Watkins took charge of everything else.

Assumpcao remembers: "Once there, I didn't have time to feel traumatised. There was a lady doctor in charge of Ayrton and she wanted to give Leonardo a briefing on his brother's condition, so I had to translate for him and also for Julian, who didn't speak Italian. The doctor explained that Ayrton had a massive head injury, they were doing their best but they couldn't operate."

Meanwhile, Watkins grabbed his colleagues Dr Servadei and Dr Gordini together and told them they would work as a team whatever unfolded in the next few hours; they were the three men who knew the most. Watkins didn't think that Fiandri had been open enough with Leonardo and that it was causing miscommunication and false hope with the family in Brazil.

When Dr Fiandri had finished talking to Leonardo, the three doctors took him, Josef Leberer, Jakobi and Lemos into a small room next to where Senna was laying.

Watkins told them he thought it best that he was completely up front and that they were fully aware of the situation. As Assumpcao translated for Leonardo, he told them that the end was near and that the situation was hopeless. Leonardo was totally unable to absorb the news. But Jakobi, Lemos and Leberer listened quietly, nodding as Sid Watkins explained. They all supported Leonardo as best they could. Jakobi was determined to be strong whilst coping with his own intense personal grief.

Leberer wanted to go in and see Senna and asked Jakobi if he could stay with Leonardo, who was in no condition to see his brother. Jakobi was really uncomfortable, but he comforted Leonardo as best he could. He wished his wife, Fiona, was there to help; he knew she was really good at moments like this.

The doctors warned Leberer that Senna did not look good because of his head injuries. But he was determined to go in and see his friend for the last time.

When Leberer got into the room, he was surprised how noisy the life support machines were. Leberer was not bothered by Senna's head injuries, which were nowhere near as bad as they had described. The massive loss of blood and stains everywhere made the facial injuries seem a lot worse.

In any case, Leberer saw only beauty. He said: "I knew every part of his body. I was there because I wanted to see him there. We were more than six years together. We were friends and I did not have a problem to go there, even if there was a big injury."

At that moment, Galvao Bueno's helicopter landed in front of San Maggiore Hospital. Hospital staff recognised Gerhard Berger and the group was quickly ushered straight through to where Senna was. The four men were led straight into a little room where Professor Watkins, flanked by Gordini and Servadei, told them bluntly that Senna was dead but that his heart was still beating. Berger remembered: "Sid Watkins told me it was very, very, very critical and basically there was no chance of getting him through." Bueno remembered: "Sid Watkins said, 'He is dead. He is brain dead, his heart stopped. We managed to make it go again, and he is kept alive with machines, but the Italian law requires us to wait 12 hours and take another ECG. Only after this can we disconnect him.' I asked him: 'But Dr Sid, will we have to wait suffering for 12 hours?' He answered that he did not believe that even with life support, Ayrton's heart would hold on for these 12 hours."

Watkins suggested they all went in to see him before that happened. Berger went first and hugged Josef Leberer, who was already inside.

As Leberer stood over him, Berger sat down by his bed with all his memories of the man who had shared his career and also been a big part of his life outside the sport. He quietly spoke to Senna's lifeless form. After spending a few minutes in the noisy soulless hospital room, he quietly said his final goodbyes and kissed Senna on the cheek. Berger said: "I spent a few minutes with him, and then that was that." As he came out, he spoke to Assumpcao, who recalls: "Berger came out of the room very shaken and said to me: 'It was truly awful, I wish I hadn't done it, I can't describe it.' I said: 'Please keep it that way. I don't want any details.'"

Then, in turn, all the others who wanted to say goodbye went in.

As he supervised access to Senna and liaised with San Maggiore's doctors, Watkins was handed a phone receiver with Flavio Lalli, Senna's brother-in-law, at the other end, on the line from Brazil. Lalli told Watkins that he was with the family at Tatui and they wanted to hear from him what was the situation. Watkins told Lalli what he had just told Leonardo, Jakobi and Josef Leberer. He told him that the situation was truly hopeless and that Senna would soon die.

Lalli told Watkins that the family were on the verge of a decision to hire a chartered jet to fly straight to Bologna. He told him it would be totally inappropriate for them to travel, as there was nothing they could do. Watkins remembered: "They accepted the tragic news with dignity, and took my advice to remain in Brazil." But they had still not grasped that Senna would die.

Betise Assumpcao kept an open line to the family, and she and Leonardo passed the phone between them. She remembers: "I spent the next three hours translating, organising, conveying messages and handling the hopes and pains of Leo in the hospital and the family in Brazil. I had Ayrton's sister on the phone telling me, 'I should pray. I should have hope. Ayrton was strong.' I simply could not make them understand the severity of the situation."

Assumpcao begged Professor Watkins to speak to the family again. She told him: "Sid, it is Viviane. She does not believe when I tell her how grave Ayrton is and I don't know what else to say. I was wondering whether you could talk to them. I am sure they will listen to you."

She continued: "Sid looked at me. He was visibly sad and in pain." Watkins told her again: "Betise, there is no hope He was already dead on the track." Assumpcao recalled: "I was speechless. I thought of nothing and simply handed him the receiver."

This time, Watkins was a little blunter with the family and told it to them straight. He had no choice. At last, they seemed to get the message.

After Berger went into Senna's room and everyone else had said their goodbyes, Watkins decided to leave, unable to take any more. His job was done. He was used to death, but this was unlike anything he had experienced. He had borne the full brunt of the tragedy. He had been first to realise Senna was dead and it had fallen to him to tell Senna's family. He then had to impart the news to people at the track. It was heartbreaking.

Now, he found he had reached his limit. Even he could only take so much. And even though Senna was still technically alive, there was nothing more he could do. It was just a question of waiting for the inevitable, which Watkins's experience told him would be within the hour. For him, his friend was already dead. He also knew that when the announcement was made, the media would be all over him wanting information, and he was far from being up for that. He desperately needed some time on his own to come to terms with the day's events.

So he took the chance of a lift back to his hotel, which was situated next to the airport.

When Watkins got back to his room, a man who had seen death many times discovered his own vulnerability as the television replayed the accident time and time again. Strangely, he found himself unable to turn the television off.

Josef Leberer was the next to leave the hospital, also unable to take any more. He went back to the track to be on his own with his memories and collect up his gear. From tonight, he was unemployed – like all Senna's employees, his contract stated that his job terminated with his employer's death.

Next to leave was Gerhard Berger, who, like Watkins, needed solitude and didn't want to be at San Maggiore when Senna's death was announced. He took a helicopter to Forli airport, where his own jet was waiting to take him home.

At the airport, in the evening dusk, he saw Senna's plane waiting forlornly for an owner that would never return. Berger broke down, overpowered by the silhouette of the plane in the fading skyline. Then he spotted Owen O'Mahoney, who rushed over to ask for news. Berger chickened out and told him he had none.

Berger, realising that O'Mahoney had been forgotten about, telephoned the hospital and got through to Julian Jakobi. Jakobi consulted with Assumpcao and she phoned Forli and told O'Mahoney to fly the plane to Bologna airport in case it was needed. She also told the pilot he had no news as to Senna's condition.

As a further precaution, Dr Fiandri decided to order an electroencephalogram to be done. An electroencephalogram is a recording of electrical activity along the scalp, measuring voltage fluctuations from current flows within the neurons of the brain. It is carried out by attaching small flat metal discs, called electrodes, to the scalp.

The electroencephalogram was necessary in case the family decided that the life support should be turned off. Under Italian law, this could not be done for 12 hours after an electroencephalogram had confirmed that there was no electrical activity in the brain.

The test showed what the doctors already knew but, by law, he was not dead; that would not occur until his heart stopped beating, which had already occurred twice and been restarted.

Dr Fiandri conferred with her trauma team and Betise Assumpcao. She had promised the media outside a bulletin about Senna's condition at six o'clock. It was very difficult as Senna was not dead but he had no chance of living, and Assumpcao did not want to raise any false hopes. They compromised with a short announcement saying simply Senna was "clinically dead" and adding nothing more by way of explanation or comment other than reaffirming that it meant he had no chance of surviving.

So at 6:05pm, Dr Fiandri, her voice shaking at the gravity of her announcement, told reporters that Senna was clinically dead. She said he was still connected to the equipment maintaining his heartbeat.

The news led the early-evening news programmes. In Britain, an hour behind Europe, the BBC waited until the last moment for a more final verdict, but when none was forthcoming, they prepared an opening segment with live interviews from Imola with Murray Walker and Jonathan Palmer. On the BBC's news bulletin at six o'clock, Moira Stuart, the newsreader, duly announced the news that shocked the people of Britain. She said: "The former world champion racing driver, Ayrton Senna, has been pronounced clinically dead after a crash at the San Marino Grand Prix." She said: "Senna suffered serious head injuries when his car left the track and crashed into a concrete wall." She added: "He is being kept on a life support machine because of Italian law, but a spokesman for the hospital in Bologna said there was 'no chance he would survive.'" The BBC's sports correspondent, Rob Bonnet, described the accident and said the loss of control seemed "so sudden and total that he was clearly powerless to even attempt a correction." Murray Walker, interviewed by Moira Stuart live from Imola, said: "This is the blackest day for Grand Prix racing that I can remember in the many, many years I have been covering the sport." Walker called Senna "arguably the greatest driver who has ever lived in the history of Grand Prix racing." He added: "To say his loss is tragic is a masterpiece of understatement."

Soon after six o'clock, Dr Fiandri had decided that if Senna's heart stopped beating again, she would not restart it – it was simply too painful to prolong a process of which everyone now knew the outcome.

She would not have to wait long.

CLINICALLY DEAD

"I never had the chance to forge a relationship with the guy. I was absolutely thrilled to be his team-mate, because I thought I would learn so much. But it wasn't to be."
                    Damon Hill
                    September 2011

CHAPTER 24

The Finality of Death

The sad announcement in Bologna

Aﬅer their second conversation with Professor Watkins, the grim reality began to sink in at the Da Silva family farm, which now had about 20 close friends and family crowding into its large sitting room. Broadcasters were picking up the phrase "clinically dead" from Dr Fiandri's announcement and repeating it over and over again.

Any thoughts of the family leaving for Europe had completely disappeared. It was now assumed that Ayrton Senna would be returning to them, and some family members started discussing the arrangements for his funeral. The others stoically awaited the official announcement, although they were all praying for a miracle. The Da Silvas were a strong Catholic family, and they believed that a miracle even at this stage was possible.

Suddenly, Neyde Da Silva stood up and said her son would need a priest to read him the last rites before he died. Viviane handed her the telephone receiver, which was an open line to her son Leonardo at San Maggiore in Bologna. She told Leonardo to ask Dr Fiandri to arrange for a priest to visit her eldest son. But Leonardo was in no condition to ask anyone anything. He didn't even understand what his mother was asking him. He handed to the receiver to Betise Assumpcao, who told Neyde she would get it done straight away. At that moment, it first dawned on Assumpcao that Senna was actually going to die. Strangely, she had not felt it before as she had been too busy looking after everybody else.

Putting that aside, she went to Fiandri who quickly got hold of the hospital chaplain who had also arrived at the hospital earlier when he heard the news on the television. He went into Senna's room at 6:15pm and gave him the last rites.

At 6:37pm, Senna's heart stopped again, and Dr Fiandri gathered her team around her and after a brief discussion told them to stand down and allow him to die peacefully. She said keeping a man who was effectively dead artificially alive was ethically very doubtful. She had had to deal with Roland Ratzenberger the day before, who had been DOA (dead on arrival) when it was obvious to her and all the doctors that he had died instantly at the track.

So at 6:40pm, Dr Fiandri pronounced Ayrton Senna dead and went into a room where the media had gathered with her medical team around her. The announcement was met with cold resignation. The hoped-for miracle had not happened.

After she had dealt with media questions, Dr Fiandri needed someone to officially identify the body for the death certificate and asked Betise Assumpcao, but she couldn't. As she said: "I said that was the one thing I couldn't do. I had done everything else, organised everything, but I couldn't do that. So Celso said he would do it." Lemos's career as managing director of licensing had come to a premature end, as Assumpcao recalled: "He was identifying his client on the cold slab in a mortuary in a country far from home. It was a horrific duty and it changed Celso."

Up to then, Assumpcao had been a model of calm, but as Lemos went to identify Senna's body, she broke down in tears as she realised it was finally all over.

She left Celso Lemos to make the arrangements for the coffin and to decide what Senna would be dressed in after the autopsy, which was required under Italian law. Lemos later said he thought fate had put him in Imola on that weekend, and God had sent him to do this particular job. So he took over, amongst other things, choosing the clothes that Senna would wear in his coffin. Lemos, clearly a man of little imagination, chose a completely unsuitable and unflattering dark suit, white shirt and tie. Assumpcao explained: "That is how Ayrton ended up wearing a black suit, something he didn't do in life."

Meanwhile, completely oblivious to what was going on in Bologna, Juraci drove Adriane Galisteu to Faro airport. When the chartered plane arrived at around 6:30pm, Adriane was waiting desperately for the plane to land on the side of the tarmac. As soon as the door opened, she scrambled on board and into Luiza Braga's arms. The pilot told them it would be a three-hour flight. On board, Luiza told Adriane that her boyfriend was as strong as an ox and that she had heard nothing more from her husband at the circuit, other than it was very serious.

But even as they spoke, Senna was already dead.

The two women sat closely together in the plane and held hands as the pilot asked them politely to put on their seatbelts. The captain taxied to the edge of the runway, and waited for clearance to take off. As he waited, a message was relayed to the plane. The pilot immediately taxied back to the terminal building without a word to his passengers.

The message to the captain was that Ayrton Senna had passed away, but he didn't want to be the one to break the news to them. He solved the problem by telling them there was an urgent call for Luiza back at the control tower. His exact words were: "I don't have authorisation from the tower. There is a call for Luiza and Adriane."

Adriane shook with fear about what the call might reveal, and Luiza rushed off the plane and ran to the tower as soon as the door opened. Adriane stepped from the plane and was overwhelmed at the silence in the terminal as she walked through. She followed in the footsteps of Luiza Braga to the control tower: "I shook all over, from head to toe," she remembered.

She waited in silence alone. Luiza Braga was pale when she returned. She took Adriane's hand and said: "Adriane." But Adriane interrupted her and said: "Luiza, only don't tell me he has died." She replied the only way she could: "He's died."

The two women hugged each other for an endless time. They spent 40 minutes in the control tower, sobbing and trying to come to terms with the devastating news. They did not know what to do next. Finally, they were driven back to Senna's house at Quinto da Lago and told the pilot to wait at Faro for instructions. When they got there, they found the whole house in mourning. Juraci, the housekeeper, who had regarded Senna as her son, was screaming. Adriane made for their bedroom and lay motionless on the bed for two hours. She remembers: "I naïvely thought I would see him arrive that night, even earlier than expected, with that beautiful smile of his, ready for a reunion after almost a month."

Captain O'Mahoney touched down at Bologna airport and went to the private aviation centre just in time to see Dr Fiandri announce the death of his boss on television. He was stoic and had seen death many times, but Senna's death really got to him and he suddenly realised how much. He said: "Ayrton got to me; he wasn't like the egotistical prats I'd been used to flying around." O'Mahoney was also in a difficult position. Like Josef Leberer's, his contract of employment with Senna specifically stated that his employment would cease 'forthwith' if Senna was killed. Now he was dead, and O'Mahoney was unemployed.

Meanwhile, a disbelieving Luisa Tosoni had just given birth to a son when she heard the news. She just couldn't believe the mild-mannered boy she had first met in 1988 would never again be checking into Suite 200. As she said: "In one way, I was happy because of my son, but in another I felt so much bleakness."

When Josef Leberer returned to the paddock from the hospital, he found it a desolate and unhappy place. Everyone was trying to come to terms with what had happened.

By that time, his death had been announced. He remembered: "It seemed like everybody was waiting and asking, 'What's happened, what's happened, what's happened?' I had to tell them what I knew."

Leberer had to cope with two grieving teams. Not only his own but also McLaren's. Ron and Lisa Dennis, and Mansour and Cathy Ojjeh, huddled around him for news. He found Frank Williams and Patrick Head in a state of disbelief. After finally getting Senna to drive for them after all these years, they couldn't believe he was gone so quickly.

He couldn't cope with too much more of it and drove his car back to the hotel as soon as he could get away.

Meanwhile, Luiza Braga spoke to her husband at the hospital, who told her there was no point going to Bologna and to pack some bags and prepare to return to Brazil for the funeral. Braga told his wife to take Adriane to their home in Sintra with one of the cars Senna kept at the villa. He said he would join them as soon as he had made the arrangements to get Leonardo back to Brazil and to have Senna's body repatriated. He told her to instruct the pilot of the chartered jet to go. Luiza explained the plan to Adriane, who agreed: "I gathered all I had brought from Brazil," she remembered: "The big suitcase, everything. The three pieces of luggage that I had just unpacked less than 24 hours before, with all I would need to spend the next five months of the European season by his side. The season that ended before it began." Before leaving, she took a T-shirt and shorts of Senna's she had worn that morning to go running.

Then she walked around the house and gardens for the last time. The garden and lawns were bathed in moonlight as they only can be in the Algarve. She walked by the swimming pool and then went into his study and checked for messages on his fax. She gazed at the photographs on his desk for the last time and his trophies. She stopped in front of his powerful Swiss stereo player and wondered what was the last music he had listened to. She pressed the eject button and out came a Phil Collins album. She slipped it into her pocket, as she remembered: "I wanted to know what had been the last CD he had listened to in life. That was one thing that I had the right to share with him. After that, I walked in tears around the house."

At around 10 o'clock, the two women left for the two-hour drive to Sintra. They were silent, thinking about what had been a terrible end to a terrible day. Just after midnight, Luiza and Adriane pulled into the drive of the Braga home, where Senna had stayed many times and had his own room.

Adriane went straight to bed, but not in his room. That would have been too much to bear. Back at the Imola track, the lights in the media centre burned brightly as more than 200 journalists prepared 200 obituaries. The pit garage, containing Senna's shattered car, was now guarded by armed police. At the hospital, it was revealed that nurses had discovered a small furled Austrian flag hidden in the sleeve of Senna's race overalls. Journalists concluded he had intended to fly it from his cockpit on the parade lap and dedicate what would have been his 42nd Grand Prix victory to the memory of Roland Ratzenberger.

Around midnight, Angelo Orsi was back in the developing room at his office. The pictures were not pleasant. He was doubtful any magazine would publish them. Representatives of the Senna family told him immediately they that did not want anyone to even see them. Orsi respected their wishes. The pictures have never been seen, except by the family and Senna's girlfriend, Adriane. Today, they are believed to be still locked in a safe in the *Autosprint* offices. Both the magazine and Orsi have turned down significant offers, believed to be well over $100,000, for the rights to them.

Orsi's decision earned everlasting respect from Galvao Bueno, who had tipped off the Senna family about their existence: "He is the only person who's got pictures of Ayrton's face developed and stashed in a safe. He has already turned down fortunes for them: he won't sell, he won't give. His superiors at the magazine understood his action, even with the fabulous offers from agencies, and I find it very dignified."

There is much more Galvao Bueno would like to say about the events of Sunday 1st May 1994, but he agreed with Milton and Neyde Da Silva that he would never discuss it. He confided to friends to whom he made mention of the events: "I shouldn't be talking about this; I have an agreement with his family."

In America, five hours behind Europe, the news spread fast, and Dale Earnhardt paid tribute to Senna after winning the Winston Select 500 at Talladega in Alabama. He dedicated his win to Senna's memory. Nigel Mansell, at home in Florida, was interviewed on the NBC nightly news: "I thought he was bulletproof," he said. "It hurts. It hurts big time."

Later that night when everyone else had been sorted out, Betise Assumpcao found herself back at the Imola circuit with Galvao Bueno, collecting her boss's possessions. As she collected his shirts and put them in his bag she saw an envelope with Adriane's name on it. She quickly scanned the contents and saw it was dated six weeks before and had obviously never been sent. She thought for a moment and then tore it into tiny pieces and stuffed them in her pocket.

They couldn't avoid the multiple televisions in the paddock that were mostly showing special programmes hastily put together. Sky News had put together a profile, showing film of Senna at his beach house in Angra. She said: "And that was when I came out of auto pilot. I started crying so hard that I was losing my breath. He was suntanned, wearing a bright yellow top with a perfect blue sky in the background. He enjoyed life so much. He looked so young and carefree and in perfect health, and I just broke down. He had such a fabulous life, and now it was all gone." Bueno was surprised; Assumpcao had suffered a lot of aggravation from Senna during his life and had often confided in Bueno what a difficult job she had and how particularly tricky her boss could be. She had always given the impression that she admired and respected him but didn't care much for him personally. Now, Bueno looked at her and said: "I didn't know you liked him so much." She tried to explain their relationship: "'Ayrton was not easy; anything he said could spark a massive reaction. He did some bad things on the track, and out of the track, too. But he was so extraordinarily talented, and also thoughtful and considerate. He was becoming more of the human being he wanted to be — that is my biggest sorrow of all."

As she and Bueno walked down the paddock on the way out, she took the tiny pieces of the envelope from her pocket and threw them over her shoulder.

The breeze scattered them across the concrete of the Imola paddock.

*"Steering, Power, What
happened to the steering?"*
Patrick Head
Sunday 1st May 1994
2.17pm

CHAPTER 25

The Steering Broke

What caused the accident?

Seventeen seconds into the seventh lap of the San Marino Grand Prix, Patrick Head shouted out the words "steering" and "power" according to anonymous witnesses standing near to him in the Williams garage. And immediately after Ayrton Senna hit the wall, he apparently turned to the engineers around him, and said: "What happened to the steering?"

Patrick Head, technical director of the Williams-Renault team, was one of the best engineer/designers Formula One has ever seen. Possibly the best after the late Colin Chapman. His stream of consciousness in those few seconds as he took in what he saw on the screen, combined with his intimate knowledge of how the Williams-Renault FW16 worked, were probably the best indication of what had happened to Senna's car. Undoubtedly, his initial diagnosis was that the steering had failed. But he must have been thinking of the relatively new power steering system; he couldn't possibly have imagined the steering column had snapped. But if he had been aware of the nature of the modifications that had been made to the car's steering column two months earlier, he might have taken a different view.

Jabby Crombac, the late French journalist and a paddock favourite, was the only non-Williams employee standing within earshot of Patrick Head that day. Crombac never talked about what happened in the garage that afternoon, even after being put under intense pressure to do so. He took the secrets to his grave. Why Crombac should have been so secretive is also a mystery. He did say to a friend: "I can confirm I was in the garage that day. I knew what happened, but I will never tell anyone."

And Head was not the only man who thought the steering had malfunctioned. Hundreds of others did as well. Italian eye witnesses in the crowd that day at Imola, who actually saw the accident, are adamant that Senna was not able to steer the car around Tamburello. These people were widely quoted in Italian publications but because none of them spoke English, what they had to say was ignored by British journalists.

There were eight marshals on duty at Tamburello that day, and they all said the same thing: Senna's car went off in a straight line towards the wall, and there was no obvious attempt to steer the car around the curve.

Regardless of whether it was the steering that failed, there is an overwhelming opinion that there was a mechanical failure both from former Formula One drivers and engineers in other teams. Whatever the mechanical failure was, it left Senna powerless to stop his car hitting the wall at Tamburello.

And this was firmly the view of the panel of experts assembled to investigate the accident. In their 3,000-page report, they blamed the failure of the steering column for the cause of the accident. The reason they gave was that it had broken where it had been modified by the Williams team, and there was substantial metal fatigue present in the column. The metal fatigue was caused by incompatible metals being used. Two investigations by independent laboratories had reached the same conclusion. The steering column had signs of fatigue over 75 per cent of the circumference and 40 per cent of the section. It was an astonishing revelation, and one that Patrick Head did not dispute. There was no question that the steering column had broken and that it had broken because of metal fatigue. Even Peter Goodman, the Williams team solicitor, admitted: "The way the steering was modified brought no credit upon my client."

The realisation about the steering column's condition must have devastated Patrick Head, who was a thoroughly decent man and a zealot where safety was concerned. The Williams team was renowned as having the best safety procedures of any team.

But there was no doubt that Williams had botched the steering column modification, the question became whether it had failed before and caused the accident or it had broken as a result of the accident. It was such a big question and it has never been satisfactorily resolved. Officially, the steering column broke before the accident and caused it – these were the findings of the panel of experts and the findings of the resulting court of enquiry. Patrick Head and Sir Frank Williams challenged these verdicts and still do to this day.

No one could deny the credibility of the panel of experts assembled to investigate the accident. They were headed by Mauro Forghieri, the former technical director of Ferrari, and Enrico Lorenzini, a professor of engineering at Bologna University. They were joined by a cross section of experts across several disciplines, including Tommaso Carletti, a former Ferrari race engineer; Professor Alberto Bucchi, an expert in road construction systems; Francesco Bomparole, of ANAS SpA, the Italian state-owned road construction company; Roberto Nosetto, a former president of the Imola circuit; Dr Rafaele Dal Monte, a professor of science and sports; and Emmanuelle Pirro, a former Formula One driver.

The panel used the facilities of Bologna University and an Italian military aerospace laboratory to carry out its investigation. The panel was of extraordinary quality, and it took the time to do the job properly. It also had the best facilities and support staff possible. The only flaw, if there was a flaw, was that it was all made up of Italians.

Despite his initial prognosis, Patrick Head and also Adrian Newey disagreed totally with the panel's opinion. They were firmly of the view that Senna effectively lost control of the car over the bumps when the rear end suddenly stepped out, catching him by surprise. They were effectively saying it was driver error. The panel of experts says it was a mechanical failure.

Of course, no one but Ayrton Senna really knows what happened to the steering. The telemetry and video film that could have proved conclusively what happened went missing. Both sides used the video footage that was available, it was coupled to the Renault telemetry to work out what Senna was doing in those few seconds before his car hit the wall and what his car was doing.

Head and Newey and the Williams team were in a minority in their view that it was effectively driver error and that Senna had not managed to keep control of the car as it went through a series of unrelated actions that affected it adversely.

Almost everyone else thought that it was mechanical failure that had caused the accident. Bertrand Gachot says it was impossible to have happened the way Williams described it. The Belgian was racing that weekend and said: "Tamburello was easily flat in the dry. It would have been impossible to crash without mechanical failure."

In the aftermath of the accident, Patrick Head's immediate instinct was to get hold of the telemetry. It appears that he quickly decided that he must deflect the view that it was the failure of the steering that caused the accident.

To be absolutely fair to Patrick Head, he had no choice but to take that position. If it was shown that the steering column broke and that Senna was left with no ability to steer his car going at 190 miles per hour, Head's career would have been over, and it is likely that the team would have been closed down and his life's work ruined. His 30 per cent share in the team was also worth in excess of £30 million – that would have been lost.

Head must have been vaguely aware that the steering column had been modified, but he would have had little idea of the detail. No one knows when he found out about the exact modifications to the steering column, but presumably he had a good look at Damon Hill's car, which had identical modifications, and didn't like what he found. From that point onwards, from when he had analysed the telemetry and examined the records, he has always maintained that Senna had lost control of the car over Tamburello's bumps.

Head's exact story was that Senna's car hit a series of four bumps in Tamburello, one after the other, which caused the car to go down on its suspension and sledge. The back end then stepped out, understeering off the track out of Senna's control. Head said: "We have checked the telemetry. He slightly lifted his foot just at that dip in the place where the tarmac changes. That caused a loss of grip from the car." Contrary to general opinion, Head never put forward the theory that it was cold tyres that caused the accident. This theory had no credibility anyway as on lap six, Senna clocked what would prove to be the third-fastest lap of the race, discounting any notion that a loss of tyre pressure, due to the cooling of the tyres whilst following the safety car, could have caused Senna's loss of control. Adrian Newey later put forward a theory that Senna could have suffered a slow puncture just before the accident, but this was little better than a blind guess.

Head has maintained his view on the basis of the telemetry that was recovered from the engine data recorder. He absolutely denied that the steering had broken, or that the steering was in any way the cause of the accident. He has always stated that the telemetry proved this. Head has always maintained that Senna was still applying torsional force to the steering column of his FW16 when he went off at Tamburello. One former team principal cast doubt on this and stated he did not believe the engine data recorder would measure the steering, but Head said there were spare channels on the Renault box that measured the steering actions.

Sir Frank Williams also denied the steering broke, although not as forcefully as Patrick Head. He said: "We as a company formed the opinion that the steering column did not break. This was decided after examining the telemetry readings and also a lot of simulations." Asked whether he had any doubts about it, Frank Williams did admit: "Absolutely we had doubts."

There were also plenty of rumours circulated that Frank Williams privately believed the steering did break but went along with the story that was put out because the consequences for the Williams team if it had been proved otherwise were catastrophic. Williams had more to lose than Head. The team was his life and he owned shares in it worth £70 million.

The defence that Williams and Head put up has remained steadfast to this day. No one at Williams, past or present, has ever broken ranks and presented a different view. Even today, 21 years later, Senna's accident is a taboo subject at the Williams factory in Didcot, England. One former staffer said: "It is just not discussed ever."

At the subsequent enquiry into the accident, Williams produced many members of its staff and freelance consultants to testify and all said basically the same thing: that the steering hadn't broken before the accident but during it. In fact, the Williams team seemed to put forward every theory and explanation they could for the accident other than steering failure.

But none of the explanations put forward explains why Senna didn't attempt to steer the car through the curve. Head's explanation was that Senna's priority was trying to keep the car in the race and not avoid an accident.

But the most credible explanation actually came from Williams witnesses Giorgio Stirano and Diego Milen, who said that he hadn't turned the wheel because he knew the braking would be more effective done in a straight line. This was of course true, but steering a Formula One car head-on towards a solid concrete wall is not something any driver would do lightly. In truth, there is little doubt that Senna, other than braking, had no control over the car as he headed for that wall – no one seriously disputes that.

Senna's team mate, Damon Hill, was in a very difficult position in the days after the crash and at the subsequent enquiry. He had an identical car and yet he managed to navigate Tamburello very successfully 58 times during the race. His view was that Senna had had a problem with oversteer as his car went over a bump on the asphalt surface of the Imola track. The bump was located just a few yards from where Senna's car began to veer off the bend at Tamburello. He said the oversteer sent the car towards the inside of the track, and Senna countered by steering away. However, his car bumped again and skidded to the right, nine degrees off the ideal line. Senna, he said, at this point decided to keep his line and tried desperately to brake. He believes also that there is no doubt that, right up to the impact, his main concern was keeping the car in the race, not avoiding the impact. But Hill's evidence doesn't quite tally with Senna's own comments after the morning warm-up, when he told his engineer not to change a thing on the car as at last it was handling well.

Stirano and Milen later told journalists there was no blame to be attached to the track or the driver: there had been an ordinary problem which destiny had made fatal. They said they reached their conclusions after examining the telemetry readings from Senna's Williams and videotapes. It was a perfectly reasonable view for them to take.

Williams engineers Gary Woodward, Dickie Stanford, Simon Scoins and Brian O'Rourke all gave evidence at the enquiry and stated the steering column did not break before the accident. O'Rourke, who is a composite-materials specialist, attempted an explanation as to why it was broken after the accident: "As the right front wheel of Senna's car hit the wall, the violent impact caused a torsion on the steering column, causing it to break." O'Rourke always strongly maintained it had broken during the accident and not before.

The Italian panel of experts contended that a modification to lengthen the steering column of Senna's Williams had broken at the entry to Tamburello, meaning Senna could no longer steer the car. They said there was a total failure of Senna's steering column as he entered the Tamburello curve at over 190mph.

The fact that the steering column did break was clear as it was dangling from the side of the car after the accident, having been pulled up by the doctors removing Senna. The two doctors who extracted Senna from the wreckage said that they did not encounter any obstacles, nor did they have to remove the steering wheel, in pulling his body out of the car. This led them to suppose that the steering column was already broken.

There was one eye witness who inspected the car in the minutes after the accident. Once he had delivered the three doctors to the crash site, medical car driver Mario Casoni had nothing else to do and was able to examine the wreck of the car in detail. At first, he said the steering column was laying on the ground by the car, but he later changed his view and said he misremembered and that it was actually dangling from the cockpit. He said: "I noticed the abnormal state of Senna's steering column, which had been uprooted and was dangling from the cockpit."

Michele Alboreto was the best qualified witness at the enquiry. He had competed in the race in a Minardi and had survived a huge crash himself at Tamburello in 1991. He was also a close personal friend of Ayrton Senna and a neighbour of his when he lived in Monaco. Alboreto rubbished Patrick Head's view and said the bumps could not possibly have forced Senna's car off the circuit. He was adamant that the crash was caused by a mechanical failure in the car. He studied videos of the crash, from both Senna's and Schumacher's car. He also studied film of previous crashes at Tamburello involving Gerhard Berger, Nelson Piquet, Ricardo Patrese and himself. He said: "Senna's shift to the right makes me think it was a mechanical failure. I am sure because I know I had the same accident as Ayrton did, and the only way you can go out at this corner is if you have a mechanical failure."

Pierluigi Martini, another former Formula One driver, said: "A driver like Ayrton Senna didn't go off the track at that point unless there was a problem. Drivers took the curve at 300kph and there was a small dip in the middle of the track, which disturbed the cars. The bump effect was perfectly normal and is common to every racing circuit in the world."

Other experts who knew Senna well have totally dismissed driver error, saying it just didn't happen, especially to a driver like Ayrton Senna. Osamu Goto, the Honda engine designer, who worked closely with Senna for six years, described him as the precisest driver he had ever known. He said, "He could feel the slightest thing. He was always like a living sensor."

A former driver, who asked for anonymity, said: "Studying the video tape, it can be seen quite clearly the car never turned into the curve. It started to leave the track at precisely the same moment and place where the driver following, Michael Schumacher, started to steer through. Senna just went straight on." John Watson, the former McLaren Formula One driver who was commentating for Eurosport on the day, said simply: "No one has ever explained to me why Senna's Williams suddenly left the track."

Gerhard Berger said: "This is not a place where you get driver error." Former world champion and Williams team member Keke Rosberg agreed: "The bend is flat out. You can't do anything wrong. You can drive through there with your eyes closed. It's not a corner."

Gerald Donaldson, a well-known Formula One journalist who has written extensively about the accident, said: "If you ease your foot from the accelerator, there is a shift of weight forwards, as a result of which the car momentarily has more downforce at the front, and when something happens in that situation, the tail is more likely to break away, but the car does not veer to the right on a left-hand bend."

Donaldson may be stating the obvious, but what he is saying is absolutely right. It is also unlikely that the power steering failed, and all the evidence is that it didn't. It's easy to see why the panel of experts came to the conclusion they did as, on the surface, every piece of evidence points to the fact that the steering column broke the moment Senna applied pressure to it, and Senna could no longer steer the car. One former team principal believes that if that did happen, Senna would have sensed it before it finally broke and brought the car to an immediate halt. But Senna was on a mission that day and retirement would haven the very last option in his mind – that day it would probably have been an acceptable risk to drive on.

It was the Italian magazine *Autosprint* that first raised the suspicion, one week after the accident that the steering column had broken. According to *Autosprint* the fracture occurred, or was beginning to occur, in the few seconds before the Williams ran off the road. At the time, Patrick Head refuted this by saying that the telemetry showed that Senna had control of the car right up to when he hit the wall. So why did the panel of experts come to the conclusion that the steering column broke, causing the accident? As one former team principal said: "Steering columns do not just break. The natural condition if one is damaged is to bend, not to break."

The *News of The World*, a British tabloid Sunday newspaper that specialised in sex scandals, was the first to reveal that the steering had been modified and that the column had metal fatigue. The *News of The World* article quoted Professor Adolpho Melchionda, a mechanical engineer, as saying: "Senna was driving a potential death trap. The cause of Senna's crash was the work done on the rod." Head vehemently denied the allegations and told the newspaper: "We are absolutely sure the car was in good order. The steering column broke after and not before the crash."

So what was the story of the steering column, and why did it become so crucial in Senna's accident? It all started at the end of February at a test session at Paul Ricard the Formula One team attended. During those sessions, Senna prepared a list of modifications he wanted done to his car. The list ran to four full A4 pages.

Senna requested more room in the cockpit and figured out himself that this could be done by lengthening the steering column by about 12mm. He asked the test team to have the modification ready for the Brazilian Grand Prix. Damon Hill must have wanted it as well as the steering column was lengthened on all three team cars.

The modification of the steering column was the direct responsibility of two young Williams engineers named Alan Young and Gavin Fisher. Fisher and Young have always maintained that the modification wasn't a rush job but was planned and executed at the factory according to Williams's own internal procedures. Whilst Young and Fisher oversaw it, Tony Pilcher was in charge of production at the Williams factory.

Under the discovery process, Williams was forced to release blueprints and drawings of the steering column to the official enquiry. The original drawings for the steering column were dated 3rd February 1994 and showed the column of the Williams Renault FW16 to be 905mm long when the car was manufactured.

When Alan Young was asked to make the modifications, the original drawings were got out and handed to him on 10th March 1994 so he had something to work from. It appears to have been his decision not to manufacture a brand new column but to lengthen the existing one. There was nothing wrong with that decision but undoubtedly it might have been a better decision to manufacture the new longer column from scratch, but in the end the decision was made to modify the existing one. It was a decision, that if the panel of experts was correct, more than likely, would ultimately cost Ayrton Senna his life.

There could have been many reasons for the decision. But the most likely one is that the factory was busy with a whole other list of modifications, and they took priority. The steering column modification was for the comfort of the driver. Modifications to make the car go faster would almost certainly have had priority.

Senna's request for the modification meant the new column measurement would be 917.3mm, an increase in length of 12.3mm, and two new elements were to be introduced to achieve this. According to the Williams team, the new assembly consisted of nine components that were manufactured simultaneously by different departments at Williams. The three new assemblies were manufactured and then inspected to assure conformity between the drawing and the finished product. Inspection is a very important part of the production process in Formula One and is carried out rigorously, and nothing suggests it wasn't in this case. If the part failed inspection procedures, it would either be reworked or thrown away. The same applied to quality – if satisfactory, the piece and its components, each carrying an ID label, would be placed in the store.

From there, the piece would be drawn from the stores for fitting to the car by the mechanics. Williams produced three column assemblies for all three of its cars, and the modifications were put on the cars sometime after 10th March, in time for the Brazilian Grand Prix.

According to Williams, the steering-column modifications had been done properly and Senna's steering column was the same as Hill's.

Pilcher said that the manufacture of the new elements for the modified column took two to three days. The new parts were machined from two types of compatible steel, T45 and EN14.

Gary Woodward was the Williams engineer who inspected the parts and also crack tested suspension and steering components after every race.

Woodward said: "Steering column modifications, which complied with the rules, were made to Senna's car. All three cars had the same modifications prior to the race in Brazil."

He added: "After each Grand Prix, the cars are subjected to a crack test, using penetrating liquids to identify any fractures in the suspension or steering columns. The steering columns are replaced halfway through the season. The tests carried out after the Pacific Grand Prix in Aida, Japan, found no defects in Senna's car." That statement takes some believing in the light of later revelations about metal fatigue in the column.

The modifications were later described in the official report as "badly designed and badly implemented". Formula One experts who saw photographs of the modified steering column post-crash, were horrified at the standards of workmanship. Effectively, the column was cut and a smaller-diameter sleeve welded inside the steel tube to lengthen it. One former team principal said: "I would have expected it to be done the other way round and a wider diameter piece welded in or, better still, both." Others believe that the only correct way to give Senna what he wanted was to manufacture a whole new column. For reasons unknown, this was not done.

Charlie Whiting, the FIA delegate, effectively in charge of inspecting cars for the governing body, was very circumspect when he appeared at the enquiry. He said that the steering had been modified without permission of the FIA. He said he had inspected Senna's car in February and March 1994, and he could not remember the modification and certainly no permission was granted for it. For their part, the Williams team denied the modification had not been approved. There was some doubt that permission for this sort of modification was needed.

Adrian Newey has only spoken about the modifications, though his lawyer, Luigi Stortoni, said: "Work was done on the steering rod. The same work was done on Hill's car. The diameters of the two pieces of pole were different. We are convinced that the welding was not the cause of it. The work was done in March, and both Hill and Senna had raced two Grand

Prix events with the modified cars, and there wasn't any problem." Patrick Head, also through his lawyer, Oreste Dominioni, said: "Damon Hill had the same modifications made to his car as Ayrton Senna. And I think he believes the job was well done. It was well done."

However, the official report of the accident said something entirely different. The panel of experts totally disagreed with Head and Newey. They were unanimous and wrote: "A modification to the steering column, which had been poorly executed, caused it to break. The steering column had been cut and a new element – which was not of the same quality metal or of the same diameter, being 18mm instead of 22mm – was welded in." It was where the new elements had been welded that the column broke. Photographic evidence backed this up.

The enquiry revealed that the modifications that Alan Young and Gavin Fisher had supervised were far from satisfactory. Tommaso Carletti, the ex-Ferrari race engineer who inspected the steering column, stated that there had been poor-quality workmanship, and the two metal extensions added to join the three sections of the column were the wrong diameter.

His view coincided with that of Mauro Forghieri and Enrico Lorenzini. The fact that the column had broken where inserts had been welded in was devastating for Williams.

Despite the fact that his former team has always stoutly defended the quality of the steering column modifications, they caused immense grief and anguish for chief designer Adrian Newey, who said: "I asked myself quite sincerely whether I should carry on. A driver had just died at the wheel of a car designed by me. I went through a really bad time. And then I did decide to carry on, but the pain is still there. I was just getting to know him when he left us. It was awful. We'll never know whether the accident was down to design error or something else altogether." These comments were made after Newey had left Williams. They could not have pleased Patrick Head as they did suggest that the Williams explanation for the cause of the accident was in doubt.

Damon Hill was eventually asked to give evidence at the official enquiry. He was a very poor witness and was clearly under pressure from Williams to say the right things and, if he couldn't, to say he couldn't remember, which he did a lot.

Hill confirmed that alterations were made to the steering column of both his and Senna's cars, but he wasn't sure when: "I can't remember the exact date. I seem to remember it being done before we ran the car. In other words, before it went to a racetrack. -I don't know when it was done. I can't tell you. I was made aware that it had been done."

When asked for his view of the accident, Hill said it was his opinion that Senna was attempting to correct oversteer when he went off the track. He said: "There are two distinct times when the car looks to be oversteering, and the steering wheel is exactly the way I would expect to see it to correct oversteer."

Hill said he had not experienced any problems with oversteer at the San Marino Grand Prix and mentioned a meeting held at the Williams factory to discuss the reasons for the accident: "I came away from the meeting with the opinion that there must have been some other reason for the accident other than the obvious one that there had been a failure in the steering."

Hill was widely criticised for being unconvincing, and critics said he seemed to have suffered from 'selective amnesia'. In truth, he was in a very difficult situation and did the best he could in those circumstances.

When it came to their turn, Patrick Head and Adrian Newey did not help their credibility when they refused to give evidence at the official enquiry into the accident. Clearly, they were advised by their lawyers not to do so. But after the missing telemetry and the missing video, it stretched their credibility to the limit, and doubts heavily influenced the enquiry's later decision against them. It seemed very poor advice and made it seem as though they had something to hide.

Previously, they had made an appearance at the enquiry on 15th April, when they spent the day listening as evidence was given by others about the state of the steering column on Senna's car. They were very interested in what other people had to say about the condition of the steering column but declined to say anything about it themselves.

Frank Williams did cooperate and appear at the enquiry. Williams was questioned closely about the modifications to the steering column: "Ayrton wanted more room in the cockpit. I remember that he was not happy about the amount of space, and there were many other things he wanted to change. He also wanted a very large steering wheel – it was one of his trademarks. It was decided to change the steering column. When it was decided, I don't remember. There would have been communication with all the relevant people. I can't be accurate or specific because I do not follow, and never have done, every operation on a daily basis."

Williams said he didn't know who was responsible for making the changes, only that many people would have been involved. When Williams was challenged about the fact that there was 40 per cent metal fatigue in the steering column where the modifications had been made, he made a very flippant reply that he was certain his own private jet he had travelled to Bologna in probably had cracks caused by metal fatigue in it. Williams said: "We'll probably never know what happened. But we think that the car probably left the road rather than suffered a steering column failure." Sir Frank's answers were strange. It is known that Williams is a very organised, safety obsessed, team. The records of the steering column changes – right from when Senna requested it, to when the request was granted and when the parts were fitted – would have been meticulously recorded. All components, especially important items like steering components, are 'lifed' and changed at the end of their predicted lives and thrown away regardless of their condition. That happens at every Formula One team.

Disregarding those processes can have serious implications for safety. There were some well-known examples of this. The Lotus team disregarded the processes in 1990 because it ran very short of money and stopped replacing components at the end of their designated lives. Because it couldn't afford to replace the parts at the end of their 'lives', it also stopped recording the lives of the components because there was no point. This was almost certainly the cause of Martin Donnelly's accident in qualifying for the Spanish Grand Prix at the Jerez circuit in 1990. In one of the most violent accidents in Formula One history, it was likely a component that was past its safe life failed, pitching Donnelly's Lotus against a barrier at very high speed. The accident was so violent that Donnelly was ripped from the car in his seat and flung onto the track. Miraculously, he survived. The Lotus team didn't and went out of business at the end of the season and was taken over by new owners who were critical of some of the processes used the previous season.

Williams was probably vague because he was instructed to be so by his lawyers. If the steering column did fail because of metal fatigue caused by poor workmanship, leaving Senna unable to steer his car, then the Williams team would probably have been out of business. It would have faced a huge lawsuit from Senna's family and sponsors would have deserted the team. And that is before the FIA would have taken any action. If it was the case that the steering column failure caused the accident then, in reality, Frank Williams and Patrick Head would have had little choice but to instigate a cover-up. No one is saying that they did, but plenty of people understood why they might have done so.

The enquiry eventually ruled that the accident was caused by the breaking of the steering column. In the 381-page written report published on 15th June 1998, the judge who led the enquiry, Antonio Costanzo, cited the reason for Ayrton Senna's crash at the 1994 San Marino Grand Prix as the breaking of the 'modified' steering column fitted to his Williams-Renault FW16B. He stated that, without that condition, Ayrton Senna's car would not have left the track at the Tamburello bend.

But there is always more to a motor racing accident than that, and last word is probably best left to Adrian Newey: "Ayrton Senna's accident was down to fate." That turned out to be, in the opinion of many, the truest statement Newey or any member of the Williams team ever made about the causes of the accident.

*"He was the one driver so perfect
that nobody thought anything
could happen to him."*
    Bernie Ecclestone
    August 1994

CHAPTER 26

Senna Goes Back to Brazil

The immediate aftermath

On the flight home to Austria in his private jet, Gerhard Berger sat in silence. When he reached his home in Austria at around 9pm on Sunday, he shut himself away. His wife and children were away and he was alone in the house. He spoke to no one. As he remembered: "I didn't talk to anyone for two days. I watched the telephone filling up with messages but I didn't feel like talking to anyone about it as nothing could change things. I just wanted to spend some time alone." Berger realised that his life had changed forever. Formula One would no longer be for him the carefree occupation it had once been. Although he had never been Senna's best friend, they had been very good friends. Senna intimidated him and carved him up on the track just like he did everyone else, and Berger had always resented it. But off track, their relationship could not have be better. Many years earlier, as his team mate, Berger had accepted Senna for who and what he was, flaws and all. He had decided that the upside of their friendship vastly outweighed the downside. It was precisely what many people felt about Senna. Everyone knew the downside but they also knew the upside, and that is what made his passing so unbearable for so many people that Monday morning of 2nd May 1994.

After two days of self-imposed solitary confinement, Berger flew to São Paulo for the funeral.

Alain Prost flew back to Paris on a chartered Renault jet that night along with the chairman of Renault, Louis Schweitzer. He was in pieces and unsure about everything in his life. For him, the fun had also suddenly gone out of the sport he loved. The events at Imola, reconciliation with Senna, and then his death had thrown him the biggest curve ball of his life. Along with all that, there was immediate pressure on him to return to the Williams team and take over his drive. Pressure was already starting to come from Renault. After all, Prost was being paid $14 million during 1994 to do nothing. To end the speculation and get Renault off his back, he was forced to announce he would never drive a Formula One car again.

Prost also had the dilemma of whether or not he should attend the funeral. He remembered: "Ayrton and I had such a history for so long that I didn't really know how the Brazilian people would perceive it: would they be upset if I went? Upset if I didn't go, or what?" That night, Jean-Luc Lagardère, the chairman of Matra, telephoned to ask him questions about Ayrton Senna's accident. Lagardère's wife, Bethy, was a former Brazilian model and she was very upset. She was the same age as Senna, and they had known each other in Brazil.

After Prost spoke to Bethy and tried to cheer her up, he was put back on the phone to Lagardère. He asked him whether he should go to the funeral. Lagardère said he would discuss it with his wife and ring him back. 15 minutes later, Lagardère was back on the phone. Bethy was adamant he should go, he told him. She grabbed the phone again and told Prost that the Brazilian people would be upset if he didn't go.

That settled it for Prost. He regarded the Lagardères as two of his closest friends and Jean-Luc as one of the sagest men in France. Prost started making preparations to fly out to São Paulo.

Julian Jakobi stayed on overnight in Bologna and flew back to London the following morning. He wife, Fiona, collected him from Heathrow airport and they talked about the weekend on the hour drive back across London to their house in Hampstead, a suburb of London. Fiona Jakobi was as devastated as her husband. Like Bethy Lagardère she loved Senna like she loved her own sons.

Jakobi told his wife he was going to book the first flight to São Paulo and leave immediately. He packed a change of clothing, had a shower and some lunch and was driven straight back to the airport. Jakobi was clear about his role in the coming days: "Because I wasn't family, but I had to keep the family going. So one kept going, really, on adrenalin and everything else."

After leaving late in the evening, Josef Leberer had driven back overnight to his home in Austria and arrived early on Monday morning. He planned to return with Senna's coffin to São Paulo but was unsure of what the arrangements would be. He waited at home by the telephone for news.

On Monday morning, a black hearse arrived at the hospital to take Senna's body to Bologna's mortuary in accordance with Italian law. The mortuary had been surrounded by fans the previous evening, after his death was announced. The body of Roland Ratzenberger was also there, awaiting its own autopsy. The outpouring of grief in Bologna was almost as it was in São Paulo. The Italians regarded Senna as one of their own, and they always had.

Antonio Braga stayed in Bologna to make the arrangements to repatriate Senna's body to São Paulo. The Bologna authorities refused to release the body immediately, insisting on a full autopsy. Leonardo Da Silva was put on the first flight back to São Paulo to be with his family. His grief was unbounded, made worse by the fact that his brother had gone to his grave with the two on bad terms over Adriane. Braga was very glad to get Leonardo on the plane and off his hands.

Adriane Galisteu woke up on Monday morning in a daze. She had slept very little. When she opened her eyes, she was unsure whether she had had a terrible dream. She hoped and prayed it had been a dream. She soon realised it was the worst kind of reality and knew that her whole future now hung in the balance. Something that seemed so sure now seemed so uncertain, and something that had given her so much pleasure now gave her more than equal amounts of grief. As far as she was concerned, her life had effectively ended – there was nothing else she could think.

The Braga house in Sintra, Portugal, was also surrounded by reporters, anxious to interview Adriane. Pictures from outside the house were being broadcast live back to Brazil. The whole world's media was interested in her story once the enormity of what had happened sank in. With the immediate family incommunicado, the focus was all on the beautiful 21-year-old blonde model, who, as far as the media were concerned, was effectively Senna's widow.

When Braga rang the house from Bologna, Adriane told him she wanted to come and see Senna's body. She told him she felt a desperate need for firm evidence, seen with her own eyes, that he was dead.

Braga advised her against it, and thought it unlikely that she would even be admitted. She took his advice, believing she would be able to see him for the last time in São Paulo before the funeral. In Brazil, it was traditional for the coffin to be left open, or at least to have a glass top. What she didn't know was that the wound to Senna's head would disturb the family. Cosmetic experts could have repaired the damage, but in the end the coffin would stay closed.

With the bedlam outside the house, Braga advised his wife Luiza that the best option was to stage a makeshift press conference outside the house for the media and then they would go away. Adriane agreed to do it, and she felt it would connect her to her boyfriend again. She relished talking about him.

But she hadn't reckoned on the insensitivity of some of the journalists from South America, who were just looking for a sensational story. Some of them had heard about the rift with the Da Silvas and their insensitivity was astounding in the light of what had happened 24 hours earlier.

One female journalist asked Adriane if she had a return ticket to São Paulo and who would be paying for her ticket. It was not the sort of question she wanted to hear or answer.

Adriane felt like she was being victimised by a hostile media looking for exclusive stories on the drama of Senna's death. She was in no state to withstand it and was clearly in great distress.

It took Miriam Dutra of TV Globo to recognise what was happening and to try and rectify it and protect Adriane. Dutra was very sympathetic to Adriane and had been dispatched urgently to Portugal to cover the story. She took over the questioning and made it clear how she felt about the way some of her media colleagues were behaving. After that, the unpleasant questions tailed off.

Afterwards, Adriane asked Dutra if she could have all the video footage of the crash that TV Globo had. She wanted to see everything she could about the accident. Dutra agreed to get it to her the following morning before she left for São Paulo.

Monday came and went for dazed Adriane, and she was sedated to help her sleep that night. The sedatives had little effect – she was still stunned from events and in a permanent state of disbelief.

Meanwhile, Antonio Braga and Galvao Bueno were desperately trying to organise the repatriation of Senna's body to São Paulo. Naturally, the family wanted it returned to Brazil as soon as possible. They thought this would be relatively simple until the Italian authorities told them the autopsy would not take place until Tuesday, and Senna's body would be released that evening. Braga and Bueno argued it out but it was no use, and they accepted the 24-hour delay. They told the Da Silva family to schedule the funeral for Thursday.

On Tuesday morning, Miriam Dutra collected the footage of the race on VHS videotape and sent it by messenger to Adriane Galisteu in Sintra. Adriane sat on the sofa and watched it over and over, accompanied by Luiza Braga and her children. She seemed obsessed with finding the reason for his crash. No one could understand why he had just driven off the circuit into the wall for no apparent reason.

Adriane also telephoned Angelo Orsi, the Italian photographer who had taken pictures of Senna after the accident. Adriane felt a desperate need for some physical proof he was dead. Orsi got permission from the family to send her a selection of the photographs. But Orsi warned her they must not leave her possession.

The autopsies of Senna and Ratzenberger both took place, as planned, on Tuesday morning. It was straightforward. The causes of death were no more complicated than in any road accident victim who had died of head injuries.

Braga and Bueno worked feverishly on the arrangements for repatriating Senna's body and, by lunchtime, it had been authorised for transfer back to Brazil. There was no shortage of offers to help. Principally there were two options: a direct flight with the Italian Air Force, or via Paris with Varig. The Italians seemed quite happy to fly the coffin straight back to São Paulo. In the end, Senna's parents would decide and both offers would be needed.

Back in Sintra, Adriane was suddenly feeling a cool wind from the Senna family in São Paulo. On both Monday and Tuesday, she had tried to telephone Senna's parents. She was told by the family's maid that both were under sedation and could not be disturbed. After a while this annoyed her, and she wondered what she had done, especially as she had shared her grief with Neyde on the Sunday.

On Tuesday afternoon, she got through to Viviane's husband Flavio Lalli, who told her it was a very difficult situation at the family house and that he was having difficulty talking to his own wife, who he said was shattered to the point of speechlessness. Lalli told her it was impossible for anyone to have any sort of conversation with either Milton or Neyde Da Silva. They had taken the news worse than anyone else. He said they remained sedated and virtually silent, almost unaware of what was going on around them.

Braga couldn't fare any better and, in the end, he made the travel decisions himself. He asked the Italian Air Force if it could get Senna's coffin to Paris to connect with Varig's flight that evening direct to São Paulo. Flight no RG723 was leaving just before midnight on Tuesday, so there was little time.

The Italians were delighted to help. Braga also asked Varig to clear out the business class cabin for Senna's coffin as he told them it was not travelling in the cargo hold. Varig's manager in Paris told Braga that there were only two people booked in first class and 12 in business class. Therefore he said the easiest thing to do was to move the 12 to first class as there were 16 seats, leaving the whole business class section free for Senna's coffin and his companions on the flight. The business class passengers were delighted to be bumped up to first class, although they were not told why.

The mahogany coffin left the mortuary at San Maggiore hospital at around two o'clock in the afternoon in a Mercedes hearse with a police escort. Galvao Bueno, Celso Lemos and Betise Assumpcao followed behind in a separate car with Senna's personal belongings, retrieved from his plane and the Williams motorhome.

Antonio Braga decided not to fly home with the coffin and, instead, he would escort Adriane back to Brazil along with his wife and children. By the time the coffin reached Bologna airport, he was on his way to Lisbon, ready to join his wife and Adriane for a flight to São Paulo for the funeral.

Word had got around and most of the route to the airport was lined with Italians saying their farewells. There seemed to be an enormous sense of guilt amongst ordinary Italians over the fact that Ayrton Senna had died in Italy.

At the airport, the Mercedes was allowed to draw right up to the Italian DC9. An honour guard of two lines of Italian policemen stood to attention as Senna's coffin was loaded on the plane. Brazil's ambassador to Italy, Orland Carbonara, saw the plane off to Paris. The DC9 took off at around 5pm for the two-hour flight to Paris.

Captain O'Mahoney was still waiting at Bologna and he asked to fly Bueno, Lemos and Assumpcao to Paris. They took off after the DC9 and followed it in to land alongside the DC9 on the runway, awaiting the incoming Varig flight. O'Mahoney had offered to fly Senna's body back to São Paulo in the HS125, which could make the trip if it stopped for fuel. But the plane's doors were not wide enough for the coffin and O'Mahoney was secretly relieved – it would have been too emotional and the job was best left to Varig. As he said: "I'm not sure I would have had the bottle to do that trip."

During the flight to Paris, O'Mahoney talked with the three and they reminisced, recalling how they had often flown from Bologna to Paris with Senna on their way home with him to Brazil after a race.

Although it had all been agreed, O'Mahoney was concerned that when it came to it, Varig would not allow the coffin into the main cabin and would insist it travelled in the cargo hold. He said captains had unofficial rules about dead bodies and some considered them bad luck to have on board. He suspected there might be a problem. They were determined it wouldn't. Bueno said he would get TV Globo to charter a private plane if Varig insisted it went in the hold.

Oddly enough, they were all looking forward to the 11-hour flight home and were absolutely determined that Ayrton Senna, as he always did, would fly home in the passenger compartment with them.

Two hours later, right on time, the Italian DC9 landed in Paris, and Senna's coffin was taken to a special part of the terminal to await being moved on board the Varig plane. The formalities were waived and the French officials paid their own respects as the coffin rested in the terminal before Senna left Europe for the last time.

The airport crew duly got ready to remove the seats when the aircraft arrived and the stewardesses issued all the business class passengers with new boarding passes. Then the trouble began. The captain, a pilot called Gomes Pinto, arrived and was briefed by Varig's Paris night manager about the unusual situation. But Pinto wasn't having it and told Bueono, Lemos and Assumpcao that the coffin would have to travel in the cargo hold, citing IATA regulations. As they argued, the Varig McDonnell-Douglas MD-11 arrived at the terminal and the incoming passengers got out and the new ones prepared to board.

There was an argument and Bueno phoned through to the family in Brazil and spoke to Antonio Braga, who was back in Portugal. Braga contacted Varig's head office. The chief executive of Varig was contacted and quickly briefed on the situation. Varig was in a difficult position. Even though it owned the aircraft and employed the captain, it could not easily override his decision. The captain of a flight is in sole charge and responsible for the aeroplane. It could not change his decision unless he changed it himself. Braga told Varig that if Senna could not travel in the cabin, then he would not travel with Varig at all and they would charter a jet or get another airline to fly him. This would have been a public relations disaster for the airline.

Varig's head office faxed the captain and advised him to let the coffin travel in the passenger section. Bueno recalled: "The captain tried everything to stop us. First, he told us it could not be done because of IATA rules. Then he demanded an okay from the family."

There was a huge row between Pinto and Bueno, but the captain finally relented when he realised the enormity of the consequences of his decision, and he was not really sure what the IATA regulations actually were. Some airline pilots, especially certain Brazilian ones, are known to have huge admiration for themselves. Pinto realised just in time that he was out of order and relented.

The six seats were removed to accommodate the coffin, and it was covered by the Brazilian flag. By then, Josef Leberer had also joined them, flying in from his home in Austria.

Meanwhile, Braga, relieved that the problem was sorted, gathered up Luiza and Adriane for the flight back to Brazil. There were no direct flights: they boarded a plane from Lisbon to Rio de Janeiro, which would continue on to São Paulo at around midnight on Tuesday 2nd May and would arrive at about the same time as the coffin. Adriane sat motionless with Antonio and Luiza Braga. The stewards were well aware of who they were and provided them with every comfort.

As soon as the Varig flight departed Paris with Senna's coffin on board, Captain O'Mahoney jumped back into Senna's HS-125 jet and filed a flight plan to Heathrow. He took off and an hour later he was at Heathrow. He changed into a dark suit he always carried on the plane and caught the first scheduled British Airways flight to São Paulo.

Senna's flight home was almost silent and broken only by prayer. The window blinds were closed and Leberer remembers: "It was something that I will never forget. We were there for 11 hours with the coffin, with the Brazilian flag and a rose on it, but you know that the soul is gone." The co-pilot joined them all for some prayers around the coffin.

When the plane reached Brazilian airspace 11 hours later, a detachment of Brazilian Air Force fighter planes formed an escort. Dawn was breaking as the MD11 descended into São Paulo, and as the pilot prepared to land, the fighters departed for their bases. The landing in half light, as the sun came up, was surreal. It was an unforgettable experience and something Ayrton Senna had done so many times in life as he came home, exhausted after yet another race.

Eleven hours after leaving Paris, Captain Gomes Pinto touched down the plane at 6:15am at Guaralhos airport. The first class and economy passengers disembarked immediately. The plane was greeted by São Paulo's mayor Paulo Salim Maluf and state governor Luiz Antonio Fleury.

At the same time, the Bragas and Adriane had reached Rio de Janeiro for a 20-minute stopover. The rest of the passengers disembarked, but the three of them were allowed to stay on board. Less than a week earlier, Adriane had flown to Portugal full of hope for the future. Now she returned to great uncertainty. She was also unsure of the family's reaction. She had not spoken to anyone since Senna's death other than Flavio Lalli, Viviane's husband, who had treated her coolly.

Whilst the plane was being cleaned and refuelled in Rio, she changed into a black suit so she could go straight to the building where the coffin was to be kept until Senna was buried the following day. The plane landed in São Paulo just 20 minutes after the Varig flight carrying Senna.

Waiting were a million citizens, who had got up early to line the six-lane motorway through the suburbs from the airport to welcome their hero home for the last time. Most were under 25.

Brazil's President Franco had already declared three days of national mourning, including a day off for schoolchildren. The Brazilian flag was flown at half-mast on all government buildings across the country.

It took 30 minutes more to unload Senna's coffin. An electric lift carried it down to soldiers from the Polícia da Aeronáutica, who carried Senna's body to a fire engine, where it was draped in the Brazilian flag. The fire engine would carry the coffin into the city centre to lie in state. At 6:45am, the fire engine moved off, preceded by 17 police motorbikes.

The policemen were wearing white leather suits and led a motorcade on the 20-mile journey into the city. On the rear of the fire engine, four cadets from the Military Police academy sat on each side of the coffin, facing fore and aft, mounting guard; five more were on the ledge at the rear of the engine. In addition, 2,500 policemen lined the route.

The policemen were to keep the crowds back, but they couldn't stop the cars. The roads were kept open as swarms of vehicles crowded the procession, getting as close as possible to the moving coffin, even on the wrong side of the carriageway, in their desperation to see the last glimpse of the coffin holding Senna's remains. Many cars had been adorned with swathes of black material on the aerials and pictures of Senna taped to the windows.

It would take the fire engine three hours to reach its destination as noisy police and television helicopters clattered overhead.

As it neared the end, the procession slowed and an honour guard of 33 mounted cavalry, carrying lances, joined the procession. The horses escorted the fire engine as it crawled between São Paulo's streets. By now, there were huge crowds welcoming their hero home. On both sides of the road they were at least 20 deep.

The fire engine was followed by thousands on foot, bicycles and motorcycles. Office workers from tower blocks showered the coffin with ticker tape, confetti and flowers. Banners and graffiti covered all available space on tunnels and bridges: 'Obrigado Senna' (thank you Senna), 'Senna não morreu, porque os deuses não morrem' (Senna isn't dead, because gods don't die). And 'Obrigado, Senna por fazer nossos domingos felizes' (thank you for making our Sundays so happy). They all shouted "Ole, ole, ole, Senna, Senna, Senna." All of the Brazilian TV channels were broadcasting the event and tensions were very high. Brazilian newspapers were reporting that the real time of Senna's death was 2:17pm and that he died at the trackside. They were saying that he was brought artificially back to life and that the race should never have been re-started. Much of it was being stoked up by Leonardo Da Silva, who wasn't thinking particularly straight, blinded by the tragedy that had befallen his family.

The coffin finally reached the state legislative assembly, where it would lie in state.

The 1950s building was set in Ibirapuera Park, south of central São Paulo. The Da Silva family were already there waiting for the coffin along with more than 20,000 people waiting in a queue to file past the coffin and pay their respects. Before that could start, the family attended a 20-minute service conducted by a pastor Sabatini Lalli, after which an old helmet of Senna's was placed on top of the coffin by his sister, Viviane.

After the ceremony, two soldiers with pikes and four with rifles, with their weapons reversed by tradition for a fallen hero, took up guard.

The people of São Paulo began to file past one side of the catafalque, and the other side was roped off for VIPs. The VIPs, with a special badge, could come and go as they pleased via a rear door. Beyond the special roped-off area was a private room.

Entry to both areas was by a special badge, with either a plain 'F' on it for Familias (family) or 'A' for Amigos (friends). The 'F' and 'A' badges were given to around 500 people who would also attend the funeral. When Captain Owen O'Mahoney arrived, Senna's mother rushed up to him and they hugged for more than five minutes. She saw that he was wearing an 'A' badge. She ripped it off and replaced it with an 'F' badge. O'Mahoney was overcome with emotion as Neyde Da Silva told him Senna had regarded him as family.

A special area and access was given to the media. A raised platform, with some chairs, had been constructed. It was crammed with TV crews and photographers, who used their regular FIA accreditation to gain entry.

Adriane Galisteu arrived and was bitterly disappointed when she discovered the coffin was closed. She said: "I couldn't understand, I couldn't believe, I couldn't accept it. I thought the coffin would have a glass lid or something that would allow me to see him for the last time. But it was completely sealed. I felt terrible disappointment; a shiver ran down my spine."

Adriane quickly became the centre of attention as she flitted in and out. She was protected from the crowds by municipal minders. She needed them, as 8,000 people were passing through the room every hour; that would continue for 24 hours.

Although relations were strained, Adriane greeted Senna's family cordially. But otherwise she kept her distance. They all had their private grief to contain. Of the family, Neyde and Viviane, his mother and sister, were in the worst shape. Leonardo simply paced the room and Milton kept his distance, stoically observing the scene, as was his way.

Senna's Brazilian personal trainer, Nuno Cobra, was distraught and his tears simply overflowed in the most public display of grief in the private area. Cobra just couldn't comprehend that Senna would not be returning the following October to resume his winter fitness routine. His face was distorted temporarily from crying and his eyes had swelled up. He was being comforted by Josef Leberer. Senna was Cobra's whole life, and that life was gone. He had no idea how he was going to cope.

In the special room, people chatted quietly, including world champions Emerson Fittipaldi, Alain Prost and Jackie Stewart. Derek Warwick turned up. He was not expected but felt he had to come. There was a poignant moment when Neyde Da Silva approached him. She told him through an interpreter: "You know Derek, Ayrton always had a special place in his heart for you."

When the current Brazilian Formula One drivers, Rubens Barrichello and Christian Fittipaldi, turned up, the crowds cheered.

Outside a huge display of floral tributes was starting to build up. There were wreaths from almost every racing organisation and from famous individuals. Some were exotic affairs. The most impressive were two huge white crosses from TAG Group and the McLaren team. The wreaths formed an avenue of flowers, together with random bunches from ordinary fans which started to form a carpet of flowers.

That morning in another room, Senna's brother Leonardo held a press conference on behalf of his family. Three days had passed and his extreme grief had turned into extreme anger. He said the family was furious that the race had been restarted when it was clear Senna had died when his car impacted the wall. He said: "The motorsport authorities are only interested in money." He condemned the governing body FIA. He said it knew the dangers the drivers were facing at Imola's Tamburello corner and that a narrow strip of grass and 20 metres of tarmac was insufficient to separate the track from a solid concrete wall. He said: "If they'd taken the correct precautions, my brother would be alive today." There was some merit in what he said, although it conveniently forgot that his brother had inspected the facilities many times and agreed with the officials that all that could be done to make Tamburello safer had been done.

Leonardo had whipped up a frenzy of anti-FIA, anti-Ecclestone and anti-Mosley fervour. He was almost irrational in his hatred. Leonardo blamed the authorities outright for his brother's death, and said that Ecclestone or Mosley would not be welcome at the funeral. Mosley decided not to come but Ecclestone wished to say goodbye to his friend.

All through that evening, night and morning, mourners filed past the coffin. Ron and Lisa Dennis, surrounded by bodyguards in dark suits, arrived and sat for 40 silent minutes, doubtless reflecting on his six years with Senna at McLaren and three world championships. Lisa Dennis was totally distraught.

Senna's family came in and out. Adriane kept vigil all night and did not sleep. She remembers: "I walked around and felt I was being looked at, watched. I didn't care. I felt like jumping into the coffin and screaming."

Friends urged her to rest overnight in preparation for the funeral, but she refused. She did, however, take a shower at Antonio Braga's nearby hotel room.

At dawn on Thursday, Frank Williams arrived to pay his respects and spoke to Adriane what words he could. Inevitably, they would be inadequate. Williams was devastated that Senna had lost his life in one of his cars. He was also distraught by what might have been. What might have been if they had signed Senna when he first tested their car and driven it so fast back in 1984? Now, having finally arrived at Williams ten years later, after four months it was all gone.

,

"He established his own limits. When he reached those limits, he wanted to beat them and establish new ones. I never knew how far he could go. I had an understanding, but I didn't know."

Alain Prost
August 1995

CHAPTER 27

A Nation's Grief

Two million Brazilians attend Senna's funeral

By the end of the public viewing, over a quarter of a million Brazilians had filed past Ayrton Senna's coffin in the state legislative building to pay their respects. The flow of people had continued through the night and could have continued for another week, such were the queues. At one point in the afternoon, it was estimated that the queue was one and a half miles long. In the 80-degree heat, it took over six hours from those at the back to reach the front

At 10 o'clock on Thursday morning, 4th May 1994, it was brought to an end by a 21-gun salute, fired by the 2nd Artillery Brigade. The gunfire rang out over Ibirapuera Park.

It signified that it was time for Senna's coffin to leave for its final resting place. Rose petals were strewn over it, and a cadre of military cadets arrived to take it from the catafalque to a waiting fire engine for the final 10-mile journey to Morumbi cemetery.

Birgit Sauer, the wife of the head of Volkswagen Brazil, had volunteered to look after Adriane Galisteu and accompany her to the funeral. The Da Silva family seemed to want to have nothing to do with Adriane, and Birgit tried to protect her from the obvious animosity. Birgit and Adriane were friends and had holidayed together and forged a very close friendship. They were now united in grief.

Adriane and Birgit got into a minibus along with Gerhard Berger and Christian Fittipaldi. The bus's curtains were drawn to protect passengers' privacy. It followed directly behind the fire engine carrying Senna's coffin. One young boy ran alongside the bus all the way to the cemetery.

The streets were lined with ordinary Brazilians, screaming grief. Many had tears streaming down their faces. Brazil had never seen anything like it, and the outpouring of grief was unprecedented.

It seemed that no one in Brazil had come to terms with what had happened in the four days since Senna's death. Like John F. Kennedy's death 31 years earlier, it was an almost impossible thing to come to terms with. Ever since Senna's death, people all over the world had been comparing it with Kennedy's. Senna's death was to Brazil what President Kennedy's had been to America. There had not been a public death like Senna's since 1963, and there hasn't been one since. Both men had died with honour just doing their jobs, and the devastation left behind had no precedent and no equal.

The day of the funeral seemed to spark emotions in São Paulo even more extreme than on Sunday. It is estimated that over 300,000 people lined the route to the cemetery, and it seemed as though the rest of Brazil was watching it on television. Clapping broke out all along the route as Senna passed by. Adriane wondered to herself if her boyfriend could hear it inside his coffin. Wherever he was, she wrote later, she thought it certain he was hearing it.

Seven planes of the Brazilian Air Force aerobatic display team, in diamond formation, laid smoke trails as the cortege crawled up the hill to Morumbi, high above the city. The last half mile was a steep winding road and, to Adriane, it seemed to take hours to climb it.

The Cemitério de Morumbi, overlooked by private apartment buildings, is a huge round park, with discreet headstones laid into the grass, horizontally in Brazilian tradition. Behind its high walls, there waited the VIP guests and hundreds more people from the world of motor racing. Many of the racing people had all flown in and assembled that morning at the Intercontinental Hotel, where specially laid-on coaches had taken them to Morumbi. Betise Assumpcao had taken charge of all the arrangements. She felt it was her last duty to her boss.

Many guests helicoptered straight in. Assumpcao arranged for the helicopters to land behind a small clump of trees. Captain O'Mahoney was surprised to find himself being given very special treatment by the Da Silva family. Expecting to catch a taxi to the cemetery, he was led off to a helicopter where he found Jackie and Paul Stewart inside along with

Alain Prost. When they touched down, they were met by armed Brazilian soldiers in grey combat uniforms wearing black caps. The soldiers closely watched over the many very important people who emerged from the helicopters.

A rope-lined pathway of light green carpet led to the open grave, where tarpaulins covered by green plastic grass protected the edges of the freshly dug grave. Prost, the Stewarts and O'Mahoney went over to where Milton Da Silva was standing to pay their respects. He shook hands with them and then beckoned O'Mahoney over to him. He handed him a small package, one of six he had on a seat next to him. Speaking through an interpreter, he told O'Mahoney: "Ayrton had many acquaintances and friends, but there were only six people he really trusted in the world. You were one of them." O'Mahoney was completely overcome. He had no idea who the other five packages were for, but he clutched his tightly for the rest of the service. When he got back to his hotel room afterwards, he found inside was a heavy gold bracelet with his name inscribed on it. It marked the beginning of a long association with the Da Silva family that has endured to this day.

When Ayrton Senna's coffin reached the cemetery, Assumpcao took charge again as it was offloaded onto a green metal trolley as the heat of the sun was deemed too much for the pall bearers to carry the coffin on their shoulders.

The coffin and the trolley were covered by the Brazilian national flag as it waited to be pushed up the hill to the graveside. It had already been decided by the Da Silva family that this would be done by current and former Formula One drivers. Assumpcao decided exactly who the pallbearers would be and who would be positioned where. She knew this was the image that would be beamed all over the world.

She didn't like the first line-up and after some careful thought, repositioned Gerhard Berger and Emerson Fittipaldi at the head of the coffin. At her signal, it moved off. Other drivers pushing the trolley and escorting it were Alain Prost, Michele Alboreto, Sir Jackie Stewart, Damon Hill, Emerson, Wilson and Christian Fittipaldi, Rubens Barrichello, Mauricio Gugelmin, Maurizio Sandro Sala, Roberto Moreno and Raul Boesel, Pedro Lamy, Derek Warwick, Johnny Herbert, Thierry Boutsen and Hans Stuck Jr.

As all this was happening, six television helicopters flew overhead broadcasting live pictures right across South America.

As the trolley pulled to a halt, the 2nd Guards Battalion of the South-Eastern Military Command stood at the ready, and three volleys of salute from the guards' automatic weapons resounded. In between each volley, the clicking camera shutters echoed round, and the empty brass shells fell to the ground.

At the graveside, a white canopy protected family and friends from the very hot midday sun. In front, some temporary chairs had been arranged. Once again, Assumpcao had gone ahead and was directing everything. At the front was the family: Milton and Neyde Da Silva, Leonardo Da Silva, Viviane Lalli and her husband Flavio and their three children, Bruno, Bianca and Paula. In the second row were Adriane Galisteu and Xuxa Meneghel, Senna's former girlfriend. Xuxa Meneghel was a television presenter and a popular celebrity in Brazil.

Xuxa had already taken her seat, and when Adriane took her designated place next to her, Xuxa immediately got up and moved to another seat. It was an extraordinary slight to Adriane, but it had been insensitive to put the two women together. It seemed as though Xuxa had been designated by the Da Silva family as Senna's unofficial widow, even though she had not seen or communicated with Senna for over two years. She had travelled to the funeral with them and left with them. In their grief, the family were trying to rewrite history and paint Adriane out of their son's life.

It reflected the coolness they all felt towards Adriane, which was only thawed a little by Neyde Da Silva, who clearly disagreed with the family's stance but was forced to accept it.

If Ayrton Senna was looking down on events that day, he would have been mightily upset – just as he was with his family's attitude towards Adriane in the weeks before his death. But no one, least of all Adriane, wanted to cause any fuss. She accepted what was going on and in some ways even understood it. It was a remarkably mature display and endeared her forever to ordinary Brazilians. She focused all her emotions on her dead boyfriend, knowing this was the last time she would be close to him.

The service was conducted by the pastor Sabatini Lalli. After he had finished, Viviane Lalli rose to speak on behalf of the family. She said:

"Brazil is going through a very bad time. No one feels like helping anyone any more. People just live for themselves. My brother had a mission, and our family is in deep emotion today because we didn't realise it had made him so greatly loved. I saw how the ordinary people showed their feelings. Some of them were shoeless; others dressed in silk. He united them, even through his death. I think that my brother is not down there but up in the heavens."

When she finished speaking, she threw up her right arm in imitation of her brother's victory salute she had seen, mostly on television, after every one of his 41 Grand Prix victories. "Valeu Senna!" she cried. And the 500 mourners responded almost in unison: "Valeu Senna!"

It had been hard for everyone to hear her as the clatter of helicopters overhead was very noisy, but they had all heard that. It was the most poignant moment and everyone was crying. At that moment, Adriane looked over the crowd of mourners and particularly noticed the grief that was etched on the face of Lisa Dennis. She had got to know Lisa during Senna's last season at McLaren, and the two women had bonded even though her English and Lisa's limited Portuguese had made communication difficult. Now their eyes briefly met, both seemingly reading each other's feelings. Adriane never forgot the look of true grief on her face.

As Viviane Lalli finished her speech, the Brazilian Air Force aerobatic team traced a big heart and a giant 'S' in white smoke against the deep blue sky. It was aerial artistry at its best and an extraordinary sight in the early afternoon heat.

But Adriane Galisteu hardly noticed as she stared at her boyfriend's coffin for the last time and she mouthed the words to herself in silence: "I love you, but you left me. I miss you. From now on, my life will be a misery."

The ceremony had lasted for just 30 minutes in bright sunlight, under a perfect blue sky.

After the service, the coffin was lowered into the ground and covered with earth. Workmen arranged the family's flowers carefully around the grave, making sure the wreaths did not cover the plaque set into the freshly laid turf. The plaque, in Brazilian tradition, read 'Ayrton Senna Da Silva 21.3.1960 – 1.5.94. Nada pode me separar do amor de Deus.' In translation: "Nothing can separate me from the love of God."

Then the family stood up in front of the small canopied area and all the mourners filed by to pay their last respects. The mourners were in no hurry to leave, but gradually one by one withdrew to the helicopters and coaches. Pointedly, Xuxa Meneghel left in an official family limousine. Adriane Galisteu appeared to attempt to join another of the family limousines but was turned away. Later she denied that she had and said she was simply saying goodbye to the family. Whatever happened, Adriane was not welcome at the family reception afterwards, and she left in the bus in which she had arrived to join the Bragas at their farm. Many people thought that the brutal display by the Da Silva family that day did them no credit. But it was the culmination of what had been a short and bitter fight over Ayrton Senna. The family had lost out to Adriane on that battle and now maybe they were taking their revenge. In some strange way, they seemed to blame her for his death. She was simply not good enough for them. Nothing she could do could change that and, in the end, she accepted it gracefully.

The apparent rejection appeared cruel, but it reflected the majority of the family's view of Adriane and the reason why Senna's last conversation with his brother had been so adversarial, something Leonardo Da Silva would have to live with for the rest of his life.

Alain Prost was the last to leave the graveside. The reigning world champion, although no longer competing in Formula One, was a magnet for the media crews, and he made sure he obliged all requests to talk about Senna's accident. He was available to every journalist that day no matter how long it took. He said: "I was shocked. He was the kind of guy you really think it won't happen to. He was the master of his job. For sure, something happened with the car. Motor racing is always dangerous, but we must minimise the risks wherever possible. I think it's time for changing a lot of things. It's not a question of rules. It's a question of philosophy, of whether you have respect for drivers."

He also talked about how he and Senna had become reconciled and were enjoying a growing warmth towards each other, culminating in an embrace at Imola on the eve of the crash. He continued: "For 10 years it was Prost and Senna. Now it's just Prost. Half of my career has gone today."

After everyone had departed, a line of vans arrived to unload the mass of flowers from Ibirapuera Park. By 1:30pm they were all laid out, apart

from one late arriving floral tribute from the American singer, Tina Turner.
The funeral had attracted over 400 regular members of the international
Formula One community who had flown in. Many had not known Senna
very well at all, and some had never even met him. And some who had
known him very well did not come.

Three significant figures had elected not to come. Nigel Mansell was in
the middle of the Indianapolis 500 race programme, a serious event in
America. Instead, Mansell sent a letter to the family. He wrote that he
fought many races with Ayrton, lost most of the fights, but even when
he won he knew that he had had the honour to defeat the best driver of
all time. He also wrote that he knew Ayrton had the habit of anonymous-
ly helping needy organisations and people. Therefore, if Ayrton's family
was thinking about starting a foundation or something like it, they should
please not consider the amount but the feeling – and he enclosed a cheque
for $5,000 to kick the fund off. Mansell's $5,000 proved to be the start and
catalyst for the creation of the Ayrton Senna Foundation.

The current world championship leader, Michael Schumacher, did not go
because he simply did not care for funerals. He said: "I can't do something
like that in public, in front of everyone. I went to his grave two years later,
before the Brazilian Grand Prix. But on my own. Only my wife was with
me."

Nelson Piquet was not a friend of Senna's in life and refused in his death
to attend his funeral. He said: "I've never liked going to funerals, and I
didn't want to act like Prost did, pretending he was Senna's friend when
they had actually spent all their lives fighting with each other."

Neither did Max Mosley, president of the FIA, attend. He had been the
subject of much criticism in Brazil for allowing the race to be restarted
after Senna's accident. The Da Silva family thought it an outrage and a
massive show of disrespect. The family simply did not realise that the
race always went on in Formula One, regardless. After all, death had been
absent from the sport for so long.

Bernie Ecclestone was also missing from the funeral service but was
holed up in the nearby Intercontinental hotel. The family had asked him
not to attend. Apparently, Senna had often talked to his father about his
relationship with Ecclestone. Senna felt it was cordial and warm on the

surface but bittersweet underneath. Senna was all too aware that, behind the scenes, Ecclestone was probably ultimately responsible for many of the troubles he faced outside the cockpit in Formula One. Sometimes, it was simply an unseen clash of egos. Formula One was sometimes simply not big enough for two such giant personalities.

But regardless of that, the two men were very close. Senna had stayed with the Ecclestone family at their London home in Chelsea Square many times. He loved the infectious enthusiasm of Ecclestone's wife, Slavica, and the way she jealously protected her family's well-being. Ecclestone's two young daughters, Petra and Tamara, were devastated by Senna's death. But Ecclestone didn't waste his trip and later met with the state governor, Luiz Antonio Fleury, to brief him on what had happened in Imola. A year later, there was a rapprochement with the family after emotions had cooled.

As the day wound down, Josef Leberer summed it up, saying to journalists he didn't believe his friend would have been afraid of death. He told them: "I remember a test in Hockenheim once, and he said to me, 'Isn't it, Josef, that we have a fantastic life? Haven't we a good life?' I said to him, 'Are you afraid that this is going to stop one day?' He replied: 'No, because I have such a good life now so whatever comes, comes.'"

A NATION'S GRIEF

"I think it's not impossible that in time we might have become friends. We shared an awful lot, and the one thing never changed, even when our relationship was at its worst, was our great respect for each other as drivers"
Alain Prost
Friday 6th May 1994

CHAPTER 28

Goodbye

Coming to terms with a different future

A fter the funeral, the Da Silva family went back to their farm at Tatui to start rebuild their shattered lives. The Bragas and Adriane went to the Braga farm in Campinas. Nothing would ever be remotely the same again for any of them. For that small group of maybe 30 family and close friends in Brazil, their life for the past 10 years had been solely about Ayrton Senna – they knew nothing else.

The Da Silva family had another problem that in reality only existed in their minds. They were scared and worried that Adriane would want to resume living at Senna's apartment at Rua Paraguai, which was the last thing they wanted. Neyde Da Silva was the only dissenting voice as the rest of the family voiced their fears. She simply told them, "No, she won't," and she was right.

Neyde Da Silva decided they had all treated Adriane very, very badly and resolved to do something about it. The following Friday, she rose early before the rest of the family had got out of bed and called for her driver. She ordered the driver to take her to Antonio Braga's farm where she knew Adriane was.

Adriane got a surprise when Neyde Da Saliva suddenly arrived without warning at the Braga house. She wanted to talk to the people who had spent time with her son in his last days. Neyde and Adriane sat down on a large sofa in the Braga sitting room and talked for a long time. Before she left Neyde arranged to meet her at Senna's apartment where they had lived together, so that Adriane could collect her things. Adriane had a lot of stuff there. She had lived with Senna for a year, and for the last month she had been alone in the apartment whilst he was in Europe.

At the gate, as she got into her car, Neyde thanked Antonio Braga and Luiza for looking after Adriane and she apologised for the way the rest of her family had behaved. As she left, Braga turned to his wife and said to her: "That is where Beco [Ayrton] got it from." Luiza nodded. She didn't need to ask what her husband meant; she instinctively knew.

After the funeral, Galvao Bueno spent a few days thinking a lot about his television career at TV Globo and asked himself whether he could carry on now that Senna was dead. Eventually, he decided he would carry on because it was what Senna would have wanted and he would do it for the other young Brazilian drivers, Rubens Barrichello and Christian Fittipaldi. Bueno was a big feature in their lives, as he had been in Senna's.

Josef Leberer also had to decide whether he wanted to continue. He stayed with Williams to look after Damon Hill until the end of the season, then rejoined McLaren.

Alain Prost was very relieved that he had taken the decision to come to Brazil. He found he was welcomed by everyone, and there had been no mention of his five-year feud with Senna.

The big question from everyone was whether Prost would come out of retirement and take Senna's seat at Williams. They seemed to be willing him to do so. He firmly discounted that: "Out of respect for him, I would never, never, never take the seat in his car."

The following day, Milton and Neyde invited Prost to join them at the family farm in Tatui. Strangely, they found the presence of their son's greatest track rival reassuring. Over the weekend, Prost and Milton Da Silva talked about his son's last weekend and his life. Prost told his father that he believed he and his son would have become good friends once they had retired. The reasons for acrimony between them did not exist outside competition in a race car.

Prost said: "I think it's not impossible that in time we might have become friends. We shared an awful lot, after all, and the one thing never changed – even when our relationship was at its worst – was our great respect for each other as drivers. I don't think either of us worried too much about anyone else. And there were those times we did have fun together, you know." To this day, Alain Prost remains a favourite of the Senna family.

Gerhard Berger and Johnny Herbert were soon gone from Brazil. They

San Marino Grand Prix: Sunday 1st May 1994

© Corbis

Left: Niki Lauda and Ayrton Senna talked seriously for more than 15 minutes in the Imola paddock on the morning of Sunday 1st May 1994. Senna was very concerned about the safety of the new breed of cars and wanted to re-form the Grand Prix Drivers Association (GPDA). He asked for Lauda's help.

Right: Ayrton Senna walks through the paddock before the drivers' briefing with former team mate Gerhard Berger. He wanted Berger's help with getting some changes to the regulations regarding use of the pace car, which had only recently been introduced to Formula One. Berger was successful in getting his proposals approved.

© Corbis

© Richard West

Above: The morning debrief in the Williams motorhome with, left to right, Ayrton Senna, David Brown, Damon Hill and John Russell. It was Senna's last debriefing, but neither his head nor his heart was in it.

Right: After Sunday warm-up, Senna had a short chat with Renault chairman Louis Schweitzer, who was attending the race having flown in from Paris. Schweitzer was two years into his chairmanship and a very big fan of Formula One.

Left: At around midday, Ayrton Senna and Damon Hill walked with Williams marketing director Richard West over to the Paddock Club where they talked to Williams team guests for 20 minutes. It was a ritual the drivers went through at every race and Senna had performed it hundreds of times before.

Above: Ayrton Senna and Michael Schumacher in the Imola paddock at the 1994 San Marino Grand Prix. Senna did not have a particularly good relationship with Schumacher. But day to day, he got on with the German driver and recognised and gave him the respect due as his biggest rival on the track.

Left: David Brown and Ayrton Senna confer in the cockpit before the race. Brown was overawed working with Senna and knew he was not his first choice as race engineer.

Above: Senna pulls on his helmet before going out in the car for the last time on Sunday 1st May 1994. Unusually, he took his helmet off when he was in the car on the grid.

Below: Ayrton Senna sits on the grid waiting for the start of the San Marino Grand Prix.

Left: The start of the San Marino Grand Prix, Sunday 1st May 1994. The startline accident is starting in the background of the photograph.

Above: Ayrton Senna leads the San Marino Grand Prix.

Right: Sir Frank Williams, Alain Prost and Renault chairman Louis Schweitzer in the Williams garage.

Below: Ayrton Senna struggles to keep ahead of Michael Schumacher's Benetton in the opening stages of the San Marino Grand Prix.

© Rex Features

Above: Ayrton Senna in the Williams Renault FW18 leads the rest of the field behind the safety car, which was brought out after the Lehto-Lamy startline shunt.

© The Life of Senna

Left: Senna's car rebounds violently from the wall at Tamburello. It was an exceptionally violent impact, bringing the car to a quick stop in a small piece of ground. The accident was so violent that the carbon fibre chassis split. The in-car camera cut out before the accident.

© F1 Magazine

Below: The suspension arm attached to the front wheel that is believed to have hit Senna just above his right eye causing a fatal injury.

Below left: The final seconds of footage from Senna's onboard camera. Senna enters Tamburello for the very last time.

© The Life of Senna

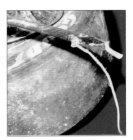

Above: The wreckage of Senna's Williams at the scene of the accident. The steering wheel is hanging loosely over the right side of the car. The non-structural cockpit cowling had been removed to allow Senna to be lifted from the car.

Above: Four doctors, including Professor Sid Watkins, attend to Senna at the trackside in the immediate aftermath of the crash.

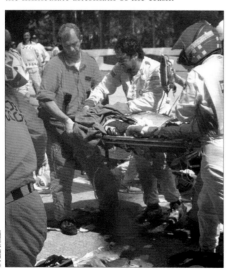

Left and below: Gravely ill with a catastrophic head injury, Ayrton Senna is stretchered off the track to the waiting helicopter.

Above and left: The shattered remains of the car are recovered back to the pits on a transporter. On news of Senna's death, the wreckage was immediately impounded by the Italian authorities pending an investigation.

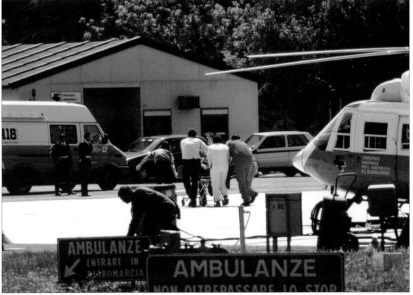

Above: The helicopter carrying Ayrton Senna arrives at San Maggiore hospital in Bologna twenty minutes after leaving the circuit. Senna was quickly transferred to a waiting ambulance to take him directly to the resuscitation unit.

Above: Nicola Larini, Flavio Briatore and Michael Schumacher on the podium hear the news from Flavio Briatore that Senna is gravely ill. It would be another two hours before it was announced that Senna was dead.

Left: Bernie Ecclestone talks to Damon and Georgie Hill after the race.

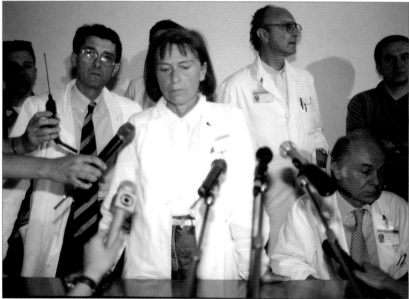

Above: Dr Maria Theresa Fiandri, Bologna's chief medical officer, announces the death of Ayrton Senna to the world's media at 6:40pm local time.

were due to attend the funeral of Roland Ratzenberger, the forgotten victim of the Imola weekend. Berger had his own demons to confront; he was unsure whether he ever wanted to race again.

Derek Warwick simply went home. His career was over; effectively, it had been ended a few years earlier by the man he had come to mourn. Afterwards, Neyde Da Silva wrote him a letter. It was all so unexpected. Warwick says, trying to explain: "I think he knew what he did to me and my career but still felt it was done for the right reasons. I don't know whether he was awkward with it or whether he just knew he had to squash something in order to survive himself. With hindsight I don't bear him any malice for that. I'm actually more angry with myself for not being tougher in certain situations. But you know, I am my character and I'm proud of what I am – but that went against me at the end of the day."

Julian Jakobi had to pick up the pieces of Senna's growing business empire. Senna had committed $47 million, and there were a lot of big decisions to make now that he was no longer there.

Senna's three-year contract with Williams was quickly paid out in full by the Williams team insurers. Also, his personal sponsorships were covered by other insurance policies. Senna had always arranged his affairs to allow for his sudden death which he always knew was a possibility.

After the business was concluded, Jakobi finally had time for his personal grief. He had been stunned by the funeral and had no idea his driver had been so revered by his people. Like many others, he recalled events in 1963 as a comparison. He said: "I remember watching John F. Kennedy's funeral in Washington in 1963, and even Winston Churchill's when I was a young boy. I'd never seen anything like this. The Senna funeral in Brazil was just quite something. You wouldn't want to be part of it because of what happened, but on the other hand, being there, it kind of put everything into perspective. Here was a guy from Brazil, which has a fledgling motor industry, who could take on and beat the industrialised world. Here was somebody, rather like Pelé, who was a world figure, who was universally respected. And, during the nine years that I worked for him, I didn't understand, being based here in Europe, just how much he was revered in Brazil."

But it was Adriane Galisteu who had the most pieces to pick up. She was the person closest to Senna at the end of his life, and she was left with nothing. Senna had left her nothing and his family was determined she would have nothing. They wished she could be erased from his history.

Despite the opposition of Senna's family, it was thought they would eventually marry. It is possible Senna had already told his family what his intentions were, and that was the reason for the friction between him and Leonardo on that last weekend.

And contrary to what the family thought, she had no intention of staying on at the apartment. Even if she had wanted it, the memories were just too brutal for her.

For nearly two weeks, Adriane stayed with the Bragas on the farm. Betise Assumpcao came to visit her and they talked nonstop about Senna's life for hours and hours. It seemed to make things easier to bear for both women.

Ten days later, Adriane met Neyde Da Silva to collect her things from Senna's flat. It was her first visit to São Paulo since the funeral. She found she had grown scared of going out, and she cowered in the car during the journey. She remembered: "The sight of the city scared me."

At the apartment, Neyde Da Silva was waiting. Adriane said: "I took the elevator and went up. The door was half open. Everything looked the same – and at the same time it was so different. There was no sign of us there. Everything was in its place. There was no life there anymore. His mother and I sat on the sofa and talked for about 40 minutes."

When Neyde asked Adriane what would she do now, she said simply she would restart her life from where it had been on Friday 26th March 1983, the day her eyes locked for the first time with the eyes of Ayrton Senna. She said later it was literally the look of love, a look that changed her world completely. No words had been exchanged between them that day but none had needed to be. It was pure fate just as the events of Sunday afternoon 1st May 1994 had been.

After they had finished talking, she threw her things into four large suitcases and asked Neyde if she could keep his toothbrush.

When the time finally came for Adriane to leave, both women cried and cried.

Outside it was raining.

THE END

From McLaren to Williams

Close Season 1993/1994

8th November 1993 to 27th April 1994

After the Australian Grand Prix and his last race for McLaren, Ayrton Senna and his girlfriend Adriane Galisteu spent a few days in Sydney before returning to Brazil. He had never been happier with a Williams contract in his pocket and a new girlfriend he was in love with; life had never been better. He was looking forward to a whole month at his beach house in Angra relaxing with Adriane.

By the beginning of December, he was back in Europe to take care of various commitments.

First trip was to Paris for an event called the Bercy kart race, a charity go-kart race organised by paraplegic former Formula One driver Philippe Streiff. The Bercy event was fraught with problems between sponsor Elf and the Shell oil company. Senna was contracted to appear in his McLaren overalls until 31st December. Elf, which would sponsor him in 1994, did not like it; and Shell did not appreciate him carrying an Elf decal on his kart. Senna took a lot of trouble personally to smooth out the differences between the sponsors so that he could compete at Bercy. Finally, the two oil giants agreed that he could drive in a neutral white kart.

During these two days in Paris, he was relaxed in a way that had rarely been seen in public. With Adriane always at his side, he laughed that he had had one of the special karts they would be driving sent to Brazil so that he could practice. "But unfortunately it arrived so late that I hardly had any time."

In the Bercy grand finale, he was dogged by bad luck; he was lying second and gunning for the lead when his kart developed a mechanical fault. He was out of the race. But he was able to joke about it: "Better here than next year in the Williams," he said.

On 8th December he was back in Paris to face the music at an FIA hearing following his fracas with Eddie Irvine at the Japanese Grand Prix. After a three-hour hearing, he was given a two-race ban: suspended for six months.

It could have been a lot worse. FISA president Max Mosley commented: "Senna rec-ognised and admitted that he had hit [Irvine]. He was honest and fair, responsible and reasonable and we all felt a great sympathy for him. But what happened cannot be allowed in the sport, and there had to be a penalty.

Irvine's attitude was extremely provocative and difficult. But Senna also opened dis-cussions in a very heated way." Senna refused to comment on the incident but sources reported that he was 'very upset' by the penalty.

He then flew to London's Heathrow airport in his plane and helicoptered down to the Williams factory for a seat fitting for 1994. It was his first visit to the factory, and Frank Williams held a little party in his office for him and Adriane. However, the visit was kept secret. Williams wanted to hold back all publicity for the official launch of the car in January.

Only the barest skeleton of the carbon fibre chassis was ready, and Senna offered his opinions on the size and comfort of the cockpit so any necessary changes could be made over the next six weeks; Adriane sat huddled on a tyre in the corner, shivering.

In mid-December, Senna returned to Brazil where he would spend Christmas and New Year before he returned to Europe on Monday 17th January to prepare for the first of the pre-season tests. As the new car was not yet ready, he would be testing the FW15D, a transitional version of the previous year's chassis.

The following evening, Senna attended a reception at the Palacio Hotel in Estoril, organised to present the team's 1994 challenge to the press. The mood was buoyant. Frank Williams again expressed his delight at Senna driving for the team. He said: "I have been an admirer of Ayrton for a long time. This gives me very great personal satisfaction. But I am fearful he will think too highly of Williams, so I hope he will not be too disappointed." Senna was not expecting to be disappointed, as he explained: "It's all going to be a bit of a guessing game this year but I suppose I have to say that if I can be as happy at the end of the season as I have felt in the past few weeks, it will have been a great year for me."

Everyone present felt that 1994 was going to be his year. A fourth world champion-ship was within his grasp. The combination of Senna and Williams was the best driver in the best car, so what could go wrong? Although firmly convinced that this would be his great year, Senna knew there could be problems ahead even before he had driven the new Williams, shorn of electronic aids. As he said: "With the new rules, the ban on electronic aids, the cards are certain to be reshuffled. Williams will certainly be more affected than others; everything will be much closer between the leaders. I don't see myself as the only favourite this year."

On the Wednesday, Renault revealed its new RS6 engine and the four-day Estoril test began. Senna had a near trouble-free four days, marred only by a couple of spins, and was very pleased with the old car and the new engine.

When the teams packed up on Sunday he was fastest with a time of 1m 22.253secs. His nearest rival was his new team mate, Damon Hill, with a time of 1m 22.662secs; the nearest non-Williams runner was the Ferrari of Gerhard Berger, almost a second behind Hill with a time of 1m 23.631secs. Michael Schumacher and the Benetton team were not present.

The launch of the new car was another month away because there were more changes to incorporate than in the past few years. Formula One was entering a new era. Driver aids, such as traction control and active suspension, had been banned at the end of 1993, after the top teams had spent massive amounts of money perfecting their systems. The ruling was supposed to cut costs and close the performance gap, but in fact it raised questions about how the new rule could be policed. Refuelling was to return to the sport, raising concerns about safety.

Out went the Kyalami and Donington Park races, and in came Aida, an unpopular Japanese track but one with great paddock facilities. Alain Prost, Riccardo Patrese and Derek Warwick had recently retired, and Heinz-Harald Frentzen, Olivier Panis and Jos Verstappen were about to make their debuts. Also on the grid were Michael Schumacher, Jean Alesi, Rubens Barrichello, Johnny Herbert, Eddie Irvine and Mika Häkkinen. The 1990s had well and truly arrived.

So where did this leave Senna? Unlike Piquet, Prost and Mansell, he would be making the transition to the new era. Approaching his 34th birthday at a time when drivers often raced on into their early 40s, it seemed that he still had time on his side and some people believed that his best was yet to come. He approved of the ban on driver aids, and he didn't think Aida was all that bad when he first visited the track, although he disliked the concept of refuelling. One thing was clear: with the sudden departure of Prost, Piquet and Mansell, he was now the dominant driver. In fact, someone pointed out to him that in 1994 he would be the only world champion racing. Consequently, he was the only real star in Formula One, and there was a lot of pressure. Although he had had run-ins with Schumacher and Irvine, he had a good rapport with Barrichello, Alesi and Frentzen. He could certainly bridge the gap.

Another characteristic of the new era was the increase in commercialism.

There had been a rise in corporate interest in the sport ever since the late 1960s, but in the early- to mid-1990s, it moved into overdrive. A driver was no longer just a driver but also a marketing tool. A computer game called Ayrton Senna's Super Monaco Grand Prix had sold 800,000 copies. There were Senna sweatshirts, Senna mountain bikes, Senna watches, Senna pens, Senna magazines and Senna motorcycles. He had designed his own Senna logo in the shape of a double 'S'. And he was not the only one. The Michael Schumacher Collection had just been launched, and in following years would provide the German's fans with everything from caps and tee-shirts to teddy bears, aftershave and toilet seats.

He had also created his own cartoon character based on himself. The character of Senninha (little Senna) was created by Brazilians Rogério & Ridaut. Rogério had previously worked with commercial designs, while Ridaut was a comic-book creator. They both liked Formula One, and both loved Ayrton Senna. So they decided to create a comic book hero that would be a copy of Senna, a little Senna, and Senninha was born. They didn't have the money to publish it, so they decided to go to the only man who could help them. They went to his office in Brazil in 1992 and arranged a meeting to talk about the project. When they met, Senna realised the two were very talented and loved their ideas. He had always wanted to do something for children but didn't really know what. It had to be educational and it had to be fun. Children needed to love it, so it had to be exciting. Senninha was the best way to express Senna's feelings towards children. They would learn ethical values in life through Senninha and have fun reading it. Brazil immediately loved it – it was something of Senna, their hero. He decided to give the first edition of Senninha free to every schoolchild, and it took off in early 1994. He said, as if needing to justify it: "Wealthy men can't live in an island that is encircled by poverty. We all breathe the same air. We must give a chance to everyone, at least a basic chance."

Senna was fully engaged in commercialism of his own in late 1993 and early 1994. He was casting around for a career after motor racing and started to set up business in Brazil.

The first few months of 1994 were spent pursuing those interests and getting the deal together. In between, he spent time with Adriane at his Angra beach house, and they had a whole month together from late January to the third week of February. In between, he was finalising commercial arrangements, with car-maker Audi and the Mont Blanc luxury goods brand, to officially handle their products in Brazil.

In the last week of February, Senna flew to Europe primarily to test the new Williams car and attend a series of business meetings, setting up more commercial deals for him to import European products into Brazil. It was the start of a business empire that would sustain him after retirement, a milestone he figured was now probably only four years away. As he told friends, he had no intention of playing second fiddle to Michael Schumacher, who was clearly emerging as his chief rival. He reckoned on two years with Williams and his last two or three years with Ferrari.

It was not until 24th February that the new FW16 was finally ready, long after some of the other cars, notably the Benetton Ford B194, had been launched. With the new chassis launched just four weeks before the first race in Brazil, Senna was faced with a hectic test schedule. It was a cold and misty Thursday at Silverstone, and after the covers came off, Senna took the car for a 15-lap shakedown test. In public he praised the team's efforts, but he privately admitted to his girlfriend Adriane: "I feel I have arrived here two years too late. The car drives funny." He continued: "I went through a lot to finally be able to sit in that car. But I feel it's going to be hard. Either I haven't adapted myself to the car yet or it's the car that doesn't suit me."

Senna had perhaps naively expected to sit down in the Williams Renault and find the perfect car, as he had done in 1988 with McLaren Honda, and to romp away with the championship. But what he found was a car stripped of all its electronic aids. Without the aids, he thought the car potentially dangerous: "It's a stupidity to change the rules. Formula One will regress." Senna told people that he thought the sophisticated electronics system was a big aid to safety. He was also unhappy with the regulations that forced cars to refuel during a race. He thought it unnecessarily dangerous and destabilising.

He also wanted to adapt the Williams team to be more like McLaren. He had grown accustomed to working with his Italian engineer, Giorgio Ascanelli, who had not been able to join him at Williams. He said: "I will start making changes slowly. It's a new team, strange faces. I want to change things gradually."

Senna knew timing was everything, and he was worried. But what sustained him was the simple lack of competition. Schumacher and Benetton were the only rivals, and he felt they would still have an inferior car. He was amazed that chief rivals Prost, Piquet and Mansell had simply disappeared. A generation change had happened without him realising, and he was the man who belonged to neither.

The first week's testing in England was followed by a trip to France, and Senna was more upbeat as he headed to the Paul Ricard track in the south of the country. He was happy to joke about the first time he had visited the French track, just over a decade earlier, when he had been a young hopeful trying out a Brabham Formula One car. He told his pilot Captain O'Mahoney on the way: "When I arrived by train in Marseille from Milan and was standing there at the station, I didn't know how to get to my hotel or the track. Today, my jet is standing by. That's not bad progress, is it?"

After the first tests of the new car, Senna had not liked the cramped cockpit (an Adrian Newey design trait) or the position of the steering wheel. After Paul Ricard, he asked for changes to be made to make more room in the cockpit and for the steering wheel to be raised. This was done by cutting away a small portion of the top of the cockpit that formed part of the monocoque and producing a new piece of bodywork. It also necessitated lengthening the steering column and changing its shape.

The modification was necessary because Senna did not like the steering wheel mounted so low, as Nigel Mansell had driven with and Alain Prost had also liked. The lower steering had also enabled a lower cockpit height, which was better aerodynamically.

Senna did not have a chance to test the modifications, which would be ready for the first race of the season in Brazil.

He was due to fly to Brazil on 13th March to incorporate all his promotional activities, but before that, he participated in the major test finale of the pre-season: at Imola, the venue for the San Marino Grand Prix on Sunday 1st May.

The Imola test ran from Tuesday 8th to Friday 11th March, with all the major players present. During the test, the drivers noticed a bump on the track at Tamburello that was causing the cars to jump. Senna and Minardi driver Pierluigi Martini went out to the corner and had a meeting with circuit director Giorgio Poggi. The event was filmed by a fan, and the film was shown at the trial investigating Senna's death three years later. It was one of many impromptu safety meetings held at Tamburello corner, often with Gerhard Berger. They always came to the same conclusion: that the corner was dangerous; there was very little that could be done, but the agreed changes were made. There was still a slight bump in the track, but the situation had been vastly improved and Martini believed the bump would only present problems for a car that was already struggling. At the time, it was a minor and routine incident. Surprisingly no one suggested that a few rows of tyres against the concrete wall might not be a bad idea.

The surprise of the test was that in the closing minutes of the very last day, Senna's fastest time was beaten by Schumacher. The 25-year-old German slashed Senna's best of 1m 21.2secs down to a straight 1m 21secs. Besides being the last pre-season test, it was the first to pit the FW16 against the opposition, and people were beginning to suggest that they had left it all too late. Senna was unruffled. He said: "The times here are not decisive. This is the end of the winter world championship. The real thing will be seen in Interlagos." But there was no disguising that the young Schumacher and his Benetton had won the winter world championship.

Senna later let slip to Brazilian journalists that the Williams team had been trying to disguise the car's true potential: he said it had never run with less than 60 litres of fuel, and its fast laps had been timed from a starting point elsewhere on the track – and from there Senna was the fastest.

Everything was not as rosy as Senna made it appear, however. Both he and team mate Damon Hill had noticed difficulties with the car. It struggled, especially in low-speed corners, was highly sensitive and twitchy, and the cockpit was cramped and uncomfortable. Hill complained: "You don't have to be very far out with the settings, and suddenly the car is not competitive. That's good and bad. Good, because it's working straight away. But bad in some ways because you can be out of bed very easily."

All the same, in the eyes of most people, Senna was still the clear title favourite. His biggest challengers were supposed to be his team mate, Hill, McLaren with its new Peugeot engine, and Ferrari. Not everyone took the testing pace of Schumacher's Benetton seriously or believed the driver aid ban would shake up things so much as to wrong-foot the mighty Williams Renaults.

But Senna, the man who had campaigned for a ban on electronic driver aids, was about to find himself wrong-footed. When he had been at McLaren, which didn't have them, he had been a vigorous opponent. Now at Williams, he could see he had got it wrong. In fact, Senna disliked the new breed of car from the start, and by the time he reached Brazil he was extremely worried. He ominously reported: "The cars are very fast and difficult to drive. It's going to be a season with a lot of accidents, and I'll risk saying we'll be lucky if something really serious doesn't happen."

Schumacher had no idea how bad the Williams was or how good his car was, and he was also downbeat: "Hopefully, we can push the Williams. Sometimes to stay close, sometimes to win a race, but, as for the championship, I think we are one more step away from that. They have the best package, but there will nevertheless be races where they don't find the right set-up and we might find the right set-up, and it will be very close. We will fight together and then, by strategies or stuff, we will win races. But too many bad things would need to happen to other teams for us to really have a chance to win the championship. Drivers like Senna or Hill, a team like Williams – they don't make mistakes."

In the absence of the 1993 world champion, Alain Prost, Williams would be running numbers 0 and 2 on its cars as 1993 constructors' champion.

Against the tradition that the more experienced and illustrious driver took the lower number, Senna would race with number 2 while Damon Hill kept his 0 from the previous year. Senna refused to drive a car labelled zero.

Senna was also nervous about his first big business venture. He had won the exclusive concession to import German Audi cars into Brazil and had invited 2,000 guests to a launch on the Tuesday after the Grand Prix. There were hundreds of small details to attend to that week.

On the Monday before the Brazilian Grand Prix, he celebrated his 34th birthday with a group of friends. Among them was Gerd Kremer of Mercedes-Benz. He recalls: "The last time I saw him was in Brazil, at the Grand Prix. It was his birthday and he told me that he was worried. He was afraid something would happen to him. He was frightened for the young drivers and that there was nothing he could do if something went wrong with his car."

The Brazilian Grand Prix also brought its own pressures. Senna was Brazil's absolute hero. Only footballer Pelé came close, and he was retired. The pressure on Senna at his home race was enormous. The fans demanded victory and to Senna even second place would be a pitiful reward for their support.

An added pressure was that it was the first race of the season – a leap into the unknown for the teams and drivers, and not least Senna, with his growing concerns about the competence of his car.

In the face of all this, Senna still wrestled the car onto pole, the 63rd of his career, with a best time of 1m 15.962secs, 0.328 seconds faster than Schumacher and 1.423 seconds quicker than the next nearest contender, Jean Alesi. Senna topped the timesheets in every practice and qualifying session of the weekend. But he knew what he had needed to do to achieve it. Driving 100 per cent all the time was dangerous, and he told his close friends so. The proof was Hill's position on the grid – nowhere. Just like the latter years at McLaren, Senna found himself carrying the team. He had made an expensive change of team for nothing.

The race was a different story. Senna made by far the best start, and pulled away into the distance as Schumacher got trapped behind Alesi's Ferrari. Two laps later, Schumacher was through and began the seemingly impossible task of chasing down Senna. The cars pitted simultaneously on lap 21 with Senna still in front, but the Benetton pit crew was exceptionally quick and Schumacher regained the track in the lead. Once in the clear air, he began to pull away and it was all Senna could do to keep him in view.

After the second round of stops, Schumacher was still out front, but Senna had not given in. In six laps he had reduced the deficit from 9.2 seconds to just five seconds. He was not going to win but that didn't stop him trying.

Then his weakness – the reason he had scored 30 per cent more pole positions than race wins – prevailed. Instead of settling down for second, he pushed and pushed and pushed too much. As he rounded the third-gear Cotavelo corner on lap 56, he half-spun and stalled the engine in the middle of the track: for all the world, a beginner's error. As Senna unfastened his seatbelts, the crowd began to go home.

Schumacher won. Senna offered no excuses for the spin. He said: "There was nothing wrong with the car. It was my fault. I was pushing too hard. For me it's the most disappointing when I can't give anything back to my fans here, who love me so much. It was obviously my mistake, but I needed to win. A second place in Brazil would have meant nothing to me."

Second would in fact have meant six points and less pressure. But his comments summed up the way he drove – a weakness that would simply increase the pressure until that fateful day at Imola.

Damon Hill was no happier with the car, reporting: "I would describe it as virtually undriveable in the slow corners. And in the quick ones, it threatened to turf you off the track at any moment. It is unpredictable."

Even overlooking Senna's mistake, however, Benetton had still run rings around Williams in the race, in clever pitwork and outright pace. It came as a surprise to many, who before the season began had believed the Williams-Senna combination was an undoubted super-team. Schumacher, assisted by rising engineer Ross Brawn and experienced designer Rory Byrne, was forging his own super-team.

But even for those who rated Schumacher's talent, the leap made by the Benetton chassis since 1993 seemed unthinkable. At this early stage in the season, the first accusations began that Benetton was running banned driver aids, including traction control. Senna heard the rumours and was disturbed by them.

He stayed in Brazil for another week after the Grand Prix. The Audi concession launch went well. For a shy man, Senna stepped confidently up to the microphone in front of his 2,000 guests and delivered a speech with the coolness of a professional speaker. It surprised his father Milton just how good he was. He was clearly enjoying his new challenge as a businessman. He was as natural at it as he was at driving. A few days later, he said his goodbyes to his family and Adriane, and headed back to Europe for essential FW16 testing.

Three hard days at Jerez were never going to solve all the problems, and a few days later Senna was on the long-haul flight to Japan for the Pacific Grand Prix at Aida, with the memory of Interlagos still fresh in his mind.

On the Thursday of the Grand Prix, Senna was spotted chatting openly to Schumacher in the paddock. It was unusual as the pair had never been particularly friendly. When questioned about the meeting later, Schumacher revealed: "He wanted to congratulate me on my win in Brazil as he had not seen me since, and we said some nice things. That is all there was to it." There was probably more to it, and some observers noted that Senna was probably trying to find out all he could about the new opposition.

One of the major news stories at Aida came from remarks in the Italian press by Nicola Larini – standing in for Jean Alesi, who had injured his neck – who implied Ferrari had some kind of traction-control system on its cars.

Harsh punishments had been promised for any team found cheating that season, but after an investigation, the FIA decided there was no need for sanctions.

In reality, at that stage the FIA had little idea of how to police the new regulations. It was all new territory.

In Japan, Senna was convinced that Benetton was using the banned traction control. He wrestled his car again to pole – the 64th of his career – although qualifying did not pass without incident. His time came from the Friday session, and luckily for him the Saturday times were slower in the higher temperatures because he spun during his first run, a move mirrored by Damon Hill. A frustrated Senna said: "I really don't know what happened. It's odd that it happened the same for both of us. But I really don't understand because the car had one of the best positions at that point of the corner throughout the weekend. It was disappointing and frustrating because it looks silly and stupid. I feel very unhappy about it... with myself. But it was better it happened today and not tomorrow."

Senna did not like being made to look stupid, especially when there seemed to be no real reason for it. It was reminiscent of his Formula Three career when he had been struggling against Martin Brundle, unable to understand why the Englishman was suddenly quicker than he was and not knowing that Brundle had received engine improvements that he had not received himself. He had crashed on several occasions in the second half of the season then. Dick Bennetts, his Formula Three team boss, said: "If we'd had the same engine rebuild six or seven races before, we wouldn't have had half the accidents that we did."

Amazingly, Senna was hopeful for the race. But it was misplaced. He didn't make it past the first corner, having starting sluggishly, and Schumacher flew past him into the lead. The German braked earlier for the first corner than Senna expected; when Senna braked, the fast-starting Mika Häkkinen ran into the back of him, punting Senna into a spin that resulted in him being t-boned by Larini's Ferrari.

Senna was furious with Häkkinen, his former team mate. "It was very irresponsible driving and shouldn't be allowed," he burst out. After his accident, he spent several laps standing at the side of the track watching Schumacher and the other cars pass. Some thought he was listening for traction control. Schumacher won the race and, with it, had claimed a maximum 20 points to Senna's none.

Before the season had begun, people were predicting that the best Schumacher could hope for after two races would be an eight-point deficit to Senna. Claims that in 1994 Senna could score 10 or 11 wins and beat Prost's all-time record were beginning to look shaky. Some less kind commentators suggested that Senna had cracked. But he could not comment on how bad the car was publicly out of deference to Williams and Renault.

Once again, the pundits had got it wrong. But it all piled on extra pressure for Imola.

After watching the Benetton for lap after lap, Senna was sure it had traction control. He had also been surprised how quickly the car had come off the line and believed it was using the banned launch control as well.

Peter Collins, the Lotus team principal, went to see Frank Williams after the race. While he was waiting, he bumped into Senna. Collins remembers it well: "I said to Ayrton that the Benetton was behaving like a car that had traction control. Ayrton, suddenly animated that I had reflected exactly what he was thinking, said to me: 'I am sure they are. I have followed it a number of times and I am sure they are.'"

Senna told Collins he was determined to beat him, no matter what. Collins says: "He saw himself as being on a crusade of integrity and honour." The conversation ended as Collins went off to converse with Frank Williams. He was convinced that Senna was resolved to do something about it.

Senna arrived back in England on the Tuesday after the race and attended the post-race briefing at the Didcot factory. Williams staffers were surprised. On the following day, he flew to Paris where he kicked off a football friendly between Brazil and Paris St Germain. From there, he returned to his home at Quinta do Largo in Portugal before he was due at the French track of Nogaro on Monday 25th April for a quick shake-down test of the reportedly improved FW16. He went from there to Munich, where on Tuesday he had meetings concerning his Audi car importing business in Brazil. On

Wednesday 27th April, his pilot Captain O'Mahoney flew him to Bologna for a clandestine meeting with Ferrari chief, Luca di Montezemolo. Then, on Thursday, O'Mahoney waited on the tarmac at Faro airport to fly him to the San Marino Grand Prix to meet his destiny.

(Appendix 1 is adapted from Chapter 29 of The Life of Senna)

FROM McLAREN TO WILLIAMS

FATAL WEEKEND

Senna's Pole Positions

65 poles from 161 starts

22nd April 1985 to 29th April 1994

Ayrton Senna didn't live long enough to hold many outright Formula One driving records. He won neither the most world championships nor the most races. But one record he did hold at the time of his death was for the most pole positions from the 161 Grand Prix races he competed in. He achieved pole in 40 per cent of his starts, clocking up a total of 65. It was such an exceptional record that few thought it would ever beaten. Michael Schumacher finally managed to achieve 68 poles but from almost twice the number of race starts at 308. Senna still holds many of the qualifying records: the most successive pole positions (eight) and the most pole positions at the same circuit (eight at Imola). His qualifying dominance over his team mates was legendary, and that record will almost certainly never be beaten. He qualified behind his team mates only 18 times out of 161 races.

Having achieved all that, interestingly Senna believed that he had never ever driven a perfect lap. As he said: "A fast lap requires a high level of sensitivity between body and mind. It is the combination of the two that gives the performance. But I have never done a perfect lap because I know, in looking back, that there was always room for improvement. It doesn't matter whether it's one-10th, or a hundredth, or a few 10ths: you always find room for it. On 90 per cent of occasions, you go faster on your second set of tyres than on your first, because of the information in your mind from the first run. It doesn't matter if the first one was already very fast. If you use properly the information, and apply all the things I described before, 99 per cent sure, you will go faster than before."

His first pole position came at Estoril in 1985 and was one of his finest moments, as he still recalled years later: "I always wanted to be in pole position for a Grand Prix. And when I got it, at Estoril in 1985, it was an amazing feeling. Then I just keep trying the same." He said every pole gave him a personal pleasure.

The spine-tingling spectacle of Ayrton Senna on a qualifying lap provided some of the most thrilling moments in the history of motorsport.

There has never been a faster driver over a single lap, nor has anyone felt or thought so deeply. His passion for pole position was palpable. No other driver put more into it, nor has anyone ever been able to explain it as well as the brilliant Brazilian, for whom the pursuit of pole was also an intellectual exercise.

So great was Senna's depth of feeling, his pure passion for pole, that just listening to him speak about his qualifying experiences was mesmerising.

When he talked about his most memorable lap – the one that left the most indelible impression on his exceptional mind – his eyes shone with a faraway look, and his voice quivered with intensity.

McLaren team member Tyler Alexander was by Senna's side for most of those pole attempts. As he recalls: "Senna always wanted to be quicker, not necessarily because somebody else had gone faster – just because he wanted to be quicker every time he went out. In the garage, we began to notice the thing he did with his belts just before he went out to go quicker than ever – usually on the last or second-to-last run. After one of the guys did up his belts, Senna would reach down and give them an extra pull to somehow make himself smaller in the car. We picked up on that, and it became something we would all just stand back and watch. Our guy would pull the lap straps as tight as possible. Senna would tug at them a couple of times and by the third or fourth pull: whoops – watch out, here we go. Everyone thought he was going to get pole – and he certainly went out with the intention of getting it – but he still had to do it. He never said, 'I'm going to go out and get on pole'. It was just, 'This is what I've got to do, and I'm going to go and try to do it.'"

Former Team Lotus mechanics Kenny Szymanski and Clive Hicks remember the days when Senna would sit in an armchair, mentally driving the Monte Carlo circuit using an invisible steering wheel, gear lever, brake, clutch and throttle. Senna admitted he was mesmerised by getting pole at every race, to the point of obsession, as he said: "It was Monte Carlo '88, the last qualifying session. I was already on pole and I was going faster and faster.

One lap after the other, quicker and quicker and quicker. I was, at one stage, just on pole, then by half a second and then by one second – and yet I kept going. Suddenly, I was nearly two seconds faster than anybody else, including my team mate with the same car. And I suddenly realised that I was no longer driving the car consciously."

Senna was qualifying for his third race in his first season with McLaren Honda, where

Alain Prost ruled supreme. The Brazilian had won the 1987 Monaco Grand Prix (with Lotus), but prior to that, Prost had won this most supreme test of driving skill three years in succession. Now, uppermost in Senna's mind, on the circuit where overtaking is near impossible, was the need to outqualify his French team mate. To accomplish this, Senna summoned all his considerable powers, then found even more, as he revealed: "When I am competing against the watch and against other competitors, the feeling of expectation, of getting it done, doing the best and being the best, gives me a kind of power that in some moments when I am driving actually detaches me completely from anything else as I am doing... corner after corner, lap after lap. This is what happened in Monte Carlo."

Senna was astonishingly fast in Monte Carlo that day in 1988 – almost stupefyingly fast – 1.427 seconds quicker than Prost, who was second on the grid. Even Prost was moved to say: "Fantastic! There's no other word for it." The Frenchman suspected Senna's exceptional performance was rooted in their rivalry; that Senna's need to prove himself quickest was similar to the way Prost had felt a few years earlier when he took extra risks to beat the then established star in the McLaren team, Niki Lauda. "In those circumstances," says Prost, "you take chances like you never will again."

But Senna took those chances, again and again, to establish his record of 65 poles.

Senna admitted he had gone too far that day in Monaco. He was already on pole by a considerable margin yet, as if in the grip of a superior force, he was unable to apply the mental brakes. Amazingly, it was done on race tyres and not special qualifying rubber. Qualifying was over two days then, and there were no lap restrictions as now. He said: "In qualifying, we used race tyres, not qualifying tyres, so I could do many laps."

As he sped ever quicker through the principality's treacherous guard rail lined streets, where the tiniest error could mean disaster, Senna was taken on a wild ride through a surrealistic tunnel into the great unknown. In his description of what followed, Senna struggled to contain an otherworldly experience within physical parameters that could not be understood. "I was kind of driving by instinct," he said, "only I was in a different dimension. It was like I was in a tunnel, not only the tunnel under the hotel, but the whole circuit for me was a tunnel. I was just going and going and going and going – more and more and more and more. I was way over the limit, but still I was able to find even more."

It was like a dream sequence, with the driver somehow detached from the act of physically handling the car and becoming a passenger along for the ride.

It was a dream that at first brought euphoria as if Senna was intoxicated by the exuberance of his own velocity. Then, abruptly, the dangerous reality of his perilous situation took on a nightmarish quality that snapped him out of his trance-like state: "Suddenly, something just kicked me. I kind of woke up, and I realised that I was in a different atmosphere than you normally are. Immediately, my reaction was to back off, slow down. I drove back slowly to the pits and I didn't want to go out any more that day."

Since he devoted so much of himself to understanding every facet of driving fast, this experience humbled Senna. He had pushed too far, lost control and broken through a barrier of comprehension. He was lost, confused and worried by feelings of uncomfortable vulnerability he had previously not known. "It frightened me because I realised I was well beyond my conscious understanding. It happens rarely, but I keep these experiences very much alive in me because it is something that is important for self-preservation."

Senna was never the reckless, unthinking madman that some of his critics – including Prost – claimed made him a danger to himself and to his peers.

He was fully aware of the perils of his profession and while he chose to meet them head-on he was not afraid to admit he was fearful of them: "The danger of getting hurt or getting killed is there because any racing driver lives very close to it all the time. It is important to know what fear is because it will keep you more switched on, more alert. On many occasions, it will determine your limits."

Yet the phenomenon of probing his limits fascinated Senna, and he found ways to use even the fear factor to extend the boundaries of possibility. His constant philosophical inquiries into the relationship between thought and deed in a racing car had much to do with his seemingly superhuman speed.

The danger factor that added an extra dimension to those watching one of his breathtaking qualifying laps was also an attraction to the man behind the wheel. As he confessed: "Because we are in a close relationship with the experience of fear and danger, we learn how to live with it better than other people. In the process of learning to live with it, you have extraordinary feelings and emotions when you get near to an accident. There is the feeling of, 'Oh! I have just almost gone over the limit'. It is fascinating and even attractive in a way. But it is a challenge for you to control it and not to exceed those things. So the feeling of living in that narrow band, of overdoing it and being too easy, is very small. The challenge to stay within that band is very much a motivation."

Senna's quest to fully explore the 'narrow band' resulted in personal revelations that were a source of ever-greater inspiration. Since his insights gained from yet more speed were never-ending, his motivation never peaked. As he once explained: "The motivating factors are the discoveries that I keep having every time I am driving. When I push, I go and find something else. I go again and I find something more. That is perhaps the most fascinating motivating factor for me. You are like an explorer finding a different world.

You have this desire to go into places you have never been before. The situation is extremely absorbing. And perhaps, because I have experienced on many occasions the feeling of finding new things – even if I thought 'OK, that is my maximum' – then suddenly I find something extra. It is the challenge of doing better all the time. That process is something almost non-stop in terms of excitement and motivation."

While Senna never stopped extending the frontiers of speed, the deep thought that matched – sometimes exceeded – the intense physical effort he put into his driving left Senna exhausted. "I do try very hard to understand everything and anything that happens around me. Sometimes, I think I know some of the reasons why I do the things the way I do in the car. And sometimes I think I don't know why. There are some moments that seem to be only the natural instinct that is in me. Whether I have been born with it or whether this feeling has grown in me more than other people, I don't know. But it is inside me and it takes over with a great amount of space and intensity. And it takes a lot of energy. At the end of every session in the car, I feel very tired because I just give everything I have. It drains me completely."

In Brazil in 1991, in front of his home crowd in São Paulo, yet another scintillating qualifying lap secured Senna the 54th pole of his career.

He then sped to victory in the race and passed Jackie Stewart on the all-time list of Formula One winners. Senna's 28th win, which at the time was second to Prost's record of 44, meant he had won exactly one quarter of the Formula One races he had entered. Yet it was the pole lap that weekend that Senna remembered most: "My heart was going hard, but my mind was cool. The perception and the reaction to such a lap is so great and it happens instantly. It is a mixture of natural instinct, macho bravery and all the technicalities it takes to do it. A billion things go through your mind and body. It all happens so amazingly fast, it is like a mystical feeling that is focused on an inner point so far away your eyes cannot see and your mind cannot project."

Laps such as this produced the maximum sensual involvement that Senna sought. In the profusion of stimuli he encountered on an all-out lap, there were occasions when he reached a state of hypersensitivity that enabled him to separate and better enjoy many of the factors that contribute to the sheer visceral thrill he got from pure speed:

"There are times when your sensitivity is higher, when your ability to feel the experience and react to the things you feel in the car is almost infinite. You can sense the car touching the track, you can smell the brakes. You can hear very clearly the engine's sound. You can feel very well the vibrations that are happening around your body, from the steering wheel or the chassis, or the turbulence from the air that touches part of your body. They are all happening at the same moment, and yet you can separate each of them in such a clear way that makes everything so fantastic and so challenging to fully understand and react to."

At Suzuka in October 1989, Senna attempted to explain how he got pole position: "The prefect lap is achieved when the driving becomes automatic because your brain controls the throttle, it knows your braking ability, your gear-change points. It depends on your eyesight before a corner, on your judgment of your speed into a corner. Sometimes you're not even looking at the rev counter when you change a gear but using only your feeling, your ear, which tells you how to be on the right revs. This is vital, because in a high-speed corner, if you look at your revs, for a split second you will not be as committed to your driving as you should. So your ear then plays an important part of it. It's not easy to describe. I think it is a matter of putting in everything that I have and everything that I am still finding that I can have."

Senna said his experiences in the car sharpened his senses and heightened the emotions that gave him so much satisfaction: "Life would be very boring without feelings, without emotions. And there are some feelings that only drivers can experience. It is a fortunate and unique position to be in, but it is stressful at the same time. Either getting pole, winning, or breaking a record, losing, going through a corner at a speed that a few seconds before you didn't think you could, either failing, feeling lucky, feeling anger, enthusiasm, stress or pain – only we can experience the deep levels of such feelings. Nobody else can, considering that in our profession we deal with ego a lot, with danger, with our health, continuously, second after second, not just day after day or month after month or year after year. Our life goes by in seconds, even milliseconds."

Ever conscious of the ticking clock, Senna also thought about when his time might run out. Before the 1994 season began, he had this to say: "If I am going to live, I want to live fully and very intensely because I am an intense person. It would ruin my life if I had to live partially. So my fear is that I might get badly hurt. I would not want to be in a wheelchair. I would not like to be in a hospital suffering from whatever injury it was. If I ever happen to have an accident that eventually costs my life, I hope it happens in one instant."

But the last word goes to the witness of most of Senna's poles, Tyler Alexander: "There was this old saying going around then that Alain Prost was the best Formula One driver around. The only problem was that Ayrton Senna was quicker."

1. 1985 Portuguese Grand Prix; Estoril   Gap: 0.413s
In the wet Friday session Senna was fastest with 1m 21.708s, almost matching Nelson Piquet's 1984 record. In the dry on Saturday he clocked a time of 1m 21.007s. His Friday time was beaten on Saturday only by the McLaren of Prost.

2. 1985 San Marino Grand Prix; Imola   Gap: 0.027s
Senna's first pole at a circuit where he would clock up a record eight was taken by the narrowest of all his margins frcm the Williams Honda of Keke Rosberg. He was to make Imola his own over the next 10 years.

3. 1985 Monaco Grand Prix; Monte Carlo   Gap: 0.086s
Senna's first pole of five at the street circuit that he would become synonymous with. He qualified over a second ahead of his illustrious team-mate Elio de Angelis in ninth, in only his second season of racing.

4. 1985 USA Detroit Grand Prix; Detroit   Gap: 1.198s
Senna took pole by over a second from Nigel Mansell's Williams, which was impressive in itself, but the gap back to Michele Alboreto's Ferrari in third was 1.697s and to Alain Prost's McLaren in fourth a stunning 2.037s.

5. 1985 Italian Grand Prix; Monza   Gap: 0.146s
A big disappointment for the tifosi as Senna was 1.384s and 2.389s faster than the Ferraris of Michele Alboreto and Stefan Johansson respectively. Senna specialised in rubbing Ferrari's nose in it in Italy particularly.

6. 1985 European Grand Prix; Brands Hatch   Gap: 0.313s
A lap that impressed many of the Formula One fraternity with its maturity and style. Only Nelson Piquet's Brabham BMW and Nigel Mansell's Williams were within a second of the Brazilian. His team-mate Elio de Angelis was left 2.845s behind in ninth.

7. 1985 Australian Grand Prix; Adelaide   Gap: 0.694s

The seven-10ths gap to Nigel Mansell's Williams in second was large but paled into insignificance compared to the margin between Senna and the rest of the field – Mansell's team-mate Keke Rosberg in third was 2.044s behind.

8. 1986 Brazilian Grand Prix; Jacarepagua   Gap: 0.765s

Senna's determination to beat his compatriot Nelson Piquet at their home race saw him emerge exhausted from the cockpit after setting his fastest lap in the closing minutes of qualifying. Predictably he stuffed Piquet.

9. 1986 Spanish Grand Prix; Jerez de la Frontera   Gap: 0.826s

An impressive gap over second placed compatriot Nelson Piquet's Williams Honda at a usually close circuit with a short lap-time. Senna's pole time was 1m 21.605s in a season where the Williams Honda was clearly the fastest car.

10. 1986 San Marino Grand Prix; Imola   Gap: 0.519s

Senna makes it three out of three for the first trio of races of the 1986 season. It was impressively his fourth pole in a row, overlapping from 1985. Made even more extraordinary by the fact that the Williams Honda was easily the best car.

11. 1986 USA Detroit Grand Prix; Detroit   Gap: 0.538s

Senna dominated the American street circuit as usual. He shone in qualifying and then topped his performance off with a win. He was particularly dominant at the tight tricky street circuits where driving skill was at a premium.

12. 1986 French Grand Prix; Paul Ricard   Gap: 0.229s

Senna took pole from the Williams Honda of Nigel Mansell with a car that was far off the pace. He struggled in the latter half of the season as Lotus concentrated all development on making the new Honda car ready for 1987.

13. 1986 Hungarian Grand Prix; Hungaroring   Gap: 0.335s

Senna took pole from Nelson Piquet's Williams Honda in his Lotus 98T with the Renault engine despite the lack of grip he continually complained of to his Lotus mechanics – who struggled to solve problems that Senna simply drove around.

14. 1986 Portuguese Grand Prix; Estoril   Gap: 0.816s
An impressive lap at one of Senna's best circuits, with only Nigel Mansell's William stay-ing within a second of the Brazilian. Despite the short lap time, 20 of the 27-strong grid could not get within two-and-a-half seconds of pole.

15. 1986 Mexican Grand Prix; Mexico City   Gap: 0.289s
A good pole in which Ayrton Senna put his Lotus Renault 98T 1.431s between himself and the sixth-placed man, eventual champion Alain Prost in his TAG McLaren. Only the car stopped Senna winning the 1986 world championship.

16. 1987 San Marino Grand Prix; Imola   Gap: 0.120s
Senna's only pole of the year, at the track where he later scored a record eight. Only Ni-gel Mansell's Williams Honda and Alain Prost's McLaren were within a second of Senna. The active suspension Lotus Honda 99T was hopeless in qualifying.

17. 1988 Brazilian Grand Prix; Jacarepagua   Gap: 0.536s
Pole for Senna at his home race and the beginning of a six-race run. Only five cars were within two seconds of his time but this became completely irrelevant when he was forced to start from the pitlane after trouble selecting gears.

18. 1988 San Marino Grand Prix; Imola   Gap: 0.771s
The gap of 0.771s to team-mate Alain Prost in second was impressive, but the gap of 3.352s to Nelson Piquet's Lotus Honda in third was amazing. It was a true testament to the combined skills of Senna and McLaren Honda.

19. 1988 Monaco Grand Prix; Monte Carlo   Gap: 1.427s
Considered by many to be the greatest qualifying lap of all time. Senna was in a trance-like situation on his fastest lap, driving his car round the narrow streets on another plane. No one came remotely close to him that weekend.

20. 1988 Mexican Grand Prix; Mexico City   Gap: 0.629s
A modest time gap to the next best by Senna's 1988 standards but substantial by any-body else's.Team-mate Alain Prost was never any threat in second.The McLaren Honda MP4 car was the class of the field that year.

21. 1988 Canadian Grand Prix; Montreal   Gap: 0.182s

Alain Prost gave Senna a run for his money at the Montreal track where he was usually the star. The Frenchman still could not wrestle away pole from his teammate driving an identical car, the McLaren Honda MP4/4 which took 15 poles from 16 races.

22. 1988 USA Detroit Grand Prix; Detroit   Gap: 0.858s

A magnificent performance on a rough track that suited the Ferraris rather than the McLarens. Senna's sixth pole in a row equalled the record set by Stirling Moss in 1959-60 and Niki Lauda in 1974. He couldn't quite get the record.

23. 1988 German Grand Prix; Hockenheim   Gap: 0.277s

After losing out twice in a row to Alain Prost and Gerhard Berger's Ferrari, Senna was back in form at Hockenheim setting his fastest lap on Friday, before the weekend's share of rain nullified the last qualifying session.

24. 1988 Hungarian Grand Prix; Hungaroring   Gap: 0.108s

A rougher than usual qualifying session for the McLarens. Senna just managed to edge pole from Nigel Mansell's Williams but Alain Prost could only manage seventh spot on the grid in his identical McLaren Honda MP4/4.

25. 1988 Belgian Grand Prix; Spa-Francorchamps   Gap: 0.410s

Times were set in the dry Friday session. Senna believed he could have gone quicker after Gabrielle Tarquini's Coloni Ford crashed impairing his fast lap. Then he didn't get a quick run on the rainy Saturday but he was still miles ahead.

26. 1988 Italian Grand Prix; Monza   Gap: 0.303s

Senna complained of traffic but still took pole from Alain Prost. It was his 10th pole of the season, beating the record of nine set by Ronnie Peterson in 1973, Niki Lauda in 1974 and 1975, and Nelson Piquet in 1984.

27. 1988 Spanish Grand Prix; Jerez de la Frontera   Gap: 0.067s

Senna snatched pole away from Alain Prost by the smallest margin of the year at this circuit famous for its tight finishes at a very difficult track to lap well. The circuit has very short straights where the Honda engine could not stretch itself.

28. 1988 Japanese Grand Prix; Suzuka   Gap: 0.324s

Senna took pole only to discover that the grid layout gave an advantage to the second-placed man, Alain Prost, something that was to rankle with him for years to come. Third-placed Gerhard Berger's Ferrari was 1.5s behind.

29. 1988 Australian Grand Prix; Adelaide   Gap: 0.132s

Senna once again pipped Alain Prost at the last minute, taking his 13th pole of the season. Nobody else was within a second-and-a-half of the brilliant Brazilian on the challenging and demanding street circuit where he excelled as usual.

30. 1989 Brazilian Grand Prix; Jacarepagua   Gap: 0.870s

Senna once again showed a considerable pace at his home event and never looked to be in any danger of losing pole position. His second fastest time would have also blown the field away, by 0.602s. It was staggering.

31 1989 San Marino Grand Prix; Imola   Gap: 0.225s

Senna's fifth consecutive pole in San Marino broke the record of four consecutive poles at a single circuit set by Juan Manuel Fangio at Monte Carlo. Apart from Prost only Mansell's Ferrari and Patrese's Williams Renault were within two seconds.

32. 1989 Monaco Grand Prix; Monte Carlo   Gap: 1.148s

Senna was once again devastating, with over a second back to Prost and 2.024s to Thierry Boutsen's Williams in third. Some thought the timing system had a glitch. Senna was a staggering 1.690s faster than his 1988 time.

33. 1989 Mexican Grand Prix; Mexico City   Gap: 0.897s

A substantial gap to team-mate Alain Prost in second meant that no one on the grid, close as they were to each other, could come near Senna's time. His normally aspirated McLaren Honda MP4/5 was far faster than the turbo of the previous year.

34. 1989 USA Grand Prix; Phoenix   Gap: 1.409s

Senna's record eighth pole in a row, a tally that Michael Schumacher came close to but could not surpass. It was also Senna's 34th pole, taking him past Jim Clark's record 33. On the Arizona street circuit no one else stood a chance.

35. 1989 British Grand Prix; Silverstone — Gap: 0.167s

Despite gearbox trouble Senna still took pole from team-mate Alain Prost, for what was his only time on top at Silverstone. He was generally successful on all types of circuit but Silverstone remained a qualifying enigma to him.

36. 1989 German Grand Prix; Hockenheim — Gap: 1.006s

On the last corner of his pole lap, Ayrton Senna ran over a kerb and ruptured one of the McLaren Honda's radiators. But his time was still over a second better than team-mate Alain Prost's closest grab in his identical car.

37. 1989 Belgian Grand Prix; Spa-Francorchamps — Gap: 0.596s

Senna's gap to Alain Prost in second was a small one for a long circuit, in an over two minute lap. Spa remains the most challenging fast circuit in the beautiful Ardennes region famous for sweeping corners. And Prost always excelled there.

38. 1989 Italian Grand Prix; Monza — Gap: 1.014s

A second's gap on this fast circuit and relatively short lap time to Gerhard Berger's Ferrari was a sensational performance. Only the top six were within three seconds of him and he was over three seconds better than his pole time in 1988.

39. 1989 Portuguese Grand Prix; Estoril — Gap: 0.591s

Senna managed to beat Gerhard Berger's Ferrari by over half a second, putting up a challenge to the rapidly improving Ferraris that the McLaren Honda MP4/5 of Alain Prost was unable to muster in an identical car and engine.

40. 1989 Spanish Grand Prix; Jerez de la Frontera — Gap: 0.274s

A smaller than usual gap to Gerhard Berger's Ferrari in second, but the 1.077s to Alain Prost in the other McLaren Honda in third was a true sign of Senna's qualifying strength in an absolutely identical car.

41. 1989 Japanese Grand Prix; Suzuka — Gap: 1.730s

Statistically Senna's best pole ever. The gap of 1.730s to Alain Prost remains the fifth largest gap of three decimal places and the biggest percentage he recorded back to second. But not compensation for starting on the dirty side of the track.

42. 1989 Australian Grand Prix; Adelaide   Gap: 0.738s
Senna convincingly out-qualified Prost, despite complaining that his now bitter enemy had blocked him on his fast lap. It was the last head-to-head between the two great drivers in identical equipment. The score was 26-4 in poles.

43. 1990 Brazilian Grand Prix; Interlagos   Gap: 0.611s
The first ever Grand Prix in Senna's home city of São Paulo. Coming off the back of an opening round qualifying defeat – to new team-mate Gerhard Berger – no one offered him any real resistance when he put in a stunning lap in the dying minutes.

44. 1990 San Marino Grand Prix; Imola   Gap: 0.561s
The 44th pole for Senna at Imola. Only Gerhard Berger was within a second of his Brazilian team-mate. Senna was to absolutely dominate pole position at Imola for many years until he lost his life there on 1st May 1994 – from pole.

45. 1990 Monaco Grand Prix; Monte Carlo   Gap: 0.462s
Still streets ahead of the rest, but it was even better than it looked as Senna's really fast lap was ruined by Gregor Foitek's Onyx Ford blocking his path at the Nouvelle Chicane. It was his fourth pole at Monte Carlo out of seven starts.

46. 1990 Canadian Grand Prix; Montreal   Gap: 0.066s
Breathtakingly close, but still a Senna triumph over new team-mate Gehard Berger in the new McLaren Honda MP4/6. Berger was fresh to McLaren and had yet to see the true brilliance of his new partner. That was to come.

47. 1990 German Grand Prix; Hockenheim   Gap: 0.236s
Although Gerhard Berger in second managed to stay reasonably close to Senna's time, the third-placed Ferrari of Alain Prost was a second-and-a-half behind. It ended a dry spell of three missed poles, his longest since 1987.

48. 1990 Belgian Grand Prix; Spa-Francorchamps   Gap: 0.583s
Senna was untouchable again at the Belgian track by half a second from teammate Gerhard Berger on a grid that was close for such a long circuit with a plus two minute lap time. Berger was in a similar position to Prost the year before.

49. 1990 Italian Grand Prix; Monza   Gap: 0.402s

After a lot of problems Senna didn't get a proper run on Saturday until the very last minutes when he snatched pole from the grasp of rival, and local Ferrari favourite, Alain Prost. It fuelled and continued the feud begun the year before.

50. 1990 Spanish Grand Prix; Jerez de la Frontera   Gap: 0.437s

Martin Donnelly crashed his Lotus Lamborghini heavily into a barrier and Senna rushed to the scene where Donnelly lay close to death in the middle of the track. The next day, he went over a second faster than he had before for his 50th pole.

51. 1990 Japanese Grand Prix; Suzuka   Gap: 0.232s

Another hard-fought Suzuka pole for Senna and still the same old problems of finding that pole was still on the dirty side of the track. His race didn't last long as he won the 1990 championship by running Prost off the road at the very first corner.

52. 1990 Australian Grand Prix; Adelaide   Gap: 0.573s

With the world championship won Senna once again excelled around the Adelaide Park circuit, taking pole from team-mate Gerhard Berger by over half a second. He retired from the race but by then it didn't matter.

53. 1991 USA Grand Prix; Phoenix   Gap: 1.121s

A stunning street circuit pole from Alain Prost's Ferrari got Senna's year off to a flier. The new McLaren Honda MP4/5B car had been finished very late and Senna had taken three months off over the winter and done little testing.

54. 1991 Brazilian Grand Prix; Interlagos   Gap: 0.383s

Senna himself described this as an 'incredible lap'. Only the Williams Renaults of Riccardo Patrese and Nigel Mansell were within a second of the Brazilian and they were the class of the field. This was a driver wringing the best from a car that wasn't.

55. 1991 San Marino Grand Prix; Imola   Gap: 0.080s

Senna's seventh consecutive pole at the Italian circuit which set an all-time record. The gap back to Riccardo Patrese's Williams Renault is testament more to the Italian hero's desire to do well at his home track than any fault of Senna's.

56. 1991 Monaco Grand Prix; Monte Carlo   Gap: 0.465s

Senna's fifth and final Monaco pole position, beating a surprising contender in the guise of Tyrrell Honda's young rising star Stefano Modena. He went on to win the race after Nigel Mansell's dominant Williams Renault had a puncture.

57. 1991 Hungarian Grand Prix; Hungaroring   Gap: 1.232s

After a lean mid-season, Senna returned to the top spot in style, with well over a second to the second quickest Williams of Riccardo Patrese. Only the other Williams of Nigel Mansell was within two seconds of the brilliant Brazilian.

58. 1991 Belgian Grand Prix; Spa-Francorchamps   Gap: 1.010s

Another pole-grabbing margin of over a second for Senna at a circuit he loved. Second Prost in a Ferrari with the Williams Renaults of Nigel Mansell and Riccardo Patrese well off the pace. Senna won the race from both.

59. 1991 Italian Grand Prix; Monza   Gap: 0.133s

There was only a narrow margin over the Williams of Nigel Mansell as the competition from the Renault engined team grew stronger and stronger. Senna was then in no doubt that he was in the second best car on the grid.

60. 1991 Australian Grand Prix; Adelaide   Gap: 0.344s

Senna's 60th pole position, taken over his McLaren team-mate Gerhard Berger by only 0.344s at one of his most competitive circuits. After two years as team-mate Gerhard Berger had pushed Senna closer than Alain Prost.

61. 1991 Canadian Grand Prix; Montreal   Gap: 0.097s

Senna's only pole of 1992. An inspired performance as he knocked Nigel Mansell off pole for the first time that year. The Williams Renaults were vastly superior to Senna's Honda engined McLaren MP4/7. No other team took a pole.

62. 1993 Australian Grand Prix; Adelaide   Gap: 0.436s

Senna's sixth pole at the Australian track, a tally beaten only by his eight at Imola. Yet again it was the only pole of the season not to go to the Williams Renaults of Alain Prost and Damon Hill. He broke a run of 24 consecutive top spots for that team.

63. 1994 Brazilian Grand Prix; Interlagos   Gap: 0.328s

A final home pole for Senna and his first for Williams Renault. The gap of three- 10ths to Michael Schumacher in second was not as revealing about the quality of Senna's performance as the gap of 1.423s back to Jean Alesi's Ferrari in third.

64. 1994 Pacific Grand Prix; Aida   Gap: 0.222s

Senna took pole without much of a challenge when Michael Schumacher failed to emerge for the Saturday session in an effort to conserve his tyres. The Williams Renault FW16 was recognised as a difficult car saved by Senna's brilliance.

65. 1994 San Marino Grand Prix; Imola   Gap: 0.337s

Senna's final pole position at the circuit where he scored an amazing record of eight. Despite not running on Saturday due to Roland Ratzenberger's fatal accident, his exceptional Friday time remained unbeaten to take pole for the very last time.

(Appendix 2 is adapted from Chapter 24 of The Life of Senna)

SENNA'S POLE POSITIONS

FATAL WEEKEND

Senna's Race Wins

41 wins from 161 starts

21st April 1985 to 7th November 1993

Winning was no accident for Ayrton Senna - it's what his whole life was about right to the end. In his last Grand Prix in Imola, on 1st May 1994, he was leading the field from pole position when he died.

Many of Ayrton Senna's 41 Grand Prix victories amounted to comprehensive driving lessons that remain textbook examples of how to win at the pinnacle of motorsport. Only death stopped him challenging Alain Prost's 51-win record and possibly putting it beyond the reach of Michael Schumacher or any other successor.

To win was what he desired more than anything else. That he was more successful at getting pole than he was at winning was a mystery to him, as it was to others. He once said: "You either commit yourself as a professional racing driver who is designed to win races, or you come second, third, fourth or fifth. I am not designed to come second or less. I race to win. As long as I feel it is possible. Sometimes you get it wrong, sure. It is impossible to get it right all the time. But I race to win because I am designed to win."

And that was probably the problem - he tried too hard to win and wore out the car or went off trying when he should have held for second and possibly inherited victory.

Senna's designs on the art of winning, his detailed planning to parlay his superlative natural talent into ultimate success, were unsurpassed. Michael Schumacher became the dominant driver of his era by emulating Senna's pioneering pursuit of excellence. But prior to Senna, none of the sport's other superstars worked as hard at winning. Sir Frank Williams only employed him for a short time, but it was long enough to realise what distinguished Senna from the team's other greatest winners Nigel Mansell and Alain Prost.

"Ayrton was the most committed of all. What was outstanding about him was his mental application. He had an air of invincibility around him. He put his entire body and mind into winning."

The Brazilian's ceaseless search for perfection involved extensive investigations into every aspect of driving, beginning with such fundamentals as the correct seating position in the cockpit and placement of the hands on the steering wheel. He believed in the classic 'quarter-past-nine' position, with his hands exactly opposite each other on the wheel. However, his distinctive cornering technique was at odds with conventional wisdom, involving quick stabbing applications of the throttle throughout the turn. From the entry, around the apex and through the exit of the corner, Senna controlled the rear of the car with the throttle and the front with the steering wheel. But it was his way of gaining control of races that most set him apart from his peers.

For Senna the race began on the formation lap, during which he deliberately worked at intimidating his rivals. While everyone else used the formation lap to warm up their tyres by weaving from side to side, Senna employed not so subtle forms of psychological warfare. By pretending to squeeze a following car out of position in a corner, feinting overtaking a car in front, or weaving ominously near a car that might venture alongside, he forcefully demonstrated his intentions and ambitions for the race. He called this aggressive behaviour 'a sort of declaration of war' and felt that such tactics would make it easier to later 'swallow up' the opposition. Senna considered the start and opening laps to be the most important parts of the race and believed they must be approached with great determination. "A driver must not wait for things to happen – on the contrary, he must act first, creating a situation that may be to his advantage," he once said. He thought deeply about the start, visualising a perfect getaway but allowing himself different alternatives 'so as not to be demoralised if things didn't work out as imagined'.

More often than not, it was his scintillating starts and devastating opening laps that demoralised his peers. The prime example of getting the jump on his rivals was his breathtaking first lap in the rain at the 1993 European Grand Prix at Donington, when he overtook every car in front of him and never looked back en route to one of his most memorable victories. Though he was capable of winning by the kind of stealth and cunning often used by his arch rival, Prost, Senna's competitive fires burned so fiercely that he favoured winning by fighting hard, preferably by annihilation. His essential philosophy was straightforward. Since the whole point of racing was to finish ahead of everyone else, he believed that if a driver was behind someone, his goal should be to overtake them, and if he was ahead then he should do everything in his power to avoid being overtaken. It was contrary to Senna's mindset to simply sit where he was and wait for the chequered flag. For him, the race was a battle from start to finish.

Unrivalled as an overtaker, Senna had an extensive repertoire of manoeuvres he employed to suit individual circumstances. While a surprise attack might sometimes work, he believed that a successful overtaking move more often came "after you have studied your opponent and discovered his weaknesses". In order to identify such flaws, he advocated staying behind for a few laps before pouncing. "The driver behind must actively create chances for overtaking and pressurise his opponent into a mistake. This is the real fascination of Formula One racing."

As much as he concentrated on continually perfecting his driving skills, Senna worked at developing a winning mindset that everyone acknowledged was on a different plane. Gerhard Berger, team mate and friend, thinks the Brazilian's secret weapon was his mentality, especially his unwavering single-mindedness, his steadfast self-belief and his absolute determination not to be beaten. When they were together at McLaren, and Williams had the technological advantage, Berger might set the third fastest time in a practice session behind the two Williams cars and then be content with that because, after all, the Williams cars were better than the McLarens. But as Berger says: "For Ayrton, Williams didn't exist. The only thing that existed was himself – and he had to be first. That thinking gave him the ability to create a power."

While most drivers tailored their performance expectations according to their car's capabilities, Senna refused to be beaten by mechanical limitations. "It is simply in your mind – believing you can do it," he said. "First of all, you've got to have the knowledge; you've got to have the experience, the basic feelings for doing it. After that it's only a question of believing you can do it, and committing yourself to it, before you actually achieve it. It's like knowing what's going to happen before it happens. Like believing things you cannot see and feeling things you are not touching. That is the key, the power."

Senna's relentless quest for ever more speed and his predilection for pushing himself harder and harder were seen by critics as potentially fatal flaws in his make-up. Often condemned for what was regarded as excessive risk-taking, he defended himself against charges that his conviction that he had a divine right to win made him dangerous.

On the contrary, Senna insisted he thought carefully about the role of fear and used it to manage the risk factor. "I always think about risk before I get in the car, especially if the circuit is one of the more dangerous ones," he said.

"I must think about this because the more calculating you can be, the less can go wrong because of an unexpected situation. There is the possibility that you could also make a mistake because your judgement might go wrong on that day. At the same time, you should not have too much fear or you cannot commit yourself."

Undoubtedly, Senna thought more deeply about his profession than any of his rivals, including Alain 'The Professor' Prost, who was renowned as a thinking driver. Throughout his career, which paralleled the increasing takeover of technology in the sport, the engineers who worked most closely with him marvelled that his mind was more than a match for any computer.

When Senna was at Lotus, the team's technical director, Gerard Ducarouge, said: "With Ayrton we don't need telemetry." Nigel Stepney, now at Ferrari, also worked with him at Team Lotus, where he recalls: "Senna's precision was unbelievable. On a debrief he could spend five or 10 minutes telling you about one lap – every bump, every entry, every apex, every exit, every line he'd taken through every corner. I think he wore Ducarouge down with his memory power and explanations of what he'd done."

Senna's insistence on lengthy debriefing sessions was legendary and his determination fully to understand the technical aspects of making a car go quickly meant he was often the last driver to leave the circuit. He would sit for hours analysing the data amassed by the engine and chassis telemetry, working out ways to improve the performance of the car and to maximise its potential. Steve Hallam, formerly with Lotus and now with McLaren, considers it a privilege to have engineered cars for Senna, whose understanding of how a Formula One car actually worked was unmatched.

"He was able to extract the maximum from all those parameters that go towards fulfilling a car's performance. In other words he would get the maximum from the brakes, the tyres, the engine, from every single part. He would consider each of them separately to find his limit and where he could extend it. Then he would combine them and channel his skills into well-defined periods of time. For a pole lap or an entire race."

Senna once tried to describe how he put everything together to help achieve those unbeatably quick laps. When his mind was in gear, it seemed he could anticipate the physical act of driving to the point where it was as if he was operating on automatic pilot. "It is always my objective to concentrate on the task, taking into account everything within me: my personality, my training, both my weak and my strong points," he said. "I can then get to a level where I am driving ahead of the next corner. I am a split second ahead entering a corner, halfway through a corner, exiting a corner – just before braking, just before changing gear, just before putting down the power. I can almost predict what I'm going to face and correct it before it happens. And that takes a lot of concentration as well as instant reactions. It means a lot of tension goes through the body, because it's like electricity. Every movement is instant and has to be 100 per cent precise, or as close to 100 per cent precision as possible.

"In this way the driving becomes automatic because your brain controls the throttle. It knows your braking ability, your gear change points. It depends on your eyesight before a corner".

On one of his really quick laps, Senna was a sight never to be forgotten. One of the most eloquent descriptions of him at speed is given by John Watson, who was driving a McLaren in the 1985 European Grand Prix at Brands Hatch where Senna, in his second season in Formula One, finished second in the race after starting from pole. Watson had just completed his own qualifying lap when he saw Senna's familiar yellow and green helmet coming up behind him at a phenomenal speed. He moved over to let the flying Lotus Renault past, and this is what he saw: "I witnessed visibly and audibly something I had not seen anyone do before in a racing car. It was as if he had four hands and legs. He was braking, changing down, steering, pumping the throttle, and the car appeared to be on that knife-edge between being in and out of control. All of this at absolutely awesome speed. It was a master controlling a machine. I saw something very special that day: a little glimpse of genius."

With the same genius for pure speed that secured a record 65 pole positions, Senna won 41 of his 161 Grand Prix races. Only very seldom did he back off and simply cruise to a victory. It was against his nature to go anything much less than flat out, an aspect of his character that was dramatically driven home to him in a lesson he never forgot. Because he was so intensely self-critical and analytical about his driving, any mistake he made caused him great mental anguish, and none more so than the one that cost him victory in the 1988 Monaco Grand Prix. Having won there the year before with Lotus, Senna was then with McLaren, where his intense rivalry with team mate Alain Prost was in its early stages. After beating Prost to pole by an astonishing 1.427 seconds, Senna was determined to destroy his team mate in the race. By lap 54, he was nearly a minute ahead of Prost, who, after getting past slower traffic, reeled off a succession of fast laps. When Senna retaliated with even quicker laps, worried McLaren boss Ron Dennis ordered them to slow down and hold their positions for the good of the team. A few laps later – while leading Prost by 46 seconds – Senna crashed.

The accident happened at Portier, the right-hander that brings the cars out to the tunnel beside the Mediterranean. There sat the abandoned McLaren, and when Prost cruised over the finish line to score an easy win. It was one victory less.

After the accident, at home in his flat he wept until he fell asleep, so disconsolate and embarrassed at making such an elementary error. Jo Ramirez remembers: "That's how intense the guy was. That's how much it meant to him. I've never known anyone with Ayrton's will to win."

There was another element to Senna's emotional state at the time that no one else knew about. It was only after he clinched the 1988 championship that Senna spoke about the spiritual transformation he had experienced at Monaco. "Monaco was the turning point in the championship," he said at the time. "The mistake I made woke me up psychologically and mentally, and I changed a lot after that. It gave me the strength, the power and the cool mind to fight in critical situations. That was when I took the biggest step in my career as a racing driver, as a professional and as a man. I have to say that it brought me closer to God than I've ever been and that has changed my life completely. I am a better human being now than I was before. I am better in everything I am and everything I do. The accident was not just a driving mistake. It was the consequence of a struggle inside me, which paralysed me and made me vulnerable. I had an opening to God and another to the devil. The accident was a signal that God was there, waiting to give me a hand. I just had to tell him what I wanted."

Senna said that from then on God spoke to him and answered his prayers through passages in the Bible. When he sought guidance and protection, the Bible would open at references to courage, determination and strength. On hearing about the depth of his religious conviction, some people ridiculed Senna, and others, Prost included, worried that he might take even greater risks and endanger himself and others because he thought God would protect him. Senna was stung by such criticisms and eventually refused to discuss the religious aspect of his life, apart from with close confidants.

Nonetheless, with or without divine intervention, following that single error in 1988, the fact remains that Senna won the following five Monaco Grand Prix events in a row.

Ramirez was particularly close to Senna and still finds it difficult to mention his name. Of all the 35 victories Senna won for McLaren, the one Ramirez remembers most is the 1993 Australian Grand Prix, in Adelaide. It was Senna's last race with McLaren before his move to Williams. As usual, Ramirez was beside Senna's car on the starting grid, helping him do up his seatbelts, when Senna confessed he felt very strange. Ramirez says: " I said to Ayrton 'You just win this for us and we'll love you forever'. He grabbed my arm, squeezed it really hard, and his eyes filled up. Mine did too."

Ramirez was worried that the emotional moment might adversely affect Senna's performance – but it didn't. He won the race to give McLaren a record 104 Grand Prix victories, one more than Ferrari at the time. Sadly, it was also destined to be the 41st and final victory of Senna's career.

It was later that night when Tina Turner sang to him 'Simply the Best'.

Jo Ramirez says he has that moment on video but has never been able to watch it.

1. 1985 Portuguese Grand Prix: Estoril, 67 laps in 2h00m28.006s

Second: Michele Alboreto, Ferrari, +1m 02.978s

Third: Patrick Tambay, Renault, +1 lap

Senna's first victory was also one of his best. In the Portuguese downpour he took a clean sweep: he won, took pole position, fastest lap and fastest practice time of the weekend and led every lap. He never looked beatable. It was a drive more than worthy of a veteran as opposed to a young driver with only 15 Formula One races behind him.

2. 1985 Belgian Grand Prix: Spa-Francorchamps, 43 laps in 1h34m19.893s

Second: Nigel Mansell,Williams Honda, +28.422s

Third: Alain Prost, McLaren TAG, +55.109s

Once again in the wet Senna was magnificent. At the ultimate driver's circuit he proved himself against the rest of the field. Even by the end of the first lap his lead looked secure. He led every lap but the ninth, when during a dry spell his teammate Elio de Angelis briefly moved into first as Senna pitted to change tyres.

3. 1986 Spanish Grand Prix: Jerez de la Frontera, 72 laps in 1h48m47.735s

Second: Nigel Mansell,Williams Honda, +0.014s

Third: Alain Prost, McLaren TAG, +21.552s

This remains the second closest victory in history. A race-long battle between Senna, Mansell and Prost that became all the more thrilling in the closing laps. Mansell on fresh rubber was catching Senna by four seconds a lap and whoever got the better kick from the final corner would be victor. Senna won courtesy of a misplaced finish line.

4. 1986 USA East Grand Prix: Detroit, 63 laps in 1h51m12.847s

Second: Jacques Laffite, Ligier Renault, +31.017s

Third: Alain Prost, McLaren TAG, +31.824s

This was Senna's first victory at one of his best tracks. It was a hard-fought win for the Brazilian around the slow and twisting street circuit. He twice lost the lead and picked up a puncture along the way but in the end he outpaced and outdrove his rivals to take his first of many street circuit victories.

5. 1987 Monaco Grand Prix: Monte Carlo, 78 laps in 1h57m54.085s

Second: Nelson Piquet,Williams Honda, +33.212s

Third: Michele Alboreto, Ferrari, +1m12.839s

In 1987 Senna took his first victory at what is considered to be his best circuit. He started in second and got away from the grid still in that position behind poleman Nigel Mansell. He inherited the lead when the Englishman's turbo gave up on lap 30. It was his first of a record six victories in the principality.

6. 1987 USA East Grand Prix: Detroit, 63 laps in 1h50m16.358s

Second: Nelson Piquet,Williams Honda, +33.819s

Third: Alain Prost, McLaren TAG, +45.327s

In Detroit, Senna took his second victory in a row in 1987. It was almost a replay of his Monte Carlo triumph. Mansell again started from pole with Senna beside him, once again took the lead at the start, and again suffered a problem – this time a sticking wheelnut at a tyre stop – to hand the lead and the victory to his Brazilian rival.

7. 1988 San Marino Grand Prix: Imola, 60 laps in 1h32m41.264s

Second: Alain Prost, McLaren Honda, +2.334s

Third: Nelson Piquet, Lotus Honda, +1 lap

The McLaren MP4/4s were three seconds better than anyone else in qualifying and after Prost had problems getting off the startline, Senna knew he could not be touched. It was a lights-to-flag victory with only his new team-mate, on the same lap.

8. 1988 Canadian Grand Prix: Montreal, 69 laps in 1h39m46.618s

Second: Alain Prost, McLaren Honda, +5.934s

Third:Thierry Boutsen, Benetton Ford, +51.409s

Alain Prost took the lead at the start but Senna was determined and executed a brilliant overtaking manoeuvre on lap 19 to wrest the lead away from the Frenchman. He completed the hat-trick of win, pole position and fastest lap in Canada to boost the championship challenge to his team-mate and rival Prost.

9. 1988 USA East Grand Prix: Detroit, 63 laps in 1h54m56.635s

Second: Alain Prost, McLaren Honda, +38.713s

Third:Thierry Boutsen, Benetton Ford, +1 lap

Another win in Detroit for the Brazilian confirmed Senna's street circuit dominance. It was another lights-to-flag victory for him to savour but it was not won without great effort. At the end of the race Senna emerged exhausted from the car in the 34 degree searing heat, from a race in which only seven other cars made it to the finish.

10. 1988 British Grand Prix: Silverstone, 65 laps in 1h33m16.367s

Second: Nigel Mansell, Williams Judd, +23.344s

Third: Alessandro Nannini, Benetton Ford, +51.214s

Silverstone was not without problems for Senna – torrential rain on one of the fastest tracks of all time, fuel consumption worries, a Ferrari resurgence in form – but he battled through to win the race all the same. It gained McLaren its eighth consecutive victory that season – the first time ever that a team had achieved the feat.

11. 1988 German Grand Prix: Hockenheim, 44 laps in 1h32m54.188s

Second: Alain Prost, McLaren Honda, +13.609s

Third: Gerhard Berger, Ferrari, +52.095s

Senna took advantage of Prost's lack of confidence in the wet to blast easily into the lead at the start. He was the master in the changeable weather conditions that Hockenheim produced and made the tricky decision of using wet tyres throughout. It paid off. He kept hold of his early lead unchallenged until the chequered flag.

12. 1988 Hungarian Grand Prix: Hungaroring, 76 laps in 1h57m47.381s

Second: Alain Prost, McLaren Honda, +0.529s

Third:Thierry Boutsen, Benetton Ford, +31.410s

At the Hungarian Grand Prix, Senna produced yet another fantastic performance. He led every lap, with Prost technically taking the lead for just a fraction of a second at the start, but it was one of the closest contests between the McLaren pairing all season. The clash fittingly made the drivers equal leaders of the championship on 66 points.

13. 1988 Belgian Grand Prix: Spa-Francorchamps, 43 laps in 1h28m00.549

Second: Alain Prost, McLaren Honda, +30.470s

Third: Ivan Capelli, March Judd, +1m15.768s

Spa-Francorchamps was one of Senna's favourite circuits. Although Prost went into first at the start, by the time they surged into Les Combes on the initial lap, Senna had taken a lead that he would not lose.There was celebration for the team when McLaren took the constructor's championship, although it had never really been in doubt.

14. 1988 Japanese Grand Prix: Suzuka, 51 laps in 1h33m26.173s

Second: Alain Prost, McLaren Honda, +13.363s

Third: Thierry Boutsen, Benetton Ford, +36.109s

Senna took one of his greatest victories and his first world title. When he stalled on the grid it looked as if the championship was over. He managed to get the car going but found himself 14th. By the end of the first lap he was in eighth, and he progressed through the field to finally take the lead from Ivan Capelli's March Judd on lap 28.

15. 1989 San Marino Grand Prix: Imola, 58 laps in 1h26m51.245s

Second: Alain Prost, McLaren Honda, +40.225s

Third: Alessandro Nannini, Benetton Ford, +1 lap

Senna's most controversial win. He made an agreement with Prost that whoever was in the lead at the first corner would be unchallenged. Senna was in front and Prost did not overtake. Then Gerhard Berger had a fiery crash and the race was restarted. Prost made the better getaway, but Senna overtook and led until the chequered flag.

16. 1989 Monaco Grand Prix: Monte Carlo, 77 laps in 1h53m33.251s

Second: Alain Prost, McLaren Honda, +52.529s

Third: Stefano Modena, Brabham Judd, +1 lap

Senna's second Monaco victory was a lights-to-flag affair and he never looked in danger. In fact he hardly seemed to be trying, despite building up almost a minute's lead before the end of the race. He lost first and second gears in the later stages, but kept pushing to the maximum so those behind would not realise he had a problem.

17. 1989 Mexican Grand Prix: Mexico City, 69 laps in 1h35m21.431s

Second: Riccardo Patrese,Williams +15.560s

Third: Michele Alboreto,Tyrrell Ford, +31.254s

Senna started from pole position and sped away from the pack at the start until a mid-field pile-up at the end of lap one meant the race was red-flagged. Senna took the lead again and led all the way to the flag while the rest of the field shuffled in from behind.

18. 1989 German Grand Prix: Hockenheim, 45 laps in 1h21m43.302s

Second: Alain Prost, McLaren Honda, +18.151s

Third: Nigel Mansell, Ferrari, +1m23.254s

After a four-race lean period mid-season, Senna was back on winning form at Hockenheim. Admittedly it was a lucky win – Prost led most of the race but in the later stages the Frenchman suffered gearbox problems and Senna flew past with just three laps to go to bring himself back into championship contention.

19. 1989 Belgian Grand Prix: Spa-Francorchamps, 44 laps in 1h40m54.196s

Second: Alain Prost, McLaren Honda, +1.304s

Third: Nigel Mansell, Ferrari, +1.824s

When the rain came down it seemed inevitable who would emerge as the winner.

Senna took the lead at the start and, taking care to avoid aquaplaning, led right until the end. The small gap to second and third places was due to a cautious spell late in the race where he slowed down considerably due to safety concerns.

20. 1989 Spanish Grand Prix: Jerez de la Frontera, 73 laps in 1h48.264s

Second: Gerhard Berger, Ferrari, +27.051s

Third: Alain Prost, McLaren Honda, +53.788s

This was far from Senna's most exciting victory – certainly not compared to his other win at Jerez in 1986 – but it was a useful and important triumph because it kept his championship challenge alive. The Brazilian was in dominant form – he started from pole, led every lap and clocked the fastest lap by 0.432 seconds along the way.

21. 1990 US Grand Prix: Phoenix, 72 laps in 1h52m32.829s

Second: Jean Alesi,Tyrrell Ford, +8.685s

Third:Thierry Boutsen,Williams Renault, +54.080s

Unusually Senna was outshone. A young Jean Alesi took the lead at the start and continued until lap 33, when inevitably Senna caught and passed him. But Alesi was having none of it.The Tyrrell driver overtook him again immediately and managed to hold the lead for another two laps. It was the sort of battle Senna enjoyed.

22. 1990 Monaco Grand Prix: Monte Carlo, 78 laps in 1h52m46.982s

Second: Jean Alesi,Tyrrell Ford, +1.087s

Third: Gerhard Berger, McLaren Honda, +2.073s

By 1990 Senna had started to prove himself invincible at Monte Carlo.Taking pole, the win and the fastest lap he was dominant throughout the weekend. In the race he led every one of the 78 laps. His only loss all weekend was when he took second in the first timed practice session to Alesi, who was once again making his mark.

23. 1990 Canadian Grand Prix: Montreal, 70 laps in 1h42m56.400

Second: Nelson Piquet, Benetton Ford, +10.497s

Third: Nigel Mansell, Ferrari, +13.385s

The track started off damp, but rather than the rain it was more a series of bizarre incidents that helped Senna to race victory, including a minute's penalty for Gerhard Berger, a groundhog that was run over by Alessandro Nannini's Benetton Ford and a series of collisions. Senna rose above it all to retain a healthy championship lead.

24. 1990 German Grand Prix: Hockenheim, 45 laps in 1h20m47.164s
Second: Alessandro Nannini, Benetton +6.520s
Third: Gerhard Berger, McLaren Honda, +8.553s
Senna took the lead at the start, but dropped back through the field during pitstops. When the race order settled down, only Nannini's Benetton lay ahead of the Brazilian, struggling on worn tyres after taking the gamble not to pit. Senna caught and passed the Italian with 12 laps to go and powered on to victory.

25. 1990 Belgian Grand Prix: Spa-Francorchamps, 44 laps in 1h26m31.997s
Second: Alain Prost, Ferrari, +3.550s
Third: Gerhard Berger, McLaren Honda, +28.462s
Ayrton Senna took pole position, the fastest lap and led every lap on the way to a totally commanding victory. The win significantly increased his championship chances. This was the 25th race victory of his career and took him above Jackie Stewart's tally.

26. 1990 Italian Grand Prix: Monza, 53 laps in 1h17m57. 878s
Second: Alain Prost, Ferrari, +6.054s
Third: Gerhard Berger, McLaren Honda, +7.404s
Monza produced yet another race where Senna led every single lap, took pole position and recorded the fastest lap in the race. It had to be started twice as Derek Warwick's Lotus Lamborghini ended up upside down at the Parabolica first time around. But Senna was unperturbed and easily kept his lead on both occasions.

27. 1991 US Grand Prix: Phoenix, 81 laps in 2h00m47.828s
Second: Alain Prost, Ferrari, +16.322s
Third: Nelson Piquet, Benetton Ford, +17.376s
Senna began his third championship-winning season in style with victory at another American street circuit. He started from pole and led every lap of the race. In winning he became the first driver ever to score 10 points for a victory and made it to the magical tidemark of 27 wins, a total only ever exceeded by five other drivers.

28. 1991 Brazilian Grand Prix: Interlagos, 71 laps in 1h38m28.128s
Second: Riccardo Patrese,Williams +2.991s
Third: Gerhard Berger, McLaren Honda, +5.416s
After years of trying, Senna finally took his first win at home. He led every lap, despite

a number of problems.Towards the end of the race his gearbox started to play up and he had to drive the final laps in sixth gear.Then it began to rain and the conditions were treacherous. He took the flag so exhausted that he had to be helped from the car.

29. 1991 San Marino Grand Prix: Imola, 61 laps in 1h35m14.750s

Second: Gerhard Berger,McLaren +1.675s

Third: JJ Lehto, Dallara Judd, +1 lap

When the rain poured down shortly before the start at Imola, it seemed inevitable that Senna would emerge the victor. He did not have it all his own way, however. Although the Brazilian started from pole, Riccardo Patrese had the better start and led the first nine laps for Williams Renault before a misfire put paid to his chances.

30. 1991 Monaco Grand Prix: Monte Carlo, 78 laps in 1h53m02.234s

Second: Nigel Mansell,Williams +18.348s

Third: Jean Alesi, Ferrari, +47.455s

Senna was back at his best track to make it four wins from the first four races of the 1991 season. He put in another seemingly effortless performance: grabbing pole position, taking the lead at the start and building up the gap to the rest of the field to take the race. It was his 30th overall career victory and his fourth in Monte Carlo.

31. 1991 Hungarian Grand Prix: Hungaroring, 77 laps in 1h49m12.796s

Second: Nigel Mansell,Williams Renault, +4.599s

Third: Riccardo Patrese,Williams, +15.594s

After his early dominance, Senna was back on form at the Hungarian Grand Prix. The records state that he led all 77 laps, but this does not show how tough a battle he faced against the Williams Renaults. Patrese harried him early on and in the closing stages let Mansell through, who hassled him all the way to the end.

32. 1991 Belgian Grand Prix: Spa-Francorchamps, 44 laps in 1h27m17.669s

Second: Gerhard Berger,McLaren +1.901s

Third: Nelson Piquet, Benetton Ford, +32.176s

It was a magnificent fifth victory for Senna in Spa-Francorchamps, although it was far from easy. He led until the first round of pitstops, when Nigel Mansell and Jean Alesi got ahead of him. Both their cars suffered later and Senna went back into the lead. Despite problems with his gearbox, he found some gears and kept going.

33. 1991 Australian Grand Prix: Adelaide, 14 laps in 24m34.899s

Second: Nigel Mansell,Williams Renault, +1.259s

Third: Gerhard Berger, McLaren Honda, +5.120s

It began to rain before the race and the start was delayed.When the cars eventually did get off it was predictably chaotic and six cars had crashed by lap eight. Two marshals were injured and following gestures from Senna and other drivers concerned for safety, the race was stopped after only 14 laps and half points were awarded.

34. 1992 Monaco Grand Prix: Monte Carlo, 78 laps in 1h50m59.372s

Second: Nigel Mansell,Williams Renault, +0.215s

Third: Riccardo Patrese,Williams +31.843s

Nigel Mansell, in the all-conquering Adrian Newey-designed FW14B, had won the first five races of the season. It seemed as if Monaco would be his, then with eight laps to go he was forced to pit with a loose wheelnut. He emerged behind Senna, and despite running close the Brazilian somehow held him off to the end of the race.

35. 1992 Hungarian Grand Prix: Hungaroring, 77 laps in 1h46m19.216s

Second: Nigel Mansell,Williams +40.139s

Third: Gerhard Berger, McLaren Honda +50.782s

The Hungaroring produced a chaotic race that saw the placings chop and change right until the final stages. Senna leapt into second at the start but found himself harried by Mansell. Mansell dropped away and when Riccardo Patrese in the other Williams spun off, Senna inherited the lead and collected yet another victory.

36. 1992 Italian Grand Prix: Monza, 53 laps in 1h18m15.349s

Second: Martin Brundle, Benetton Ford +17.050s

Third: Michael Schumacher, Benetton +24.373s

Senna led just six of the laps and was never a match for the Williams Renaults of Nigel Mansell and Riccardo Patrese in terms of speed. However, a double hydraulic failure for the Williams pairing meant he snatched the lead in the closing stages.

37. 1993 Brazilian Grand Prix: Interlagos, 71 laps in 1h51m15.485s

Second: Damon Hill,Williams Renault +16.625s

Third: Michael Schumacher, Benetton +45.436s

This race did not start well. He got off in second, was overtaken by Damon Hill and then received a 10-second penalty for overtaking under a yellow flag. He emerged from the pits in fourth just as a storm brewed up. Senna took the lead in the confusion that ensued as the cars switched to wets and then back to slicks again as the track dried.

38. 1993 European Grand Prix: Donington Park, 76 laps in 1h50m46.570s
Second: Damon Hill,Williams +1m23.199s
Third: Alain Prost,Williams Renault +1 lap
Senna's greatest victory. He suffered a poor start and was in fifth as the cars moved off the sodden grid, struggling to hold on to even that place. But by the end of the first lap he had overtaken the four cars in front, no lesser drivers than Michael Schumacher, Karl Wendlinger, Alain Prost and Damon Hill.The rest of the race was irrelevant.

39. 1993 Monaco Grand Prix: Monte Carlo, 78 laps in 1h52m10.947
Second: Damon Hill,Williams Renault +52.118s
Third: Jean Alesi, Ferrari, +1m03.362s
Senna had crashed heavily in Thursday qualifying and was suffering from a sore thumb. He managed to race and gained places not from star driving but from Alain Prost stalling during a penalty stop and Michael Schumacher suffering hydraulic failure. It was his record sixth Monaco crown and his fifth in a row.

40. 1993 Japanese Grand Prix: Suzuka; 53 laps in 1h40m27.912s
Second: Alain Prost,Williams Renault, +11.435s
Third: Mika Häkkinen, McLaren Ford, +26.129s
Suzuka saw a race-long challenge between Senna and Prost, first one and then the other taking the upper hand. However, the occasion was more famous for the Brazilian punching Eddie Irvine for getting in his way than the victory. It was the 103rd win for his McLaren team, which took it equal with Ferrari at the top of the all-time tally.

41. 1993 Australian Grand Prix: Adelaide; 79 laps in 1h43m27.476s
Second: Alain Prost,Williams Renault, +9.259s
Third: Damon Hill,Williams Renault, +33.902s
Senna led for the full distance, barring pitstops, on what was an emotional occasion. It was old rival Alain Prost's last race before retirement and it was a touching moment when they met on the podium for the last time. Few would have guessed that the race would also mark Senna's final victory and that he would be dead three races later.

Ayrton Senna's nearly wins

As memorable as some of the victories are the races that Ayrton Senna should have won. He could have taken his first ever Formula One victory for Toleman Hart at Monte Carlo back in 1984. He was catching race leader Alain Prost at an unbelievable speed but the race was stopped on lap 31 due to heavy rain. In 1988 two silly accidents lost him races in McLaren's best ever year. After receiving a pit signal to slow down, he crashed into the barriers at Monte Carlo from a huge lead in the later stages of the race. Then at Monza he collided with backmarker Jean Louis Schlesser's Williams with just two laps to go. At Suzuka, in 1989, he fought hard to take back the lead from Alessandro Nannini after controversially crashing with Alain Prost at the chicane but was excluded after the chequered flag for 'dangerous driving'. On that occasion the loss of the race cost him his championship chances.

(Appendix 3 is adapted from Chapter 25 of The Life of Senna)

SENNA'S RACE WINS

FATAL WEEKEND

Senna's Racing Philosophy

His odd personality

Ayrton Senna always realised he had an odd personality but thought it a consequence of being the best driver in the world. As he said: "I have applied my personality in motor racing so many times – it's one of my qualities. Sometimes it has cost me a race or a good result, but it is my personality and that's what I am."

Senna said that before the start of a race, he would concentrate so hard that he felt as though the bodywork of the car became a second skin. "This carbon-fibre incarnation could sometimes prompt acts of folly," he said. "In 1988, at Monte Carlo, I was in pole position. But I was on a cloud.

Pointlessly, I stepped up the chase again, only to wake up and realise that the others weren't going too slowly – I was going too fast. I'd let the intensity of the emotion get the better of me, and I'd overstepped my limits."

Years later, Senna revealed that in 1989 at the Spanish Grand Prix, he was weighed down by too much pressure. He says he won without really savouring the victory. So the next morning he got hold of a Fiat Panda and went back to the circuit. He explained: "During the Grand Prix I felt no joy. I said to myself 'You can't leave here without enjoying yourself '. So I went back on the track. There was no one there. It felt good. I savoured it."

That his whole life was focused around motor racing was never a doubt in Senna's mind. He admitted it controlled him rather than him controlling it: "Everything in my life is aimed at the point when I sit in my car on the grid.

It's a focused situation, where you want to search deeper and deeper inside in order to find the next step. This situation takes you to a different world.

You have this desire to go into places where you have never been before. It is something that is very lonely in a way, because once you get in a car, on a circuit, it is you and the car, nothing else. That situation is extremely absorbing. Perhaps it's because I have experienced, on many occasions, the feeling of finding new things. Even if I thought 'OK, that is my maximum', suddenly I found something extra. That process is almost non-stop in terms of excitement and motivation."

Senna saw it as an asset even when it cost him a race win, as it did many times. Although most motor racing commentators attest to the fact that he rarely made a mistake, close examination of his record does not back it up. It also comes back to the fact he scored a third more poles than race wins.

When his record is properly examined, not only in races but practice and qualifying, it is clear that Senna made plenty of mistakes, mostly going faster than he should have been. But he was always unrepentant: "The main thing is to be yourself and not allow people to disturb you and change you. You have got to be yourself, even though many times you make a mistake due to your own personality. You learn, and you must learn through your mistakes and get better.

"I believe if you have the ability to focus strongly on something then you have the ability to gain from it. It's been like that all my life – it's always been a question of improving. There is no end; as you go through, you just keep finding more and more. It's fascinating. We are made of emotions and we are all looking for emotions – it's just a question of finding a way to experience them."

The Brazilian hated making mistakes and admitted they got to him afterwards. The most public one was in Monaco in 1988. He once said: "Those things can get to you if you're not careful because you really see how fragile you are – you have no power, you are just there. You can be gone in a fraction of a second so you realise suddenly you are nobody and your life can have a sudden end."

He claimed he had always confronted problems and never run away from them: "You are faced with some unexpected situations and you have to face them – it is part of your life and you either face it or you just drop it and don't do it anymore. I happen to like what I do so much, I can't drop it."

Jackie Stewart believed this absolutely and says he often saw an imprisoned look in Senna's eyes. "I never thought he looked like he was getting the degree of pleasure he deserved because he worked as hard as any man could work at mastering his art. I've seen a lot of other people who, while doing that, have also had a quality of life and an appreciation of life that might have been fuller than Ayrton gave himself the privilege of having. I think that's what made the difference because in all the great drivers, they've all been given a gift from God. Some have manicured and massaged that gift to the highest level of their potential. Ayrton did it more recognisably through sheer hard work and it would almost seem aggravation to him. He had his ego factor, which everybody has but it looked like it wasn't a pleasure. He was sometimes what I would call a rushed driver. He didn't look as though he had the same time in the cockpit as Jim Clark to do things. Everything was more hurried, more abrupt, more nervous. I don't think his reactions were faster – or braver. It's just that he drove right on the limit. And I believe he went closer to the limit than a lot of other people would. He survived them all but I was always waiting for the accident. Not the kind of accident that happened at Imola. I was waiting for the type of accident where he would use too much of the kerb and the thing would flick on him."

That comment strikes right at the heart of what Senna was. He believed in his ultimate superiority over any man and any machine. He believed it was his divine right to win in Formula One from 1988 onwards, and when he didn't, he always looked for the answer. It was his inquisitiveness that stood him apart from other men. And it made him one of the most unpredictable men alive. No one ever knew where they stood when he was around. He said in 1990: "The newest machine in the world will never match the human being. Therefore, really, what we are all looking for is how we function, how we operate: why this, why that? There is a logical way of looking at it, there is the spiritual way of looking at it – through religion, through God, and it's a process with no end."

Senna rethought the process of life more often than any other driver of his era and possibly ever in Formula One. He was constantly not only trying to learn about his cars but also about himself. He called it a 'non-stop process'. But he admitted there were many things about the way he behaved and how he could drive faster than others that he simply didn't understand.

He didn't understand why he could never accept coming second and why he won far less races than he won pole for. He said: "There are so many things to which you just cannot find the answers."

His religion gave him some of the answers he craved. He read the Bible primarily to find answers and, in religion, found a new way of life. He said in 1989, after he lost the championship that year to Alain Prost: "I still want lots of answers but I think I have a new road where I am finding those answers slowly. I believe there are many things about which you're not aware, human qualities that were given to you by God. If you get to understand just a little bit, it makes so much more sense: it makes things so much more peaceful to understand the difficulties – particularly – and to better enjoy the good moments. Unfortunately, I had not experienced that before: I wish I had."

In Montreal in 1991, Senna told journalists: "Winning is like a drug. Do I think I am totally addicted? Maybe, I don't know the meaning correctly in English, but I am totally dependent at this moment on winning." It was that philosophy that made him what he was – the good and the bad. He was like a drug addict who would commit any crime to get his fix. It was the single thing that drove everything he did.

Ayrton Senna was a hugely contrasting and complex man. One minute absorbed and lost in the Bible, the next ruthlessly disposing of fellow competitors on the race track, sometimes to the extreme unpopularity of the journalists who observed his every move. Only his vast talent and intelligence excused his behaviour on many occasions. Senna's formidable intellect was one of the secrets of his speed. His career was a triumph of mind over matter and his philosophy of life and words of wisdom are among his most important legacies. Senna believed there was some truth in the old saying that the ideal would be to have two lives because in the first life you would learn how to live and then you would use that experience to live the second life to the full. But, typically, that wasn't enough for Senna. He said:

"You need a third life and a fourth because you wouldn't ever get to the bottom of it." His wisdom went far beyond his years, and he managed to pack more into his short lifetime than most people achieve in a longer life.

He was able to do this because he applied his exceptional intelligence to thinking about the whole business of living, not just racing.

However, his passion for his sport was so all-consuming that it was inevitable that his greatest insights about life would come from racing. With Formula One as the catalyst his powers of reasoning were honed and the framework created for the development of his personal philosophy. His superior intellect was ideally suited to the fast-paced world of Formula One, where quick-thinking is a way of life, and his racing experiences sharpened his senses and accelerated his intellectual development.

He once said: "One thing that happens in our lives as racing drivers is that we do a lot of things in a short period of time. So we have to live our lives very intensely. And by living very intensely, everything happens so fast. The difficulty is doing it right all the time. With so much pressure and stress it's quite easy to get it wrong. That is the major challenge. To do it properly, do it right, positively, constructively. You don't always manage it but in the end the aim is really to do the best you can all the time. Because then you are at peace."

Senna said that as a young boy he didn't even know who he was, a knowing observation that in itself reveals the concern for self-understanding which went on throughout his life. For Senna, his relentless quest to explore himself, to push his personal limits and discover how far he could go was key to becoming one of the greatest racing drivers in history. Beyond that, his search to find himself was a prime reason for living, a motivational force that went far beyond his fundamental need to win races. "I think I am a complex person," he said, "because I am never convinced that 'this is it'. I don't sit and wait for things to happen. I'm always searching for more, particularly within myself. In this area it is infinite. Because where do you stop? You don't know what capability you have in your mind. What you read, what you can learn about - we only use a fraction of our capabilities, our competence. So this research is fascinating. It's a continuous feeling that 'there's more, there's more'.

Wherever and whenever he found more, Senna, like a true explorer, became excited by his discovery, especially if the revelation came behind the wheel of a Formula One car. "This situation takes you to a different world," he said. "You have this desire to go into places where you have never been before. It is the challenge of doing better all the time."

When a racing driver continually pushes himself he is also exposing himself to greater danger. It is the nature of drivers to take one of three approaches to this most difficult of dilemmas. The easiest way, and the most common, is to slow down, to never exceed the personal limits of safety they feel comfortable with. Obviously that would never work for Senna, a man who once said: "The motivating factor is the discoveries that I keep having every time I am driving.

When I push, I go and find something more. I go again and I find something more. That is perhaps the most fascinating motivating factor for me."

The second way drivers handle the danger factor is to virtually ignore it. They do this either through having a lack of imagination (or deliberately repressing it) about what might happen to them in a big accident, or refusing to believe they could ever be seriously injured or killed in a racing car. Unfortunately, drivers who are ignorant of danger or believe they are invincible tend not to last long.

Like most thinking drivers Senna was fully aware of the dangers and he was not afraid to admit he was fearful of them. Typically, he used this as a way to improve his driving. "The danger of getting hurt or getting killed is there because any racing driver lives very close to it all the time. It's important to know what fear is because it will keep you more switched on, more alert. On many occasions it will determine your limits."

But just as he went faster than nearly anyone else, perhaps in order to be able to get his mind in gear to be able to do that, he went further than anyone else when dealing with the fear factor. He was fascinated by it and chose to meet it head on.

"Because we are in a close relationship with the experience of fear and danger we learn how to live with it better than other people. In the process of learning to live with it you have extraordinary feelings and emotions when you come near an accident. There is the feeling of almost going over the limit. It's fascinating and even attractive in a way. But it's a challenge to control it and not exceed it. The feeling of living in that narrow band, of overdoing it, is very small. The challenge to stay within that band is very much a motivation."

Senna had a highly developed sense of personal values, which he attributed to his parents giving him the proper upbringing and to his religion. "I can put my hand on the Bible and say that everything I have done, everything I have said and everything I believe has been done in the straight way of life.

This is the honest way, the professional way, the sporting way. It respects people and it respects their way of life."

When others contravened his personal code of conduct, or committed what he felt was an injustice – to himself or others – Senna was never afraid to speak out. After Roberto Moreno was unceremoniously fired by Benetton to make way for Michael Schumacher in 1991, Senna was the only driver to speak out against what he considered was a morally corrupt and ethically incorrect act by Benetton.

As much as he devoted his life to racing Senna thought his sport paled in comparison to the plight of the poor and the oppressed people and the environmental problems of the world. "Formula One is nothing compared to those things," he said. "People have to have a chance, a basic chance at least, for education, nutrition, medical care. If this does not begin to happen then there is little hope for the future and little wonder that the problems become greater and that violence arises. Unfortunately, I am not blessed with the powers to solve the problems. But it touches me deeply and worries me considerably."

Though he refused to talk about it publicly, he spent millions of dollars of his own money to help the poor children in Brazil. In the last year of his life he spent over $5 million developing his 'Senninha' (little Senna) project and publishing comic books detailing the adventures of the crusading cartoon character, patterned on himself and dedicated to fraternity, good sportsmanship and the defeat of wickedness.

As for such problems as drugs he thought he could contribute on another level: by setting an example. "The best way to help, if you are in a position that gives you credibility, is to do your own activity in a way that is consistent with good values. In other words, I don't need drugs to be successful. I don't need drugs to go fast. I don't need drugs to have feelings or happiness or emotions."

Experiencing the full range of emotions was one of the major satisfactions Senna found in racing. "Life would be very boring without feelings, without emotions. And there are some feelings that only we can experience. It's a fortunate and unique position to be in, but it's stressful at the same time. Either winning, or breaking a record, losing, going through a corner at a speed that a few seconds before you didn't think you could, failing, feeling luck, feeling anger, enthusiasm, stress or pain – only we can experience the feeling and the level of it. Nobody else can, considering that in our profession we deal with ego a lot, with danger, with our health, continuously, second after second, not just day after day or month after month or year after year. Our life goes by in seconds or milliseconds."

Because he thought so deeply about his profession, Senna was able to find in it greater rewards than most drivers. But his profound commitment also brought him more than his share of despair. While he found driving immensely stimulating he also acknowledged that there was a negative side to this essentially solitary pursuit. "Once you get in a car on a circuit, it is you and the car, nothing else. It is very lonely in a way."

Just as he was in a class by himself in the car, Senna's superior intellect set him apart from others out of it. It was lonely at the top and sometimes his sense of isolation made him feel vulnerable so he turned to others for help and strength. His family in Brazil was a great source of inspiration and comfort. He was closest to his father Milton and his brother Leonardo but once described his sister Viviane and his mother Neyde as his two best friends. He had faith in the family unit as a way of life, loved children – "they are the honest ones" - and wanted to have his own, probably with his last girlfriend Adriane Galisteu, because he "needed someone to share his life".

But Senna also sought, and found, inner peace and spiritual nourishment through his belief in a superior being. "Psychologically or physically you can be the strongest man in the world but, especially in my profession, you cannot do it on your own. It's such a fight all the time, such a stress, such a tension, there are moments when you need help. You've got to have the source of power. And the only source of power that is with you all the time is God."

His relationship with journalists was far from good. His original confidants, Brazilian Reginaldo Leme and photographer Keith Sutton worked closely with Senna in the early days but later became disillusioned.

Both men gave him everything early in his career when he was an unknown and then found themselves frozen out when they would not bend to his will once he was famous and successful. He often ranted at the press when they failed to take his side and it was something that dwelled on his mind. He often took it too seriously and thought about it too deeply, especially when he tried to explain to a group of journalists the problem: "I really want it to be properly understood, because... it means automatically that this is going to go through, and flow through, the system – which is where you guys are responsible – in order that it gets to the other end. And that is one of the small contributions that, from time to time, I feel I can give, and that I feel strongly about. And I feel really unhappy, or frustrated, when I see that it doesn't get through, or if it gets through, it gets completely wrong. Sometimes I am angry with myself, not necessarily with you guys... with myself, because I see afterwards that the way I did it wasn't right, I made a mistake the way I put it, because I wasn't clear enough, or ... the way it was passed to you guys gave you an opportunity to interpret it the wrong way. So it's not only your responsibility to have got it wrong there. I am also responsible because I should have done different, to get you to understand what I was trying to say."

Because he was such a deep thinker he found it hard to answer a question simply. They were always long answers but usually worth listening to.

He found the continual demands on his time very stressful but didn't shirk his duties. As he said: "It's not just being a racing driver that is stressful... Yesterday, when I arrived at the circuit, I was there at 11.30am. But before 2.30pm I could not sit with my engineers to talk about racing, talk about my racing car... I couldn't, because I had to attend to a certain amount of requests. There was no end. And I couldn't cope, I couldn't fulfil the need, no matter how hard I tried... I got out after three hours of work, not only tired and totally down, with no energy, but also frustrated because I felt that I couldn't cooperate the way I would like and would wish... with everyone. And yet it wasn't over, because at 4pm I was in a press conference. And after the press conference was over, a number of people were still around me. And today I am here, for a half-hour interview, and I don't know how long we have been here. And no matter how long we remain here, there is still so much. I tell you, it takes a hell of a lot out of me to do that."

(Appendix 4 is adapted from Chapter 27 of The Life of Senna)

SENNA'S RACING PHILOSOPHY

Ayrton Senna leaves Italy on Tuesday 3rd May 1994

Above and right: The coffin of Ayrton Senna is loaded onto an Italian military DC9 jet at Bologna airport for the first leg of its journey home. The coffin was flown to Paris and transferred onto a Varig flight to São Paolo, Brazil, on the evening of Tuesday 3rd May 1994.

Left: Hundreds of Italians gathered to pay tribute as Senna's coffin was driven through the streets of Bologna on the way from the mortuary to the airport. The Italians regarded Senna as one of their own and were devastated when he was killed in their country.

Right: On Monday 2nd May 1994 fans placed flowers, T-shirts and a Brazilian flag at the exact spot where Ayrton Senna's Williams-Renault FW16 hit the wall at Tamburello curve the day before. The tyre marks were still visible on the concrete wall, a sign of the terrible tragedy that had overtaken Formula One when the sport's greatest driver was killed.

Left: Ayrton Senna's coffin lying in state at the state Legislative Assembly building in Ibarapuera Park, São Paolo.

Below: Brazilian Formula One drivers Cristian Fittipaldi, Raul Boesel, Rubens Barrichello and Portuguese driver Pedro Lamy pay their respects to Ayrton Senna before the funeral.

Below: Thousands of Brazilians gathered at the gates of São Paulo Legislative Assembly as they await the arrival of the funeral cortege carrying the coffin bearing the body of Formula One driver Ayrton Senna.

Ayrton Senna's funeral - Thursday 5th May 1994

© Reuters

© Rex Features

Above: Milton and Neyde Da Silva, Ayrton Senna's parents, along with Viviane Lalli, his sister, stand by the coffin at the public viewing in São Paulo on Wednesday 4th May 1994. Shortly before that, Viviane had placed one of her brother's racing helmets on his coffin.

© Corus

Above: Ayrton Senna's coffin was carried from the airport on a fire engine when it arrived in São Paulo on Wednesday 4th May 1994. The funeral cortege was seen by 2.5 million people lining the route.

Above: Xuxa Mengehel was Ayrton Senna's girlfriend for two years. The Da Silva family adored Xuxa and she was the unofficial widow at his funeral in Sao Paulo in 1994.

Right: Adriane Galisteu says her goodbyes to her boyfriend of 13 months. She was expecting the coffin to be open at the viewing and was very disappointed when, at his family's request, it was not.

© Rex Features

Left: The funeral cortege leaves São Paulo airport for the drive into the city.

Below: Ayrton Senna's coffin is carried by former team mates and drivers: Emerson Fittipaldi, Gerhard Berger, Damon Hill, Derek Warwick, Alain Prost, Thierry Boutsen, Michele Alboreto and Jackie Stewart.

Above: Viviane Lalli, Senna's sister, takes the helmet from his coffin.

Below: Alain Prost, Sir Jackie Stewart and Emerson Fittipaldi gather at the graveside of Ayrton Senna on Thursday 5th May 1994.

© Rex Features

Above: The final resting place of Ayrton Senna, Morumbi Cemetery, on the outskirts of São Paolo, Brazil. The grave is always covered with flowers placed there by fans.

Above: Inside the Third Appeal Court of Bologna during the appeal trial over Senna's death in November 1999. The prosecutor calls on the court to confirm the original requested sentences, which the judge had ignored.

Left: Mauro Forghieri with members of the inquiry demonstrate the actual steering column of Ayrton Senna's car and how it broke during the accident.

Far left below: Ayrton Senna's helmet, which took the full force of the impact.

Far left bottom: Senna's steering wheel with the remains of the steering column attached.

Below: The shattered remains of the cockpit of the Williams Renault FW16.

Above and left: Adrian Newey, Patrick Head and Sir Frank Williams were in a difficult position after the accident. The steering column of Senna's car had broken before or during the accident because of metal fatigue. They were later accused of culpable homicide - manslaughter - in the Italian courts.

Above: Bernie Ecclestone's mission in life was that the show must go on. Brazilians were unhappy that the race was not stopped after Senna's accident. He also got in a muddle by telling Senna's brother, Leonardo, that Ayrton was dead before he had actually been pronounced dead.

Above: Max Mosley did not play a big role in the events of the 1st May 1994, but he instigated huge changes in Formula One safety culture afterwards.

Above: Professor Sid Watkins was closer to Ayrton Senna than he was to any other driver. He was the first to realise that he was not going to recover from his injuries after his accident on 1st May 1994.

Senna's Self-belief

He feared nothing
except God

A yrton Senna feared very little in life – just two things in fact: God, and life itself. He wasn't afraid of death but he was afraid of serious injury and incapacitation. In Adelaide he once said, and then repeated it in a slightly different way in Estoril six months later, that he could never accept not living a full life, the sort of life he already lived. Now the words he used are haunting and worth repeating again: "If I am going to live, I want to live fully, very intensely, because I am an intense person. It would ruin my life if I had to live partially. So my fear is that I might get badly hurt. I would not want to be in a wheelchair. I would not like to be in hospital suffering from whatever injury it was. If I ever happen to have an accident that eventually costs my life, I hope it happens in one instant."

After the kind of accident he suffered at Imola on Sunday 1st May 1994, inevitably he would have preferred the fate he got. He always made that clear.

Senna did feel fear, but always on the day before he got in a Formula One car, as he admitted: "I always think about risk the day before I get in the car, especially if the circuit is one of the more dangerous ones. I must think about it because I am exposing myself to a certain risk. The more calculating you can be, the less can go wrong because of an unexpected situation." Despite those fears, come race or practice day, Senna's mind was clear and the fear gone. It was the way he prepped for a race.

Although, apart from Elio de Angelis's death in testing in 1986, he did not experience death at a race track until, ironically, the very last weekend of his life, he knew the dangers and often used to talk about them. Above all, he was aware of the charmed life he led – something denied to most other people. He said: "I don't really know the meaning of fear in English, but the way I see it, the danger of getting hurt or getting killed is there because any racing driver lives very close to it all the time. It is because we are in a close relationship with that experience, consistently, that we learn how to live with it better than other people."

The Brazilian had an incurable fascination with accidents that caused injury. In the few times a driver was injured during his time in Formula One, Senna was always close to the action. It might have been considered morbid behaviour by those unfamiliar with his personality. But he thought that by being there and learning what had happened, he could understand the process of an accident – and how to survive it. This particular characteristic was never more apparent than during his last weekend at Imola, when there were two serious accidents. One where the driver – Rubens Barrichello – went to hospital and the only serious consequence was him missing the race; the other where the consequence was rather more severe and the driver, this time Roland Ratzenberger, effectively died in his car. Senna was immediately on the case, visiting the site of Ratzenberger's accident in the pace car (and getting into trouble for it) and was right by Barrichello's side when he regained consciousness after flying into a barrier and being hospitalised. For him, it was more a learning process than human concern.

The faster he drove, the nearer he was to having an accident and he was more aware of that than any other driver: "You have extraordinary feelings and emotions when you get near an accident. If you know why you are doing it, and how you are doing it, then you feel fine. You know the limits – you have it in your hands. It's fascinating in a way – even attractive. But it's a challenge to control it and not exceed those limits. The feeling of living in that band, which I think is very narrow, is a real challenge – and maintaining it very much a motivation."

Senna was always adamant that the fear was gone once he stepped into a racing car – any fear he had existed entirely outside the cockpit. As he said: "You should have no fear because if you have fear, you cannot commit yourself. It's important to know what fear is because it will keep you more switched on, keep you more alert. On many occasions it will determine your limits." When Senna got frightened he was always stopped, as he was at Monaco in 1988.

The Brazilian admitted he often reached the extreme limits in his driving, as he undoubtedly did on 1st May 1994. Whatever went wrong with the car, and no one will ever know what really happened, he might have been able to save the situation if he had not been driving on the absolute limit. But as he said: "We live in extremes: we tend to go to extremes. It is attractive to go to those extremes, particularly with strong emotions, because it becomes a challenge to bring the emotion back to the centre. By going to the extremes, and then being able to bring it back to the centre, you get the performance. It's important to have the feeling of fear, in a way, because it keeps part of you in an area where you can hold yourself in equilibrium."

Senna rarely hurt himself in an accident. Twice in 1991 he was mildly hurt, but until 1st May 1994 he had never drawn his own blood in a Formula One car. He had suffered far more serious accidents on his jet-skis than he ever did in a car. Again he was always aware of what danger he was in but believed he was basically in charge: "Once you sit in a racing car, you know you are taking risks, and you know you are exposing yourself to the possibility of having an accident. Of course you never think you are going to have a bad accident or get injured. But you always have it in the back of your mind. And in most cases it determines the limits you establish for yourself... how fast you go in a corner or over a full lap... in a qualifying lap or during a test. And that is a very important feeling to have, because in a way it helps you stay together and not overshoot in many situations. It is self-preservation but without disturbing your concentration and commitment to driving."

In 1988, when Senna won his first world championship, it had a dramatic effect on him. He started talking a lot about God to journalists whereas he had hardly mentioned religion before. He found God as he found success – the inference was that God had given him the world championship and he did not think much of himself until he had won it. It was as if he changed from that day on. He tried to explain it: "I believe we should choose the right moments to talk about such things very carefully. And we shouldn't let it flow completely naturally all the time. There are times when you should hold back a little bit because it won't do any good. What you try to do may go completely the other way if you do not choose the right moment."

It was very hard to understand what he meant but he became increasingly eloquent as he grew older and started talking about it in greater detail. In one press conference, in 1988, he rambled for a good half-hour about his beliefs and what they signified: "In life, people believe in many different Gods. All over the world there are different ways of praying to, or believing in, a superior power. My belief is that there is only one God, and he is the king of kings – the most powerful of them all. In the world generally there is the good power and the bad power; good things and negative things. All that we see, all that is part of the world – the sky, the sun, the moon – has been created by this God. He controls everything: the bad things only happen if he allows them to happen. His reasons and his desires, his objectives, can only be understood by him. We do not have the ability to understand his objectives for us. He knows what goes on in our hearts and minds before we can feel it.

And he is the only one who is able to know. I have always been religious, because of my family, but I was what I would call a superficially religious person. However, over the past year-and-a-half, two years, I have started to devote more of my time to my psychological side, my spiritual side, and tried to learn more about this way of life. I have been fortunate enough to have some good people close to me that know a lot more than I do, to give me the help to start at the right place, and learn the right way. As I've been doing it, I have had, on different occasions, situations that have proved [his existence] to me. I was fortunate enough to see things... I wouldn't have believed it if it was just by theory or discussion. I needed the proof to believe in the first place. And I was fortunate enough to have the proof in different situations, on different occasions, of happiness and frustrations, disappointments, doubts and confidence. I had signals that showed me his desire and his power, more than anything his power, to control anything and everything. Of course, talking is fine. Some people, I'm sure, will know what I'm talking about because they have also experienced it. Some won't because they've never had the experience, and they will not believe. What is important to me is to give people the facts that I have been through, let's say the experience I have been through. I'm not doing anything more than relating the experience that I have had so far, as facts. That has changed my life, progressively, and it is still changing my life. I am today a different person, a much better person, and I know tomorrow I will be even better."

It was apparent that he swaged his religious commitments by reading the Bible as he was not a churchgoer. His devotion to God was totally on his own terms – he belonged to no specific religion and had nothing to do with any church. He said explaining: "I share my beliefs with people who have the same feelings as I have, people who see things the same way I see them. These people know a lot more than I do. I have started to learn, to have help from these people, so I can progress and improve."

Senna craved understanding and found it in the pages of the Bible, as he admitted: "The best thing I have ever read is the Bible – it's the best book, the all-time best-seller. There you can find all the explanations and all the answers you are looking for. I don't think a lifetime is enough to read it all properly."

Prayer became ever more important to him right up to the end of his life.

As he said: "When things are difficult for me to understand, I try to pray and try to talk to him [God] to ask him to show me my way of life, give me some sign, some light, some understanding. And reading the Bible, I swear to you, many times I got the answers to questions that I could not understand or accept. Opening the Bible, he [God] is immediately there, talking to me about what I am asking, giving me the understanding. That is the beauty of this way of life, to be able to have such a contact. Reading the Bible, he talks to you. It's even stronger than if someone is standing in front of you and talking to you. That has happened not once but many times with me.

Psychologically you can be the strongest man in the world, or physically, but on your own you cannot do it, especially in my profession where it's such a fight all the time, such a stress, such a tension – there are moments when you cannot do it by yourself, you've got to have the source of power. And the only source of power that will be with you all the time is him."

After the race in Monte Carlo in 1988, when Senna crashed out of the lead dramatically, he claims he met God. He called it part of the learning experience: "I am learning about it. The more you learn, the more you want to learn, the more you experience it, the more you want to experience it. It's more than power, it's peace: an equilibrium in which your mind and body go into a different level of living. It's natural that you want more – you want to go deeper and live more of this life. So today I face so many frustrating and difficult moments, and yet I find the power and the strength to carry on fighting. I know on some occasions that I would not be able to do it, physically or mentally, just by myself. And if I am doing it, and finding the power and the strength, it's because someone is behind me, and ahead of me, and on my left and my right. I can feel it – and it is a beautiful experience to be able to live this way."

Senna almost became an evangelist because he was so passionate about his beliefs and thought that everyone could reach out to what he had: "It is something that is available to all of us, not just me. It is just a question of asking for it, and of opening our minds and our hearts for him [God]. He is there all the time just waiting for us to say."

He was also reconciled to the fact that it was not always positive and admitted that he had doubts when that happened: "When you have a hard time, you suddenly have doubts. But his [God's] reasons, on many occasions, are only his reasons. Only he [God] knows why things should happen, even if they seem like a bad thing. But in the future it will be a good thing for us. Our understanding is so short, so small, compared to his, that on many occasions we cannot understand. That is where faith is everything. I finally found that in my life, that is what gives me strength to go through the nice times and the difficult times. This year on many occasions I was winning a race when suddenly, boom, something went wrong. I am sure in different years I would get out of the car mad, completely upset, and talk a lot and criticise. I did the opposite this year. I was disappointed, of course, but I had equilibrium and I was at peace. I was able to accept it in a constructive way. I was able to give the people who work with me part of the power that I had to keep whole and look to the future. And that is something I was not able to do a few years ago. What's the difference? The difference between a few years ago and now is that I have finally found him [God], and I have him, like I said before, all around me."

After 1988 Senna appeared to have referred to God in everything he did. He said: "I had not experienced that before: I wish I had found it before [1988]. That's the proof to me. I know my character. I know the way I am, the way I behave. And suddenly I start to find the way I am behaving strange because it's not me. I am much more aggressive and much more pushy when something goes wrong. But suddenly I accept things when they go wrong – I am disappointed but I rationalise it and accept it and look at it as something that will count positively some time in my future even if I cannot understand it in my small mind. That makes all the difference in life."

Somehow Senna always seemed ready for death. As he said: "The day it arrives, it will arrive. It could be today or 50 years later. The only sure thing is that it will arrive."

(Appendix 5 is adapted from Chapter 28 of The Life of Senna)

SENNA'S SELF BELIEF

FATAL WEEKEND

The Trial in Bologna

A search for the truth

n 1996, two years after the accident, the then 39-year-old Maurizio Passarini, Bologna's state prosecutor, brought charges against six people over the death of Ayrton Senna on 1st May 1994. The charge contended that a sub-standard modification had been made to the steering column of Senna's Williams. The column then suffered from metal fatigue brought about by poor workmanship. This suspect modification finally led to a total failure of Senna's steering column as he entered the Tamburello curve at over 190mph. Passarini said that Senna was unable to steer due to a useless steering wheel and unable to brake sufficiently due to the design of the track surfaces, the track edge acting like a launching ramp. Even Senna's skills could not save him from what proved to be a fatal impact with the Tamburello wall. The state prosecutor had a legal duty to find out why Ayrton Senna was killed and if anyone was culpable. That is the way it is in Italy. A death on a motor racing circuit is the same legally as a death on a public highway in Italy.

When a racing driver is killed in Italy, there is always the threat of a trial, but only if a prosecutor can find someone to blame. It is the nature of the country. Italy is the one place that Formula One team-owners fear going because of the legal ramifications if anything happens to their drivers. From a legal point of view, for the Williams-Renault team, the San Marino Grand Prix was the worst place for Ayrton Senna to meet his end. And that was the problem for the defendants as the rules were very different to English law. At virtually every hearing, there was detailed comment in newspapers and on television, some of it hysterical and clearly, by English standards, prejudicial.

Peter Goodman, Williams' English lawyer, who masterminded the team's defence, said: "There was a great deal of television in Italy both before and during the trial, which left the whole of Italy apparently convinced that the English team had killed the great Ayrton Senna and were getting away with it by means of an Anglo Saxon conspiracy."

The Williams team, through its lawyers, always contended that the car hit a series of four bumps in Tamburello one after the other in a random pattern, never done before and never repeated since, in a freak incident that had a million to one chance of happening. They maintained it caused the car to go down on its suspension and sledge, understeering off the track out of Senna's control.

There were plenty of irregularities throughout the legal process. Patrick Head and Adrian Newey were not allowed to examine the wreck of the car from the moment of the accident to the date of the trial. Adrian Newey and FIA circuit director Roland Bruynseraede were interviewed as witnesses without warning them that they could be charged.

The six defendants were charged with 'culpable homicide': three members of the Williams team – team principal Frank Williams; technical director Patrick Head; and the car's designer Adrian Newey – and three others faced different charges for the same offence: Roland Bruynseraede, the FIA circuit director at the 1994 San Marino Grand Prix; Giorgio Poggi, the director of the Imola circuit; and Federico Bendinelli, head of Sagis SpA, the company that operated the Imola track.

All in all, five lawyers represented the six men, and not only did they have to disprove the charges, it was the nature of the legal situation that they also were obliged to shift the blame among themselves. By the time of the trial, Adrian Newey had decided to go and work for the McLaren team and had been placed on gardening leave by Williams. He was not exactly on the best of terms with his old colleagues as a result. It made life difficult for the Williams defence as Newey had engaged a separate lawyer to defend himself against the charges.

Initially the lawyers for Williams, Head and Newey were forced to blame the circuit for Ayrton Senna's death as part of their defence, and the lawyers for Poggi and Bendinelli needed to blame the car. It seriously handicapped the defence. It was not until the middle of the proceedings that Peter Goodman had persuaded all the defendants' lawyers to work together to get a collective positive verdict.

The FIA itself was also effectively on trial through its representative, Roland Bruynseraede. A guilty verdict for him would have been a guilty verdict for the FIA. It would almost certainly have meant the FIA would have withdrawn its endorsement of any motor racing in Italy, making the whole country a motorsport backwater. No one wanted that. Formula One needed Italy almost as much as Italy needed Formula One. The country was a crucial part of the commercial and sporting jigsaw. No one could foresee what would happen without it. As FIA president Max Mosley explained: "The difficulty is that in Italy, a small degree of blame in someone's death is still a criminal offence – that means involving either a gross degree of negligence or some deliberate act that was likely to lead to the death, but not serious enough to lead to a charge of murder. The problem is that although culpable homicide in Italy is seen as a relatively small thing, when it is reported in other countries - particularly in countries where an English-style legal system prevails - it is like manslaughter, which nobody wants to be accused of, and it becomes front-page news. So I think there is a feeling now in Formula One that it is not even a question of whether the accused are acquitted or not. Nobody wants to be put on trial for what is really an honest sporting mistake. A lot of people find it very difficult that such a thing can result in criminal prosecution. So the whole situation is under discussion at the moment, irrespective of the outcome of the trial."

Mosley and the FIA were powerless to prevent the trial going ahead - they simply had to go along with the Italian legal process and hope that good sense would prevail; as it had in all the other fatal accidents in Italy over the years. "Clearly one cannot have a situation where any perfectly ordinary person pursuing a sport in an honest and decent way can expose themselves to criminal proceedings," said Mosley. "They cannot be blamed for anything on moral grounds. It is absurd to think that any of them would deliberately do anything to jeopardise the life of a racing driver."

The stakes were high for all the defendants. For Patrick Head and Adrian Newey, it was the first time a driver had died in a car they had designed. Patrick Head could not comprehend a guilty verdict on his record. As he said: "The charge is quite serious, you know. It is a criminal charge, not under civil law, and we obviously have to defend ourselves to the maximum. If we don't believe it is the case, we have to put full effort into proving to the judge that it is not appropriate charge. It is certainly not something I want to have on my record."

The Senna family had appointed a lawyer to represent them but he didn't turn up every day. The lawyer was merely acting as an observer for Milton and Neyde Da Silva and their daughter Viviane. The family had no real interest in the trial because, as Viviane Lalli said, "It won't bring him back to us."

Although Williams was represented in court by Italian lawyers, the team retained English solicitor Peter Goodman, then of Schilling & Lom and later of Pictons, to run its defence. Goodman had long-standing links with the Williams team and Patrick Head and Frank Williams. He also had close links with the Senna organisation, following the lengthy negotiation of Senna's contract with Williams in 1993 and became a business associate of Senna's manager, Julian Jakobi, in 1999. Goodman took no direct part in the trial, but had a watching brief to make decisions on the spot for the team. He hired the Italian lawyers, who were necessary as much of the trial was conducted in Italian.

Goodman interviewed most of the witnesses and prepared them for trial and probably knew more about the case than anyone. He attended every day of the proceedings. In one year, he made 90 international flights in connection with the case.

Goodman believed that the nature of the charges were unsound and stemmed from a lack of understanding of the way Formula One cars are built, modified and prepared for racing. No one denied that the steering column had broken, but Goodman and his clients believed it was impossible to know whether it had happened before or after the accident.

The state prosecutor said it happened before and the Williams team said it happened afterwards; and each claimed he could prove it. In reality, neither could, as the trial made clear.

But the state prosecutor came close. The weakness in the Williams argument was the presence of metal fatigue and some experts' dim view of the way it had modified the steering column. Other technical directors privately criticised the way the modification had been executed, from pictures of the crash. The professional reputations of Head and Newey remained intact as it was clear they had had nothing to do with the modifications, which were carried out in the Williams factory. It was the Williams team as a whole that suffered a reputational loss.

Maurizio Passarini had appointed an impressive panel of technical experts to assess the evidence. It was headed by Mauro Forghieri, the former technical director of Ferrari, and included Enrico Lorenzini, a professor of engineering at Bologna University; Tommaso Carletti, a former Ferrari race engineer; Alberto Bucchi, a professor at Bologna University and an expert in road construction systems; Francesco Bomparole, a representative of the state road contractor; Roberto Nosetto, former president of the Imola circuit; Dr Rafaele Dal Monte, a professor of science and sports; and Emmanuelle Pirro, a former Formula One driver. The team had had the run of the 900-year-old Bologna University's facilities and an Italian military aerospace laboratory to carry out its investigation and prepare its report. The panel was all Italian and none were currently involved in Formula One. But for almost a year, it was a full-time job that demanded a presence in Italy, which limited the number of people who could serve on the panel.

The trial began on 20th February 1997 in a down-at-heel ballroom, hastily converted from a Saturday night dance venue as the local courthouse was not big enough.

The charge was culpable homicide, or manslaughter in English parlance. The penalty under Italian law for manslaughter varied from six months to five years imprisonment, but there were precedents indicating the penalty could be a fine, as had happened in other such cases. However, nobody believed it would come to that.

The opening day of the trial was marked by a lone man standing in silence at the entrance to the makeshift courtroom holding a placard with a picture of Ayrton Senna and the words 'tell us the truth' underneath.

As in any motor-racing event involving Formula One, a collection of the world's media turned up, bristling with cameras. The presiding judge was Antonio Costanzo and he swiftly ordered them out of the courtroom. He decided that two fixed television cameras would film events, except where witnesses objected.

The defendants and witnesses were not obliged to turn up and attendance was voluntary. Only one defendant put in an appearance on the opening day – Federico Bendinelli, director of the company that operated the Imola circuit. But he had only to walk to the courtroom from his office.

He had a lot to lose. If the defendants were convicted, no one would come to race at his circuit any more. A conviction would merely inconvenience the other defendants. His livelihood was on the line.

Bendinelli told reporters outside the circuit the obvious dangers for Italy of a successful prosecution. He said that in Italy criminal investigations were obligatory and stated that no one should be held responsible for the accident: "The risk exists that all races in Italian territory will be banned if we are convicted."

The lawyer representing the Senna family told the court they had decided not to stand as civil plaintiffs, which would have been their right.

The evidence ran to more than 3,000 pages. The size of the document prepared by the panel of experts was astounding. It stated that the accident was caused by a modified steering column failure, which caused the driver to lose control of the car. The case against Williams, Head and Newey was simply that the car's steering column snapped. The three race officials were charged with not ensuring that the circuit's safety requirements were met.

A large-screen television as set up in the room so it could show second-by-second the last minute of Ayrton Senna's life. It showed video footage coupled to the Williams telemetry recovered from the engine data recorder box. Passarini said: "Each split second, we will know what Senna was doing – hitting gas, braking, turning wheels or changing gears."

The first day saw a challenge from lawyers representing Frank Williams and Patrick Head that evidence from tests on the wrecked car should be thrown out because the defendants were not present during the appraisals.

Two more sets of lawyers argued that the case against Newey and Bruynseraede should be thrown out as they had not been told early enough that they were defendants. Newey's lawyer Luigi Stortoni argued that his client had been improperly questioned by state prosecutor Passarini in order to obtain evidence. He argued that Passarini had interviewed Newey as a witness, not as a defendant, and had not warned him he could face prosecution. He said: "This is a scandal. It should not happen in a civilised country." That was the view of almost everyone in the court.

Filippo Sgubbi, Bruynseraede's lawyer, claimed that his client had given evidence under similar circumstances. But Francesco Pintor, the assistant prosecutor, maintained: "All rules and regulations were strictly adhered to."

Oreste Dominioni, the principal lawyer for Frank Williams and Patrick Head, said: "We are absolutely sure the car was in good order. The steering column broke after, and not before, the crash."

Maurizio Passarini said he planned to call as witnesses Damon Hill, Bernie Ecclestone and Michael Schumacher, and said the witnesses would testify in the last week of April when the people concerned were due to attend the San Marino Grand Prix. Around 40 other witnesses were also expected to give evidence, including Nelson Piquet, Gerhard Berger and Riccardo Patrese.

The Senna trial was not scheduled as one long hearing, rather as a series of mini-hearings lasting one or two days. It would eventually take nearly 40 days and last almost a year.

After a gap of seven days, the trial resumed on 28th February. Judge Costanzo rejected the challenges from the two defence lawyers for Williams, Head and Newey. There was a new challenge on territorial jurisdiction from Newey's lawyer, stating the trial should be moved to Bologna, where Senna was declared dead in hospital; this, too, was rejected.

With that, the trial was adjourned for another week to 5th March. On 5th March, the prosecution was finally able to present its case. None of the accused was present when state prosecutor Maurizio Passarini laid out his principal case, which was that faulty engineering by the Williams team and a defect in the track were responsible for Ayrton Senna's death. He stated: "A modification to the steering column, which had been poorly executed, caused it to break." He claimed the car left the track because the asphalt surface was not on the same level as the trackside. "There was an angle with the side of the track," he said.

Williams and Patrick Head's lead lawyer, Oreste Dominioni, immediately rejected the accusation that the car was at fault, claiming that the state of the track was to blame and that investigators had failed properly to test its surface. He said: "They should have determined whether the characteristics of the course were such as to make the car lose stability and leave the track."

Dominioni called for a new technical investigation of the circuit.

The move against the track was promptly countered by a group of lawyers representing Poggi, Bendinelli and Bruynseraede, who said that ample checks had been carried out on the Imola circuit. Passarini said his case was that the steering column of Senna's Williams car had been badly designed and was not strong enough to withstand metal fatigue. He said: "The steering column had been cut and a new element – which was not of the same quality metal or of the same diameter, being 18mm instead of 22mm – was welded in. It was where the new element had been welded in that the column broke. When Senna had a steering wheel dangling in his hands, he was doing 192mph. He braked and hit the wall at between 130mph and 136mph. If the track had been completely flat, he would have been more able to brake and his speed could have been reduced to 105mph.

Dominioni denied that modifications to the steering column had been done 'fast and furiously' before the Imola race and also pointed out that the steering column was identical to that used by Damon Hill in the other Williams car that season. He said he would be able to demonstrate that the steering column had broken after the crash, not before.

Roberto Landi, the lawyer for Bendinelli and Sagis, denied there had been anything wrong with the track to cause the accident. He declared: "All the world's circuits are like Imola."

Adrian Newey's lawyer demanded a new forensic examination of the steering column on the grounds that Newey had not been able to appoint his own expert to attend the original tests, as he had not been warned he was under investigation and might face charges.

Passarini, who spoke for over an hour and a half, also said he wanted to counter suggestions that he was waging a vendetta against motor racing by pointing out that no prosecution had resulted from Roland Ratzenberger's fatal accident the day before Senna was killed.

Passarini said that Ratzenberger's accident occurred because of damage to the car sustained when it left the track, rather than because of design or construction errors, and that only in the case of Senna had the investigations demonstrated a case of manslaughter.

He proceeded to admit various pieces of evidence, including a film taken by a camera on Senna's car, analysis by consultants and a digital reconstruction of the accident using television pictures taken from several angles. He said he also wanted to use as evidence records regarding crashes on the same bend by drivers in previous years: Nelson Piquet in 1987; Gerhard Berger in 1989; Michele Alboreto in 1991; and Riccardo Patrese in 1992.

In addition, Passarini wanted to refer to television pictures showing cars grounding on the corner and sending up showers of sparks. Finally, he wanted to admit film showing an object thrown into the air by the wheels of either Senna's car or Schumacher's close behind. He said: "I wish to clarify that I do not attribute any causal significance to the small object on the track."

Passarini also laid several other rumours to rest: Senna had not taken any drugs, did not make a driving error and did not pass out. He said the telemetry told him that "Senna desperately tried to stop the car until the end."

Dominioni said he would be calling as a witness Massimo Angelini, who was driving the safety car around the circuit before the race restarted. Judge Costanzo put off his reply to Williams' lawyers, led by Dominioni, who had asked for a new expert investigation of the Imola circuit.

A week later, on 11th March, the defence presented its case through five sets of lawyers – but not before Passarini had made some more damning allegations, irrelevant to the case being tried, against the Williams team's engineering prowess. He told the court that a metal plate was welded onto the rear suspension after it was damaged during winter testing at the Paul Ricard circuit at Le Castellet in France. He explained: "I mention that not to say that the rear suspension was the cause of the accident but to note that, despite the fact that these are very sophisticated vehicles, when a problem occurs it is patched up with a metal plate."

Among the early witnesses was Mario Casoni, the driver of the medical car that day at Imola. He said: "I noticed the abnormal state of Senna's steering column, which had been uprooted and was dangling from the cockpit." Williams' lawyer Oreste Dominioni countered: in 1994, he asserted, Casoni had said the column was lying on the ground. Casoni replied that he had made a mistake in his statement given to a police officer at the time.

Dominioni had a difficult job. He had many ways of defending his client and one of them was to continually try and defer blame onto the track and therefore to Federico Bendinelli, managing director of Sagis, which operates the Imola circuit. Dominioni pointed to the track-surface problems, saying they had not been fully investigated. But seemingly unknown to Dominioni, Bendinelli's lawyer Roberto Landi produced an amateur video shot at Imola on 9th March 1994 when the Williams team was testing prior to the Grand Prix. The video, taken by a fan, showed Senna talking with track director Giorgio Poggi, apparently discussing track conditions on the Tamburello curve. Another witness, police inspector Stefano Stefanini, head of Bologna's traffic accident unit, said Senna was complaining about dips in the asphalt, which were taken care of the following day by track workers.

Passarini also took the trouble to prevent the defending lawyers citing the condition of the tyres as a possible reason for the accident. He asked Stefanini about Senna's lap times before the accident. Indicating that Senna was driving absolutely on the limit to put some time between him and Schumacher in second place, Stefanini told the court that Senna, with a fully-fuelled car, had posted a time of 1m 24.887secs on the sixth lap of the restarted race.

"That was a very good time," he said. "Only two drivers bettered it – Damon Hill and Michael Schumacher – and that was at the end of the race."

Traffic police commissioner Marcello Gentili was asked about the car's trajectory and signs of braking prior to impact to ascertain whether problems with the tarmac could have caused the accident. Gentili said there was a 21cm angle between the track and the trackside, and there were intermittent signs of braking.

Two doctors who pulled Senna from the wreckage testified that they did not encounter any obstacles, or have to remove the steering wheel, in pulling his body out of the car. This led them to suppose that the steering column was already broken.

The trial resumed the next day with Passarini calling Pierluigi Martini to testify as a former Formula One driver knowledgeable of both the Imola circuit and the Tamburello curve. Martini said: "A driver like Ayrton Senna didn't go off the track at that point unless there was a problem. A lot of things can happen during a race, but in this particular case, I don't know what the problem could have been. Drivers took the curve at 300kph and there was a small dip in the middle of the track, which disturbed the cars. The bump effect was perfectly normal and is common to every racing circuit in the world.

"I was at Imola with Senna and others weeks before the race when we noticed a small bump in the Tamburello bend. The circuit officials were very efficient and had the asphalt smoothed out, which was the only thing they could do. The cars still touched the ground and were disturbed so you just had to hold your line." He continued: "The repairs had only slightly improved the situation. Senna had complained to me three weeks before Imola at Aida [Japan], that his car was nervous and the cockpit narrow. But Tamburello could have only created problems for a car that had problems. The people at Imola did everything they could to give us drivers what we asked for."

Martini felt he could not say that the Tamburello bump had caused Senna to veer off the track. There was only one line into Tamburello and the bump could not be avoided without leaving the track. He added that Senna's fast lap time indicated that his tyres were fully warmed up.

Eight course officials who were present at the Imola race were then asked by Passarini whether they had been aware of anything in the path of Senna's car and whether they believed his Williams Renault had left the Tamburello curve in a straight line. All felt that Senna's car went off in a straight line towards the wall, and all said there had been nothing in his way.

The trial then adjourned for the customary week's break until 17th March.

When it resumed, crucial evidence was heard concerning the recovery of the car's two data recording boxes. The first, belonging to Williams, was designed to record data from the chassis and gearbox; the second, belonging to Renault, stored information on the V10 engine.

The wrecked chassis was initially brought back to the parc fermé and locked in the stewards' garage, before being impounded by the Italian authorities after Senna's death was announced. Imola circuit engineer Fabrizio Nosco testified that he had removed both black boxes from Senna's Williams after the crash, having obtained permission from FIA race director Charlie Whiting. The black boxes were then handed over to Williams personnel, who had arrived in the garage with Whiting, and they took them away. They were not handed over to the authorities, as they should have been under Italian law, although at that stage no one knew Senna was dead, or even seriously injured. Nosco stated: "Apart from a few scratches, both were intact." This vital evidence was refuted by almost everyone else who saw the boxes. Williams' witnesses were adamant that once the power was removed, the data, being RAM, was lost. Peter Goodman, Williams' lawyer said: "The blow was so significant that it caused the chassis to split. The box was severely damaged in the impact."

Bernard Duffort, a Renault engine-electronics expert, was the first to see both boxes. He claimed that the Williams box showed signs of impact and had been damaged. When examined, it contained no data. Duffort said the data from the Renault box was transferred onto a computer disk on the day of the crash and a copy handed to the Italian authorities on 18th May 1994, along with the data recorder. By that time, however, the recorder's information had mysteriously been wiped from its hard disk. Duffort said that tests done on the recorder in Paris shortly after the accident, on an engine test bench, had erased its data. Taken at face value, it was all scarcely believable, as the looks on the faces of the prosecutor and the judge reflected. The defending lawyers were embarrassed. But perhaps it wasn't explained well enough. Renault engineers maintained its black box was merely a recording device, and once the data had been downloaded to a floppy disk, the recorder was totally irrelevant. A lot of people didn't believe it, but it was undoubtedly true. Peter Goodman said after the trial: "People didn't understand that the box is simply a recording instrument. There was no interest in the box, which was a standard instrument and undamaged. The interest was in the data, and this was removed from the [Renault] box in the usual way and put onto a computer disk. The box was then reused. Nothing was mysteriously wiped from its hard disk."

The day's star witness was Italian Michele Alboreto, who had survived a violent crash at Tamburello himself in 1991 when driving in Formula One. He testified that he believed Senna's fatal crash was caused by a mechanical failure in the car, not a track defect. This opinion, he added, was formed from his many years' experience of Imola and other tracks round the world.

The Italian gave his verdict after viewing a video of the crash, replayed in the courtroom, and in particular pictures from a camera on board Michael Schumacher's car, which was close behind Senna's. Film was also shown of previous crashes at Tamburello involving Gerhard Berger, Nelson Piquet, Riccardo Patrese and Alboreto himself.

Outside the courtroom, he told reporters: "Senna's shift to the right makes me think it was a mechanical failure. The situation at Imola was not exceptional – we've raced in much worse conditions than those. I hope this trial helps us understand what really happened to Senna, because it still isn't clear. Mechanical failures are frequent, given the nature of the races and the fact that people always aim for the limit. But no engineer can ignore safety."

Alboreto went on to describe as 'minor' the bumps on the track surface just before the curve, which had been the subject of Williams' lawyer Oreste Dominioni's questions to him, and said they could not have forced Senna's car off the circuit.

The following day, 18th March, had as its star witness FIA race director Charlie Whiting. Initially, he was questioned about the modification Williams had admitted making to the steering column. Passarini asked him if he had known about it. In his testimony, Whiting said that Senna's car had been modified without permission before the race, but that the modification would have been reported at the next regular check. Whiting said that he had approved Senna's car in February and again in March.

His evidence conflicted with that of the Williams witnesses, who claimed the team had already informed the FIA and could prove it. But after looking at photographs of minor changes to the chassis, Whiting told the court: "I don't remember this on Senna's car."

When asked to explain why he had allowed the data recording boxes to be removed from the car by the team before it was handed over to officials, Whiting replied that he had done so because of the overriding need to make sure the other Williams car might not suffer the same strange loss of control that had apparently affected Senna's.

He confirmed that he had authorised the Williams engineers to remove the two black boxes immediately after the accident, but one had been damaged in the crash and the recorder was blank. The problem apparently was that the separate battery that powered the databanks had become disconnected, wiping all the memory.

Whiting's statement contradicted Fabrizio Nosco's testimony the previous day that both data recording boxes were intact when he removed them from Senna's car. Electronics expert Marco Spiga was called and disputed Whiting's claim: he felt the data should have been available. He said it had taken a month for Williams and Renault to hand over the boxes to the investigators, and when they had received them, both were blank. He told the court: "The Williams box was totally unreadable when we got it back."

The confused Passarini asked for a further investigation of the data recorder, and all the parties involved were summoned to an examination of the unit at the engineering department of Bologna University on 24th March.

After the subject of the black boxes had been exhausted, the findings of the autopsy on Senna were read out by pathologist Corrado Cipolla. He said Senna's injuries were caused by a massive blow above the right eyebrow. He affirmed that Senna had not died from the impact of the crash but from a blow to the head by a blunt object. He showed a photograph of a part from the front suspension. He said the blow crushed the front part of Senna's brain, killing him instantly, although his heart and lungs continued to work assisted by a life-support machine, which was eventually turned off. He therefore gave the official time of death as 2.17pm, although 'cardiac death' occurred at 6.40pm.

Other experts said Senna's blood indicated perfect health and a total absence of banned substances and that his helmet complied with specifications.

This testimony appeared to lay to rest rumours that Senna had been taking performance-enhancing drugs and had a light, illegal helmet to save on weight.

The court resumed again on 2nd April when the subject returned to the black boxes. Maurizio Passarini called on electronics expert Marco Spiga to demonstrate how the external sockets of the data recorder worked. These were the sockets reportedly damaged in the crash. New pin connectors were supplied by Williams expert Giorgio Stirano. However, it emerged that a data card was needed to transmit the information to a computer, and this was not supplied. Maurizio Passarini said: "Why are we only told today that we need a card? Williams has never told us this before. Why wasn't it made available?"

Giorgio Stirano replied: "Because we were only asked for the pin connectors."

The judge took a dim view of the state prosecutor's much-vaunted technical advisers not be able to work that out before the trial.

Edda Gandossi, a lawyer acting for Williams, said: "It would be pointless to try and cast any suspicion or inferences regarding the behaviour of the Williams engineers. This has always been polite and courteous." The day was therefore a write-off and the trial adjourned until 15th April.

Peter Goodman subsequently explained the day's events by saying that, after weeks of listening to ridiculous theories and what he saw as defamatory accusations, he had decided to use the moment as an opportunity to illustrate that the prosecutor's team of experts, however illustrious, were not familiar with modern racing cars. The Williams engineers co-operated by supplying the lead that Marco Spiga had requested, knowing full well that the lead would not help him prove his theory. The intention was to discredit him publicly and also, by implication, the technical expertise of the prosecutor's team of experts. This was important to Goodman as the trial was about to move into quite complex technical areas.

When the 15th of April dawned, there was a surprise as the two principal defendants, Patrick Head and Adrian Newey, appeared for the first time and spent the day as observers, very interested in evidence that was due to be given regarding the steering column. Passarini called one of the panel of experts, Tommaso Carletti, an ex-Ferrari race engineer, who said: "There are three possible causes of the break: poor quality work, the quick movement of the steering column and a too small diameter of the joins between the three sections of the column."

Another one of the experts, Mauro Forghieri, ex-technical director for Ferrari, said: "I believe that Ayrton Senna turned his steering wheel firmly to the left shortly before the crash. If he had not done so, he would have crashed immediately. Senna would have realised the steering on his Williams Renault was functioning abnormally and after twice easing off the accelerator, he began to brake."

Enrico Lorenzini, professor of engineering at Bologna University, also gave technical evidence for the prosecution. The following day the defence put its case regarding the steering. Two Williams engineers, Giorgio Stirano and Diego Milen, said that Senna had had a problem with oversteer as his car went over a bump on the asphalt surface of the Imola track. The bump was located just a few yards from where Senna's car began to veer off the bend at Tamburello.

The Williams engineers said the oversteer sent the car towards the inside of the track and Senna countered by steering away. However, his car bumped again and skidded to the right, nine degrees off the ideal line. They said Senna, at this point, decided to keep his line and tried desperately to brake. There was no doubt that right up to the impact, his main concern was keeping the car in the race, not avoiding the impact.

After the hearing, Stirano and Milen told reporters there was no blame to be attached to the track or the driver: there had been an ordinary problem which destiny had made fatal. They said they reached their conclusions after examining the telemetry readings from Senna's Williams and videotapes.

Their view directly opposed that of members of the expert committee – Forghieri, Carletti and Lorenzini – who claimed that Senna's steering column was already 60-70 per cent damaged by metal fatigue and simply stopped responding after the car hit the second bump in the track.

During the trial, there appeared to be a small change of opinion amongst the experts that Senna did have some control of the steering but didn't dare use it because he realised it was about to snap. Forghieri told the court: "Senna realised that if he had tried to steer the car in a way to spin it round, the steering would have snapped."

It was a big admission and the panel of expert's lost some credibility as a result. But in reality, it still meant that Senna had no real control of the steering and therefore could not take the curve as he would have done

It was a valid assumption to make and Forghieri was a powerful witness in Italy. Outside Italy, he was regarded as an emotional man who enjoyed drama and the court room in Imola had become his latest stage. Lawyer Robert Landi, acting for race organiser Federico Bendinelli, said the bumps on the track were no different from those drivers had to contend with on other circuits around the world.

Outside the courtroom, Adrian Newey spoke for the first time, telling reporters: "Ayrton Senna's accident was down to fate. My defence lawyers will give my opinion on what happened on 1st May."

In the last week of April, Bernie Ecclestone was due to testify, but the hearing was postponed and then delayed again by a lawyers' strike.

When the trial finally resumed again on 14th May, it opened with Maurizio Passarini accusing the Formula One Constructors' Association (FOCA) of withholding evidence. Bernie Ecclestone did not arrive – instead three FOCA TV personnel appeared. The court was told Ecclestone would not attend in person but would give his evidence by means of written questions and answers, via official channels, known as an international 'rogatoire'.

The FOCA staffers at Imola on Sunday 1st May were Alan Woollard, the director; Eddie Baker, the production manager; and Andy James, the engineer. All appeared as witnesses. It is believed that a deal had been done beforehand that guaranteed the three men would not be arrested. In 1995 at the San Marino Grand Prix, Italian police had tried to arrest Alan Woollard in an attempt to force FOCA to reveal more tapes, which Passarini believed existed. FOCA had initially been very reluctant to release any on-board footage. In the end, it had been forced to do so by the persistence of Brazilian journalist Roberto Cabrini of TV Globo, who knew it existed.

All three men told the court it was pure coincidence that the videotape was changed in the split second just prior to the fatal crash. They all said that the tape from the camera on Senna's car was turned off at almost the precise moment his Williams Renault left the track, 0.9 seconds prior to impact with the wall at the Tamburello curve. It was the moment when one camera cut and another was waiting to cut in.

Passarini told the court there were 1.4 seconds of indistinct pictures and greyish lines, which were apparent on the tape when the view switched from Senna's camera to Berger's. It was at the onset of this period that the accident occurred. The explanation given for this interference was that it was the pause between camera switches. At the time, FOCA TV supplied in-car footage to the national television networks before the advent of its own digital TV network. It also owned the copyright to other filming at the circuit. Thirteen cars out of the 26 were carrying in-car cameras at the race, and four could be viewed and recorded at any one time. Transmissions from three of these could be chosen to be relayed to the network broadcaster.

The restrictions lay in the system. The signal was sent from the cars up to a helicopter in the sky and then relayed down to FOCA's equipment at the track. There were only four channels. Therefore, only four of the 13 cameras could be used at any one time and Woollard switched the signal between them. As fate would have it, he cut Senna's at the split second before the accident.

FOCA had eventually handed the tape over to TV Globo, and it was broadcast. But the version of the tape it handed over to Cabrini ended 12.8 seconds into the fatal lap – or at least the record states that. Information taken from Senna's on-board computer confirmed the crash had occurred 14.2 seconds into the lap, so there was a period of 1.4 seconds before the impact with the wall at Tamburello. The tape FOCA TV sent to the Italian authorities ends 0.9 seconds before impact, the court records that 0.5 seconds of new footage remains unaccounted for.

The decision to switch the camera shot coming from Senna's car to that of Japanese driver Ukyo Katayama was taken approximately 10 seconds before, as Senna was leading the race and there was nothing of interest ahead of him.

But in fact, Passarini said, the next shot on the tape was from Gerhard Berger's car, not Katayama's, and it too showed an empty track. "What, if I might say so, is the point of the shots if they have not been tampered with?" he asked.

According to the court records, the three FOCA witnesses all said that wrong button was pressed, thus mistakenly selecting pictures from the camera on Berger's car and creating the interference, which explains the 1.4 seconds of indistinct pictures between the last shot from Senna's camera and the first from Katayama's. FOCA executives Andy James and Eddie Baker dispute this and have restated that it was the pause in the changeover.

Passarini's claim that the videotape was supplied to the Williams team 15 days after the accident, but only received by the court on 9th September, was met with the reply that the request had been interpreted as being for pictures of the impact, which did not exist. It was obvious to all in court that Passarini didn't believe a word of it. It was also revealed that better quality tape could be provided if the court had the facilities of a Betacam professional recorder. The FOCA men agreed to release a Beta version of the tape that was of immeasurably better quality.

Speaking to reporters outside the courtroom, Passarini said: "I am certain that the pictures supplied by FOCA are incomplete. Several details show this to be the case, and I shall say so in the hearing." He implied that he was considering bringing other charges in connection with the videotape. He never did.

On 2nd June, the court reconvened, ready to hear the much-anticipated evidence of the reigning world champion Damon Hill, who had been Senna's team mate that fateful day. The day started with a disagreement after Michael Breen, Hill's lawyer and manager, insisted that all television cameras be cleared from the courtroom. The cameras were removed so that Hill could begin his testimony.

Hill's day in court was marked by a poor translator who at times turned the proceedings into farce. Hill, usually the most eloquent of men, proved he had a very poor memory of such a momentous day in his life. Hill told the court that alterations were made to the steering column of both his and Senna's cars in the 1994 season. Passarini asked him exactly when the steering column had been modified. Hill said: "I don't know exactly. I think it was before we went to the first test, but I can't be sure." Passarini pushed him. Hill said: "I can't remember the exact date. I seem to remember it being done before we ran the car. In other words, before it went to a racetrack." Pushed further to confirm it was before the season started, Hill said: "Yes." There was a moment of high drama as the translator misinterpreted the 'yes' as a 'no'. Luckily, there were enough bi-lingual people in court to correct his error.

Passarini asked him when he had known about the modifications. He answered: "I don't know when it was done, I can't tell you. I was made aware that it had been done." Passarini asked him who had informed him of the change, and Hill said he couldn't remember. He said he could not remember whether Senna had complained about the handling of his car after the steering-column modification, although he could remember details of a meeting he attended with the Williams team.

Passarini then turned the subject to power steering, and Hill confirmed the car had it. But amazingly, under oral testimony, he couldn't remember whether the car had had it the previous year, when he debuted with the team. Passarini then reminded Hill of a statement he had given to the prosecutor in June 1994 that the system was new that year.

The power-steering question was important. It has long been the view of many that the cause of the accident was a power-steering malfunction that locked the steering at the Tamburello curve just before the accident, explaining why Senna went straight on and didn't take the corner. There had certainly been problems in-race with the power steering, as revealed by the telemetry from the Renault black box. The electronic system was only in its third race. There had been previous problems with it, as there would be with any new system. Steve Nichols, the former McLaren car designer, asked to comment on it by The Guardian's investigative reporter Richard Williams in 1995, had revealed the pressure had risen suddenly and then fallen suddenly in the few seconds prior to the accident for no apparent reason. Nichols said in 1995: "If the power steering broke, you'd expect the hydraulic pressure to go straight to zero."

Passarini had no evidence to back this theory but pressed the point to Hill. He asked him: "In the two previous races in 1994, did you race with or without the power steering?" Hill replied: "I honestly don't remember."

Hill also said that Patrick Head had told him to switch off his power steering as he waited on the grid after Senna's accident for the restart of the race. The power steering was activated from the cockpit. He said: "It was obvious at the restart that they wanted to be sure things were all right in the car. I didn't ask for a reason. I just did what I was told."

Passarini then asked him whether he had talked to Senna about the car or if Senna had complained about it. Hill said: "I don't remember." Asked about the car, he said: "We found it very tight in the car – in my case the problem was that there was very little room between myself and the steering wheel."

He said he had viewed the video footage at a meeting with Williams engineers at the team's Didcot headquarters less than a week after the tragedy. In the courtroom, more than an hour was spent viewing the film from Senna's on-board camera, and Hill was invited by Passarini to comment on it.

Hill took the view immediately after seeing the film at the Williams factory and in the courtroom that Senna was attempting to correct oversteer. He said: "There are two distinct times when the car looks to be oversteering, and the steering wheel is exactly the way I would expect to see it to correct oversteer."

Asked whether the apparent oversteer in Senna's car was due to low tyre pressure or the state of the Imola track, Hill answered: "You cannot separate the two. My idea looking at it is that the car seems to oversteer when it crosses the place on the circuit where there are some marks." Hill said he had not experienced any problems with oversteer at the San Marino Grand Prix.

His testimony tallied with Williams' defence lawyers, who, in March, had claimed Senna's death was due to anomalies in the asphalt track surface.

Hill also undermined another of the prosecution's claims – that FOCA TV had failed to supply the complete film shot by the on-board camera in Senna's car – stating that the footage he saw during the meeting at Williams also ended before Senna's car left the track.

Bombarded with questions by state prosecutor, Maurizio Passarini, Hill repeatedly answered: "I cannot remember. It was too long ago."

However, he was clear about Passarini's assertions that a weld made to shorten the column snapped moments before impact: "I came away from the meeting with the opinion that there must have been some other reason for the accident other than the obvious one that there had been a failure in the steering," he said.

Hill was unconvincing, and afterwards he was accused of 'selective amnesia'. At times, his continual answer of 'I don't remember' met with laughter. In reality, he was in a very difficult position and was just trying to get through the ordeal as truthfully as he could.

The following day, 3rd June, there was a reconstruction by Michael Guttilla, director of vehicle simulation products at Mechanical Dynamics Motorsport Group, the company that developed a customised software package called ADAMS used by Formula One teams. Diego Milen claimed the reconstruction showed Senna's Williams had suffered from oversteer, forcing him to correct the trajectory on two occasions. This eventually led to the car leaving the track and impacting with the wall at the Tamburello curve.

Maurizio Passarini challenged the simulation and the validity of the data presented, saying that the Imola track surface is of diverse gradients whereas those used in the reconstruction were flat. Therefore, these facts would influence the outcome of a car travelling at 310kph.

Passarini had all his wits about him that day and dented Michael Guttilla's credibility. In the reconstruction, Senna was said to have achieved pole position in qualifying on the Saturday; in fact, he had achieved the best time on the Friday and had refused to continue qualifying on the Saturday after the death of Roland Ratzenberger. The blunder embarrassed the Williams lawyers. Guttilla was also challenged by Bendinelli's lawyers, acting for circuit operator Sagis, who challenged the validity of the circuit data used in the reconstruction, which they defined as arbitrary and unverified. They maintained Williams had obtained its data through unofficial sources.

At the end of the day, the court saw the better quality Betacam tape of the Senna car footage, supplied by FOCA TV. The pictures were much clearer and revealed much more. Michele Alboreto had also seen the new tapes privately – he was reportedly shocked when he viewed the new images and, due to the improved quality, noticed the sideways movement of Senna's steering wheel.

The hearing resumed on 25th June and was preceded by a programme the previous night on Italian prime-time television that analysed the trial so far. The programme, called 'Senna Trial: The Black Hole', was broadcast on Italia 1. The defendants were also being tried on Italian television – clearly prejudicial to justice, but apparently normal in Italy.

On Wednesday 4th June, testimonies continued about the modifications made to Senna's steering column. Witnesses were called by the Williams defence lawyers, the first being Tony Pilcher, in charge of production at the Williams factory. Pilcher was asked by Williams lawyer, Dominioni, if he was involved with the manufacture of modified parts for the steering-column assembly. Pilcher replied that he was responsible for their production. Stortoni, Newey's lawyer, objected – asking whether Pilcher was under investigation – and the judge immediately overruled him. Dominioni continued, showing two drawings of the steering assembly to Pilcher, who explained them to the court. He said the original drawing was dated 3rd February 1994. It showed the steering column of the Williams Renault FW15 to be 905mm long. This was elaborated from the plans of Alan Young and was given to him on 10th March 1994 for production.

Pilcher explained that Senna had requested a modification – the new column measurement was to be 917.3mm and two new elements were to be introduced. The assembly consisted of nine components, manufactured simultaneously by different departments at Williams.

The assembly was manufactured and inspected to assure conformity between drawing and product. If the part failed inspection procedures, it would either be reworked or discarded. The same applied to quality – if satisfactory, the piece and its components, each carrying an ID label, would be placed in the store.

From there, the piece would be drawn for fitting to the car by the mechanics. Williams produced three column assemblies and the modifications were executed immediately after 10th March, in time for the Brazilian Grand Prix.

Williams' lawyers showed that the steering-column modifications had been done properly and that Senna's steering column was the same as Hill's.

Maurizio Passarini then questioned Pilcher about the dates of the modifications and the materials used. Pilcher testified that at least two to three days were required for that type of modification. The parts were machined from two types of compatible steel, T45 and EN14.

Another Williams witness that day was Max Nightingale, who was responsible for aerodynamics and hydraulic steering. Nightingale was asked about the tests done after the Senna accident with respect to the steering and suspension. He said: "Patrick Head asked for the tests to be performed. Our data was based on the high peaks of Senna's telemetry, which were probably due to bumps on the track. These are incompatible with a break, otherwise they would have been reset." He confirmed that, as a precaution, the power steering on Hill's car was disabled after Senna's crash.

The next witness was Williams employee Simon Wells, responsible for hydraulic tests. He testified that he had not found any signs of stress on the steering of Damon Hill's car, but he had not carried out a test. In a strange outburst, Passarini accused Wells of being "a technician who conducted an examination that he was unable to accomplish."

On Thursday 3rd July, Williams engineers Gary Woodward, Dickie Stanford, Simon Scoins and Brian O'Rourke testified for the defence. They said that the crash in which Ayrton Senna died was not caused by steering column failure. Gary Woodward, who was responsible for the interior mechanics of Senna's car, testified that the column in his Williams Renault was carefully checked before the race. He said: "After each Grand Prix, the cars are subjected to a crack test, using penetrating liquids to identify any fractures in the suspension or steering columns. The steering columns are replaced halfway through the season. The tests carried out after the Pacific Grand Prix in Aida, Japan, found no defects in Senna's car."

At that point, Maurizio Passarini asked him if he was aware of the modifications made to Senna's steering column. Woodward replied: "Steering column modifications, which complied with the rules, were made to Senna's car. All three cars had the same modifications prior to the race in Brazil."

Simon Scoins, a Williams electronics engineer responsible for downloading telemetry, admitted he had received the Williams data recording box from Senna's car after the crash. He said: "I was shocked when I lifted the material cover from Senna's car. The Williams data recorder was above the gearbox, 180cm from its natural position. Three of the four connectors were disconnected or damaged. I carried it to the garage where I attempted to connect it. It was useless. I tried inserting the RAM card but without success. I have no knowledge of the Renault data recorder."

Composite-materials specialist Brian O'Rourke said: "As the right front wheel of Senna's car hit the wall, the violent impact caused a torsion on the steering column, causing it to break."

The following day, Maurizio Passarini again showed the enhanced Betacam video images. They were taken from Senna's in-car camera and, according to the prosecution, showed anomalies regarding Senna's steering column.

Two fixed points were shown located on Senna's steering wheel: a yellow button and a V mark, the first with a distant radius 83mm from the centre of the steering wheel, the second 55mm.

Relative arcs showed the shift of the points indicated with reference to two moments in the race, the period behind the safety car and the first lap of the restarted race.

Then Passarini produced a new video regarding the evidence. The circumference traced from the yellow button was relative to the movement of the chassis, whereas just before the crash the yellow button lowered to the level of the V, which represented a deflection of 28mm.

Dominioni introduced a video brought from the factory: the steering of Senna's car showed it had a flexibility of 15mm. Mauro Forghieri told the court angrily: "Any driver would have refused to drive with steering in that condition."

The following Wednesday, 9th July, was destined to be the last day in court before the summer recess: the hot courtroom proved explosive. The witnesses called were Mr Nosetto and Professor Rafaele Dal Monte for the prosecution; and Mssrs Minelli, Marchionna, Saliti (general secretary of the Italian Motorsport Commission, or CSAI) and Muscioni (an FIA safety inspector) for the circuit.

Roberto Causo, defence lawyer for FIA delegate Roland Bruynseraede, who was in court for the first time, attacked the conditions with regard to the concrete run-off area and the escape route from the track at the time of the crash.

Roberto Nosetto was a director of Santerno, the company responsible for the circuit, between 1980 and 1989. He explained: "There were two rules: that of the CSAI of 1962 and an international one which had evolved with time. The wall at Tamburello into which Ayrton Senna crashed met the standard. It was constructed of resilient cement, made to absorb any impact at an angle not exceeding 30 degrees. Senna's impact was 22 degrees."

Nosetto told the court that in 1989, when he finished his administration, to the rear of the grass border a course layer of wide cement was constructed, measuring 9-13 metres. This area was to allow for emergency procedures.

Passarini asked Nosetto for his opinion on the way Senna's Williams Renault left the track. He told the court that the Williams flew, in the sense that the front wheels rose and fell, leaving visible tyre tracks. It then crossed over the grass/cement areas, with a braking distance of 38.5 metres, which happened in 0.6 seconds. On the track, the deceleration was 4G, on the grass/cement it was 0.8G. Bendinelli's lawyer, Roberto Landi, objected: "The word 'flew' is misleading. Better to say 'a slight lifting.'"

Professor Dal Monte told the court: "The Williams lost ground adhesion. The average gradient of the track then was plus 3.1 per cent, the average of the escape shoulder plus 2.1 per cent. At Tamburello, there was not a way of escape as denoted by the regulations. There was not enough space to reduce the speed of the car."

Nosetto added: "The escape area should have had the same inclination as the track. There could be some undulations provided that the ideal line of track continuation was consistent, without gradients and with a maximum radius of 50 metres."

Then the defence lawyers for the Imola circuit produced a CD, based on the telemetry data, full of diagrams which gave the real and optimal braking times. According to this data, Senna hit the wall at 188kph (116.8mph) against the 216kph (134.2mph) calculated by the prosecution's experts. In ideal conditions, Senna would have crashed at 167kph (103.7mph), against the 140kph (86.9mph) estimated by the prosecution. But in both cases, the front right wheel of his car would have become detached, hitting his head at the same point and with enough force to kill.

After a long summer break, the trial resumed on 16th September. When it opened, there was drama as David Coulthard failed to appear as a witness. The day had been planned to examine Coulthard's evidence and recall Michele Alboreto, whose earlier evidence conflicted directly with Coulthard's.

Williams' lawyer, Oreste Dominioni, maintained that as Coulthard would not be available until the end of the Formula One season, his written statement should be accepted. This did not go down well with state prosecutor Maurizio Passarini, who clearly felt Coulthard had been nobbled. He stated that as Coulthard lived in Monaco, he shouldn't have a problem with travelling 400 kilometres to attend the trial. However, if his written deposition added nothing to that already offered by the defence, then it should not be admitted.

The no-show put Dominioni in a difficult spot: he required Coulthard to refute Alboreto's evidence as they were in direct conflict over the movement shown on Senna's steering wheel.

The judge was also unimpressed by Coulthard's non-attendance. He said: "People involved in Formula One don't want to be thought hostile towards the environment. No one will go to prison for this, and that is logical as the whole sport entails risks hardly avoidable. But this trial is obliged to at least defend the memory of two drivers, I talk also of Ratzenberger, as they cannot defend themselves. It bothers me that people are defending positions which are indefensible."

In the event, Passarini recalled Michele Alboreto to the stand. On 17th March, he had testified, after viewing a VHS video of the crash, that he felt mechanical failure made Senna unable to negotiate the Tamburello curve. Now he was recalled because he had had a chance to view the much-improved Betacam version of the tape and had made public his views based on that. Passarini wanted them put into the court record. Alboreto was again adamant that there was a technical failure. "You don't go off on that bend unless there is a mechanical failure," he said. He also stated that on circuits like Imola, the stresses and strains on the steering column would cause flexing "in the order of two or three millimetres."

Oreste Dominioni then read out the written statement that former Williams test driver David Coulthard had made, which stated that the amount of movement seen on the steering wheel of Senna's car was normal. The statement said that the steering wheel in the McLaren, which Coulthard drove in 1996, behaved similarly. Coulthard's statement directly countered Alboreto's evidence.

Alboreto, very direct and impassioned, replied that movement was allowed, considering the torsion inflicted by the arms of the driver and the composition of the material. Oscillation could depend on the distance from the support, but only by two or three millimetres.

Coulthard supported the Williams theory that the movement as seen on the Betacam video was perfectly normal. Judge Costanzo accepted his testimony, provided that he subsequently appeared in person.

During Alboreto's testimony, film was also shown of previous crashes at Tamburello involving Gerhard Berger, Nelson Piquet, Riccardo Patrese and Alboreto himself.

Outside the court, Alboreto said he was convinced Senna's crash was caused by mechanical failure, not driver error. Being semi-retired allowed him to speak freely, he said. This was in reference to Coulthard's statement, which Alboreto implied was obtained under duress.

He told reporters: "I'm even more convinced that it was a technical problem that caused Senna to crash now that I have seen the video. There is a tape which shows the flexing movement of the steering wheel was two to three centimetres. No steering wheel moves a few centimetres. Should the court accept this film as evidence, it will prove that something was wrong with Senna's car." It was clear outside the court how close Alboreto and Senna were, as he declared: "I hope this trial will come to the defence of a man, a great driver, who is no longer with us. Shortly after his death, I heard ridiculous stories – that the crash was caused by Ayrton fainting or because he was thinking about his fiancée. Senna deserves the recognition that he was not to blame for his own death. I don't want to see anyone go to prison, but his memory must be protected." Alboreto refuted Coulthard's statement, claiming he was being told what to say to safeguard his future in Formula One. "Coulthard has the prospect of a long career in Formula One," he said.

Others felt at the time that Alboreto's testimony was so vehement because he had a long-standing past grudge against the Williams team over a drive that was promised but never materialised. Whatever the truth, Alboreto has taken it to his grave. In 2001, he was killed in a testing accident in Germany, driving an Audi R8 Le Mans car.

The debate over the Coulthard no-show set the scene for an argument between Passarini and Williams' defence lawyers, who produced experts to conduct a simulation to prove that the behaviour of Senna's car was similar to that of the simulator. This followed on from Mike Guttilla's testimony.

Passarini displayed the images from Senna's in-car camera to prove that he steered to the right. A Williams expert said the movements visible were not only circulatory as dictated by the force of the torsion.

Finally, Williams' lawyers screened a video of a 1994 car taken from the team's museum. It featured a driver (David Coulthard) at the wheel simulating the movements made in a race. According to the defence, it reconstructed the oscillations of Senna's steering wheel before the accident, with the yellow button that moved in a springy compatible way conducive to the materials used and the imposed effort from the driver. In his written statement, Coulthard said the steering wheel in his 1996 McLaren behaved similarly. Passarini was not impressed. "The film shown today has the same value as the defendant who says 'I wasn't in that place on that night'", he said. "It remains the comment of a defendant."

The court reconvened on Monday 22nd September to examine the Williams computer simulation shown on the 16th. Passarini called Professor Pietro Fanghella of the University of Genoa to question engineer, Diego Minen.

Professor Fanghella said: "My graphs showed that when superimposing the traces of the real telemetry onto those of the simulation, there was a temporal difference of 1.5 seconds. Regarding Tamburello, the responses in the simulation do not relate to those of Senna. In comparing the two graphs, there were discrepancies of 25 per cent, 50 per cent and in some cases 100 per cent. The simulation captures only the course of the vehicle, not the corrections made by the driver. The steering wheel is not in relationship with the angle of the steering wheel in the program."

Minen replied: "The relationship between the steering trajectory and the steering wheel is not comparable due to the unstable track surface – a phenomenon that happened only once but which, for Williams, is the reason Senna left the track. The temporal difference in the telemetry real-simulation is of 1.2 seconds and this is not relevant. It is impossible to quantify the angle of the steering applied by the driver by looking at the yellow button on the steering wheel."

The following day saw first questioning of two defendants, Federico Bendinelli and Roland Bruynseraede. Passarini reminded the court that Bendinelli was managing director of Sagis, the company that runs the Imola circuit, and that Bruynseraede was the FIA delegate present at Imola on Sunday 1st May 1994. Also due to attend was Giorgio Poggi, the circuit manager, but he was ill.

Passarini repeated his claim that Senna's accident was initially caused by steering-column failure, the secondary cause being his inability to brake sufficiently – a result of the raised edge of the track, which stopped the car's wheels from gripping the surface.

First to testify was Bruynseraede, who granted the FIA licence to the Imola circuit in 1994. He stated that he had inspected the track two months before the race and that circuit officials had always observed any demands made to improve safety. He said the final track inspection was made on the Wednesday preceding the race, and nothing was found to cause concern. He said: "The FIA had never required alterations to Tamburello, and I had never received complaints from the drivers regarding that part of the track." He added that in any case, he had not been involved in the bureaucratic procedures through which the Imola circuit obtained its licence from the FIA.

Bendinelli stated that the Imola circuit had been modified but that all alterations were made with FIA approval. He said that the FIA had never found fault with the angle at the track's edge, before or after Senna's crash.

Adding that Imola and many other circuits had modified their layouts after 1994, he explained why: "Critical situations were being created for the cars, most likely because of the abolition of active suspension. The FIA took remedial action with changes to the circuits, especially the faster ones, and also to the cars. The FIA felt that drivers were relying too much on computers and therefore the human element was being lost from the sport."

He said Senna himself had welcomed the abolition of active suspension and was one of its most vocal opponents.

Bruynseraede told the court that in 14 years he had received only one request to alter the circuit. It came from Alain Prost, who in 1989 was acting as the drivers' representative. Prost requested that a grass verge at Tamburello be cemented over to allow drivers to brake more quickly and give more control should they exit the track at that point. Bendinelli's lawyer, Roberto Landi, asked his client about the modifications to Tamburello after the 1994 fatal accident. He replied: "Tamburello is now different but the track gradient with the run-off area is the same as before the alteration."

The day ended with Passarini making presentations regarding David Coulthard, and his previous protestations that he could not attend before the season ended on 26th October. He said that unless Coulthard attended the trial session on 28th October, his statement should not be admitted as evidence.

The judge said that the trial would resume on 3rd October, when Frank Williams, Patrick Head and Adrian Newey would attend. When 3rd October dawned, it took only five minutes for Judge Costanzo to adjourn the session after Frank Williams, Patrick Head and Adrian Newey all failed to turn up. Lawyers told the court that due to a ceramics trade fair being held in Bologna, all hotels in the Imola area were booked up; their clients had found it impossible to secure accommodation. The lawyers told the court that they would attend on 29th October. To avoid a wasted day, the judge and lawyers spent two hours finalising the trial's schedule as it neared its conclusion: on 7th November, Maurizio Passarini would begin his summing-up for the prosecution; then on 10th, 11th, 12th, 14th, 17th, 18th and 21st November, the defence could sum up its case.

As scheduled, on 28th October, David Coulthard finally arrived to testify. Pressure had been put on a reluctant Coulthard to attend in person by the Williams' lawyers because his evidence was vital. Coulthard said the movement shown by Senna's steering column/wheel was perfectly acceptable. Coulthard stated that in 1994, it was normal for the Williams' steering column to move both up and down and left and right by several millimetres and for the driver's hands to rub against the cockpit. As the steering wheel was constructed of carbon fibre, this would also flex. He said the regulations had since been changed, and the collapsible steering wheels were much stiffer.

Passarini asked Coulthard if he knew how much 'play' there was in the steering column, independently of the steering wheel. Coulthard retorted: "No, I have never done that test because I have never driven a car without a steering wheel." His remarks brought the house down – even the dourest of the Italian court officials finding some mirth in his remark.

The court was shown the video of Coulthard sitting in a stationary Williams Formula One car, showing the movement in the steering wheel. After reading Coulthard's oral testimony, Michaele Alboreto had told reporters outside the court room that he had never before experienced that behaviour in a steering wheel.

On 29th October, the trial resumed amid great anticipation: Frank Williams, Patrick Head and Adrian Newey were due personally to testify. In the event, neither Newey nor Head turned up – they informed the court via their lawyers that they had exercised their rights not to answer questions, and opted to submit written statements at a later date. But Frank Williams had arrived in Italy the previous day in his own plane and apologised for being late arriving from his hotel. The trial was adjourned to await his arrival, expected by late morning.

When he finally arrived, Passarini asked him about the Williams team's own internal investigations. Williams said: "We were looking for as much fact as possible and were anxious to see as much television footage as we could. We, as a company, formed the opinion that the steering column did not break. This was decided after examining the telemetry readings and also a lot of simulations."

Williams went on to say that the team had considered various explanations, but he did not offer a theory for the cause of Ayrton Senna's crash. He did say he remembered that alterations were made to the steering column after 1st May: "I remember that all the remaining cars were checked and were okay. Even so, we decided to change the columns and manufacture different versions to remove any doubt about integrity."

Asked whether he had any doubts about Senna's steering column, Williams replied: "Absolutely, we had doubts. That's why we're here today, trying to find out what happened."

Passarini asked Williams why Senna's steering column was modified. Williams said: "Ayrton wanted more room in the cockpit, and it was decided to change the steering column. When it was decided, I don't remember. There would have been communication with all the relevant people. I can't be accurate or specific because I do not follow, and never have done, every operation on a daily basis."

Williams said he didn't know who was responsible for making the changes, only that many people would have been involved. "Senna made three or four pages of recommendations to make the car go faster after every practice session. I remember that he was not happy about the amount of space, and there were many other things he wanted to change. He also wanted a very large steering wheel – it was one of his trademarks," he said.

Williams said that he was not aware changes had been made until after the race. Passarini offered a judgement on Senna's opinion of the car, which Williams rejected, saying: "The driver did not say he could not drive the car, rather that he would like more space so he would be less tired in the latter half of the race."

Passarini brought up the fact that the Williams team's own experts had discovered over 40 per cent metal fatigue in Senna's steering column. Williams said: "But I'm certain that the plane I arrived in yesterday had cracks in it."

Pushed further about any action he would have taken had he known the extent of the metal fatigue in Senna's column, Frank Williams restated that he was not responsible for technical issues.

Speaking to reporters later outside the court, Williams said: "We'll probably never know what happened. But I made it clear in court today that we think that the car probably left the road rather than suffered a steering column failure."

Williams was effectively the last witness for the trial. The summings-up were scheduled to begin on 7th November. Maurizio Passarini gave his closing statement. The state prosecutor first recapped the events leading up to the fatal crash, again focusing on the steering column modifications made by Williams. He referred to the events of that tragic Imola weekend: the death in qualifying of Roland Ratzenberger; the initial accident at the start of the race; the deployment of the safety car and the race restart.

Passarini said that driver error must be excluded. Two investigations by independent laboratories reached the same conclusion. The steering column had signs of fatigue over 75 per cent of the circumference and 40 per cent of the section. Reference was made to the testimony given by defence witness David Coulthard regarding the normality of the two centimetres of oscillations shown on a Williams steering column.

Almost certainly with a view to undermining comments made earlier by Frank Williams, Passarini made a point of highlighting the fact that after the race restart, Senna clocked what would prove to be the third-fastest lap of the race, discounting many theories – including Williams' – that a loss of tyre pressure, due to the cooling of the tyres whilst following the safety car, could have caused Senna's loss of control.

Passarini also introduced the multimedia evidence showing the behaviour of the car, telemetric information and Senna's last moments at the wheel. He made it clear that he was unhappy with some aspects of the defence, for example the data recorder installed in Senna's Williams-Renault. This box was said to have been smashed during the accident, with vital information it contained thus lost.

Passarini said that Senna's data recorder contained 20 memory chips, but only two were damaged – those whose data would have been retained even when the power supply failed. "It must be a coincidence, but it makes you wonder if someone was very jealous regarding its contents," he said.

In a surprise move, the state prosecutor announced that certain officials from the Formula One Constructors' Association (FOCA) were to be investigated over alleged false testimonies. The probe was to be carried out by the Bologna attorney's office.

Passarini talked about the problems he had encountered in obtaining the final footage from Senna's in-car camera. He claimed that the responses given by the FOCA TV employees were "disconcerting or downright comic, if not tragic." He said that Bernie Ecclestone, at one time expected to be called as a witness, was not directly concerned with the investigation. He did indicate, however, that letters Ecclestone has sent to the legal authorities would be examined to see if there was a separate case to answer.

This could relate to the film taken from Senna's on-board camera. The Williams team was provided with the footage within a week of Senna's death, Passarini's office took over six months to obtain the tape. He said: "This is typical of the disdain with which the Formula One world has treated this enquiry."

Passarini also attacked Francesco Longanesi Cattani, the FIA's press supremo, and said he may face an investigation. He did not say what for. Passarini always contended that the footage supplied from Senna's in-car camera was incomplete because it stopped 0.9 seconds before Senna's fatal impact. He said that nine minutes had been spent following Senna's Williams and, therefore, it was comical to believe that it was "sheer coincidence" that FOCA TV staff decided to switch shots just before impact.

He did not believe the testimonies given by the FOCA TV employees, who maintained that the car camera was switched from Senna's vehicle to that of Gerhard Berger's by chance. "A moment later Ayrton Senna was dead," he said.

The state prosecutor maintained that the camera was still running at the time of the crash and said he believed the missing footage would have proved his case: that the steering column snapped whilst Senna was still on the track.

Then dramatically and without warning, Passarini recommended that all charges against Frank Williams, Roland Bruynseraede, Federico Bendinelli and Giorgio Poggi be dropped. He said that as both Frank Williams and Federico Bendinelli merely dealt with the administrative side of the business they could not directly be held responsible for the crash that claimed Ayrton Senna's life.

Passarini said that although safety standards at Tamburello were questionable, Poggi and Bruynseraede did not commit any crime. Senna was killed not by his car's impact with the Tamburello wall but because a piece of suspension pierced his helmet, causing fatal head injuries. He said that the question was whether, if his car had been travelling at a lower speed, Senna would still have died: as this issue was in doubt, charges should be dropped.

Pasarini then went on to say that both Patrick Head and Adrian Newey should be convicted as they were both ultimately responsible for the design changes made to Senna's car. The state prosecutor claimed that the fact that Senna asked for modifications didn't reduce the responsibility of the accused. He recommended that the court award one-year suspended sentences to both defendants. The maximum sentence is five years. "Newey and Head designed the steering column modifications badly, and especially, did not check how the plan was put into execution," he said.

There was no guarantee that the judge would take Passarini's advice to acquit four men, but from that point on it was deemed a formality. Federico Bendinelli said afterwards: "I was convinced the circuit bore no responsibility for what happened and neither did Frank Williams. His position was the same as mine. I was calm and confident from the start."

Friday 14th November saw Adrian Newey's lawyers, Landi and Stortoni, argue that Newey was not directly involved with the alterations to Senna's steering column. The prosecution, they maintained, should have taken account of the actions of the two technicians responsible for the steering modifications, namely Young and Fisher.

Stortoni said the prosecution felt that, although Newey had not worked on the modifications directly, he was ultimately responsible. But there was no proof that Newey ordered the job. In fact, when Williams held an internal investigation into the cause of the accident, Newey wasn't even asked to attend.

The final session for the defence came on 18th November with closing statements from Patrick Head's lawyers, Dominioni and Gandossi. Dominioni's strategy was to try and dissect the prosecution's case. He launched a lengthy attack on the prosecution's technical advisers, saying that Passarini had never asked them whether a lack of stability in Senna's car, due to the track surface, could have caused the fatal crash.

Dominioni told the court: "Passarini's reconstruction of the incident which cost the life of Ayrton Senna has no basis in proof; it is unfounded and those accused must be cleared." He said that Senna's steering column was the same as Damon Hill's, both having been designed prior to the start of the 1994 racing season. Looking at the testimony of one of the prosecution's experts, Dominioni said it was not possible to say whether a part constructed with the safety equal to a coefficient of one could have broken.

The fatigue on the piece emphasised by the prosecution should have been revealed at 350,000 cycles (a cycle is any fit application that provokes wear on the part); but the steering column, inspected after the first two Grand Prix races of the season, had experienced 27,000 cycles, a value clearly lower than the safety limit. The question then was when and why, because up to the last control check with the penetrating liquids, this had not been highlighted. "Unfortunately in life, there exists the unpredictable, the unforeseen event and the inexplicable," Dominioni said.

He asserted that there were contradictions within the prosecution's case, above all those of Forghieri concerning the tyre pressure. On the fundamental point of the tyre pressure, he said the prosecution's experts had relied on presumptive evaluations, not actual data. The Goodyear tyre company disagreed with Forghieri, claiming that the prosecution's reconstructions were wrong. The temporal logic and dynamics of the incident, which began at the time of 11.24 seconds as a consequence of a violent collision on the track, caused one swerve of the car and the resultant oversteer as Senna tried to correct.

Dominioni said the prosecution maintained that the steering column broke causing Senna's Williams to veer to the right, and in his 60 metres off the track Senna didn't try to steer. The defence maintained that this was not because the wheels didn't react to the steering, but because Senna with great clarity kept the wheels straight to achieve the best possible braking.

He said it was useless to compare the Friday session times with those of the accident because conditions were unequal. As Senna's on-board camera was not fixed rigidly, the film was not reliable due to optical illusions.

Dominioni recalled that Michele Alboreto had accused Coulthard of not speaking the truth about the oscillations of the Williams' steering wheel. He stated that Alboreto in turn was unreliable and prejudiced. He said: "I therefore ask for the acquittal of [Frank] Williams and Head for they have not committed any crime. The incident didn't occur through the breaking of the steering column."

Dominioni said that the cause of Senna's fatal loss of control was still unknown. He reiterated the theory given by Frank Williams, who had earlier stated that Ayrton Senna's crash could have been the result of a combination of cold tyres and the uneven track surface.

On 19th November, the defence lawyers continued their summing-up speeches. Although the prosecutor had cleared Giorgio Poggi, his lawyer and nephew Manrico Bonetti still went ahead. He said that after a long career, which started in 1973 as a track inspector, Poggi was due to retire after the Imola race on 1st May 1994. He maintained that Poggi was a scrupulous executive and there was a limit to his responsibilities. He asked therefore for a full acquittal.

On Wednesday 12th November, Roland Bruynseraede's lawyer, Roberto Causo, said the personalities of the prosecution's team of experts had strongly conditioned the investigation. He argued that if the prosecution's case were to be believed, then the Imola track was in breach of the regulations and would have to be demolished and rebuilt.

Landi, for Sagis, concluded that Bendinelli and Poggi had had operational roles since 1980. Then the alterations to the circuit, requested and designed by Nosetto, were already approved and under construction. Their activities had always been subject to FIA scrutiny.

On 21st November, at the penultimate hearing of the trial, Maurizio Passarini replied to the defence's closing statements. The state prosecutor told the court that the Tamburello curve, even though subjected to alterations in 1989, was still a very dangerous place, exposing cars to high mechanical stress. The modifications previously undertaken should have encompassed the elevating of the shoulder by 30-40cm to conform to the regulations.

Passarini disproved the objections raised by the Williams defence, saying that it was untrue that the prosecution's experts had not considered the theory of instability, which in one out of 50 cases could account for a car leaving the track.

He said that all aspects of the track had been examined, and everyone was aware that the underside of the car had made violent contact with the ground.

The state prosecutor maintained that Williams' reconstruction of the incident must be discounted. He claimed that the team's data was disproved by the telemetry, which did not show that Senna, whilst trying to correct an oversteer problem, had understeered. He said it was in fact quite the opposite – what impressed about Senna's car was that, with the diminution of the lateral acceleration, the torsion applied to the steering column reached zero, which signified that Senna had abandoned using the steering. Passarini said Senna did this not to achieve optimum braking but because, at this point, the steering column broke. Had the steering column been performing normally, the telemetry should have shown this.

He said it was permissible to have doubts about when and where Senna's steering column was modified, but that it was pointless to say that the steering column on Hill's car was of the same standard. He said: "It is not a valid defence to say that this breaking is considered an unpredictable phenomenon and that there is not a causal link between the incident and the death of the driver. The breaking of the steering column was the main cause – without this, the car would not have left the track. Because of the senior positions held by Head and Newey at Williams, they cannot claim to be exempt from the responsibilities of quality control."

Adrian Newey's lawyer quickly concluded the day's proceedings: the defence's main argument was unassailable, he said. Williams and Head's lawyer had done most of his talking for him.

On 26th November 1997, the nine-month trial into Ayrton Senna's death drew to a close. State prosecutor Maurizio Passarini repeated his request for Adrian Newey and Patrick Head to be found guilty of manslaughter, having dropped the charges against Federico Bendinelli, Giorgio Poggi, Roland Bruynseraede and Frank Williams.

Asking for the acquittal of their respective clients, the various lawyers for the six accused gave their final statements. Judge Antonio Costanzo retired to consider the verdict, which he said he would announce at 1.30pm on 16th December 1997. At the appointed time, he delivered the verdict everyone had expected, clearing all six defendants of manslaughter charges arising from Ayrton Senna's death.

The judge had ignored Maurizio Passarini's recommendations for one-year suspended sentences to be delivered to Patrick Head and Adrian Newey. He said he would publish his reasons within 90 days. None of the defendants was present to hear the verdicts.

Peter Goodman, the Williams team solicitor, who had observed the whole proceedings at the front of the courtroom, said: "We had a good hearing; all the facts came out, and I'm sure the right verdict was reached." Roland Bruynseraede's lawyer, Roberto Causo, said: "By this verdict the judge has recognised that Formula One is an extremely dangerous sport."

Giovanni Carcaterra, representing the Senna family, said: "The Senna family only wanted to discover what actually happened – they were not interested in sentences." Passarini said he looked forward to reading the judge's report: "I need to see whether the judge ruled that the incident was due to the breaking of Senna's steering column, although there was no criminal responsibility, or if he felt that the column did not break. In that case, I would be even more disappointed." Few doubted the verdict was right. A guilty verdict may have ended top-line motor racing in Italy, perhaps for ever. The FIA issued a statement: "The FIA has noted today's decision of the Imola court, but will not comment until it has examined the full text of the decision and studied its implications."

Williams as a team said: "Williams Grand Prix Engineering is pleased to confirm that Frank Williams, Patrick Head and Adrian Newey have been acquitted of all charges which were the subject of the Imola trial. Our legal advisers inform us that the prosecution has an automatic right of appeal.

Clearly, we would hope that this matter will not be pursued any further."

Ferrari Team Principal, although not involved in the trial, issued a statement afterwards: "I haven't commented during the trial because I felt I should wait until the verdict. It has been rather laborious and lengthy and is therefore a judgement of conscience, which has to be accepted and respected. It is not easy to give an opinion on a motor race when you know of the dangers and risks involved. My comments are positive because the fact is there has been a very careful examination of all the events and because of the outcome of the trial," he said.

Damon Hill said he believed the judge's decision would help Formula One's image after the recent controversies: "I know this trial has been hanging over Williams and this vindication expresses a feeling about the team's utter integrity and the standard of its engineering. I never had any doubts about either."

FATAL WEEKEND

Veteran team-owner Ken Tyrrell expressed his pleasure on behalf of the other team owners: "I, like other team bosses, am delighted that they brought in the correct verdict. The idea that Williams, the most successful team with probably the best engineered car in Formula One, would have made a mistake was unthinkable," he said. "I would have been apprehensive racing in Italy if this decision had found Williams guilty of manslaughter. I realise that in Italy someone has to be held responsible in the event of a death, but it is a quirk of the law, and the authorities need to look at that."

In the 381-page written report published on 15th June 1998, six months after the verdict, Antonio Costanzo cited the reason for Ayrton Senna's crash at the 1994 San Marino Grand Prix as the breaking of the 'modified' steering column fitted to his Williams-Renault FW16B. He stated that without that condition, Ayrton Senna's car would not have left the track at the Tamburello bend.

With the publication of the official report, the chief prosecutor, Maurizio Passarini, had the right to appeal against the judge's decision to find the defendants 'not guilty'. No one thought he would seek an appeal after all that had happened and considering the dangers for Italian motorsport if he succeeded. But he did. He wanted what he saw as the bad design and workmanship of the steering-column modifications carried out on Ayrton Senna's Williams-Renault to be punished. In response, Williams also appealed against the factual finding.

The appeal was heard in Bologna on 19th November 1999. Three days later, the appeal court absolved Patrick Head and Adrian Newey of all charges related to the death of Ayrton Senna. The decision was based on paragraph two of Article 530 of the Italian penal code – "when no more evidence is presented during an Appeal session, and when the first session has concluded with full absolution, the accusation has to be declared as non-existent." The defence simply utilised the knowledge that the prosecution would have no chance of submitting new evidence.

The Williams's lawyers believed that the success of the appeal had also reversed the original judge's view that the actual steering was broken, and they were adamant that the team and defendants were completely vindicated.

Whether that was true or not was unclear. Peter Goodman says: "We don't consider it to be a mystery any more. It was not a failure in the car."

On 14th March 2002, the wreck of the Williams Renault FW16 was recovered from Bologna police station and returned to the Williams factory, some eight years after the accident. The car is believed to have been destroyed and the engine returned to Renault.

(Appendix 6 is adapted from Chapter 33 of The Life of Senna)

THE TRIAL IN BOLOGNA

FATAL WEEKEND

Bibliography

Bower, Tom, No Angel-The Secret Life of Bernie Ecclestone
(Faber & Faber) 2011 Hardback 432 pages ISBN: 978-0571269297

Cavicchi, Carlo & Orsi, Angelo, Senna Veri (CL Conti Editore)
1994 Hardback 168 pages

Collings, Timothy, Schumacher (Bloomsbury Publishing Plc)
1994 Hardback 200 pages ISBN 0 7475 1965 X

D'Alessio, Paolo, Obrigado Ayrton Simply The Best (Giorgio Nada Editore)
1995 Hardback 116 pages ISBN 88 7911 141 8

Dodgins, Tony, Ayrton Senna – All His Races (Evro Publishing)
2014 Hardback 304 pages ISBN: 978-0-992820-90-9

Donaldson, Gerald, Formula 1: The Autobiography (Weidenfeld & Nicholson) 2002
Hardback 360 pages ISBN: 978-0297843085

Donnini, Mario, Ayrton Senna – A Life in Pictures (Giorgio Nada Editore)
2014 Hardback 208 pages   ISBN: 978-8879115940

Donnini, Mario, Senna & Imola (Giorgio Nada Editore) 2015 Hardback 112 pages
ISBN: 978-8879116138

Folley, Malcolm, Senna versus Prost (Century) 2009 Hardback 416 pages
ISBN: 978-1846055409

Galeron, Jean-François, Magic Senna (Editions La Sirène) 1994 Hardback 95 pages
ISBN 2 84045 095 X

Galisteu, Adriane, Adriane – My Life With Ayrton (APA Publishing)
1995 Hardback 96 pages ISBN 0 646 214 209

Giaccon, Mauro, L'ultimo Ayrton (Giorgio Nada Editore) 1996 Hardback 96 pages
ISBN 88 7911 164 7

Hamilton, Maurice, Alain Prost/McLaren (Blink Publishing/McLaren) 2015
Hardback 320 pages ISBN978-1-905825-98-1

Hamilton, Maurice, Ayrton Senna/McLaren (Blink Publishing/McLaren)
2014 Hardback 256 pages ISBN 978-1-905825-87-5

Hamilton, Maurice, Frank Williams (Macmillan)1998 Hardback 290 pages
ISBN 0 333717163

Hawkins, Richard & Hugh Gollner, Senna – Portrait of A Racing Legend
(Oxford International Publications Ltd) 1994 Hardback 94 pages ISBN 0 952867 0 9

Hayhoe, David & Holland David, *Grand Prix Data Book 1997*
(Duke Marketing Ltd) 1996 Hardback 567 pages ISBN 0 9529325 0 4

Henry, Alan, *50 Years of World Championship Motor Racing* (Hazelton Publishing) 2000
Hardback 336 pages ISBN 1 874557 78 0

Henry, Alan, *Ayrton Senna – Portrait of a Champion* (Hazelton Publishing)
1988 Hardback 94 pages ISBN 0 905138 60

Henry, Alan, *Remembering Ayrton Senna* (Weidenfeld and Nicholson Ltd)
1994 Hardback 95 pages ISBN 297 83450 9

Higham, Peter & Jones, Bruce, *World Motor Racing Circuits – A Spectators Guide*
(Andre Deutsch) 1999 Hardback 192 pages ISBN 0233 99619 2

Hilton, Christopher, *As Time Goes By* (Haynes Publishing) 2009 Hardback 304 pages
ISBN: 1-85960-611-3

Hilton, Christopher, *Ayrton Senna* (Haynes Publishing) 1999 Hardback 304 pages
ISBN 1 85960611 3

Hilton, Christopher, *Ayrton Senna – His full car racing record* (Patrick Stephens
Limited) 1995 Hardback 192 pages ISBN 1 85260 543X

Hilton, Christopher, *Ayrton Senna – The Hard Edge of Genius* (Corgi Books)
1991 Paperback 282 pages ISBN 0 552 13754 5

Hilton, Christopher, *Gerhard Berger – The Human Face of Formula 1*
(Patrick Stephens Ltd) 1995 Hardback 288 pages ISBN 1 85260 515 4

Hilton, Christopher, *Senna's 50 Poles* (CBS/Sony Publishing) 1990 Paperback 96 pages
ISBN 4 7897 0608 7

Koike, Norio, *Ayrton Senna – Official Photobook* (Forme) 1995 Hardback 160 pages
ISBN 88 86682 00X

Mansell, Nigel, *2001 Formula 1 Annual* (European Press Ltd) 2001 Hardback 672 pages
ISBN 0 9541368 0 2

Mansell, Nigel, *Nigel Mansell – My Autobiography* (Collins Willow) 1995 Hardback 352
pages ISBN 0 00 218947 4

Mansell, Nigel, *Staying On Track* (Simon & Schuster) 2015, Hardback 384 pages
ISBN: 978-1471150227

BIBLIOGRAPHY

Moncet, Jean-Louis, *Life in the Fast Lane* (Hutchinson) 1989 Hardback 176 pages
ISBN: 978-0091740146

Mosley, Max, *Formula One and Beyond* (Simon & Schuster) 2015 Hardback 384 pages
ISBN: 978-1471150227

Noble, A, *They Died Too Young – Ayrton Senna* (Parragon Books) 1995 Hardback
76 pages ISBN 075250 699 4

Nye, Doug, *McLaren – The Grand Prix, Can-Am and Indy Cars* (Hazelton Publishing)
1988 Hardback 324 pages ISBN 0 905138 54 6

Paolo, Bobby, *Ayrton Senna Da Silva – A Worldwide Myth* (Bobby Paolo, Club Ayrton
Senna) Paperback 128 pages

Ramirez, Jo, *Memoirs of a Racing Man* (Haynes Publishing) 2010 Hardback 320 pages
ISBN: 978-1844252381

Rendall, Ivan, *Ayrton Senna – A Tribute* (Pavilion Books Ltd) 1994 Hardback 174 pages
ISBN 1 85793 517 9

Rodrigues, Ernesto, *Ayrton: O Herói Revelado* (Objetiva; Edição) 2004 Hardback
640 pages ISBN: 8573026022

Santos, Francisco, *Ayrton Senna* (Libros Cupula) 1994 Paperback 224 pages
ISBN 84 3291347 2

Senna, Ayrton, *Ayrton Senna's Principles of Racing Driving* (Hazelton Publishing) 1991
Hardback 208 pages ISBN 0 1874557 40 3

Sturm, Karin, *Ayrton Senna – Goodbye Champion, Farewell Friend* (Motor Racing
Publications) 1994 Hardback 160 Pages ISBN 0 947986 1

Sutton, Keith, *Ayrton Senna – A Personal Tribute* (Osprey Automotive) 1994 Hardback
214 pages ISBN 1 85532 507 1

Sutton, Keith, *Everlasting Hero – Ayrton Senna* (Sony Magazines Inc) 1994 Hardback
198 pages ISBN 4 7897 0922 1

Tremayne, David, *Echoes of Imola* (Motor Racing Publications) 1996 Hardback
160 pages ISBN 1 899870 05 9

Tremayne, David, *Rubens Barrichello: In the Spirit of Senna and the Shadow of
Schumacher* (Haynes Publishing) 2005 Hardcover 356 pages ISBN: 978-1844252008

Watkins, Sid, *Beyond The Limit* (Macmillan) 2001 Hardback 224 pages
ISBN 0 333 901188 6

Walker, Murray, *1994 Grand Prix Year* (Hazelton Publishing) 1994 Paperback
144 pages ISBN 1 874557 01 2

Watkins, Sid, *Life at the Limit* (Macmillan) 1996 Hardback 258 pages
ISBN 0 333 65774 8

Watkins, Susan, *Bernie* (Haynes Publishing) 2010 Hardback 416 pages
ISBN: 978-0857330338

Williams, Richard, *The Death of Ayrton Senna* (Bloomsbury Publishing)
1999 Paperback 216 pages ISBN 0 7475 4495 6

BIBLIOGRAPHY

FATAL WEEKEND

Index

INDEX

Nightingale, Max 352
Norio Koike 139
Nosco, Fabrizio 193, 195, 196, 342
Nosetto, Roberto 221, 336, 353

O

O'Mahoney, Owen 30, 33, 37, 38, 52,
53, 54, 55, 74, 133, 179, 206, 214,
241, 243, 250, 251, 270, 276
Ojjeh, Cathy 214
Ojjeh, Mansour 214
Onassis, Aristotle 32
Orsi, Angelo 216, 152, 239

P

Paddock Club 74
Paletti, Riccardo 109, 111
Palmer, Jonathan 207
Panis, Olivier 267
Passarini , Mauroizio 333, 336, 337, 338,
339, 340, 341, 343, 344, 348, 349,
350, 352, 353, 359, 360
Patrese, Riccardo 225, 267, 338,
339, 343
Paul Ricard Circuit 270, 340
Pelé 9, 272
Pilcher, Tony 351
Pinheiro, Teresa 1
Pinto, Gomes 242
Pinto, Jose 182
Pintor, Francesco 338
Piquet, Nelson 11, 112, 225, 267,
338, 343
Pirro, Emmanuelle 221, 336
Poggi, Giorgio 270, 339, 340, 363, 365
Polícia da Aeronáutica 244
Portuguese Grand Prix 27, 48, 58
Portuguese TV 182
President Franco 244
Prince Albert of Monaco 35
Princess Caroline 35

Professor Jose Pratas Vital 161
Professor Pinto da Costa 161
Prost, Alain 8, 23, 24, 25, 26, 27, 35,
39, 40, 91, 133, 134, 135, 136,
137, 153, 154, 184, 235, 236, 251,
254, 260, 267, 270, 271, 281, 297

Q, R

Qalanjo, Khadija 100
Quinta do Lago 14, 47, 48, 51, 130, 154
RAF 52
Ramirez, Jo 22, 41, 181, 302, 303
Ratzenberger, Margit 110, 137
Ratzenberger, Roland 95, 99, 100, 103,
104, 105, 106, 107, 108, 109, 111,
115, 116, 121, 127, 130, 133, 137,
151, 158, 162, 212, 215, 237, 239,
261, 339
Ratzenberger, Rudolf 110, 137
Renault 23, 70, 145, 167
Reynard, Adrian 97
Rindt, Jochen 101, 167, 195
Rindt, Nina 167
Rix, Brian 176
Rogério & Ridaut 268
RTL TV 74

S

Sala, Maurizio Sandro 251
Salcito, Domenico 141
Salo, Mika 100
Salzburger Nachrichten 103
San Maggiore Hospital 108,154, 158,
160, 165, 166, 177, 178, 180, 182,
183, 201, 204, 206, 207, 211, 240
San Marino Grand Prix 21, 57, 107,
108, 187, 219, 231, 233, 129
Sassetti, Andrea 97
Sauer, Birgit 249
Schilling & Lom 335

INDEX

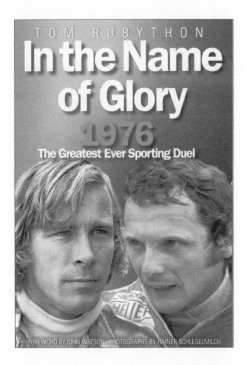

In The Name of Glory

As the sun set on the 1975 season James Hunt was down and out of Formula One. He had no drive for 1976 and was all washed up. In contrast Niki Lauda, the new world champion of 1975 was in an entirely different position. A full year's contract ahead of him and Enzo Ferrari begging him to sign a new lucrative one for years into the future. Lauda was hot favourite to win the world championship again in 1976.

No one but no one would have named Hunt as a possible contender. Then there was a life changing experience for Hunt as Emerson Fittipaldi decided to break his McLaren contract and leave the team. It was the opportunity James Hunt needed and he seized it with both hands and with the help of his friend John Hogan at Marlboro cigarettes grabbed the drive with both hands.

Fittipaldi had unwittingly set the stage for the greatest duel in sporting history when two drivers fought an epic battle for the 1976 Formula One world championship which in the end was decided by a single point over a 16 race season. It was all done in the name of glory.

The Life of Senna

Ayrton Senna was in many people's opinion, the most brilliant Formula One driver who ever raced. His death on Sunday 1st May 1994 was as shocking as it was public. Over 200 million people watched him perish on television, and the knowing realised he was dead as soon as his car came to rest. In this first full account of the life of Ayrton Senna, the author and his collaborators examine each detail of the driving maestro's life - from his earliest days to his first race, his pole positions, his world championships and, finally, his death and its aftermath. It is a story that has never been fully or properly unravelled. And it is a story that needs to be told.

This book is about his life, his victories and his loves. It is the first proper story of a man the world revered and whose like will never be seen again.

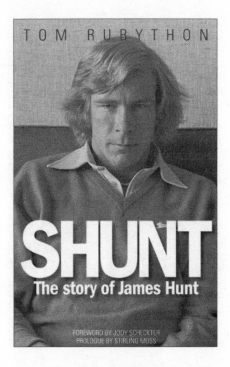

SHUNT

James Hunt is remembered more for his girlfriends and wild personal exploits than for his skills in a race car. But the excesses of his glamorous life cannot hide the fact that he was, in many people's opinion, the fastest driver on the Formula One circuits in the 1970s. In an era dominated by the likes of Emerson Fittipaldi, Niki Lauda and Ronnie Peterson, Hunt stood out in terms of raw speed and his seemingly effortless ability to plant a Formula One car on pole position. In this full and comprehensive account of the life of James Hunt, the author and his researchers have examined every detail of the driver's life – from his very earliest days to the last hours of his existence – as well as the lives of the people he left behind. It is the story of a man who started his racing career penniless, earned millions in a lifetime of success, but, in an astonishing twist of fate, at the end of his life, died exactly as he had begun – penniless. It is a story many have tried to tell; but never in such a complete way. This is that story.

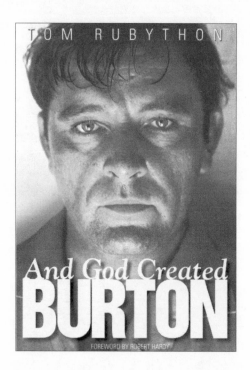

And God Created Burton

A sweeping saga spanning 1898 to 1984, stretching from the mining fields of South Wales to the film sets of Hollywood, and from the playhouses of Cardiff to the grand theatres of Broadway - this new and far reaching biography rakes over the coals of the life of Britain's greatest ever actor, Richard Burton. And God Created Burton is the first complete biography of the greatest Welshman who ever lived. The man conquered Hollywood in a way that no British actor had before or since, rising to become the highest earning actor Britain has ever produced. His achievements were considered all the greater as they were accomplished in the era of great British actors, such as Laurence Olivier and John Gielgud. All the more so as Burton's prowess uniquely spanned theatre, film and television in a way no other actor has before. Burton became a genuine legend in his own lifetime and, in the mid sixties, for one year, he stood at the very pinnacle of Hollywood as the world's most bankable actor. He also loved and lost some of the most beautiful and talented actresses of the era, including Elizabeth Taylor, Claire Bloom and Susan Strasberg. But he could have achieved even more but for his addiction to alcohol, a fate that was inherited from his father which stayed with him right to the end of his days, eventually killing him and tarnishing an otherwise extraordinary career.

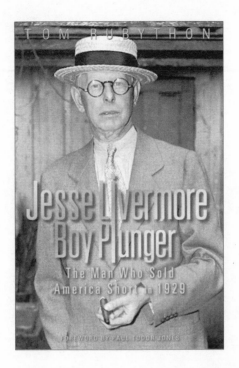

Jesse Livermore - Boy Plunger

In the summer of 1929, people believed that the stock market would go up forever. An eight-year winning run had seen the Dow Jones increase 500 per cent. The Dow peaked at 381 on 3rd September and later that day the most respected economist of the era, Irving Fisher, declared that the rise was "permanent". One man vigorously disagreed and started a process that would see him sell $450 million of shares short. Two weeks later, the market began falling and rising again on successive days for no apparent reason. This situation endured for a month until what became famously known as the three 'black' days: On Black Thursday 24th October, the Dow fell 11% at the opening bell, prompting absolute chaos. The fall was stalled when leading financiers of the day clubbed together to buy huge quantities of shares. But it was short-lived succour and, over that weekend, blanket negative newspaper commentary caused the second of the 'black' days on Black Monday 28th October when the market dropped another 13%. The third 'black' day, Black Tuesday 29th October, saw the market drop a further 12%. When the dust had settled, in the aftermath of the 24th to the 29th October, Wall Street had lost $30 billion. The man who had sold $450 million of shares was Jesse Livermore. He made nearly $100 million. It remains, adjusted for inflation, the most money ever made by any individual in a period of seven days. This is the story of that man.

TOM RUBYTHON

Tom Rubython is best known as the author of *The Life of Senna*, the definitive biography of Brazilian racing driver Ayrton Senna. *The Life of Senna* has become the biggest-selling third party biography of a racing driver, with over 250,000 copies sold worldwide. Eleven years after its publication, it still sells over 12,000 copies a year. Before he started writing books, Rubython was well known in magazine publishing, spanning the worlds of sport and business. Aside from his work in Formula One, he has been a specialist business writer for thirty years. In business, he is the former editor of *BusinessAge*, *EuroBusiness* and *Spectator Business*. In sport, he has edited *F1 Magazine*, *BusinessF1* and *SportsPro*. Rubython now specialises in non-fiction storytelling and has written biographies of racing driver James Hunt, British actor Richard Burton, and the Wall Street financier Jesse Livermore. He is passionate and methodical about the process of researching and writing books. Starting out with a determination to tell the full story, he emphasises what is important and de-emphasises what is not - the crucial tools of any non-fiction writer.